Raid on America

Other Books by the Authors:

DONALD G. SHOMETTE
Pirates on the Chesapeake
The Othello Affair
Shipwrecks on the Chesapeake
Flotilla
London Town: *A Brief History*
Shipwrecks of the Civil War

ROBERT D. HASLACH
Netherlands World Broadcasting
Nishi, no kaze, hare: *Nederlands-Indische inlichtingendienst contra agressor Japan*

Studies in Maritime History

WILLIAM N. STILL, JR., *Editor*
Stoddert's War: *Naval Operations During the Quasi-War with France, 1798–1801*
BY MICHAEL A. PALMER

The British Navy and the American Revolution
BY JOHN A. TILLEY

Iron Afloat: *The Story of the Confederate Armorclads*
BY WILLIAM N. STILL, JR.

Confederate Shipbuilding
BY WILLIAM N. STILL, JR.

A Maritime History of the United States:
The Role of America's Seas and Waterways
BY K. JACK BAUR

Raid on America

The Dutch Naval Campaign
of 1672–1674

DONALD G. SHOMETTE
AND
ROBERT D. HASLACH

UNIVERSITY OF SOUTH CAROLINA PRESS

Copyright © University of South Carolina 1988

Published in Columbia, South Carolina, by the
University of South Carolina Press

First Edition
Manufactured in the United States of America

LIBRARY OF CONGRESS
Library of Congress Cataloging-in-Publication Data

Shomette, Donald
    Raid on America: the Dutch naval campaign of 1672–1674 / Donald
G. Shomette and Robert D. Haslach.
        p. cm.—(Studies in maritime history)
    Bibliography: p.
    Includes index.
    ISBN 0-87249-565-5
    1. Dutch War, 1672–1678—Naval operations, Dutch. 2. Dutch War,
1672–1678—Campaigns—America. 3. Great Britain—Colonies—America-
-History—17th century. 4. Netherlands—Colonies—America-
-History—17th century. I. Haslach, Robert D. II. Title.
D277.5.S54 1988
937.2′4—dc19   88-17107
                                                              CIP

For Carol and Linda

Give me a spirit that on life's rough sea
Loves t'have his sail filled with a lusty wind.

Contents

PREFACE

The conduct of the campaign in the Americas by Commander Cornelis Evertsen the Youngest of the Admiralty of Zeeland, during the Third Anglo-Dutch War, was an event that is neither well known nor fully reported on in the annals of American maritime history. The reasons for such neglect are many, some ephemeral and difficult to discern, others long lasting and quite obvious. Initially designed as a surprise attack on the rich English East India Company fleet, the Evertsen Expedition was launched with only three men-of-war and an equal number of lesser support craft. As a secondary but equally significant objective, the squadron was assigned to conduct raids on practically every major English and French colonial establishment in the Western Hemisphere. With fewer than 600 men, the secret expedition sailed from the Dutch port of Vlissingen in late December 1672. Aborted in his primary mission by battle with a superior English force in the Cape Verde Islands, Evertsen turned his attentions upon the Americas. Equipped with navigational aids and directions over 40 years old, the raiders were obliged to conduct their voyage along coasts barely sketched in on the charts. Indeed, when Evertsen and his Zeelanders sailed into American waters, the great age of discovery had barely passed. The age of colonization was in its adolescence. The Virginia colony was in its 66th year, Maryland in its 39th, New York in its 49th, and Massachusetts in its 43rd. The Leeward Islands of the Caribbean had only recently been cleared of their native populations through European enslavement and mass annihilation. It was a time when anything was possible.

The expedition against the American colonies of England and France, ironically, was intended as nothing more than a raid on enemy shipping, a state-sponsored foray against the merchant marine of the enemy powers, in waters where they were likely to be the most vulnerable. The objective was specifically designed to supplement the depleted treasury of the war-torn State of Zeeland and to cause as much damage to the foe as possible while sustaining the least cost to the expedition. Quite by accident, and with the aid of a squadron of Amsterdam men-of-war led by an enterprising Friesian named Jacob Benckes, the raid on America became far more than its designers had ever intended. It became, in fact, a campaign of conquest in which the former Dutch colony of New Netherland, comprised of New York, New Jersey, and Delaware, was recaptured for the United Provinces of the Netherlands and provisional government established.

Before all was said and done, Evertsen and Benckes subdued three English colonies, depopulated a fourth, captured or destroyed nearly 200 enemy vessels, inflicted a serious injury upon the Virginia tobacco trade, wiped out the English Newfoundland fisheries, and caused unending panic in the New England colonies. Yet, Cornelis Evertsen did not return to the acclaim of his countrymen. Unlike the famed Piet Hein he had not returned home with a vast treasure-laden fleet of captured galleons, nor had he inflicted a stunning defeat upon the numerically superior armadas of the enemy as had the great De Ruyter. Instead, he returned to Europe, during the precise moment of The Netherlands' near military and economic collapse, with a colonial responsibility that the Fatherland neither sought nor could afford to protect. The cries of 6,000 New Netherland Dutch for protection counted for little in the hearts of a government beset on all sides by powerful invaders and charged with the survival of nearly two million souls.

It is not surprising, then, that the States General and the Prince of Orange, Willem III, were receptive to Spanish suggestions that Evertsen's amazing recovery of New Netherland be relinquished to obtain peace with England. It mattered little to a Dutch government, bent on simple survival in the face of overwhelming odds, that Spanish efforts were designed to remove for all time a major commercial rival and sometimes enemy from the Western Hemisphere. Indeed, with the signing of the Treaty of Westminster and the eventual return of New Netherland to England Dutch influence upon the course of history in the Americas all but evaporated.

For England, the ignominy of the defeats and captures inflicted by Cornelis Evertsen and Jacob Benckes in Chesapeake Bay, New York, and Newfoundland was considerable. Reports of their depredations were frequently diluted, undoubtedly for the self preservation of those at the helm of government or officers charged with military command.

It is thus not unexpected that the English record of the Evertsen-Benckes raids is frequently less than complete, and occasionally unreliable. And owing to the language barrier, few English or American historians, with a handful of noteworthy exceptions, have sought to penetrate or interpret those Dutch records concerning the totality of the campaign. Some, such as John Romeyn Brodhead and Mrs. Schuyler Van Rensselaer, have incorporated the excellent Dutch resource base with commendable clarity and accuracy as it pertains to regional history. Unhappily, no English or American historians have sought to provide a complete narrative of the campaign and its consequences. This, then, is the principal objective of the authors of this work.

Cornelis Evertsen the Youngest, quite fortunately, was not without his champions. Principal among them was C. De Waard, who incorporated Evertsen's ship journal of the voyage of *Swaenenburgh*, various pertinent minutes of government council proceedings, official letters, secret state proceedings, and the like, into a fully annotated collection. This collection, published as *De Zeeuwsche Expeditie naar de West onder Cornelis Evertsen den Jonge, 1672-1674*, has been fully translated in its entirety by Robert D. Haslach, and forms the principal foundation upon which this study is constructed. Indeed, any work on the Dutch raid on America could not be produced without it. Of substantial value to an understanding of the guidelines under which Evertsen operated is the Evertsen Papers in the Bontemantel Collection of the New York Public Library. These important papers, including two sets of secret instructions, were transcribed and translated by Victor Paltsits in the 1920s. The secret instructions provided the framework within which Evertsen was obliged to operate, and hence, a major structural feature of this work.

Cornelis Evertsen the Youngest was one of three contemporary Zeeland naval commanders who bore both the same first and family name. His father was the first to bear the name Cornelis, and was designated as Cornelis Evertsen de Oude (the old). Cornelis de Oude's brother was Admiral Jan Evertsen, who named his son Cornelis. He became known as Cornelis Evertsen de Jonge (the younger). When Cornelis de Oude's own son was born, he too was named Cornelis, and became known as Cornelis Evertsen de Jongste (the youngest). Upon the death of Cornelis de Oude during the Battle of Lowestoft in 1665, Cornelis de Jonge became the eldest to bear the name and "de Jonge" was dropped. Cornelis de Jongste then became Cornelis de Jonge. The alteration has not been noted by some historians, causing unending confusion. Hence, the authors of this work have chosen to refer to him as Cornelis Evertsen the Youngest, even though during the raid on

Preface

America he was technically Cornelis Evertsen the Younger. It is hoped that confusion will thus be avoided.

A similar problem occurs with two of Evertsen's ship commanders. Both are related, and both bear the same first and family name. Evertsen's brother is called Evert Evertsen Cornelis' Zoon, and commanded *Swaenenburgh* as captain until his death at sea. The captain of the man-of-war *Suriname* was Evert Evertsen Frans' Zoon and may have been a cousin. Both are always referred to in the text by their full names.

Another confusing element that the authors have been obliged to address was that of calendar variations. In 1582, Pope Gregory XIII ordered that ten days be omitted from the calendar to bring the calendar and sun into correspondence, creating the Gregorian Calendar used today by most western nations. However, many of the Protestant countries, with the exception of The Netherlands, stuck with the Julian, or Old Style, calendar format, some for nearly two centuries. Hence, Dutch and English records differ by ten days, a point overlooked by a number of historians who have failed to bring the dates into line regarding the Dutch proceedings in the Americas. The New Year, accepted by some in the seventeenth century such as Great Britain, as beginning on March 25 and by others as beginning on January 1, has been brought into line with the Gregorian, or New Style, Calendar, for the sake of utility. The authors have also chosen to employ the English calendar dates for the same reason, except in citations and notes where both dates are given.

Distances are computed in Dutch miles, that is a degree of latitude divided into 60 nautical miles, or 15 leagues of 4 miles each. This has been done because only the course of the Evertsen and Benckes squadrons have been followed extensively, and reflect data presented in the journal of the *Swaenenburgh*.

Every effort has been made to retain the correct national spelling of all proper names as they are used. Hence, the Dutch town of Vlissingen is referred to rather than the English version Flushing; the Spanish island of Gran Canaria is not referred to as Grand Canary; the French Ile d'Ouessant has been used in lieu of the Dutch Ouessant or the more common English Ushant; the Dutch Suriname is used over the English spelling of Surinam, and so forth.

As the threads in the fabric of written history are often intricately and elegantly interwoven by numerous persons, it is impossible to produce a garment worthy of note without generous assistance. So it has been with this work, which, without the rich input and guidance of numerous individuals, would have suffered immeasurably. The authors

Preface

would like to thank, first and foremost, Margrit B. Krewson, German/ Dutch Area Specialist, European Division, Library of Congress, for bringing the two authors together for the first time, a meeting without which this work would never have come to fruition. Special thanks should also be given to Mrs. M. C. van Hoof, of the first section, Algemeen Rijksarchief, in The Hague, Dr. R. M. Vorstman, of the Rijksmuseum "Nederlands Scheepvaart Museum" in Amsterdam, Dr. J. R. Bruijn, Professor of Maritime History, Leiden University, and David J. Lyon, Curator of Naval Ordnance, National Maritime Museum, Greenwich. It is also important that the staffs of the many great institutions that have provided enormous assistance to the research effort involved in the production of this work be acknowledged. These include The Netherlands Ministry of Foreign Affairs at The Hague, the Koninklijke Bibliotheek, also in The Hague, the Public Record Office, Kew, London, and the National Archives and Record Service and the Library of Congress in Washington, D.C.

A special word of thanks must be extended to a longtime associate and friend, Jennifer Rutland, for her critical reading and typing of much of the manuscript.

And finally, the authors would like to extend their heartfelt appreciation to their wives, Carol Shomette and Linda Haslach, for having patiently endured the deluge of papers, notes, books, pictures, and miscellaneous oddities that have flooded their normally pristine homes during the many months this work was in progress.

1

PROLOGUE: MAD FOR A DUTCH WAR

On March 17, 1672, the England of the Stuart monarchy of King Charles II formally declared war on its commercial archrival, the United Provinces of the Netherlands. It was the third such declaration in less than two decades. These were turbulent years, characterized by dynamic competition for trade, precipitous social evolution, colonial expansionism of unparalleled proportions, revolution, and of course, military conflict. To the two great North Sea powers, however, the onset of the Anglo-Dutch Wars brought to a head the issues of commercial and maritime domination and the consequent rewards of a vast, largely untapped American empire. The victor would rule a colonial entrepôt that would thrive and grow for over a century. The loser would have nothing less than an end to aspirations of commercial dominion in the Western Hemisphere. And in the far-flung colonies, from the profitable sugar islands of the West Indies and steaming enclaves on the South American mainland to the bountiful fisheries of the Newfoundland coast—indeed, wherever the great warring powers could find advantage or opportunity—they raided, plundered, and burned crops, crofts, ships, and towns.

Though largely fought for commercial ends, the Anglo-Dutch Wars germinated in the bloody soil of political upheaval, revolution, and the disruption of traditional authority between the two nations, once closely allied against the might of Hapsburg Spain and Bourbon France. The seeds were planted in 1648, when the Peace of Munster officially acknowledged that which had long been fact: the Eighty Years War between Spain and The Netherlands ended in Protestant Holland's successful revolt against the Catholic Hapsburgs. Independence of the United Provinces of The Netherlands, the first major European republic of the seventeenth century without a sovereign prince, was assured.

The United Provinces comprised seven sovereign, and often rival, provincial states: Gelderland, Utrecht, Groningen, Overijssel, Friesland, Zeeland, and Holland. It was a nation as diverse as the names of its states. Indeed, the name Holland, which was and is often given to represent The Netherlands as a whole, means "hollow land," and designates a low central trough lying between the nation's upland regions on the east and coastal dunes to the west. The central trough or hollow was polder area, once sea bottom, enclosed and reclaimed by the industrious Dutch to rich agricultural lands through the construction of an intricate system of dikes. The universal sobriquet for The Netherlands was The Lowlands, for, indeed, the highest elevation in the entire country was barely 300 feet above sea level. But it was in its coastal waters and rivers that its future and fortunes as a maritime power lay.

The coast of the United Provinces, fronting on the North Sea, was extremely irregular. In the north a windswept arc of islands, called the West Friesians, marked a once-continuous offshore sandbar that had been ruptured by storms during the thirteenth century. Behind these low-slung islands were miles of hostile, wide mud-flats, that were usually submerged at high tide. Along the Zeeland coast to the south, the shoreline was also typified by low-lying islands, but unlike the West Friesian Islands, these were born from the ancient sediments deposited by the Scheldt, Maas, and Rhine rivers.

If The Netherlands was to be called a maritime state, it was also, of necessity, a riverine state, for it literally sat astride and controlled the strategic outlets of some of Europe's most important rivers. As the Rhine entered the country, it divided into two main branches, the Lek and the Waal. The Meuse, flowing from France through the Spanish Netherlands (modern Belgium), emptied as the Maas into the sea south of Rotterdam. The estuary of the Scheldt, which was primarily a Belgian waterway, was also in The Netherlands. And in the north was the Zuider Zee, an enormous, shallow, saltwater sea that would be closed off centuries later, drained, and turned into productive farmland. Linking these waterways, primarily in the central and southern Netherlands, was a series of canals, which provided an excellent network for inland waterborne transportation. The Netherlands of the seventeenth century were typified by a moderate marine climate, with westerly winds and the warming waters of the North Atlantic Drift sweeping the coast. Laced with high humidity, it was also subject to frequent sea fogs. And, swept away by the salt sea breezes, the young Dutch nation's ships sailed with clerks and soldiers, entrepreneurs and speculators, to the four corners of the earth, successfully challenging their mighty rivals, England, France, and Spain, for the fruits of empire.

Perhaps it was The Netherlands' unique form of republican government, which emerged from the Eighty Years War, that permitted its precipitous rise from a tiny state, outnumbered, outpopulated, and surrounded by many powerful enemies with far more resources in hand. Each state or individual provincial Parliament of the Republic varied somewhat in its makeup and in the manner of the selection of its deputations to the central assembly, the States General, but all valued their right, and supported one another's right, to independent action above all else. In the two major maritime provinces of Holland and Zeeland, the delegations to the States General were nominated by regents of each of the major towns in the respective provinces. An additional delegate representing the nobility in each of the two provinces was also permitted, guaranteeing the domination of representation by an urban patriciate. In the province of Friesland, the major landowning farmers exercised the weightiest influence, while in Gelderland it was the nobility that manipulated the balance of power. Each of the remaining provinces varied in its selection processes and in the power force that managed it in diverse ways. Yet in all seven provinces, the urban patrician class asserted the inordinate influence and authority that fueled the engines of commerce, government, and war. In Dutch towns, magistrates were elected by municipal councils, and judicial and rural civil service posts were filled by the provincial governments.[1]

The strength of the Republic lay in the mutually recognized sovereignty of each provincial state by the rest. The stability of each provincial government was practically insured by the control of municipal government, the root system of authority, by the upper middle class, upon whose business and trade the province depended. As the noted historian C. R. Boxer suggested, the mutually accepted recognition of each provincial state's sovereignty insured the domination of the Republic by the upper middle class, producing, in effect, a monopoly of all provincial and municipal posts by an oligarchy of 10,000 individuals.[2]

They were a prudent, sober, conservative lot, whose faces peer emotionless from the paintings of Rembrandt and Frans Hals. Yet they were driven by a self-righteous pride and patriotic devotion to their respective cities, ancient centers in which generation after generation of the ruling class had prospered, passing on their industry and acumen, authority and sinecures to the next in line.

As a nation, the seven provinces were unified only by the States General, in whose hands was entrusted the foreign policy of The Netherlands, which epitomized the image of solidarity that the world saw. Composed of a varying number of delegates from each of the provinces (though each of the seven delegations had only one vote), the States General was, in reality, a prisoner of the will of its sovereign members, who were in turn bound by instructions dictated by their respective states. When an issue concerning the "Generality," or the Republic as a whole, required attention, or when a delegate proposal not covered by some provinces' directions was mooted, a unanimous vote was required for the resolution or proposal to be validated. Frequently, delegations were obliged to refer such matters back to the municipal councils of their respective provinces before reaching a decision. And, as no province was required to obey any directions of the States General unless mutual consent by the entire body had been achieved, it was often difficult to function effectively—especially when provincial interests outweighed national objectives.[3]

Among the principal drawbacks that frequently shackled the States General were the conflicting provincial interests that repeatedly deadlocked major issues, usually issues relating to admiralty, commercial, or maritime affairs. Five of the seven provinces fielded their own navies, which were administered by their own admiralties and supported by provincial taxation, the largest of which were those of Holland and Zeeland. During war, combined operations often resulted in an overabundance of leaders, all of equal admiralty or flag rank but under the command of an admiral appointed by the Grand Pensionary of the States General, usually a Hollander with a bias toward his own province's admiralty. Commercial rivalries were equally divisive. In such instances, a strong individual, group, or political block was called upon to render a decision and push it through to acceptance by all parties. The most influential leadership was frequently supplied by the State of Holland, which carried the largest portion of the Republic's financial burden (and consequently great political clout), and the princely House of Orange-Nassau. Often, the city of Amsterdam dominated the leadership of Holland through its highest official, the Grand Pensionary, (Raad Pensionaris), who cooperated with a working committee elected by the States General.[4]

With such a decentralized government, it was something of a miracle that the Republic was able to field great armies and navies at all, or to pay for them through taxation. Indeed, as one historian has suggested, it was only through the dedication and sense of destiny of the stern Calvinist oligarchy of the States that the system held together and flourished at all.[5] With each of five provinces fielding its own navy, it was equally miraculous that cooperation at sea was possible. Only

Prologue: Mad for a Dutch War

through the iron-fisted and brilliant leadership of such naval geniuses as De Ruyter, and the Tromp and Evertsen families, and political leaders such as Willem I, Willem II, and Johan de Witt were such disparities forged in the fires of continuous warfare and beaten into a single national sword. It was a system that somehow not only worked, despite its many weaknesses, but that carried the United Provinces to a pinnacle of commercial, cultural, and military influence on the world stage. Yet the success of the Republic was also rooted in its people, whose watchwords, unlike those of England, France, and Spain, were freedom of trade, toleration, and security. By the mid-seventeenth century, religious wars were no longer as important as trade to the Dutch, who saw Catholic, Protestant, and Jew alike as worthy trading partners. Commerce, even in the midst of conflict, was acceptable if it was beneficial to the Republic's merchants.

It is not surprising that, although the republican Netherlands were a novelty at the time (Venice and remote, agrarian Switzerland excepted), revolution and civil war did not end in northern Europe with the success of the Republic. In 1649, a year after the United Provinces achieved recognition, Charles I was beheaded and the monarchy abolished in England. Surprisingly, this act of regicide (or patricide as some Dutch preferred to call it) did not find universal favor in Holland. Surviving Stuarts and Royalists fled before the armies of Oliver Cromwell to France and to republican Holland. In The Netherlands they received the protection and monetary aid of the House of Orange-Nassau and consequently the sympathy of the Dutch people. Unfortunately for the late King's heir, Prince Charles, the sympathetic Stadholder, Prince Willem II of Orange-Nassau, died in 1650, just before his own son was born. Thus, circumstances that were destined to carry Holland closer to pure republicanism had the effect of leaving the impecunious Stuart exiles in the United Provinces more tolerated than admired.

Though Princess Maria, widow of the late Stadholder, assumed the regency for her infant son Willem III, the United Provinces quickly drifted toward government by the States General, in the control of which it would remain until 1672. During this golden age of republicanism, a core of wealthy merchants and republicans in the proud city of Amsterdam employed the opportunity of the regency to terminate the hereditary Stadholdership as an institution, and with it the singularly powerful influence over Dutch affairs of the House of Orange-Nassau. In place of an executive Stadholder, the provinces and their States General (a hybridized executive and legislative unit) would manage the nations' policies and future. The bankers, investors, and merchants of the wealthy city of Amsterdam held effective control over the city's representatives and domination of the delegation of Holland. Holland, in turn, became the most dominant of all the Dutch provinces, and sagaciously exercised its influence and power to enormous effect. The decentralizing result that evolved was government by regents, or boards of directors—a corporate state of 1.8 million people, approximately 42 percent of whom lived in cities oriented by their merchant leaders toward international mercantile and fiscal success.

The open and dynamic economy of The Netherlands incorporated an urban life attractive to many. Immigrants, at first from Flanders, and later from Scandinavia and Germany, brought to Holland's cities their wealth and skills. In the seventeenth century, immigrants accounted for a third of all persons marrying in the city of Amsterdam alone. The urban melting pot had soon successfully congealed into a dedicated national entity based on capitalism and private incentive. In regard to immigration and urban capitalism, The Netherlands presented a stark contrast to England, her principal rival on the North Sea. Urban population growth exceeded that of England until 1700, a year in which the latter's total population was more than three times that of The Netherlands. Real wages for construction in southern England stood in sad but dramatic relief when compared to those in the Province of Holland. Wages paid in England, in fact, would not exceed Holland's until the nineteenth century.[6]

Despite their apparent political and religious similarities after 1650, the two titanic republican and Protestant states of northern Europe found it increasingly difficult to walk arm-in-arm, let alone continue friendly relations. Increasingly, England viewed its upstart rival's economic success as its own failure. Economic theory of the day dictated that there was but a finite amount of business possible. Market expansion was unknown, communications were agonizingly slow, storage of goods unreliable, and distribution relatively primitive. Production of what few durable goods there were was in the hands of trade and craft guilds. Thus, what one country put into its own coffers was thought to have been taken from the other's. Central to England's quarrel with the Dutch was that they kept inventing new mechanisms, means, and processes to increase their own rate of success, improving their profit margins to England's great economic detriment, and they had done so almost from the moment of the birth of the Dutch nation. While England endured the full force of a precipitous plunge in real wages in the sixteenth century, the economy of The Netherlands between 1580 and 1620 climbed steadily, even though mired by military conflicts, with a vigorously expanding trade and industry.[7]

Prologue: Mad for a Dutch War

The Dutch had long heard, and were inured to, English complaints that they were less than grateful for England's important assistance in achieving their independence. But such English attitudes ignored the Netherlanders' enormous competence at sea and the indomitable Dutch will to survive. When, in 1639, a Dutch fleet under Admiral Maarten Tromp encountered the largest Spanish fleet since the Invincible Armada in the Downs, 47 galleons and 24,000 men strong, under the command of Admiral don Antonio Oquendo, England was stunned by the outcome. Thirty-two Spanish ships were lost or run ashore on the English coast, and 10,000 Spaniards had perished. Spanish seapower was forever destroyed as an element in the reckoning of European power politics.[8] But the Dutch answers to England's complaints were not only military. The Netherlands had developed the skills, systems, and boats to exploit and dominate the North Sea fisheries and the rich Baltic timber and grain trade while England remained backward. The differences, national biases aside, were also technological. English fishing boats of the age were relatively small, unsafe in heavy Channel and North Sea weather, unable to fish far from port, and the fishermen were unable to derive the maximum benefits from the fruits of their labor through a flexible marketing system such as the one developed by their rivals across the North Sea. By midcentury, the Dutch had developed an excellent multipurpose, threemasted merchant ship called the *fluit*, or flyboat, which was easy to handle, needed fewer crewmen than the English vessels, and was superb for use as an auxiliary military transport for fighting fleets because of its great carrying capacity. The Dutch then excelled in all of the maritime arts and sciences. Dutch mapmakers, such as Wagenaer, were renowned in all nations for their sea charts, which were in common usage on English ships where they were known as "Waggoners." As mariners, the Dutch were equalled by none, and drew oblique praise even from those who intended otherwise. In 1652, one English visitor to Holland, in a generally abusive pamphlet entitled "A Brief Character of the Low Countries under the States, being three weeks observation of the Vices and Virtues of the Inhabitants," grudgingly stated of the Dutch that "almost all among them are seamen born, and like frogs can live on both land and water."[9]

Not long after republicans assumed the reins of government in England, they began to take aggressive actions to remedy their commercial shortcomings and to expand their own naval and maritime power by attempting to curb a growing Dutch trade with English colonies. Oliver Cromwell and the British Parliament had good reason to be concerned. In 1644, one pamphleteer stated, the United Provinces could boast of a merchant marine of 80,000 seamen, a thousand topsail merchantmen and a fishing fleet of 6,000 herring busses and inland vessels. Another thousand vessels were suitable for warships. The Netherlands East India Company, almost a government unto itself, could field, on its own, 150 ships, and employed 15,000 people, many of whom were seamen.[10]

On April 27, 1651, a delegation from the Protectorate and Parliament of England appeared in The Hague with a proposition, superficially aimed at the renewal of the nonaggression and peace treaty dating from 1495 between the British Crown and the Dutch province. Cromwell's grand objectives were republican in sentiment, for in his policy of *unus gens una republica* he sought union with The Netherlands, but a union resulting in the subservience of the lesser to the greater. Early on, the delegation from the States General determined that negotiations had reached an impasse.[11] The ancient fifteenth-century treaty had contained six clauses, to which the British desired to add a seventh. The additional article sought agreement by the United Provinces not to aid "enemies of England" in any way, including refugees and rebels. The clause was clearly directed against the Stuarts and their supporters, who had found consolation, shelter, and monetary assistance from the powerful House of Orange-Nassau. Such a demand placed the Dutch in a quandary, for the ousting of the Stuarts might prove bad for business, as England's American colonies, Maryland and Virginia in particular, with whom the Dutch had a substantial trade, had not yet submitted to the republicans.

The formal proposition of May 10, 1651, was not acceptable to The Hague, and the States General offered, and vigorously debated, its own alternative treaty. There were important differences between the two proposed treaties, the most apparent being that of length. Where Parliament's offered seven articles, the States General's "permanent, irrevocable and Eternal" treaty of "Friendship, Unity [and] Correspondence" proposed thirty-six. But in its second article, the Dutch proposal laid its intentions bare: it was to assure existing or future freedoms of defense, commerce, navigation, and national interests. In return for far-reaching guarantees on free navigation and commerce, including a specific Dutch right to trade directly with England's colonies in the Caribbean and the Chesapeake, both countries would agree not to aid each other's rebels, which, in the context of the times, referred solely to England's problems with the Royalists.

Whether it was this last issue that proved too much for the English or whether it was the guaranteed freedom to uncontrolled and unlimited fishing rights everywhere for the Dutch, including in English waters, the Parliament in Westminster could not accept the States General's proposal. In response, the English Ambassador drafted the first Navigation Act, a piece of legislation destined to influence the course of European and American history for decades to come. With Dutch cooperation obviously not an immediate prospect in The Hague, Cromwell's Council of State passed, on October 9, 1651, an act for increase of shipping and encouragement of the navigation, the start of a series of so-called Navigation Acts designed to both promote English shipping and to cut into Dutch trade supremacy, especially with England's own colonies.

At the same time, the English began overt seizures of Dutch merchantmen on the grounds that they were conducting illegal trade with England's colonies, something that was true from the English point of view, but only a technicality from that of the Dutch. A number of the American colonies had not agreed to be ruled by Cromwell's protectorate, and the republic had yet to force them to submit. After the failure of the treaty ploy, England's demands on The Netherlands became quite simple: ten percent of the herring they caught in English waters, continued salutation of the English flag, and no Dutch commerce with English colonies. England pursued a strategy of strict enforcement of its new policy to ensure Dutch compliance. After Parliament brought Virginia under its dependency on March 13, 1652, and carried out a series of seizures of Dutch merchantmen in English waters for alleged trading with the enemy Royalists, the *casus belli* between the rival commercial states was given form and substance. England's claim to the Right of the Flag, the pretended right that ships of all other nations should lower their topsails and strike their national colors whenever they should encounter a British warship flying the flag of England, became the trip-wire of war. And the man who tested the Lion's teeth in May 1652 was none other than the pride of the Province of Zeeland, Admiral Maarten Tromp. In a fateful encounter with England's Admiral Robert Blake, Tromp refused to strike his flag and battle ensued.

The First Anglo-Dutch War officially began on May 19, 1652. The smaller Holland and Zeeland ships did not fare too badly in the three major engagements of that year: off Plymouth in August, in the Downs at the Battle of the Kentish Knock in September, and off Dungeness in November. Both sides claimed (and still claim) these as decisions, if not victories. But in February 1653, the gallant and outgunned Tromp lost the Three Day Battle off Portland, the Battle of the North Foreland in June, and then his life in the Battle of Ter Heide in late July. If it had not been for the outbreak of war between England and Spain in 1654, it is probable that the Dutch might have lost everything, especially in

Raid on America

America, before the Peace of Westminster was signed on April 15, 1654. In fact, Cromwell had sent an expedition to New England to enlist colonial support in the conquest of New Netherland (a vast, sparsely settled region in what are now the states of New York, New Jersey, and Delaware). The New Englanders were more than pleased with an opportunity to gain control of wealthy New Amsterdam, the administrative center of the colony, on the tip of Manhattan Island. Indeed, a force of 900 men and a troop of cavalry were preparing to leave Boston when peace intervened.[12] But the Dutch had learned much from the war, particularly regarding the imperfections of their fleet. Under the leadership of the Grand Pensionary, Johan de Witt, the United Provinces set out upon a major shipbuilding program, which culminated in 1655 with the fielding of the 90-gun *Zeven Provinciën*, commissioned at Delftshaven for the Admiralty of the Maas.[13]

It is not surprising that the British profited more from its war with the weakened and bloated Spanish Empire than it did from that with the young and resilient Holland. In 1655, England captured the island of Jamaica and obtained its first important foothold in the northern Caribbean. In the same year, Parliament formed the Board of Trade to bring some order to its hitherto largely freebooting commerce in the West Indies, something the efficient Dutch had organized far more successfully in their East Indies and West Indies Companies. England's colonies, some of whom had to be threatened into obedience to the Protectorate, however, were not pleased with the practical effects of Cromwell's Navigation Act on their own welfare and prosperity. Virginia planters, for instance, were still complaining in 1656 that "unless it be a little dispenct withall," the Navigation Act would ruin rather than improve its trade.[14] The Dutch had effectively integrated the small and efficient merchantmen, the fluit, with a free-market economy. Compared with the English, they could build ships more quickly and more cheaply, and they could operate them efficiently with smaller crews at lower cost. They kept their import duties low so that business, especially the maritime trades, was encouraged. From bases in New Netherland, they could and did ply the coasts of the English colonies (which for Cromwell was certainly justification enough to eject them from that place) or sailed directly from Europe to purchase for cash or kind whole crops and then distribute them to the western world from Amsterdam at a profit. The English, by contrast, seemed largely inefficient shippers, monopolistic mercantilists who offered fixed prices to the producers but proved short of hard cash to pay their debts. Apart from war, their usual response to the Dutch challenge was to tighten ever more firmly the screws in the Navigation Acts.[15]

English mercantilists were delighted with the new laws, for enforcement of their restrictions on trade meant the difference between prosperity and power and poverty and weakness for the competing European states. The colonies, both in the Western Hemisphere and in Southeast Asia, were intended to be producers and suppliers of raw commodities needed by the industries and traders of Europe. Basic foodstuffs such as fish, fruit, sugar, and salt (a necessity for food preservation) were, perhaps, the most important. The list of key consumer goods also included such luxury items as dye-woods, cotton, fine woods, furs, tropical produce, and, in ever-increasing volumes, tobacco. Sugar, dried fish, and tobacco were among the principal export commodities of the American colonies, high-value goods for European traders, which increased in demand in a developing European economy with expanding extra-personal income that could be spent on nonessentials.

If for England, France, and The Netherlands, sugar was sweet gold, the West Indies was the gold mine. In British-owned Barbados there were 745 plantations in 1667, ranging in size from several hundred to a thousand acres, producing sugar for export. A slave population of over 82,000 provided the labor force necessary to keep the plantations producing. As early as 1650, the Barbadian crop was valued at over £3,000,000. By the onset of the last quarter of the seventeenth century, Jamaica, with 200,000 acres granted to 717 families for plantations, boasted of 70 sugar works on the island, while the French West Indies produced 5,350 long tons a year.[16]

But it was tobacco that bonded America, England, and The Netherlands together in the seventeenth century as consumers and middlemen, and then pitted them against one another. With the exception of Brazil for a short few years, The Netherlands possessed no colonies in the Western Hemisphere capable of producing large quantities of tobacco. Instead, it succeeded in becoming the vital link as a tobacco importer, exporter, and manufacturer, a position achieved with the cooperation—indeed, the collusion—of the English colonists.

King James of England first recognized the importance of tobacco to his realm in 1620 with the appointment of the "Nicotianae Commission" and engaged in a formidable attempt to regulate its trade. Like many later edicts, James's "proclamation for restraint of the disordered trading of tobacco" had little effect on the business. In 1622, he was obliged to appoint a committee of the Council to control navigation and trade with England's infant American colonies. The Dutch, with more commercial shipping and active traders and the capability to build on an important warehousing industry at home, were already skimming the best tobacco Virginia had to offer. The English effort at regulation had a pitifully insignificant effect. Another proclamation, issued in 1624 and followed at a later date by Orders in Council, prohibited the use of foreign ships to freight Virginia tobacco to the marketplace. The effort proved to be an escalatory measure built upon sand. Finally, James was obliged to ban the import of tobacco grown elsewhere, a ban that his successor, Charles I, repeated for good measure soon after his investiture. Each year the Crown seemed to produce another proclamation on tobacco: once in 1626, twice in 1627, and again in 1630,[17] but the effect of England's efforts to control her colonial trade was quite limited. In 1632, a recommendation in the Virginia Assembly to trade with the Dutch was accepted. The crown countered in 1633 with two more attempts to stop the free-market movement in which the Dutch played their usual entrepreneurial role. For England, such efforts at control proved fruitless throughout the 1630s.[18]

An effort to put more force behind the regulations, and the first movement toward what later became codified in the fatal Navigation Acts, was initiated in 1641. In that year a number of English merchants urged that the rules established in the 1630s controlling the shipping and selling of tobacco be embodied in an Act of Parliament. After all, such protectionist measures were meant to assure their own monopoly and to prevent Dutch competition. To achieve their ends, however, it was believed that the American intra-colonial commerce, an incestuous triangle that involved the Chesapeake Bay colonies of Maryland and Virginia, New Netherland, and New England, and dealt in everything from fish and furs to tobacco and wine, continued unabated and therefore had to be stopped. In 1644, the Long Parliament banned shipment of fish oil, fins, and gills from the colonies in foreign ships as well as the import of wine, wool, and silk from France. These measures were meant to boost English shipping, at the expense of the colonial fishing industry in America. The detrimental effects of these regulations, from the colonists' point of view, was that they would no longer be able to enjoy the cheaper Dutch shipping rates to move their products to market. In an attempt to soften the blow, the Long Parliament also passed a measure which allowed goods to be exported duty-free from England to the colonies, as long as they were carried aboard English vessels. To eradicate the illegal trade through New England, parliament also voted to levy taxes on Tidewater tobacco imported through New England by Dutch middlemen in New Netherland.[19] The net result for those in the colonies who adhered to the regulations was to raise the cost of doing business. For the home country merchants, however, it was a blessing.

Matters remained that way until the death of King Charles I in 1649. Upon Cromwell's assumption of power, Parliament passed an act that prohibited trade with England's American colonies in an effort to shut down all commerce completely until they acknowledged the Protectorate's authority.[20] After attempts to negotiate a treaty with The Netherlands failed, almost exactly one year later the implementation of the first Navigation Act formally codified England's mercantile politics.[21] It was unabashedly anti-Dutch and pro-English, stating that only those ships of which the owner, the captain, and the majority of sailors were Englishmen or English colonials had the right to carry on trade between England and her colonies; the coasting trade, whether between British or colonial ports; and England's foreign trade, so far as it concerned the plantations. The only exception to the regulations was the right of other nations to import in their own ships the products and commodities of their own countries. But such actions were also anti-Dutch, since Holland, a nonmanufacturing nation, could claim the manufacture of little more than woolens. Cromwell and his associates assumed that these steps would deny the rival Dutch the England-colonial freight business and, with any luck, extinguish their flourishing warehousing and entrepôt trade, and shift it to England.

It was one thing to pass an act but another to see it enforced. In this case, enforcement actually encouraged New Netherland's illicit trade in tobacco with Maryland and Virginia. The presence of the wealthy Dutch trading colony on the Hudson, firmly and strategically planted between the Chesapeake and New England and very active in the Caribbean trade, enabled their partners in the English colonies to evade the 1651 Navigation Act with ease. For, despite England's demands, Maryland had no ships of her own and was forced to rely on Virginia merchant ships, New England vessels, and Dutch merchantmen to export her produce. There were thus enormous opportunities for illegal trade.

As might be expected of a trade that was largely outside the law, there are few reliable figures for trans-Atlantic tobacco shipment in the seventeenth century. Colonial statistics were often imprecise on purpose: alleged floods, drought, spoilage, Indian attacks, and plagues of insects could be relied on to help portions of crops disappear from the books. Although English statistics depended upon their colonies' obedience to the regulations and proper bookkeeping, there was room for imprecision at the other end, too. The English importers' greatest profit did not come, in fact, from evading the Navigation Act but rather the high English import duties on tobacco. The most effective technique was to land tobacco and immediately reexport under a paper transaction to a nearby duty-free port, such as the Isle of Man. From there small boats would bring it in smaller quantities into England duty-free. It is generally assumed that the relatively small amount of duty collected in England on its own intercolonial trade demonstrated general English collusion in tax evasion.[22]

Massachusetts, Connecticut, and Rhode Island at first prohibited exports to both the Dutch and the French in America. And, although under the terms of Virginia's surrender to Parliament on March 12, 1652, the colony technically possessed the right to free trade, Virginia too was forced to apply the Navigation Act. There was, however, general discomfort with the Act, even in England. In 1652, the city of Newcastle had already requested reinstatement of "such ancient libertyes and fredomes in their trade with the Low Countryes" and the City of London had preceded Newcastle with public objections to the Act, as it deprived them of their profitable business with the Dutch market.[23] Enforcement was notoriously ineffective. After 1654, the American colonies resumed business as usual with the Dutch. Rhode Island picked up her profitable trade with the Dutch; New England traders and Virginia planters shipped Virginia tobacco to New Amsterdam for reshipment to Holland, and Massachusetts made sure it did not lose any business, either.[24]

The restoration of the Stuarts to the throne brought The Netherlands no relief from the English trade war, although that country had sheltered the English during the Protectorate. Charles II, who had begged assistance from the House of Orange-Nassau, now renewed the 1651 ordinance as the "Navigation Act of 1660." This revival of the anti-Dutch measure was now intended to provide the Crown with badly needed revenue, to rebuild the Royal Navy, and to help reestablish England's place of power in Europe. Indeed, when it was debated in August 1660 in the House of Commons, the Speaker stated that the Act "will enable your Majesty to give the law to foreign princes" and "to enlarge your Majesty's dominions all over the world."[25] To do so, it added new and tougher clauses to improve Cromwell's 1651 act.

Vessels now had to be owned by Englishmen, and each ship's master and three-fourths of her seamen had to be English subjects. Logically, for a country already short on ships, captured vessels built abroad were also included, except for those built by colonists, for there was no way of telling whether a "reflagging" deal had been made in the colonies to benefit the partnership of a colonial entrepreneur and a Dutchman. London issued clarifications to prevent misunderstandings of this clause on captures. In fact, one of the Committees on Trade and Plantations' most important jobs was to prevent foreigners from resuming the England-colonial trade through the rules on passes, denization and naturalization, and foreign-built ships.

The British sought to block every possible loophole. The colonies' most important raw-material exports were listed in the Enumeration of Commodities clause, added only on the third reading of the act. Sugar, tobacco, cotton, fustic and other dye-woods, and cocoa (which was added in 1672 when chocolate-drinking became the rage in England) could be shipped directly and only to England. The 1663 Navigation Act tightened this clause by stating that all European goods bound for the colonies had to be shipped first to England and unloaded and physically put on shore there before they could be shipped on. The purpose was to make sure that British middlemen took part in each transaction and to prevent the colonies from finding independent, non-English sources of goods.

The Navigation Act also required a bond and security from all ships leaving England for the colonies and for all ships leaving a colonial port with a cargo of goods listed in the Enumeration Clause. To ensure this clause was enforced, colonial governors were granted one-third of all goods they confiscated on the grounds of illegal trading. The Act of 1663 also required English governors to take an oath before assuming office to do all in their power to enforce the laws under penalty of £1,000 sterling, loss of office, and ineligibility for another governorship. Instructions given in England in 1662 by King Charles II to Virginia's governor, Sir William Berkeley, reveal that, at least in Virginia, the Acts of Navigation had failed to stop colonials from carrying on illegal trade with the Dutch. Berkeley was directed to limit production of tobacco in his colony, to encourage the planters to produce other staples, and, above all, to observe the acts of trade, providing facts and figures in annual reports to England.[26] Covering all angles, another piece of legislation, the 1662 Act of Frauds, stated that

> No sort of wines (other than Rhenish), no sort of spicery, tobacco, potashes, pitch, tar, salt, rozin, deale boards, fir timber, or olive oyle shall be imported into England, Wales or Berwick from the Netherlands or Germany upon any pretence whatsoever in any sort of ships or vessels whatsoever.[27]

The English colonists, of course, were not alone in their independent trade practices. Dutch traders, too, were sidestepping the East Indies and West Indies companies' duties and levies on their own business activities with the same creative evasions and questionable bookkeeping. In a memorandum dating to about 1670, an anonymous Dutch clerk summed up the problem of the West Indies Company:

> Virginia-bound ships, which seldom depart from here, and return loaded as a rule with tobacco, pay 30 stuivers for each 400 lb barrel of tobacco, and as this is paid against value, it has happened that on the pretext that the tobacco is spoiled, moderation [of the amount due] is permitted, but only on condition that the Board of the Admiralty is given a percentage of the auction proceeds; this is done after the fact, being intended, after all, to prevent all the dirty tricks which usually are concealed beneath such pretexts.[28]

In 1672 the English instituted yet another refinement of measures to control colonial trade. Aroused by reports of illegal commerce in tobacco, the Parliament enacted that in case the usual bond or promise to carry the enumerated commodities directly to England were not given, a duty of a penny per pound of tobacco should be paid to the collector at the port of clearance and earmarked for the Royal Revenue. The intention was to stop yet another colonial subterfuge. Since all goods had to first be landed in England, some planters were simply shipping their goods from Europe (often from Holland) to another plantation in the Americas, landing them there, and then shipping them home so that they would technically have been on English soil and thus in compliance with the Act. The circumventing loophole was, of course, discovered and blocked in 1675, after the last Anglo-Dutch War, with a proclamation that prohibited the import of European commodities that were not loaded in England into any of His Majesty's plantations in Africa, Asia, or America. It also reaffirmed all other laws relating to the trade of the plantations.[29]

War tensions between Holland and England intensified precipitously after the new round of Navigation Acts. In July 1663, several Stuart lieutenants explored the possibility of seizing New Netherland for King Charles II's brother, James, Duke of York, and eliminating the Dutch "cancer" amid England's American colonies. In January 1664, they reported that the operation was both feasible and likely to succeed. In April, King Charles II and Lord Clarendon created a commission to deal with the project. Members of the commission were Colonel Richard Nicolls, Groom of the Duke of York's Bedchamber and the governor over the as-yet uncaptured colony; Colonel Robert Carr; Colonel George Cartwright; and Samuel Maverick. The commissions' mission was twofold. Its first objective was to heal factional strife, civil and ecclesiastical, between Massachusetts and Connecticut, and to resolve boundary and charter disputes among New Plymouth, Rhode Island, and Providence Plantation. They were also authorized to visit all of

Prologue: Mad for a Dutch War

England's American colonies, to report on the laws, manners and customs of the local governments, and to find new ways of making the colonies more profitable to the Crown.[30]

The second objective, issued in private instructions to the four commissioners on April 23, 1664, was

> the possessing Long Island, and reduceing that people to an entyre submission and obedience to us & our government, now vested by our grant and Commission in our Brother the Duke of York, and by raising forts or any other way you shall judge most convenient or necessary soe to secure that whole trade to our subjects, that the Dutch maye noe longer ingrosse and exercise that trade which they have wrongfully possessed themselves of.[31]

Dovetailing the commission's instructions, the Duke of York optimistically issued deeds of lease and release on June 24, 1664, (after the expedition sailed) for a portion of the New Netherland colony to be known as Nova Caesarea, or New Jersey, to Sir George Carteret and Lord Sir John Berkeley, while conveying the Delaware region to William Penn, son of Vice Admiral Sir William Penn.

The commission's goals were clear enough as they sailed from Portsmouth on May 15, 1664, aboard the frigate *Guinea*, accompanied by three other armed vessels and three companies of seasoned troops. They were to gain control of the strategic Dutch colony between New England and Maryland, to eliminate opportunities for English planters and traders to sell directly to the Dutch and defraud the Crown of revenues that it badly needed, and to gain control of the Dutch trade with the Iroquois Confederacy of the Mohawk, Oneida, Onondaga, Cayuga, and Seneca tribes. Two months later, on August 26, the flagship of the little squadron dropped anchor in Nyack Bay (modern Gravesend Bay), between Coney Island and New Utrecht. Upon the arrival of the remainder of the squadron, Nicolls received a message from New Amsterdam's governor, Peter Stuyvesant asking the purpose of their presence—for there was no war between the two nations. Nicolls replied haughtily, stating that it was an affront to King Charles II

> to Suffer any Forraigners how near soever they may be Allyed to usurp a Dominion and without his Maties Royal Consent to inhabit in those or any other his Maties Territoryes, hath Commanded me in his name to require a surrender of all such Forts, Towns or Places of Strength which are now possessed by the Dutch under your Commands And in his Maties Name I do Demand the Town scituate upon the Island commonly known by the name of Manhatoes [Manhattan] with all the Forts thereunto belonging to be render'd unto his Maties Obedience and protection unto my hands.[32]

Raid on America

With few defenses capable of resistance, Stuyvesant surrendered the fort and city without bloodshed on August 29. Soon afterwards, Nicolls dispatched Sir Robert Carr with *Guinea,* the armed merchantman *William Nicholas,* and 100 soldiers under the joint command of his brother, Lieutenant John Carr and Ensign Arthur Stocke, to reduce the Dutch garrison on the Delaware at New Amstel. The governor of the place, Alexander d'Hinoyossa, however, refused to surrender, but after three days of negotiations, on October 1, was attacked and subdued in his fort. Thereafter Sir Robert, to his eternal disgrace, conducted a program of wanton looting and robbery, consummated with tasteless excesses, against a people with whom his nation was not even at war.

But war had been sought, and war it would be.

Most officials in the British government supported England's race to engage the Dutch, and as then Clerk of the Admiralty Samuel Pepys noted, most of the English Court and Parliament held only contempt for the Hollanders and were "mad for a Dutch war." War fever had also swept the common English layman into its midst. Though the king was lukewarm to such adventures, he confessed that "the truth is they [the Dutch] have not great need to provoke this nation, for myself I believe there is scarce an Englishman that does not desire passionately a war with them."[33] Not only had fighting, instigated by England, broken out in America, but on the West Coast of Africa as well, where the crown hoped to secure strategic Dutch slaving and trading stations. For his own part, the cautious Pepys was not so exuberant. "All the news now," he confessed to his diary, "is what will become of the Dutch business, whether war or peace. We all seem to desire it, as thinking ourselves to have advantage at present over them; but for my part I dread it."[34]

In December 1664 hostilities spread to European waters when the king ordered Sir Thomas Allin to assail the rich Dutch convoy from the Levant, known as the Smyrna Fleet, then homeward-bound, in the Strait of Gibraltar. Dutch ships in English ports were seized and their cargoes confiscated. In late February the crown finally moved to declare war, which was officially announced on March 4, 1665.

For the United Provinces, torn by political bickering among the various provinces, hostilities came at the worst possible moment. A state of unreadiness pervaded the navies of the republic, which were swept by dissensions and rivalries, particularly between the admiralties of Amsterdam and Zeeland. The Dutch entered the contest with 103 men-of-war and eleven fireships (generally smaller than the English warships), mounting 4,869 guns, and manned by 21,556 officers and seamen. England had nearly 160 ships, 5,000 guns, and 25,000 men. But owing to provincial rivalry, the Grand Pensionary Johan de Witt, a Hollander, divided the fleet into seven separate squadrons, to prevent command from falling to Admiral Jan Evertsen, a Zeelander.[35] The initial effect was disastrous. On June 3, 1665, off Lowestoft, on the North Sea coast of England, the Duke of York's fleet humiliated that of Lietuenant Admiral Jacob van Wassenaer, Lord Obdam. The action resulted in the death of the illustrious Zeeland Admiral Cornelis Evertsen de Oude. The onset of the London Plague[36] slowed the English war machine somewhat that summer, but in the West Indies, where the sagacious privateer Henry Morgan was commissioned by the Governor of Jamaica to plunder, pillage, and seize all Dutch possessions in the region, The Netherlands' fortunes continued to plummet.

The sea battles of 1666 in European waters began more propitiously for the Dutch than had those of the preceding year. With the appointment of Lieutenant Admiral Michiel de Ruyter to the post of Commander in Chief, a military genius took charge of the disparate elements in the Dutch navy and bound them together. From June 1 to 5, De Ruyter defeated the Duke of Albemarle, Admiral George Monck, during the epic Four Day Battle off North Foreland, in one of the bloodiest, most fiercely-contested naval engagements in history.[37] On July 25, Monck returned to re-engage De Ruyter in the Two Day Battle between the North Foreland, at the entrance to the Thames, and Dunkirk, on the coast of France. Although managing to maintain the upper hand and free the river from a Dutch blockade, the English failed to inflict anything resembling defeat upon their foes. The following month, however, a British squadron under Sir Robert Holmes caused enormous damage to the Dutch marine—damage that was destined to be repaid in kind tenfold. Acting on information provided by a traitorous Dutch renegade named Captain Laurens Heemskerk, Holmes entered the Zuider Zee, behind the West Friesians, or Wadden Islands, and sailed through the Vlie, where he destroyed over £850,000 in property and burned more than 150 merchant vessels sheltered there and at the island of Terschelling.[38]

Once again, however, Charles II's government, drained by the war effort, faced bankruptcy. The general debt was approaching £2,500,000, of which £1,000,000 was for the navy alone. Unable to sustain a major fleet without the assistance of Parliament, with which the crown shared little love, the king resolved to lay up the first- and second-rate ships of the Royal Navy and rely upon commerce raiders to break the Dutch. Despite objections from the Duke of York and others, much of the English navy was called in. Yet it was the Great Fire of London, which began on September 2, 1666, in Pudding Lane, not far from London Bridge, that all but paralyzed the English war effort.[39] Shattered by the war, bankruptcy, plague, and fire, England was ready to sue for peace.

Negotiations began at Breda in the spring of 1667, under arbitration of the Swedish government. As old issues were raised and debated unceasingly, The Netherlands brazenly moved to strike the final military blow of the conflict, thereby securing the most beneficial terms. With much of the English fleet laid up or demobilized, De Ruyter saw his opportunity. On June 4 he left the Texel with a grand armada of 86 ships, 3,330 guns, 17,416 officers and men, and a force of Dutch marines. Three days later he arrived at the mouth of the Thames. His bold objective was to raid the Royal Navy's main fleet anchorage in the Medway, and possibly threaten London. On June 10 Sheerness was successfully stormed and captured along with its magazines and storehouses. The following day, aided by renegade English pilots, a division of ships under the command of Lieutenant Admiral Willem van Ghent prepared to enter the Medway. After forcing his way through an iron-chain boom and five scuttled ships laid across the waterway, Van Ghent pushed on for Chatham. The countryside and river towns were panic-stricken; streets leading away from Sheerness, Gravesend, Chatham, and other urban centers on the river became clogged with people fleeing with their possessions. At the Chatham Navy Yard, the Dutch found (among other things) 13 of England's finest warships, including the 100-gun flagship *Royal Charles* (now reduced by lack of funds to 32 guns), laid up or at anchor and deserted. They set about their work with vigor, ultimately taking or destroying 16 ships and inflicting one of the worst humiliations possible upon the enemy. The damage to England's prestige was incalculable.[40]

Londoners were terrified, and rumors circulated with abandon. Some even claimed that the king had abdicated and fled. Making the affair even more disgraceful was the fact that English seamen, many of whom had gone unpaid for months, deserted in large numbers to join the Dutch (who paid and fed their seamen with regularity), crying "Heretofore we fought for tickets now we fight for dollars." For several weeks De Ruyter blockaded the Thames, strangling commerce and securing control of the Channel for the homeward passage of the rich Dutch East India fleet. Peace was now a necessity England could not refuse.[41] On July 21, a month after the debacle on the Thames, the Treaty of Breda was signed.

The treaty signed on that summer day in the city of Breda was not, in light of the defeats they had suffered, particularly unpalatable for

England. First and foremost, it recognized all conquests made by each of the countries. England kept its plum, the strategic colony of New Netherland on the coast of North America. The Netherlands received the steamy jungle colony of Suriname on the South American mainland, which had been seized by Commander Abraham Crijnssen that spring. England conceded to the Dutch demands in West Africa. The French, who had been allied with the Dutch but who had failed to provide the slightest support, were granted Arcadia in Canada. But most importantly, the treaty modified British trade laws in favor of The Netherlands and provided for various commercial concessions while recognizing Dutch dominion over the East Indies. England's proud claim to the Right of the Flag was now limited to home waters. The ships of the United Provinces of the Netherlands, it appeared, were again free to sail unchallenged.

2

OUR BUSINESS IS TO BREAK
WITH THEM

From all appearances, the United Provinces of the Netherlands emerged victorious from the Second Anglo-Dutch War. Unhappily, the peace that followed, like that of the first war, only nurtured the roots of renewed hostilities, for England's economic problems, one of the causes of conflict, had been seriously exacerbated. Charles II began almost immediately to search for more subtle ways to defeat the Dutch while preparing for another military effort. For The Netherlands, the war had been one of survival, not conquest, and had produced a hollow victory. Although Dutch negotiators had eagerly demanded revocation of the Navigation Act, they had totally ignored any mention of the 1662 Act of Frauds in their rush toward peace, which proved sorely injurious to Amsterdam's warehousing and distribution business. Indeed, it seems quite probable that the Dutch negotiators, in their haste to conclude an acceptable treaty after the Medway, were ill-informed on this act and on the various amendments to the 1660 Navigation Act. Such oversights were destined to prove detrimental to The Netherlands and provided England with opportunities to expand upon old restrictions not addressed in the treaty.[1]

Johan de Witt, Grand Pensionary of the State of Holland, felt the flush of personal achievement after the Treaty of Breda, for it was he who was directly responsible for its terms. His popularity and influence were at their peak, and he was not slow in capitalizing on it to achieve his political ends. Trying to complete the work begun in 1650, while riding the crest of victory, he pushed through the States General the "Eternal Edict," which officially ended the hereditary office of

Stadholdership for the House of Orange-Nassau. With the advent of republicanism, royalists and bankers, he hoped, would no longer be the dominant factor. Merchants and republicans had triumphed.

Johan de Witt, Raad Pensionaris of Holland. *Courtesy Royal Netherlands Embassy.*

The winds of war, however, were never entirely subdued or far from The Netherlands. By the late summer of 1667, the powerful armies of King Louis XIV of France had begun to overrun the Spanish Netherlands. Fearing a possible Franco-Dutch alliance and partition of the Spanish empire or, worse, the complete subjugation of the Rhine delta by the growing might of the Sun King, many in England were alarmed and pressed for negotiations with the Dutch to form a military alliance, despite their commercial rivalry. The first move, however, was initiated by De Witt, who conveyed his objectives to the English Ambassador to The Hague in the fall of 1667. The Dutch, it appeared, were as fearful of a Franco-English alliance as were the English of a Franco-Dutch alliance. By the end of 1668, a military treaty with Holland was concluded at The Hague, to which Sweden later became signator. Faced by this Triple Alliance of Protestant states, France was forced to sign the Peace of Aix-la-Chapelle in 1668 and to evacuate the Rhine delta.[2]

Unlike Charles II, whose objective was to defeat The Netherlands to achieve commercial superiority, Louis XIV was intent on no less than the total destruction of the Dutch nation. Stung by the failure of his designs against the Spanish Netherlands, he began by dispatching Charles Colbert de Croissy to replace the Marquis Henri de Massue Ruvigny, the French Ambassador to England. De Croissy's principal mission was to break up the Triple Alliance and isolate Holland. Louis's efforts were received warmly by Charles, as was Charles's favorite sister, Henrietta-Anne, or "Minette," as he called her, the Duchesse d'Orleans, the wife of the Sun King's brother Philippe, Duc d'Orleans. The Duchesse and De Croissy had soon won Charles over to Louis's grand design. Sweden was detached almost as easily. In late spring, Minette sailed for England on a singularly important mission.

On May 22, 1670, a secret treaty was signed between England and France at Dover, an agreement as callously slippery and treacherously deceitful as any in history. In the document Charles agreed to support Louis' claim, through his wife's rights, to the monarchical possessions of Spain, for which England would receive, in turn, several territories in South America. France, however, was not to directly violate the Treaty of Aix-la-Chapelle, thus enabling Charles to remain superficially faithful to his own recently concluded alliance. Yet at the same time, the two nations pledged to wage a future war against The Netherlands. The arrangements for naval and military cooperation, however, were to be directly linked to Charles' willingness to proclaim himself a Catholic, "being convinced of the truth of the Catholic religion and resolved to declare it and reconcile himself with the Church of Rome as soon as the welfare of the kingdom will permit." In return, Louis promised a subsidy for the barren English war chest to support the effort against the Dutch (half in advance) and land troops if necessary. It was concluded that the combined attack on the United Provinces would follow, rather than precede, the declaration. This was small concession for such a diplomatic deceit. And as no time frame was given, the effort was open-ended, permitting both nations to prepare well for the contest.[3]

A formal treaty, however, was felt to be necessary—one intentionally lacking in features certain to prove difficult for Charles to explain should it be made public. On December 21, 1670, five of Charles's intimate ministers, popularly known as the Cabal—Sir Thomas Clifford, Lord of Chudleigh; Henry Bennet, Earl of Arlington; George Villiers, Duke of Buckingham; Lord Anthony Ashley Cooper (later Earl of Shaftsbury); and John Maitland, Earl of Lauderdale—signed a second treaty with France. This document, detailing the specifics of allied action against the United Provinces, even to troop movements, served, in effect, as a coverup for the initial agreement. England was to provide a fleet of 50 warships and 6,000 soldiers. France was to provide its own naval contingent of 30 ships and the bulk of land troops. Louis, having already determined upon his strategy for the mainland, agreed to permit England to manage the conduct of the war at sea, and in return Charles would receive as his share of territory the Zeeland islands of Walcheren, Cadzand, and Sluys, near the mouth of the Scheldt. The clause in the secret Treaty of Dover concerning Charles' acceptance of the Catholic faith, however, was not included, and was indeed veiled from the eyes of those ministers, such as Buckingham and Ashley, who might prove less than supportive. Neither was the treaty made known to Parliament or to the public. Nor, again, were there stipulations as to when such a war should begin. It was, in fact, to be a war of convenience. As for the alliance with France, Charles justified it to his Council by saying simply, "The French will have us or Holland always with them and if we take them not, Holland will have them."[4]

Unaware of the duplicity of its so-called ally, the United Provinces considered itself secure in the strength of the Triple Alliance, and as late as the autumn of 1671 hoped that the tripartite treaty would prove the ultimate defense against a French attack. Alarmed, however, at French rearmament, the States General began to reevaluate its own land and sea forces. On November 21, 1671, challenged by the Sun King, The Staten, or, States General, defended its actions in a letter that failed to reach Louis for a month. He received the communique with mock indignation and replied with provocative threats.

Late in 1671, as many in the States General began to feel the cold chill of war blowing once more across The Netherlands, the all-important issue of naval preparedness was once again addressed. A proposal for naval defense was called for. Representatives of the admiralties of Amsterdam, Zeeland, the Maas, the Northern Quarter, and

Friesland submitted their needs in December. The naval defenses of the United Provinces would require 72 warships of from 40 to 80 guns, 24 frigates and as many fireships, galliots and snaauws and other vessels, manned by no fewer than 10,000 men. The cost to the nation for the eight-month season during which such a force must be fielded was estimated at 7,893,992 guilders.[5]

The deputies to the Staten were soon engaged in deep and occasionally heated discussion, particularly on two key points: money and who was responsible for it; and whether the young Prince Willem III would be accorded the traditional—but since 1650 forbidden—title of Captain and Admiral General of the United Provinces. The landlocked provinces were, of course, opposed to spending their money for the benefit of Holland's and Zeeland's fleets when their own garrisons already stood in need of funds and troops. Finally, though the drift toward war seemed irreversible to many, the States General declared that it would fund a fleet of 48 warships—the size of the 1671 peacetime fleet. There would be no provocative action, such as a massive rearmament campaign, to jeopardize the already-fragile peace. The force outlined by the Staten would include only 36 warships of 60 to 80 guns, each with crews of 360 sailors and 80 soldiers; 12 other ships of war manned by 200 sailors and 50 soldiers; 24 fireships with crews of 22 each; 24 snaauws with crews of 25 apiece; and 24 hired galliots to carry messages and supplies. The Staten also shortened the season for which the fleet would be funded from eight months to seven. A total of 4,776,248 guilders was allocated for the navy.[6] The matter concerning the title for the young Prince of Orange was also hotly contested and introduced a new and explosive ingredient that neither the English nor the French had considered in their planning. Compounding the old partisan sentiments, the House of Orange was strongly connected by family with the State of Zeeland, the principal rival of the all-powerful State of Holland and the hub of anti-Orangist sentiments. The divisive issue concerning the elimination of the position of Stadholder by the Eternal Edict was one that had, in years past, thrown the States General into a confrontation before it had been adopted. Now, the resurrection of a solemn, popular young Orangist as a potential commander-in-chief of Dutch forces was a widely-acclaimed move calculated to draw the nation together.

Born in November 1650 to Willem II of Orange-Nassau and his princess, the daughter of Charles I of England, Willem III was an aggressive young man who had asserted his noble right to provincial office at his legal majority. The Republic remembered well his illustrious lineage—William the Silent, the soldier Prince Maurice, Frederick

Our Business is to Break with Them

Henry, and his own father Willem II—men whose leadership had guided the nation through precarious times. So, too, they decided, must the young Willem (born six days after his father's untimely death), whose future they would entwine with their own. Supporters of the Orangists also reasoned that Willem's own office might even produce a more positive stance from his uncle, the king of England. Thus, in February 1672, as hostilities again loomed large on the horizon, the 21-year-old Prince was appointed Captain General and Admiral General of all Dutch forces in the field.[7]

War had yet to be declared, for to do so England required provocation, an incident, to arouse the public and, undoubtedly, to soothe the national conscience. Almost any event, manufactured or otherwise, would do, for, as Lord Arlington succinctly put it, "Our business is to break with them yet to lay the breach at their door."[8]

When the royal yacht *Merlin* was dispatched to bring Lady Temple, wife of Ambassador to The Hague Sir William Temple, home to England, one such engineered incident almost succeeded. The captain had been directed to sail into the path of a Dutch squadron commanded by Admiral van Ghent (the same commander who had bravely forced the defenses of the Medway in 1667) and to fire at the squadron if it failed to lower its colors to those of the English. The intended act was clearly a violation of the Treaty of Breda, since it was to be undertaken in Dutch water. Upon encountering the yacht, Van Ghent did not salute. *Merlin* fired. Determined to evade an obviously contrived incident, the Dutchman swallowed his pride and lowered his flag. The Netherlanders thus carefully avoided giving England her longed-for excuse. The English, however, were not to be put off in their quest for war.[9]

In early March they were given another opportunity. Word had recently arrived that the Dutch Smyrna fleet, escorted by a squadron of six warships, was approaching the English Channel. Sir Robert Holmes was immediately ordered to sail from Portsmouth with all the warships he could assemble.

When Holmes put to sea, he was ordered to call upon any other English ships he might meet to assist him, and to intercept the Dutch. His squadron consisted of H.M.S. *St. Michael*, a second-rate 90-gun flagship; *Resolution*, commanded by the Earl of Ossory; *Cambridge*, Sir Fretchville Holles; *Fairfax*, Captain George Legge (later Earl of Dartmouth); and *Gloucester*, Captain John Holmes, third-raters all. In addition, there were also four smaller fourth- and fifth-rate warships. Off the Isle of Wight, Holmes chanced to encounter Sir Edward Spragge with six men-of-war bound home from the Mediterranean.

Raid on America

Had anything been seen of the Smyrna fleet, Holmes asked? Spragge replied that he had, in fact, been sailing in its company, and it was not too far distant astern. Without requesting his assistance or revealing his instructions—for he did not wish Spragge to share in his enterprise or in the booty—Holmes sailed on.[10]

On the morning of March 12 the British sighted the Smyrna fleet, 66 merchantmen escorted by six small Dutch men-of-war. The two warships in the Dutch van were commanded by Captain Eland de Blois, a crusty veteran of the Medway. The center two warships were under the direction of another veteran, Captain Adrian de Haese. And the rear was under a sagacious, 30-year-old Zeelander named Cornelis Evertsen the Youngest, one of the line commanders at Lowestoft and the Four Days Battle, and a member of one of the most illustrious naval dynasties in Dutch history.[11]

It was, perhaps, a trick of fate that Cornelis Evertsen the Youngest, the focus of this chronicle, was to be a participant in the sea fight that would initiate the Third Anglo-Dutch War, for he was also destined to promulgate the last major sea battle of that conflict as well. That he was a warrior born is without doubt, for his lineage was a mixture of saltwater, gunpowder, and blood. His great-grandfather, Evert Hendrickz (b. ca. 1550; d. ca. 1601), one of the original Dutch Sea Beggars, had become a Captain in 1572 and served on the North Sea. His grandfather, Captain Jan Evertsen de Oude (b. ca. 1572; d. 1617) had participated in the attack on the Spanish fleet at Antwerp in 1600, and later operated in the English Channel, the Atlantic, and Mediterranean against pirates, finally falling in a battle against French freebooters. He gave the Netherlands' navy no less than five of his sons, among whom were two of the most prominent admirals of Dutch naval history, Jan Evertsen and Cornelis Evertsen de Oude. Jan Evertsen, destined to rise to the rank of Lieutenant Admiral of Zeeland, had served The Netherlands well, battling Barbary Pirates, the Spanish, and the Portuguese whenever called upon. He had escorted the fabulous Silver Fleet taken by Piet Hein past the enemy at Dunkirk in the face of deadly odds in 1628. He had fought the English in the first two wars with England, and he would have commanded the entire Netherlands navy had not his loyalty to the House of Orange and to his province blocked promotion. Jan died fighting gallantly in the Two Day Battle in 1666. His son, Cornelis Evertsen de Jonge (1628–1679), was of equal stature, having been appointed Captain in 1652, fighting pirates and Englishmen alike. Having conducted himself with distinction at both Lowestoft and the Four Days Battle, he was appointed in 1666 to the post of Vice Admiral of Zeeland. He would participate in every major

Our Business is to Break with Them

Admiral Cornelis Evertsen the Youngest. This undated portrait by an unknown artist, once housed in the Stedelijk Museum, Middleburg, was destroyed during World War II. *Copy courtesy Library of Congress.*

fleet engagement of the Third Anglo-Dutch War, in De Ruyter's expedition to the West Indies, and in operations in the Baltic. In 1678, at the end of his career, he was to command a squadron for Spain in the first French Sea War.[12]

Born to Cornelis de Oude on November 16, 1642, Cornelis Evertsen the Youngest had, like others in his illustrious family, been bred to the sea. By the outbreak of the second war with England, he was barely 23 years of age, but had already earned for his bravery the nickname that was to remain with him throughout his career: "Kees the Devil" Evertsen.[13] Kees the Devil seemed to be ever in the midst of the fight. In the first sea action of the Second Anglo-Dutch War in February 1665, a minor engagement between three English men-of-war and two smaller Dutch vessels, the young Evertsen, commanding the 32-gun *Eendraght*, was taken prisoner after a redoubtable effort. His bravery was soon applauded even by the king of England. On March 20, John Evelyn the inveterate diarist and court favorite, visited Whitehall with letters from the Duke of York and was called into the King's bedchamber. He later recorded the encounter. "I showed the letter written to me from the Duke of York from the fleet," he noted, "giving me notice of young Evertsen . . . newly taken . . . I went to know of his Majesty how he would have me treat them, when he commanded me to bring the young captain to him."[14] Four days later, Kees the Devil was presented to the king of England in the royal bedchamber. The king

> gave him his hand to kiss, and restored him his liberty; asked many questions concerning the fight (it being the first blood drawn), his Majesty remembering the many civilities he had formerly receiv'd from his relations abroad . . . . Then I was commanded to go with him to the Holland Ambassador [who had yet to depart], where he was to stay for his passport, and I was to give him 50 pieces in broad gold.[15]

Brought next before the Duke of York, Evertsen answered, when it was observed that a bullet had passed through his hat, "that he wished it had gone through his head, rather than been taken."[16] Fortunately for The Netherlands, it had not, for Evertsen was to serve with distinction at Lowestoft, where he was named flag captain for his father. Upon his father's death in the bloody Four Days' Battle, he assumed command of his ship. He had been among those who had dared to beard the lion in his den at the Medway in June 1667. And now, he was about to participate in the first battle of yet another war with England—a war in which he was destined to capture a frontier empire for his fatherland.

When the English fleet closed with the Smyrna convoy, Sir Robert Holmes peremptorily ordered Captain de Haese to board him. The Dutchman wisely declined, sending a junior officer in his place. No excuses were given, and *St. Michael* opened with a crushing broadside. De Haese replied in kind, and the engagement became general. The stolid De Haese fell in action, but the pennant of the United Provinces continued to fly. Sir Robert maintained the engagement against a determined resistance until sunset, failing to capture a single merchantmen while suffering severe damage. With dawn the action resumed. Four English warships, which had hung back the day before, now entered the fray; soon one was disabled. The Dutch, outnumbered nine to six, did not escape unscathed, suffering the loss of the 44-gun *Klein Hollandia*, and Captain Eland de Blois the use of his left hand. Four of the smaller merchantmen were captured (but only two proved of any value). Nevertheless, by dark, Evertsen and his associates had managed to extract 62 merchantmen from harm's way. As for Holmes, whose ship had been badly disabled and whose effort, carried out without a declaration of war, could only be construed as nothing less than piracy, "he had little advantage."[17]

There was now no turning back. On March 17, 1672, England declared war on the United Provinces. Ten days later, France followed suit and was soon joined by the German states of Cologne and Munster.

The Dutch met the first land attacks with fewer than 60,000 troops under arms. At sea, the allied fleets of France and England under the Duke of York and the comte d'Estree numbered 98 ships-of-the-line and frigates, and approximately 30 fireships, mounting 6,018 guns and manned by 34,496 officers and men. Against this force, De Ruyter commanded 75 ships-of-the-line and frigates, 36 fireships, 4,484 guns, and 20,738 seamen, almost double the peacetime force authorized by the States General. The French strategy was to drive north into the Generality lands of Brabant and then to take Amsterdam while the English attacked from the sea, landing on the coast, and flanking the Dutch from the west. Beset on every side, the United Provinces' principal trade routes would also be sorely threatened, and without commerce, even if the enemy was fended off, the nation's lifeblood might well be drained in a war of attrition.[18]

By the end of April, Louis XIV had left his residence for the front, and before mid-May his troops under Generals Turenne and Chamilly were on the march to Vise. The 120,000-man French juggernaut seemed unstoppable, bypassing and besieging whatever did not fall before it. Notoriously under-funded, Dutch defenses were totally inadequate to hinder the foe and they fell, one after another.

On June 8 the Dutch fell back to the famous Hollands Waterlinie, giving up the provinces of Gelderland and Utrecht to the French after less than a month of war. Four thousand French cavalry under Rochefort immediately took advantage of the open, flat landscape, occupied Utrecht on June 1, and galloped north into the heart of the country as far as Naarden, Leerdam, and Asperen.

In the east 30,000 men from Munster and Cologne invaded with equal success, taking Zwolle and Kampen with only token resistance, and Deventer after conducting a heavy bombardment. In July a treaty with Munster handed the captured provinces to that city, and private deals gave Deventer to Cologne and Kampen to Louis XIV, who now laid claim to all of the provinces of Gelderland and Utrecht.[19]

Early in the war, The Netherlands suffered more than the loss of territory. The land was in desperate need of cash. The hostilities, especially the successful French drive to the very gates of Amsterdam, had panicked into flight the international capital invested there. Since Amsterdam's sophisticated banking and investment climate had attracted much of the capital and the capitalists that had created the Dutch mercantile system, and because purely Dutch capital was liquid, it was both sensitive and mobile. Those of wealth, however, responded to the reality of French invasion by seeking safety in flight. Some, such as the Florentine investment community, more prudent than most, had withdrawn their funds as early as February. By June the flight of investment and investors was liberally laced with panic.[20]

"Within these 3 or 4 days," wrote one observer of the scene,

above 10 millions of gilders in money and gold have been conveyed from The Hague to Amsterdam, and all the Jewes and Rich Merchants drawes all the Money they can out of Amsterdam upon Venice Legorne and other places, the Exchange from Amsterdam upon Venice was the last Post at 105 pence for a Ducat, having been the Weeke before at 85.[21]

Another wrote:

You many easily believe that they are in a desperate condition when they doe at this time give from 10 to 17 per cent. to have bills for Antwerp or any of these Countrys for monies, as quite despairing of their own.[22]

But the foreign capitalist was not alone in this panic: Dutchmen were fleeing Holland with their assets as well, for such unlikely places as London and Hamburg. And the usually blue-chip bonds of the province of Holland, often employed as a medium of exchange, sank to as much as 30 percent of their par value, while East India shares were dumped on the market at half their prewar price. But the panic of 1672 failed to break the Bank of Amsterdam.[23]

The war at sea was as total as the land war. At the outset the five admiralties were directed to seize British ships whenever found, and in particular on the River Elbe, at Hamburg. The East and West Indies Companies were empowered to attack and capture British and French ships, forts, and possessions in Europe, Asia, Africa, and the Americas. Channel markers and beacons on all rivers and inlets were removed and picket frigates were stationed to prevent surprise attacks inland. The admiralties were directed to work day and night to fit out their fleets. However, old debts, rivalry, and the unwillingness of the inland provinces, beset by their own problems, to provide emergency funding delayed this process. Only Amsterdam and the Maas managed to field fleets before the end of April 1672.[24] Friesland readied only one ship and the Northern Quarter four. For Zeeland, a total lack of funds retarded efforts to get ships to sea. But of equal significance was the hope that privateering, which the States General had forbidden at the outbreak of war in order to assure that the admiralties had first call on vessel and manpower resources, would quickly be opened again.

Our Business is to Break with Them

The State of Zeeland was by far the greatest privateering province of The Netherlands in the seventeenth century. In the First and Second Anglo-Dutch Wars, the State did nearly treble the business of Amsterdam, its nearest rival in privateering. And as it was clearly Amsterdam's junior partner in world trade and in the East and West Indies Companies, privateering furnished much of that island province's income. Lacking Amsterdam's strong treasury, banking, and finance, Zeeland was obliged to pay for its share of the war from current accounts, which directly influenced the degree and structure of its contribution, as well as the strategy and objectives of its independent operations.[25] Despite (or perhaps because of) the ban on privateering, Zeeland fielded six ships-of-the-line, two frigates, four fireships, and two snaauws in behalf of the national war effort, but only after marines and soldiers were provided to fill out their complements.[26] Zeeland was, even then, hesitant to dispatch her naval contingent to serve with the main fleet, fearing that such a move would leave her island province exposed to enemy attack and occupation, which, indeed, was the very plan proposed by the Anglo-French alliance.

The United Provinces could no longer wait upon Zeeland. In mid-April Admiral de Ruyter took the Amsterdam fleet out and rendezvoused at Texel with the ships of the Maas, Friesland, and the Northern Quarter. Dropping south along the low, monotonous Dutch coast, hoping to encounter the Zeeland squadron under Lieutenant Admiral Adrian van Trappen Bankert, the 65-year-old De Ruyter reviewed again and again his instructions from the States General. His primary mission was to fall upon the British fleet under the Duke of York, anchored in the Thames, before it could sail to join the French squadron under the comte d'Estree. Failing in that, he was to engage the English at sea before the fateful juncture might be made. It was not until May 2, however, that the Zeeland contingent was able to join the main flotilla. By May 5 the Dutch were in the Downs off Dover, but learned to their disappointment that the Duke of York's and d'Estree's two fleets had already effected a juncture off St. Helens in Isle of Wight and had sailed east only hours before.

A change of strategy was called for. Off Dover, the Admiral assembled a council of war to discuss the order of battle. The conference, delayed by a storm, only served to emphasize the danger in which the Dutch found themselves, for the enemy continued to grow more superior in number and size of ships and in firepower with every passing day. De Ruyter decided to sail back into the North Sea and station the fleet five or six miles off the Dutch coast between Zeeland and the

Michiel de Ruyter. *Courtesy Library of Congress.*

mouth of the Rhine. He would await the enemy in the shallow, familiar waters near home and harbor.[27]

Another revision in plans was brought about by lack of contact with the enemy fleet and by Johan de Witt's grand scheme to attempt a reprise of the successful raid on the Thames of 1667, a design pressed upon the admiral by the Grand Pensionary's brother Cornelis, who was assigned to the fleet as a commissioner. Now, admirals Van Ghent, Cornelis Evertsen de Jonge (cousin of Captain Cornelis Evertsen the Youngest), and Van Nes were detailed to prepare for a surprise raid on the Thames. After a day of fog and other delays, Van Ghent, with his flag flying from the frigate *De Leeuwen*, took his squadron from its station off the mouth of the Thames up toward six British ships. The Dutch could proceed no farther than the fort at Sheerness, which produced such effective covering fire that it was clear the English were well prepared for such a raid. De Ruyter's fleet spent the next two days cruising off the mouth of the Thames in frustration.

Well to the north, James, Duke of York, had put in at Southwold Bay (or Solebay, as it was commonly called) on the coast of Suffolk. Here he was to revictual before pressing on to his intended station on the Dogger Bank, off Holland. James's flagship was the spanking-new 100-gun *Royal Prince*, which led the Squadron of the Red, with Sir Edward Spragge as his vice admiral on *London*, also of 100 guns, and Captain Sir John Harman, in the 90-gun *Charles*, serving as rear admiral. The comte d'Estree, Vice Admiral of France, was Admiral of the White and sailed aboard *St. Philippe*, with 78 guns and men. The Rear Admiral of the Fleet and Admiral of the Blue, aboard the 100-gun *Royal James*, was the Earl of Sandwich. The allied fleet consisted of 87 ships-of-the-line and frigates, 13 smaller warships, 24 fireships, and 28 ketches and flyboats, mounting 5,100 guns in all. Of these, 26 line ships, 4 frigates, 5 smaller warships, 8 fireships, and 4 flyboats were French. Opposed to the generally larger and more heavily manned and gunned allied fleet, De Ruyter would command 133 ships during the coming battle: 61 warships of between 50 and 80 guns, 14 frigates, 22 armed dispatch boats, and 36 fireships, mounting a total of 4,484 guns.[28]

Anchored in Southwold Bay on the morning of June 7, James felt reasonably secure from attack as long as the wind was in the west, but he had earlier cautioned his captains to be ready to stand to the east and anchor the line of battle should it shift to the east. Through his scouts, De Ruyter learned of the disposition of the Allies. When the wind suddenly shifted to the northeast, the weather gauge now in his favor, he fell upon the surprised enemy soon after 7:00 A.M., before their lines could be formed. Bottled up in the bay, with little room to maneuver, the English were immediately thrown into chaos and were saved from total destruction only by a last-minute shift in the breeze. Despite the confusion, De Ruyter concentrated his forces on the few English ships that could be brought into line. The admiral, with several of his support ships in company, immediately closed with James's *Royal Prince*, and by 11:00 A.M. the English flagship had suffered over 200 casualties and could no longer continue the fight. His royal highness was soon obliged to transfer his flag to Sir Robert Holmes' *St. Michael*. In the meantime, d'Estree and his second in command, Admiral Abraham Duquesne, ordered the White Squadron's cables cut and bore away to the southeast—away from the fight! De Ruyter dispatched Admiral Bankert and his Zeelanders, including Kees the Devil Evertsen, with a score of ships to keep an eye on the French and then returned his full attention to the Red and Blue Squadrons of the English. By midday, both James and Sandwich, having been taken by complete surprise, were able to maneuver only 20 ships into line to meet the Dutch onslaught, and suffered severely. Of the two commanders, Sandwich would pay for the surprise, after a desperate and brave fight, with his life. Admiral van Ghent, who had exchanged close broadsides with Sandwich, was also killed. *Royal James*, having fended off repeated attacks by Dutch warships and fireships, sinking several, finally succumbed to a fireship attack, and burned to the waterline. Elsewhere, *St. Michael*, pounded by a double line of Dutch warships and severely injured in her hull and rigging, was obliged to leave the fight with five feet of water in the hold. Again James moved his flag, this time to Spragge's *London*, but she too was soon disabled in a fight with Admiral van Nes.

At 7:00 P.M. De Ruyter shifted his attention to the French and bore away to join the Zeeland squadron, which had engaged them to windward. James immediately began to assemble 25 to 30 warships and pressed to join d'Estree. By nightfall, however, both sides had parted. Losses between the two opponents were about equal; the English had lost five ships, the Dutch four, and, for all their caution, the French had lost two vessels. With both sides short of ammunition and bearing heavy damages, the engagement was not renewed on the following day. Instead, James returned to Sheerness to refit, and De Ruyter sailed back to The Netherlands.

Although both sides suffered similar losses, the Battle of Solebay saved The Netherlands from a devastating, perhaps fatal, invasion by sea. The allied fleet would remain immobilized for the next month—a month in which the desperate United Provinces would be given new hope.

Throughout the remainder of the summer and autumn, De Ruyter, with fewer than 70 vessels, maintained a close vigil on the Dutch coast, even as the manpower needs of the Dutch army drained seamen from his ships. His fleet, devoid of funds, equippage, and supplies, dwindled in strength. In the meantime, James returned to sea, took station off the Dogger Banks, and commenced cruising off the Friesian Islands, hoping to intercept the rich homeward-bound Dutch East Indies fleet. Not long afterwards, while at Blankenburgh, De Ruyter also learned of the approach of the Indiamen and, hugging the coast, slipped out without being disovered by the English, to meet and conduct the fleet safely into Delfzyl in the West Ems. Frustrated by the cagey Dutch commander, degenerating weather, diminishing provisions, and crews more dead from scurvy than alive, the Duke of York returned to port in early August and laid up his fleet for the winter.

Though De Ruyter's victory at Solebay destroyed any possibility of an allied invasion by sea, the Dutch faced what seemed a hopeless situation ashore. Four provinces were occupied, trade was all but destroyed, East Indies Company stocks were plumetting and State securities were following suit, and the French were poised to administer the coup de grace. When a band of French skirmishers entered Muyden, on the outskirts of Amsterdam, the end seemed near. The invaders, however, were driven from their forward position at the eleventh hour. In a last fit of desperation, the Dutch defenders opened their dikes. As the waters spread across the face of the Fatherland, the French were stopped cold. But the crisis continued for Holland.

With the French army at the gates, the Dutch people turned, as they so often had in the past, to the House of Orange-Nassau. On July 2, Prince Willem III of Orange-Nassau was elected Stadholder of Zeeland, and two days later the State of Holland followed suit. On July 8 he was confirmed as Captain General and Admiral General of the union. Support for the republican De Witt brothers evaporated. On August 4 Johan de Witt resigned from his office as Grand Pensionary. Two weeks later, he and his brother Cornelis were brutally murdered by a mob in the streets in The Hague.

A new order had been established, and, thanks to De Ruyter and the flooding of the lowlands, a breathing spell had been granted for it to take root and grow. During that brief interval, a desperate scheme of bold proportions was set in motion—a scheme aimed at no less a target than had befitted such daring sea rovers as Hein, Drake, and Hawkins. It was a scheme to capture no less a prize than the fabulously rich English East India fleet to pay for the next year of war. But it was also a plan to conduct a daring raid on the lifeblood of English and French empire, the colonies of the far-off Americas. The expedition was to be carried out by a young, ambitious commander, renowned for his fighting ability, sagacity, and impetuosity—the dark, brooding, but stolid Zeelander named Cornelis Evertsen the Youngest, Kees the Devil.

3

SIMPLE SURRENDER

The Zeeland Islands lay low on the chilly North Sea. In December they were gray, misty, damp, and cold. The stormy sea was nowhere more than a few miles from clusters of brick houses huddled behind protective dikes. Waves often pounded seawalls just yards from the snug, dim parlors where Zeelanders lived for six months of the year behind tightly closed doors and windows. For the most part, the people of Zeeland were neither farmers nor soldiers. They were, instead, merchant traders and seamen whose lives had for centuries been intricately entwined with the sea, its bounty, commerce, and protection. Indeed, their dominance as a maritime people was insured by the very insularity of their country—where land was scarce and costly and where people invested in trade rather than in real estate.

In the seventeenth century, trade was not a loosely defined concept, especially for these insular people whose commerce and industry were dependent upon their ability to coexist with the sea. For the Dutch—even those small businessmen and merchants not directly involved—trade offered opportunities for investment all but absent in other nations. Great enterprises were often built up with both large and small sums of capital placed in shares in a *rederij*. This innovative Dutch investment vehicle, similar to a modern joint venture or corporation, was used frequently and for many purposes: to erect a mill, to finance a forge, or to build, buy, charter, or freight a ship. A rederij might finance a fishing venture, a trading voyage, or, in wartime, it might field a privateer (or *caper*) to search for rich enemy prizes.[1]

A *caper* was a colloquial name for a Dutch ship sailing under letters of marque and reprisal, or *Commissievaart*, as privateering was called in The Netherlands. The act of privateering was a legal expedient employed by most European nations during wartime to inflict damage upon an enemy's maritime trade—and hence the opponent's economic ability to make war—by fielding privately owned ships of war to serve as commerce raiders. Sponsored by wealthy individuals or syndicates and acting singly or in wolf packs, the capers of the Third Anglo-Dutch War first operated under commissions issued by the States General and, after July 1672, by Prince Willem III.[2] The capers successfully inflicted enormous damage upon the commerce of both England and France, forcing the allies to divert large amounts of naval resources and funds to protect their maritime trade.

Zeeland, owing to its centuries of maritime industry, and its strategic location dominating the North Sea approach to the English Channel, became the leading province in The Netherlands for fielding capers during the Third Anglo-Dutch War. It was a large and well-organized business. From 1665 onward, there was in Vlissingen, the principal port of the province, a corporation or syndicate of holders of commissions called the "Directie van de Nieuw Equipage," which made up the fulcrum of the privateering industry during wartime. Commissievaart was, like rederij, a business, and its chief operating officer, the *boekhouder*, or bookkeeper, was responsible for the operational and fiscal aspects of a privateering voyage. In The Netherlands of the seventeenth century, the bookkeeper was the cornerstone of national economic success and corporate empires. Usually important men in their own right, they frequently counted among their numbers individuals active in the management of both the East and West Indies Companies. Men such as Abraham van Pere and Pieter van Rhee, leading merchants of Vlissingen and patroons of the island colony of St. Eustatius in the West Indies, were typical of the lot. Van Pere was not only a regent of Vlissingen, but also an extremely wealthy individual who had earned spectacular profits from the commissions he held.[3]

It was the bookkeeper who found the financing, chartered the ship, saw to its fitting out, and hired the *commissievaarder*, the captain-adventurer who would command it, usually a seasoned mariner upon whose talent, skill, and honesty a privateering venture depended. The selection process was not lightly undertaken, for the bookkeeper was obliged to deposit a 20,000-guilder surety with the Admiralty. The captain-adventurer sailed under direct orders of the bookkeeper, not only to prevent the crew from plundering the bookkeeper's prize cargoes, but also to prevent him from operating on his private account. The captain was required to keep a log, and upon his return to the Fatherland was to submit it to the bookkeeper and all the way up the chain of naval command to the Admiralty. A single privateering voyage could well involve an entire town of seamen, victuallers, officers, investors, and craftsmen of every type. Indeed, it might well involve an entire province such as Zeeland.

During the Second Anglo-Dutch War, Amsterdam held 37 commissievaart commissions; smaller Zeeland held 93. In the course of the ensuing war, Amsterdam held 75, and Zeeland 184. Of the Zeeland commissions, 25 captain-adventurers were active in both wars.[4] It was not uncommon for certain Zeeland families to dominate such activities, producing generations of merchants, investors, and capers. Some, such as the ancestors of Jan Evertsen, managed to sandwich lucrative privateering voyages between regular naval service.

The navy of The Netherlands arrived late on the scene of European affairs, although the Dutch "sea beggars" had long been famed for their readiness to cast aside their fishing nets for sword and pistol. Naval warfare under sail or oar, however, was a seasonal thing for all the nations bordering the North Sea and the English Channel: the howling winter was a time during which fleets were normally put up, refitted, and readied for the coming season's campaign. For some (particularly the Dutch, who paid for their fleets to be fielded for only seven to eight months of the year), it was a time in which expeditions of limited objectives, usually to warmer climes and undertaken by capers or provincial admiralties, could be launched with minimal hazard of interception in home waters.

During the Third Anglo-Dutch War, the Netherlanders frequently sought to capitalize on English and French antipathy towards the winter weather. Vessels of war were occasionally hired out by state admiralties during the late fall and winter seasons to nonbelligerents or allied nations for service as convoy escorts, thus providing much-needed capital to help finance the war effort. Small winter squadrons were fielded to carry out commerce raiding, similar to operations undertaken by the commissievaarders, thereby generating additional revenues for the state through the sale of prize goods and vessels. Such expeditions were expected to not only injure the enemy, but to pay for themselves in generated revenues as well. Indeed, it was not uncommon for individual ships or squadrons of commissievaarders and state warships to operate in concert, under formal agreements, sharing in the proceeds between them. By late 1672, commerce raiding had, in fact, become a de facto, if not a recognized, integral component of Dutch naval strategy. It stifled English and French trade, forced the foe to reallocate his naval resources, injured his economy, and demoralized his merchant marine. Complementing such efforts, the Dutch had become masters of one of the principal maxims of military strategy—

strike the enemy where he is weakest and least expects it. Of necessity, however, they had added their own major corollary: make it profitable.

By the fall of 1672, Zeeland, like Holland and the rest of the United Provinces, was approaching the brink of economic collapse. Taxation was able to meet only a portion of the State's military expenditures, and the coming year was certain to be worse. By winter, the financial outlook was grim at best. "This Countrey," noted one observer,

> is in a very sad condition, which makes many resolve to leave it. Commerce stands still. Tradesmen have very little work, [and in the] mean time Taxes are encreased beyond belief, but where to find the Money, appears not. All the ready Money, that People have, and can get, is daily conveyed away out of the Countrey. The two hundredth penny [tax] which was paid five times the last year, must this year be paid as often as the States shall Demand it, upon promise, as we are told, that the States will hereafter allow Interest for it, and the War being ended that even the Principal shall be repaid. In Amsterdam they sell daily to the loss of 20, 30, 40 per Cent.[5]

Amsterdam, of course, was not alone in its dilemma. By the late fall of 1672, it had become painfully obvious to Secretary of Zeeland Caspar de Huijbert that what was needed to keep his own State afloat in the coming year—both fiscally and physically—was a massive infusion of revenue. The defeat of the allied fleets at Solebay in June had proved a temporary reprieve from direct naval assault for Zeeland, and the opportunity to field a small winter squadron with the objectives of commerce raiding to enlarge the State's coffers could not be ignored. All that was necessary was a rich, vulnerable target and an able commander capable of capturing it.

Exactly who first conceived of the idea of intercepting the richly laden homeward-bound ships of the English East India Company, or failing in that, conducting a swift commerce raiding foray against the enemy's colonies in the Americas is uncertain. That such a plan might render a rich return, capable of buttressing the faltering economy of the State in a single bold stroke, was a possibility few in the government of Zeeland apparently doubted. If conducted with good organization, leadership, and a healthy dose of good luck, such an expedition might even prove the salvation of the state's economic distress.

Since the beginning of the seventeenth century, England and The Netherlands had been vicious competitors for the wealth and trade of the Orient. The Dutch United East India Company (Vereenigde Oost-Indische Compagnie), better known as the VOC, was chartered in 1602 by the States General specifically to organize trade and to combat Spanish and Portuguese power. The VOC readily secured rights amounting to trade monopoly and outright political sovereignty, with armed fleets and troops to defend its geographic and commercial hegemony. From its great center at Batavia, VOC dominance spread, taking Ceylon and Malacca from the Portuguese, and in 1652 establishing a colony on the strategic southern tip of the African continent, at the Cape of Good Hope. Valuable trade concessions were won in Sumatra, Persia, India, China, and Japan. But such gains were not exacted without competition from such powerful rivals as England, Spain, Portugal, and France. Indeed, the English East India Company, chartered in 1600 by Queen Elizabeth, posed a constant problem. Since 1622 the English had concentrated their efforts on the Indian subcontinent, and by the end of the Second Anglo-Dutch War had effectively eliminated the Dutch from that region. Thus, the interception of the rich, homeward-bound fleet of the East India Company would prove doubly rewarding.

Successful interdiction of richly laden East India merchant ships was not without precedent. As early as the late sixteenth century, such captures had been effected with incredibly rewarding results. In 1592 a capture of legendary proportions was carried out by an English squadron against a single Portuguese carrack, *Madre de Deus*, which carried a cargo valued by the English Treasurer and Controller of the Navy, Sir John Hawkins, at nearly half a million pounds. Cargoes of such ships ranged from exotic spices such as coriander, cinnamon, mace, nutmeg, ginger, cloves, and pepper, to rare woods, musk, silk, jewelry, pearls, diamonds, gold, and silver. The English East India Company ships were heavily armed, but usually sailed in small numbers, and were accompanied by Royal Navy escorts only upon reaching the more dangerous waters of North Africa and Europe. Obliged to avoid both pirates and the ships of rival nations in the waters of the Orient, they sailed westward across the Indian Ocean, around the Dutch-held Cape of Good Hope, then north along the west coast of Africa, arriving, usually in March, at the isolated South Atlantic island of St. Helena. This barren, rocky pinprick was, in 1672, the only revictualling station between Cape Town and the Cape Verde Islands. There fresh water, citrus fruits, and wild goats provided a welcome respite for the scurvy-plagued mariners who had survived the arduous voyage from the Far East. Thus, the island had been assured an importance far beyond that which its actual situation or size would have otherwise warranted.

Early in their quest for commercial empire, the Dutch recognized the strategic value of St. Helena for the respite and revictualling of

their VOC ships, and had garrisoned it accordingly. Upon the establishment of the Cape Town settlement, the island was relinquished to
the English, whose own East India Company ships now employed it as
their own revictualling and rendezvous center in the South Atlantic.
Being such a vulnerable, weakly garrisoned, and splendidly isolated
post, at which some of the richest vessels in the world were obliged to
call, made it the most opportune target the leaders of Zeeland could
have picked for their winter raid.

In the early fall of 1672 the Raden, the councilors or governing body
of Zeeland, took up the task of developing a comprehensive plan for the
interception of the English East India fleet at St. Helena. On October 2
the Lords of Zeeland adopted a secret resolution providing the mecha-
nism to set such an expedition in motion, and for the next five weeks,
they labored to draft instructions designed to guide a small force of
men-of-war against the powerful English East India Company's 1672
homeward-bound squadron. In the event the Zeeland expeditionaries
failed to achieve their primary objective, the Raden wisely included an
alternative of less economic potential, but of equal value in distressing
the enemy—a naval raid on the British and French colonies in the
Americas.

In the weeks that followed the passage of the October 2 resolution,
both the Raden and the Admiralty of Zeeland moved forward with a
singleness of purpose to prepare for the coming expedition. A competent commander had to be selected, a squadron assembled, outfitted,
and armed, and instructions drafted. Ships had to be watered, vict-
ualled, and manned. Secrecy was paramount, for the slightest information leak could lead to the complete failure of the expedition; the element of surprise was imperative for success. Thus the project was to be
carried out independently by the state of Zeeland, without the knowledge or consent of the States General or any of the other United Provinces. The mission would be undertaken with Zeeland men-of-war,
seamen, and officers. And, most important, the financial rewards
would solely benefit Zeeland.

The selection of a field commander for such a daring mission was
undoubtedly difficult, and doubly so in that it had to be made in the
utmost secrecy, for there were many excellent Zeeland naval officers
from which to choose. The command was, of course, one that might be
considered a plum; if the mission was successful, not only would the
coffers of Zeeland be enriched, the pockets of those who participated,
from the commander down to the lowliest seaman, would be lined
with a share of the booty. Yet without question, the criteria for the

selection of a commander were, as always, based on politics and influence as well as competence. That no less than three members of the Evertsen family, heirs to one of the most ancient and respected naval dynasties in Dutch history, were selected as commander and captains bears mute testimony to the power of position and connections. With a powerful political base in the Zeeland capital of Middleburg, key support from the all-important port of Vlissingen, and close ties with the ascendant House of Orange, the descendants of such national naval icons as Admirals Jan Evertsen and Cornelis Evertsen de Oude were logical selections. The promotion of the capable and daring Captain Cornelis Evertsen the Youngest—Kees the Devil—to the post of expedition commander was made, undoubtedly after a spate of political maneuvering by Evertsen supporters in the Raden. Fortunately, while politically acceptable, young Evertsen was also a combat veteran of two wars, a leader experienced in squadron command, and a mariner of proven bravery and skill. His first mission, upon acceptance of command, was to man and prepare his fleet for duty.

Evertsen was assigned a squadron of six vessels (two of which had been captured from the English during the last war) and a core of experienced mariners, marines, and "militia." The flagship of the little fleet was built by Francis Bayle in 1666 at Bristol, England, as the fourth-rate man-of-war *St. Patrick*. Constructed under contract to the Royal Navy Board of Commissioners, she was 621 tons burthen, 102 feet in length, 33 feet 10 inches abeam, 14 feet 6 inches in hold, and drew 16 feet 6 inches of water. Upon being commissioned, *St. Patrick* was placed under the command of Captain Robert Saunders, an aggressive fighter, in the summer of 1666 and sent on a shakedown cruise.[6] Upon conclusion of this brief voyage, Saunders certified for the Navy Commissioners "that the *St. Patrick* is as good a contract ship as possible, and answers all expectations as to strength and stoutness of sailing."[7] Mounting 48 guns on two gun decks—20 24-pounders, two 18-pounders, 22 nine-pounders, and four four-pounders—she could toss a total of 365 pounds of metal in a single broadside.[8]

Saunders had quickly earned for his ship a reputation as one of the best frigates in the Royal Navy, a warship at once feared and respected by the foe. He employed the *St. Patrick* with both skill and daring, and in August 1666, while escorting the Virginia and Barbados fleet into the Soundings, he met six French privateers awaiting the convoy in ambush. In a dashing encounter, *St. Patrick* sank three of the attackers, sent two more as prizes into Portsmouth, and took the last, a 30-gun ship, on as a consort. In December, she topped off the year by capturing a powerful Dutch man-of-war.[9]

Simple Surrender

In early 1667, the big frigate sailed again, with less than her full complement of 220 men, in company with the fireship *Malaga Merchant*, Captain William Seeley commanding. Off the North Foreland, near the mouth of the Thames, the two patrol ships fell in with a pair of Dutch warships on scout duty. The two Dutchmen were the Zeelanders *Delft*, 34 guns, Captain Dirck Jobsen Kiela, and *Schaeckerloo*, 28, Captain Willem Hendrickssen. Captain Saunders, possessing the greater firepower, engaged quickly, but more intent on taking valuable prizes than on sinking them, sailed alongside *Delft* and attempted to board. Captain Seeley, who might have played a role in the battle, hauled his ship off and watched the engagement from afar, even as *Schaeckerloo* moved in to grapple the English frigate's exposed side. The hand-to-hand melee that ensued was fierce, with many casualties on both sides. Eventually, the contest began to turn in favor of the Dutch. Both Saunders' son, who had been aboard, and the ship's surgeon later reported that had the English stayed at their guns throughout the fight, the ship might have been saved. But when the captain fell mortally wounded, some 30 crewmen fled into the hold and the battle was lost. Even as he succumbed to his wounds, Saunders sought to deny the enemy his ship and in a last effort managed to blow up her forecastle. It was not enough, for after two bloody hours of fighting, *St. Patrick* was overwhelmed and carried into Vlissingen.[10]

St. Patrick's reputation and demonstrated fighting ability did not go unnoticed in Zeeland. Repaired and refitted, with gilded wood and brilliant paintwork and her new decorations glistening in the sun, she soon became a welcome addition to the Zeeland Navy. Renamed *Swaenenburgh* after a 30-gun Zeelander that had exploded in battle in 1666 and after a major town of the province, she was reduced to 44 light-caliber guns, but was destined to be the largest warship in Evertsen's squadron. Given the nepotism that dominated the selection of officers in all of the Dutch admiralties, it was not surprising that the big, three-masted frigate would not only carry Evertsen's flag as squadron commander, but would be captained by his brother, second in command of the expedition, Evert Evertsen Cornelis' Zoon. Her complement consisted of 120 noncommissioned officers and crew, 64 marines under Captain Anthony Colve, a veteran of service in Suriname, and two "militia" men, Lieutenant Joan Becker and a sergeant.[11]

In a peculiar twist of fate, the second ship of the squadron was none other than the pinnace *Schaeckerloo*, the same vessel that had been instrumental in the capture of *St. Patrick*. Built in 1661, she had served out the previous war armed with 28 guns—8 eight-pounders, 18 six-pounders, and two four-pounders—which could fire a broadside of 90 pounds of metal. For Evertsen's expedition, she was outfitted with two additional guns, bringing her total to 30. Both the pinnace and her commander, Captain Passchier de Witte, like the Evertsens, had sailed under Admiral van Ghent and were no strangers to combat. *Schaeckerloo* was manned by a crew of 90 and carried a marine contingent of 64 under Ensign Carel Quirinssen. Two militiamen, Lieutenant Willem Snel and one sergeant, were also onboard.[12]

The third warship of the squadron, *Suriname*, like *Swaenenburgh*, was an English-built vessel, originally called *Richard and Frances*, captured in 1666 by Captains Abraham Crijnssen and Boudin Keuvelaer. This vessel was also commanded by an Evertsen, Captain Evert Evertsen Frans' Zoon. Named for the colony Crijnessen had taken from the English in the last war, *Suriname* was outfitted with 25 iron cannon of various calibers and manned by a crew of 80. She too carried a contingent of 64 marines, under the command of Ensign Antonij Malepart. A small detachment of 12 militia soldiers and a sergeant under the command of Lieutenant Carel Epesteijn and Ensign Jeronimus de Huijbert were also placed aboard. Both Epesteijn and De Huijbert, the latter probably a relative to Secretary de Huijbert of Zeeland, had been assigned to *Suriname* by a special decree of the Delegated Raden of Zeeland. Considering that the vessel had been designated to carry the bulk of prize goods expected to be taken at St. Helena, it is likely that the two officers and special detachment had been assigned to the expedition for the sole purpose of maintaining a vigil over the plunder.[13]

The fourth member of the squadron was the long, low snaauw *Zeehond*, a swift shallow-draft vessel that was to prove of enormous value as a scout boat, and later as a small raider and pursuit craft. A uniquely Dutch craft type, the narrow-beamed snaauw had evolved, possibly as early as the 1630s, from the simple shallop commonly employed in the Low Country. By 1656, however, the armed, shallow-draft, double shallop of war, which was even then being termed a snaauw, was in common usage. Built and fitted for fast pursuit in the shoally estuaries and coastal waters of the Low Country, the snaauw was readily adapted for privateering and pirate-chasing. Often described as a large sloop (and not to be confused with the later brig-rigged snow), the craft type was occasionally undecked, and varied in displacement from two to 50 tons. Such vessels were often propelled by sweeps, or a combination of sweeps and sails, manned by crews of up to 25, and armed with two to ten guns. Under the command of Captain Daniel Thijssen, *Zeehond* mounted six iron three-pounders and carried 400 rounds of three-and one-pound shot. She was manned by a crew of 22 and carried no marines or militia.[14]

The fifth vessel of the squadron was the little ketch *Sint Joris*, commanded by Captain Cornelis Eewoutsen and manned by a crew of 34. Though intended to be converted to a fireship before the attack on St. Helena, the ketch, with her six iron three-pounders and 600 rounds of shot, was to be employed initially as a dispatch boat, and thus carried no militia or marines.[15]

The last vessel of the tiny armada was the hoecker *De Eendracht*, commanded by Captain Maerten Andriessen. Armed with four iron three-pounders and carrying only 150 rounds of shot, this ungainly, short, tubby vessel was to serve as the squadron's larder.[16]

With its full complement of seamen, marines, militia, and officers onboard, the six-ship squadron of Commander Cornelis Evertsen carried only 586 men and 115 guns.

The Lords of Zeeland planned the expedition thoroughly. No less than three separate sets of secret instructions were prepared in conformity with the October 2, 1672, resolution. Each set of instructions detailed at great length every step that was to be taken by the squadron, as well as alternative actions in the event of failure or unforeseen circumstances. The instructions were iron-clad in their rigidity and intentionally left little room for the expedition's commander to take it upon himself to design his own course of action.

Of the three sets of lengthy instructions, only the last two have survived the passage of centuries to provide the specifics of the missions. The first set of instructions, which are believed to be no longer extant, and which are only implied as having existed by reference to them in the text of the second, was at least 17 articles in length. It detailed such major issues as the course the expedition was to take from Vlissingen, via the English Channel and the Canary Islands to the Cape Verde Islands. It may have discussed the vessels to be employed, the chain of command, the overall objectives of the mission, and such potential problems as unauthorized plundering of prize cargoes. The first two sets of orders were apparently to be opened just prior to the squadron's departure, for there are no indications in later logs of the voyage of such important actions having taken place after the squadron put to sea.[17]

Broken down into 19 separate articles, the second set of instructions was explicit in its every detail. After sailing from the Cape Verde Islands, the squadron was to set a course for the Equator, avoiding the treacherous Bight of Guinea on the coast of Africa on the one hand, and Brazil, "whose jutting bars it is very necessary to avoid," on the other. The pilots were to follow the course normally set by vessels sailing to the East Indies, and each ship was to be provided with a "passage map, on which it is noted down in writing how and where the Equator can be most easily passed," together with instructions on the fastest route. Once at the Equator, they were to set course to the Tropic of Capricorn, "which can be performed quicker in the months of December, January and February than during the summer months, as has been shown by experience." Sailing through the Tropic of Capricorn, they were to press on until meeting the west winds. Riding these they were to proceed to St. Helena, taking care not to overshoot their destination, for beating back would only signal difficulty and probably defeat of the expedition's objectives.[18]

Speed and timing were of the essence if they were to intercept the annual East Indies fleet, and the officers of the squadron were directed to constantly "admonish, stir up, and if need be oblige" the pilots to guide their ships to their destination as quickly as possible. The principal operations of the squadron were to be conducted at and near the Island of St. Helena, for the expedition "has for its chief purpose the observing and capture of the English East India return ships which cannot well succeed unless the Squadron arrives in time at the said Island, and conquers the same." Thus is was ordered that only experienced pilots who had already sailed to the Cape of Good Hope be consulted and employed.[19]

Once St. Helena was sighted, the vessels of the squadron were to raise both English and French flags "to entice some people away from the land," to detain and interrogate them concerning the island's defenses. A landing was then to be made on the north shore coast to take the small English fort there, but in a fashion to be determined prior to the attack by a secret Council of War composed of the squadron's senior commanders. To facilitate a better understanding of the situation of this remote island outpost of the English East India Company, the Lords of Zeeland provided the expeditionaries with the most reliable descriptions of the island that were available, descriptions made by Admiral Verhoeven in 1608, W. J. Bontekoe in 1624, and Zeijgert van Rechteren in 1632. To take St. Helena, Cornelis Evertsen was obliged to rely on data 40 years old or older.[20]

Should the squadron, upon its arrival, encounter any French or English ships, they were to be immediately attacked and overpowered before enemy landing parties had an opportunity to erect shore batteries for their defense. To facilitate such an eventuality, the squadron was to be provided with the ketch *Sint Joris*, which was to be outfitted as a fireship prior to the attack. The squadron leaders were to take particular care, however, "since their Noble Mightinesses expect to find here richly laden merchant vessels rather than men of war," that *Sint Joris* not be employed unless absolutely necessary.[21]

Once the island had capitulated, the squadron was to immediately take on enough water to sustain itself and be ready to sail at any time or upon any eventuality. If the Council of War should think it necessary, a small captured vessel might be dispatched to the Cape of Good Hope to take on fresh water, cattle, and fruit and return to rendezvous and reprovision the main fleet at St. Helena. In the meantime, special inquiry was to be made on the island concerning the English garrison's signalling practices to and from arriving ships. Once the enemy's signals were learned, they were to be employed in decoying his ships into Dutch ambush. Lookouts were to be placed on the highest points of the island to watch for and provide timely warning of their arrival. The Lords of Zeeland left it to the field commanders as to the tactics to be employed in capturing the foe when they were sighted. Upon their capture the least valuable ships were to be immediately unloaded and their cargoes transferred to *Suriname*, while the Council of War took special precautions to prevent fraud and theft during the unloading and loading operations. All valuable cargoes that occupied little space, such as pearls and diamonds, were to be transferred to *Swaenenburgh*.[22]

The squadron commanders were warned twice, in both the first and second sets of instructions, about the improper ransacking of enemy ships and the breaking open and embezzlement of goods, merchandise, silver, gold, pearls, diamonds, or anything else "outside the seamen's perquisites." There were to be no exceptions. Books, bills of lading, charter parties, lists of cargoes, and other similarly important documents were to be meticulously saved for an exact accounting to the government upon the squadron's return. The officers were instructed to "also show their indignation against, and . . . punish those who shall be found to have connived at similar transgressions, or who themselves have committed any faithlessness or fraud." Merchants, ships captains, and first officers of captured vessels were to be conveyed to the Fatherland. It was optimistically assumed that the squadron would meet with little resistance, and that surprise would be enough to elicit the capitulation of even the richest of ships. Indeed, the Lords of Zeeland were confident enough in their anticipation of success to think that a rich victory might be purchased cheaply, "because it is not apparent that these hoped for hostile ships shall be captured after any hard fighting, but just through a simple surrender."[23]

The victuals of the captured ships were to be distributed among the Zeelanders. *Suriname* was to take onboard all of the English and

French prisoners from both the island and the prizes, and sail for Brazil, Angola, or some other uninhabitable coast. The remainder of the squadron was to continue at St. Helena until May 22, 1673 (June 1, New Style), unless news of the imminent approach of additional English East Indiamen arrived. The squadron, however, would not be permitted to remain beyond May 31, unless the Council of War, "for some evident reasons and impelling cause," determined otherwise.[24]

The commanders were specifically instructed that "good care shall be also taken that the prisoners be not abused but treated decently according to the usage of war." While at St. Helena, sick crewmen and prisoners alike were to be disembarked on the island to be refreshed and restored with fresh meat, fish, vegetables, oranges, and lemons. Recognizing the value of the fresh citrus fruits in combatting scurvy almost a century before the English, the Zeelanders were directed that special care be taken that the fruits and herbs sent with the squadron's provisions "shall not be ruined, spoiled or immediately squandered." The commanders were also ordered to take special care regarding hunting and capturing game on the island to insure that a proper distribution of fresh meat be made among the squadron's seamen and soldiers.[25]

Anticipating "that the enemies might also intend to dispatch thither some ships for the protection of the Island and the expected return ships," the Lords of Zeeland further directed that the squadron must always be kept in perfect shape. It must be prepared to meet "a strong and equal enemy" or to evade a more powerful foe, in order that the island and the prizes be defended. Should it be impossible to do both, they were to evacuate the island, but only as a last resort to prevent the squadron and its prizes from falling into the enemy's hands. Thus, it was deemed necessary to prohibit unlimited shore leave, and to insure that a sufficient number of sailors and marines always be kept on board to meet any emergency.[26]

Upon the squadron's departure from the island, no more than six Englishmen were to be left behind, along with ten or twelve Dutch volunteers (who were to be promised a little more pay), and one of them would be designated commander. All would be obliged to swear allegiance to the States General. All slaves upon the island, with the exception of a few for the use of the little garrison, were to be removed. One or two of the English vessels found at the island were to be left, as was a suitable quantity of arms, munitions, and victuals.[27]

Upon the departure of the squadron from St. Helena, the secret Council of War was to open the second set of secret instructions, which were adjoined to the first set, and they were "to regulate themselves according to its contents."[28] Ironically, it was in this second set of instructions that the format for the campaign against America, which would govern the proceedings of the squadron for the bulk of the voyage, had been set down—more as an afterthought than a plan—in a single article.

4

PUT EVERYTHING TO RIGHTS

On the morning of Saturday, November 30, 1672, as the quartet of government officials hurriedly made their way toward the Vlissingen waterfront, the crisp North Sea wind was blowing out of the east. Even from a distance, over the roofs of the clustered buildings that blocked the direct approach to the harbor, they could see the mastheads of the Zeeland winter squadron, which lay in wait for their final inspection. After nearly two months of preparation and delay, Commander Cornelis Evertsen's little fleet was ready to sail. Zeeland Council Secretary de Huijbert, accompanied by Councilmen van der Beke, Stavenisse, and Engelse, had come to see the fleet off personally, for with this tiny force sailed Zeeland's hopes of recouping the terrible economic losses incurred by the season of war.[1]

Secretary de Huijbert was well aware that the squadron's complement had been filled only with great effort. Competition for able seamen had, in recent months, been horrendous, and it was certain to get worse. He reminded himself that the State's costly shipbuilding program at Vlissingen, necessary to field a strong fleet for the defense of the Fatherland next year, was well underway, with no less than 16 frigates under construction or nearing readiness for launch. Elsewhere on the waterfront, he noticed, seven or eight capers also being built and readied for sea. But the war was rapidly and effectively sapping the vitally important economic manpower resources that permitted Zeeland to build and field such weapons. Indeed, every able-bodied soul who could be collared had become grist for the war machine necessary to save the Fatherland. Commissievaart and state navy recruiters vied for the few suitable men left, and the better-financed capers usually won. As one observer of the predicament later noted, "These Capers being so numerous, do make Middleburg and Flissingen so dead,

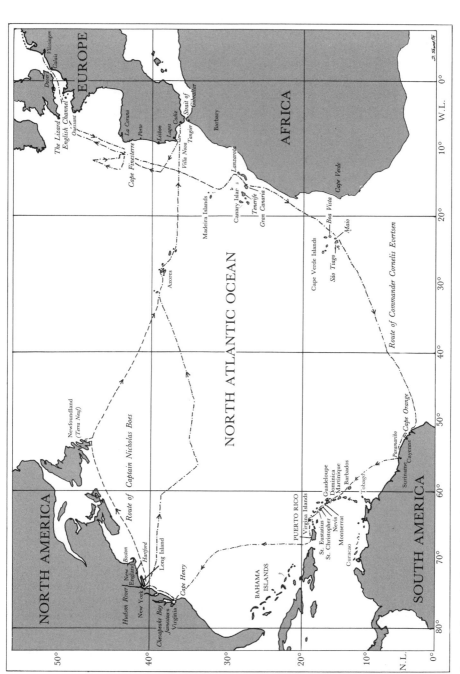

Route of the Zeeland Squadron of Commander Cornelis Evertsen, 1672–1674.

and so unpeopled them of Men, that it appears not how our Fleet can be Manned."[2]

Despite the problems, the four government officials went through the necessary stately, and almost ceremonial, final inspection of the men and ships "mustered" for the highly secret mission. Though no record of the scene is known, it was doubtless similar to thousands of departures of men-of-war and their crews, bound for distant and hostile shores, that had occurred before and would be repeated many times after the sailing of the Evertsen Expedition.[3]

The ceremonies over and goodbyes said, at 3:00 P.M., Evertsen ordered anchors raised. Accompanied by a small flotilla of capers, the squadron sailed from Vlissingen harbor into the Scheldt and by dark had reached Dishoecke, in the municipality of Kouderkerke, on the Walcheren coast. There it would remain for several days, delayed by adverse winds, sleet, and fog. Finally, on Thursday, December 5, the weather broke, and by evening the flota had sailed out of the Deurloo and into the North Sea.[4]

Evertsen exercised caution as he prepared to slip south through the narrow, 20-mile-wide Strait of Dover, one of the classic naval chokepoints of Europe. He was well aware that on either side, at both Dover and Calais, were extensive enemy fortifications, and even in winter, enemy naval patrols were likely to be encountered there or in the English Channel beyond. On Friday morning, the cliffs of Calais, several hundred feet in height, and the South Headland of England were sighted. By 8:00 P.M., the lights of Dover could be seen flickering in the distance.[5]

On the following day, the first of many encounters with the enemy occurred off of the Isle of Wight. At around midday, a British warship was sighted approaching the squadron from the south. Evertsen immediately altered course to meet him, but the sight of several large, oncoming Dutch men-of-war was apparently enough to give the English commander second thoughts. He quickly turned and fled. Evertsen, "in order not to get distracted with hunting but rather to promote our journey," immediately gave up the chase and resumed his course. By midday Sunday, the squadron was seven and a half miles off the Lizard, the southernmost tip of the Cornwall Peninsula of England. They had successfully slipped through the English Channel, and the frosty, apparently empty Atlantic lay before them.[6]

As the fleet pressed on into the open ocean, it was initially greeted by southeast winds and clear weather, and the first of many opportunities to take enemy prizes. Two ships, one of which Evertsen thought might have been the former Dutch galley *Van Middleburg*, believed to have been separated from a convoy, were sighted and pursued. The chase proved not only fruitless, but drew the Dutch far from their chosen course. Finally, off Ile d'Ouessant (Ushant) on the coast of Bretagne, France, the chase was abandoned.[7]

On the evening of the 9th, the weather turned bitter. Laced with rain, heavy winds, and sleet, the Atlantic exhibited its full fury for the newcomers. *Swaenenburgh*, barely ten days out of port and bound for several of the most isolated and distant regions of the globe, began to leak incessantly. The storm continued unabated, and the squadron was buffeted without respite. On the 12th the chains securing the standing rigging were broken on the leeward side of the flagship's foremast. With only a single set of lines to absorb the strain on the opposite tack, there was a strong danger of the foremast snapping with a sudden shift of wind. Evertsen responded instantly by ordering the ship to fall off leeward, permitting the crew, during a brief lull in the storm, to drop the foresail and bring down the foretopmast to make repairs.[8]

After a short respite, the winds again began blowing hard. The tubby, heavily laden hoecker *De Eendracht*, which had wallowed in the rear of the squadron, fell even farther from view. Again *Swaenenburgh*'s forerigging was damaged, and again the big frigate was forced to fall to leeward to effect repairs. *Sint Joris* was next to slip from sight amid the gray winter sleet and wind. Evertsen's brother, the captain of *Swaenenburgh*, fell seriously ill and was incapacitated. On Saturday morning, the 14th, Evertsen thought he sighted a yacht to the north, but on coming up, was delighted to find that the ship was Eewoutsen's battered but intact ketch. While sailing alongside the little dispatch boat, the flagship sighted yet another sail off to the lee. This time, the squadron had encountered its first bona fide prize of the voyage. The vessel, which was promptly taken, proved to be an English fluit out of London, called *Isaac and Benjamin*, Captain Jan Plofver (John Flower) commanding. She had been bound in ballast for Virginia with a crew of 29.[9]

Evertsen was undoubtedly pleased with the prize (even though it was empty), particularly because some of the English prisoners taken with her had readily agreed to enlist onboard his squadron for the duration of the voyage. A prize crew of 16 men was transferred to the fluit, and those English who had not enlisted were distributed around the fleet, undoubtedly to prevent the possibility of a prisoner uprising from taking place onboard a single ship. The crew of the flagship was, of course, equally delighted, for under the terms of both Dutch capering and regular admiralty prize law, a one-sixth share of the price brought by the sale of the prize at auction was to be divided among the captain and crew of the vessel that made the capture.[10]

Two days later, off Cape Finesterre, Spain, when a sail was sighted to the southwest, a second chase proved equally rewarding. By evening, with the help of a good topsail wind, *Swaenenburgh* had come up with the stranger, which proved to be an English-owned, but Spanish-built, bark called *St. Maria*. Commanded by Captain Robert Lesley and manned by a crew of nine, the vessel had been en route from Boston, Massachusetts, to Bilbao, Spain, with 188,000 pounds (850 kintals) of dried and salted fish in her hold. A mate (*stierman*) and eight men were placed aboard as a prize crew as the English prisoners were taken off.[11]

For the next several days the squadron was obliged to make long tacks to the east and west off Cape Finesterre to combat the southerly and southwesterly winds. The actual advance southward was minimal. The waters off the cape, however, were well-known in the 17th century as the frequent haunts of Turkish (Moorish) corsairs, and attacks on fat merchantmen were not uncommon. Indeed, as recently as 1669, two such pirates, flying Dutch colors to fool their prey, had brazenly assaulted the rich 300-ton French East India Company ship *St. Paul*. Though the Dutch lookouts in Evertsen's squadron kept a wary eye for such potentially troublesome encounters, the only excitement for several days was another brief sighting of a sail to the north on December 19, and an equally brief but futile pursuit.[12]

Though the squadron made little progress in the teeth of the southerly winds, worse weather lay ahead. On December 20, fog closed in and all but five of the fleet disappeared into the mist. Early the next morning, the worst nightmare a mariner could have envisioned nearly materialized for Cornelis Evertsen. At the beginning of the dogwatch (4:00 A.M. to 8:00 A.M.), as *Swaenenburgh* cut through the dense fog, a strange ship suddenly loomed up dead ahead. The flagship's helm was put hard over to prevent a crippling, perhaps fatal, collision. Her crew responded smartly, and for a brief instant, the Zeelander came parallel to the stranger on an easterly course. Before the mysterious ship could be identified, however, the weather suddenly closed in and again turned dark with a hard, pelting rain. By midday, neither the stranger nor the remaining vessels of the squadron could be seen from the decks of *Swaenenburgh*. Evertsen brought his ship back on a westerly tack, but southerly progress against adverse winds was still limited, and by the end of a most harrowing day, after much beating about, the flagship found herself still barely 50 miles west of Cape Finesterre.[13]

December 22 dawned off the northwesternmost point of Spain with newer more vicious winter storms threatening out of the south. Once again *Swaenenburgh* was obliged to humble herself to the winds to prevent damage. On December 23, in the midst of a gale, orders were given to hoist the flagship's foresail, set it at halfmast, and run before the storm. Suddenly, "as soon as the sail filled it burst into shreds in a tremendous blow, so that we were forced to fall off to the east so that the ship under sail wouldn't capsize." Again *Sint Joris* disappeared from view. Finally, as night came on, the tempest subsided and the wind, though still powerful, swung around to the west.[14]

The following day the gusting continued strong, with high seas imposing the maximum stress upon the squadron. During the preceding evening, it was soon discovered, both *Isaac and Benjamin* and *De Eendracht* had disappeared. Though *Swaenenburgh* "barely made headway a piece to see whether they were in our lee," neither the fluit nor the hoecker were anywhere to be seen. Relocating the two vessels was not Evertsen's only problem, for the recent tempest had caused serious damage to the frigate's mainyard, cracking it in the middle. The piece had to be brought down and splinted. By the afternoon of the 25th, it had been repaired and returned to its place.[15]

By December 27, *Swaenenburgh* had been blown, sailed, and drifted to within four miles of Cape Finesterre. Now it was *St. Maria's* turn to disappear, for on the following day, yet another gale struck and continued for three full days. Not until January 1, 1674, was it possible to estimate the squadron's position at latitude 46°33', Cape Toriana bearing 59 miles southeast by south.[16]

Finally the weather moderated and on January 3 two sails were sighted to the lee. Evertsen ordered pursuit, and the two vessels were overtaken. They proved to be Dutch capers commanded by Captains Cornelis Lijncoert and Jan Pietersen Pits. The two privateers, operating in concert, had found the hunting off the Iberian coast good, and had taken four prizes, which, though empty, had been sent into La Coruña, Spain, to be adjudicated and sold by a special Dutch commissioner there appointed by the States General. Evertsen was probably pleased to learn of the capers' successes, but more so that they had fallen in with the hoecker *De Eendracht* eight days earlier.[17]

On Sunday, January 5, with Cape Finesterre estimated at 41 miles northeast by east of the squadron, Captain Pits broke off to continue hunting on his own, but Lijncoert remained in company. Two days later, the squadron's position was estimated to be less than 60 miles west of Cape St. Vincent, Portugal, the southwesternmost point of continental Europe, and once considered the limit of European navigation. But even these waters were no strangers to commerce. At dawn on January 9, a sail was sighted to the south, and yet another chase was initiated. This time, Lijncoert's swift privateer, which had been sailing ahead of the main flota, made the capture, an English fluit en route from Malaga to England with raisins.[18]

Evertsen took the opportunity of the departure of the prize, which was to be sent by the caper into La Coruña, to post letters to the Raden of Zeeland, and a copy of same to the Commissioner of the States General stationed there, Nicolaes van Hoorn. Evertsen's report was brief, describing progress to date and the apparent loss of the two prizes, *Isaac and Benjamin* and *St. Maria*, and the recent tempest. It was a matter of some importance to Van Hoorn, who was commissioned to manage the accounts of all prizes captured on the coasts of Biscay and Galicia. Should either of the two prizes have survived and arrive along the coast, it was his responsibility to manage their adjudication and sale.[19]

The squadron pressed on, and on January 10, Evertsen adjusted course in hopes of sighting Porto Santo, northernmost of the Madeira Islands. On the following day, a fine, misty rain began to fall. Nevertheless, the lookout signalled land ahead, and Evertsen ordered the leerail under to make all speed on a southerly course. By midday, however, it was discovered—undoubtedly much to the lookout's embarrassment—that the squadron had been attempting to make landfall on a cloud bank on the distant horizon! Clearly, there had been some error in navigation, but as the fair sailing and clear weather offered splendid opportunity to rectify the mistake, Evertsen ordered all of the mates and navigators of the squadron to board *Swaenenburgh* and take a sighting at the same time. From a consensus taken, the correct position of the fleet would be determined.[20]

On January 11, Evertsen's mates and navigators lined up along the sunny rail of *Swaenenburgh*, and each computed what he perceived to be the frigate's position on the globe and in relation to the next expected land to be sighted, the Portuguese-held Madeira Islands. Below these lay the Canary Islands, their first planned landfall. There was, as expected, little difference in the computations of latitude, but a wide disagreement on longitude, with one faction proclaiming the squadron to be east of Madeira and the other west. Evertsen, siding with his own intuition and experience, decided to run southeast under short sail. As was often the case, his instincts proved correct. The following day, he estimated that the Madeiras lay behind him. On the 14th, "3 glasses into the morning watch sighted the land of Lancerota in the SSE, about 8 to 9 miles from us." They had reached their first major objective of the expedition, the northeasternmost of the Canary Islands, where they had planned to take on water.[21]

The Canary group, the easternmost island of which lay approximately 60 miles off the northwest coast of Africa, consisted of seven islands—Gran Canaria, Fuerteventuar, Lanzarota, Tenerife, La Palma, Gomera, and Hierro—and six small islets. It was an exotic archipelago characterized by steep coasts, extinct volcanoes, lava fields, deep valleys, elevated plains, and a salubrious climate. Citrus, palm, and the native dragon tree, as well as flora much like that of northern Africa, predominated in the lowlands, while the rich volcanic soil readily lent itself to limited cultivation of a wide variety of staples. From the earliest of classic times, when Carthaginians came to visit and colonize, the islands had held a particular attraction to European and African conquerors. Not until 1495, however, was the full hegemony of Spain established over all of the islands. It was a domination that was to last well into the twentieth century.

To seventeenth-century European eyes, the Canaries could boast of little apparent fertility, for rain was a rare event, and there were no natural rivers to grace the landscapes of any of the islands. A French writer wrote imaginatively in 1674 that

> the shortage of water is compensated by a Tree prodigious in size. It has very large leaves and very long branches. A cloud always surrounds this Tree, and, in touching its leaves, causes water enough to refresh the thirst of the inhabitants and beasts of this island.[22]

To others, including a Swede who wrote glowingly of the islands in the 1650s, the Canaries were a paradise of fresh and exotic foods, offering oranges, lemons, potatoes, bananas, sugar, syrup, wine, and tobacco. And to his wonderment, the leading citizens were accompanied by black slaves bearing sunshades.[23] But to the pragmatic seafarers who called there, the islands were a Godsend where life-sustaining water, victuals, and wood were to be had, albeit sometimes at great cost. Cornelis Evertsen was neither as credulous as the French traveler nor as naive as the Swede, for he knew what the Canaries had to offer and how to obtain their goods.

On January 15, the Dutch squadron sighted the pinnacles of Gran Canaria and set course for it. The volcanic cones of this island, as well as those of La Palma, and the majestic 12,162-foot Pico de Teida on Tenerife, were navigation points visible from 60 miles or more out to sea. With little difficulty, the squadron sailed into the roads of Gran

Raid on America

Canaria's capital town, Las Palmas, and about nightfall anchored in ten fathoms of water with coral bottom. Lieutenant Becker was immediately dispatched ashore to the Spanish castle that guarded the harbor to formally report the arrival of the squadron and to secure permission to take on water and procure other necessities.[24]

The following morning at dawn, a white flag was run up *Swaenenburgh's* masthead to signal the captains of the squadron to report their needs. Lieutenant Becker was again sent into town, this time accompanied by a clerk, to see if the goods requested were ready. If so, he was instructed to have them sent aboard immediately. Unfortunately, while Becker was ashore, a storm blew up out of the northwest, and high seas made it impossible to come ashore with boats to bring off the goods. Nevertheless, in the evening, Evertsen dispatched *Swaenenburgh's* sloop to shore

> to see whether there was any chance to get the clerk sent with Lieutenant Becker back on board, but because of the high waves breaking on the shore, there was great danger of losing the sloop and crew, but still the sloop overcame the danger and was brought up on dry ground.[25]

By midnight the weather had cleared, and by dawn on January 17, the sloop had returned with the clerk and a note from Becker. Negotiations with the governor of the island had gone well; permission to take on water had been given. Since *De Eendracht*, carrying much of the squadron's provisions, had yet to appear, Captain Evert Evertsen Frans' Zoon was dispatched to take on victuals purchased at Las Palmas as quickly as possible. By 9:00 A.M. the squadron, except for *Suriname*, had completed its business in the roads and had sailed for the watering place, five miles distant.

Despite the governor's permission, securing water would prove more of a problem than anyone had anticipated. Arriving at the watering place in the afternoon, the Dutch discovered that the local Spaniards had dammed the flow of a small stream a mile and a half above the beach. Evertsen dispatched a sergeant with the letter from the governor to the officer in charge of the local village, "to request him so kindly to see to it that matters were put right, as water had to be loaded." The following day, at about midday, the sergeant returned to *Swaenenburgh* accompanied by the local captain. The Spaniard made it clear that if the Dutch wanted water they would have to pay the civilian inhabitants for it. Evertsen was wise enough not to quarrel, and had soon reached an agreement with the captain, whereupon word was sent to open the sluice and let the water run. Another full day was lost before the trickle of water reached the beach. On the 19th, gusting winds and treacherous surf retarded the transport of barrels to the shore and threatened the loss of men and boats alike. Only nine barrels were loaded that day, and that with the greatest difficulty. But the dangerous work had to proceed.[27]

At about midday on January 20, as the Dutch seamen and marines labored, the governor of Gran Canaria, several military officers, two Catholic priests, and two city officials from Las Palmas came aboard the flagship. Their mission, as suggested by the presence of so many important men, was clearly not to make a social call but one which, when presented to Evertsen, may have caused a slight chuckle. The Spaniards informed the young Dutchman that a Turkish corsair had recently been cruising about the island causing great mischief. They had come to humbly request that the squadron "cruise for a day or two to see whether we could trap the Turk." Evertsen, who was undoubtedly mildly chagrined at having to pay for water, now had a solid stick with which to beat the Spaniards into provisioning his ships—at his tempo. He thus replied that he must first attend to securing the promised water and firewood, and that *Suriname*, which was waiting impatiently off Las Palmas for victuals, would have to join the fleet fully laden. Only then could he attend to the problems of the Spanish. The governor quickly assured the commander that he would "put everything to rights," and that the victuals at Las Palmas would be sent aboard the ship there with all haste. He proved as good as his word.[28]

Delighted with the turnabout, Evertsen turned his attentions back to the business of watering and wooding. On the 21st, amid showers, *Schaeckerloo* was dispatched to nearby Mas Palombas Bay to begin cutting firewood, for there was none to be had along the barren shores facing Evertsen's anchorage. When Captain Lijncoert informed the commander of his intentions to part company with the fleet, Evertsen took time to prepare another report for the Raden of Zeeland, which was to be delivered via Cadiz. Soon afterwards, the caper sailed, presumably with the commander's blessings and communiques.[29]

Watering continued, if with less success than had been hoped, for it was soon discovered that part of the supply taken onboard had been contaminated by seawater from extremely high flood tides and heavy surf, which had salted the little freshwater reservoir near the beach. Yet the victualling of *Suriname* at Las Palmas had been consummated with far greater speed than could have been hoped for. Shortly after Lijncoert's departure, the Zeelander arrived carrying the victuals for the fleet.[30]

On Wednesday, January 22, Evertsen settled accounts with the Gran Canaria merchant, Senor Diego de Roo, who had provided the victuals for the squadron. This he did not do in hard currency, but through a paper transaction that exemplified the sophistication of the Dutch banking and mercantile system of the late seventeenth century, and its ready acceptance by merchants of many nations. De Roo's bill was covered by a debiture certificate drawn on the firm of Jan Baptist van Herten and Company. Van Herten was a partner with Abraham de Meyer of Vlissingen, in a Dutch trading house, and co-owner of one of the largest and wealthiest operations in Cadiz as well. Since Van Herten and De Meyer were well-known in Cadiz and their paper was good, De Roo had readily agreed to the transaction.[31]

In the afternoon, soon after *Suriname* had taken on additional ballast, *Swaenenburgh* and the remainder of the squadron sailed for Mas Palombas Bay to join *Schaeckerloo*, but owing to the onset of darkness they did not sail in. On the following day, the squadron entered and began taking on firewood, but found the fresh water there salty and unpotable. Late in the afternoon of January 24, the fleet prepared to sail from the bay on a stiff easterly breeze, "but as our anchor touched the bow," Evertsen wrote later that day, "the wind suddenly came about to the west with such force that it was as much as we could do to keep off the beach." With difficulty, the squadron managed to escape safely into the open ocean. Leaving the Canaries behind, the Dutch pressed south, skirting to within half a dozen miles of the Barbary Coast of Africa, which was briefly sighted on the 27th.[32]

The task of commanding a squadron of warships in foreign, largely unfamiliar waters, where difficulties presented themselves at every turn, would have been challenge enough for most men, but for Cornelis Evertsen there had been the added personal burden of the continuing illness that in mid-December had seized his second in command, his own brother, Captain Evert Evertsen Cornelis' Zoon. Captain Evertsen had suffered through a month and a half of freezing winter storms and heaving seas, only to expire on January 31. Cornelis Evertsen noted his brother's passing quite simply: "At about 9 o'clock at night my brother died after being sick 6 weeks." There would be no burial at sea, however, for Kees the Devil was determined that his brother would be interred in Dutch soil.[33]

Still the squadron slogged on, unaffected by the death of a single leader, for there were certain to be many more such losses. The Cape Verdes, everyone knew, lay somewhere ahead, and beyond them the distant, rocky shores of St. Helena. No one could know what lay in store. When the island of Boa Vista, the first of the Cape Verdes, was sighted, few aboard could guess that their entire mission was about to be radically altered.

5

TO THE LAST MAN

The *harmatten*, the dry east wind from the North African interior that swept across the barren, volcanic Cape Verde Islands in January and February, did not hinder the approach of the Zeeland squadron in the least. The crescent-shaped, sparsely-populated archipelago of ten islands and three small islets was held by the Portuguese, under whose dominion they had been maintained since their discovery and colonization in the mid-fifteenth century. The Barlavento, or Windward Islands, were composed of Santo Antão, São Vicente, Santa Luzia, São Nicolau, Sal, Boa Vista, and the islets of Branco and Razo. The Satovento, or Leeward Islands, consisted of Maio, São Tiago, Fogo, Brava, and the islet of Secos. All were mountainous and inhospitable, with only Sal and Maio boasting of any level terrain whatsoever. The 9,300-foot-tall Cano Peak on Fogo, an active volcano, provided the highest elevation of the widely scattered chain and from time to time erupted in violent "Flames of Fire." But the Dutch were more interested in the salt, water, and firewood to be had here, the terminus of the second important leg of their mission, than the view.

At dawn, on February 5 the squadron sighted the island of Boa Vista, and by midday had come close under it. Soon thereafter, Evertsen ordered Captain Passchier de Witte in *Schaeckerloo* to press on ahead to São Tiago, the principal island of the archipelago, in search of Maerten Andriessen's hoecker and the prize fluit and to alert them of the squadron's safe arrival. Thijssen's snaauw was dispatched to Boa Vista to purchase salt, and then to rendezvous with the fleet at São Tiago.[1]

By midday, February 8, Evertsen and the squadron had dropped anchor in 14 fathoms of water with a sandy holding ground in São

Raid on America

Tiago Bay.[2] The location, famous to Atlantic travelers of the seventeenth century, was a welcome respite from the open ocean. The noted buccaneer and diarist William Dampier would describe the site six years later thus:

> On the East-Side of the Isle St. Jago is a good Port, which in peaceable Times especially is seldom without Ships; for this hath been long a Place which Ships have been wont to touch at for Water and Refreshments, as those outward-bound to the East-Indies, English, French and Dutch; many of the Ships bound to the Coast of Guinea, the Dutch to Surinam, and their own Portuguese Fleet going for Brazil . . . but few Ships call in here on their return to Europe.[3]

There were on the island two large towns and several small villages, and, for such an isolated place, a great many inhabitants; here mariners in need of provisions could expect to barter with the country people for their precious staples. Bullocks, hogs, goats, fowls, eggs, plantains, coconuts, and the island's principal product, wine, were to be had from the inhabitants in exchange for such necessaries as shirts, drawers, handkerchiefs, hats, waistcoats, breeches, linens, and other cloth. Dampier warned, however, that "Travellers must have a Care of these People, for they are very thievish; and if they see an Opportunity will snatch any Thing from you, and run away with it."[4] São Tiago was under the administration of a governor whose authority extended over the entire archipelago, and whose duties, especially during visits by warring European powers, were often trying at best.

Evertsen had every reason to assume that he might obtain the necessary firewood and water here without difficulty, and dispatched the sloop ashore to make the arrangements. When the landing party reached the beach, however, the local officer informed them that the governor of the island, then in town two miles away, must first be informed of their request. A man was dispatched to follow up on the order, and, since the sloop was already ashore with its empty water barrels, the beach officer generously permitted the crew to fill them while they awaited the expected permission. Meanwhile, in the harbor, anticipating the delay to be nothing more than a bureaucratic formality that would soon be addressed, the Dutch were a-bustle with activity. Work parties quickly started to bringing the water barrels up out of the holds. Slings were rigged to drop empty barrels into waiting boats and haul up filled ones. Soon the once-trim fighting decks of *Swaenenburgh* and *Suriname* began to take on the appearance of cluttered merchantmen offloading in the Maas. Guns were rolled back from the gunports to make way for the deck work, and empty barrels rather than the accustomed iron tubes were clustered along the sides. It was a moment of extreme vulnerability, but an operation of absolute necessity for the completion of the mission ahead.[5]

At approximately 2:30 P.M. two shots were fired from the Portuguese castle fort overlooking the harbor, which Evertsen assumed to be the signal that permission had been granted to wood and water. Thus, he ordered *Swaenenburgh*'s boat to shove off for shore with another load of empty barrels. Unfortunately, affairs did not proceed as he had hoped, for when the landing party again reached the beach, they found the governor awaiting them. Until he had spoken with a captain or an officer of the ships in his harbor, he stated arrogantly, he would permit neither water nor firewood to be taken.[6]

Something, Evertsen must have sensed, was wrong. The Cape Verdes, as a colonial outpost of Portugal, was neutral territory, and as a rule permitted normal provisioning for ships of all nations, even belligerents. Yet the governor's word was law, and the Dutch were not interested in provoking an incident. The landing was not without its benefits, however, for when the shore party returned to the squadron, it brought not only the governor's directives, but word on the possible whereabouts of *Schaeckerloo*. De Witte, they had learned, had earlier anchored in the bay off the main town of the island, but had failed to locate either Andriessen's hoecker or the prize fluit. Evertsen had little time to worry about the pinnace or her captain, and immediately dispatched Lieutenant Joan Becker, from *Swaenenburgh*, ashore in the boat, still laden with empty barrels, to negotiate with the Portuguese official. Welcome though it may have been to the crews, the enforced leisure caused by the negotiations could readily turn into disaster, for, like an oasis in the desert, São Tiago, with its water and wood, could easily bring mortal enemies together unexpectedly.[7]

The wait for Becker's return seemed to stretch on interminably as the sun lowered to the horizon. Then, two hours before sundown, with Becker still ashore, *Swaenenburgh*'s lookout sighted a most unwelcome visitor—an English warship. Flying both pennant and royal standard, the enemy frigate was observed rounding the headland of the bay and preparing to proceed. Almost simultaneously, the Englishman recognized the vulnerable ships at anchor in the roads as Dutch, immediately came about, put her bow toward the open sea, and drifted. Within minutes she was joined by three more powerful ships-of-war, a fireship, and a prize. After a flurry of signals between them, they formed up, came about, and, running before the wind, bore down on the momentarily stunned Zeelanders to engage.[8]

Ironically, the British squadron that had appeared at São Tiago at Evertsen's most vulnerable moment was on a mission almost identical to that of the Zeelanders. The squadron was under the command of Captain Richard Munden, a veteran Royal Navy commander, onboard H.M.S. *Assistance*, a fourth-rate frigate, and included the hired ships-of-war *William and Thomas*, Captain Thomas Piles, *Mary and Martha*, Captain John Butler, *Levant Merchant*, Captain William Hobbes, and the fireship *Castle*. Munden had sailed in utmost secrecy from the Downs on or about January 15 upon a mission known to only a few at the highest levels of the Admiralty. His objective was nothing less than to effect the capture of the enormously rich and important homeward-bound Dutch East India Company fleet at the island of St. Helena.[9]

For Evertsen, the unexpected arrival of Munden's squadron was yet another nightmare every commanding officer hoped never to experience in reality. The ships under his command had been surprised at their most vulnerable moment, anchored in an unfamiliar bay and beset by a numerically superior and better-armed enemy with the wind at its back. Part of his company was ashore, and his own fighting decks were so cluttered with tackle and barrels that running out a single gun was all but impossible. And the exact whereabouts of one of his strongest ships, *Schaeckerloo*, were unknown.

Having permitted himself to be completely surprised under such adverse conditions was an error that could only be rectified by immediate and flawless action. With one eye on the oncoming enemy, Evertsen instantly ordered the anchor cables chopped through with axes and the Zeeland squadron to make all possible sail. With a major piece of luck, some of *Swaenenburgh*'s crew managed to haul her sloop onboard, even as others raced up the ratlines and clambered out on the spars to unfurl her canvas. There was no time, however, to recover the boat or the ship's skipper, nor *Suriname*'s boat, nor *Sint Joris*'s sloop.[10]

In the mad scramble to get underway, Evertsen ordered the decks cleared for action. Immediately the crew began to throw everything possible overboard, making room on the fighting decks to run out the guns. Their only hope, and a slim one at that, was to run before the wind close along the coast and to find *Schaeckerloo*. Though they might not long avoid the enemy's guns, they could at least prevent the humiliation of being cut out.[11]

Owing to remarkable seamanship, the tactic worked, and the English, who had smelled an easy victory only moments before, were soon left far behind as the sun began to set. It was dark before Evertsen skillfully maneuvered *Swaenenburgh* before the little town where *Schaeckerloo* had been reported that afternoon. There were, however, neither lights nor sign of the pinnace. Anxiously, he ordered a series of signal charges fired to warn De Witte of the danger sweeping in from behind. But all was silent. With only two men-of-war against the enemy's four, the outcome of any engagement seemed too dismal to consider. There was, of course, the hope that the boats and sloop left behind in the rush to escape might encounter *Schaeckerloo* somewhere in the bay and inform her of the predicament—hopefully before the English did. But for the Dutch, the terror in the dark had only begun.[12]

At about 10:00 P.M., as *Swaenenburgh* poked cautiously along in the darkness, an enormous shape loomed suddenly, crossed her bow, and, at the command of a disarticulated voice, came alongside. In an instant, a second equally ominous shape hove up on the opposite side of the Dutchman. Munden had found his prey.

The two English frigates opened on *Swaenenburgh* with shattering broadsides and musketry. The Dutchman's decks were no longer cluttered with tackle and gear, and her guns were loaded and ready for fight. Evertsen replied in republican fashion, answering the enemy in kind from both port and starboard guns. Even in the darkness, lit only by the crimson flashes of exploding gunpowder, it was clear to Kees the Devil that his able gunners were scoring clean hits. Then all was suddenly quiet. The Englishmen had broken off the engagement and come up into the wind, perhaps content to finish off their prey in the daylight. *Swaenenburgh* only shortened sail, Evertsen wrote caustically, "in the hope that the ship *Schaeckerloo* might leave the roads to join us to do his duty."[13]

With the dawn of Sunday, February 9, the English presence on the bay was still painfully obvious to the Dutch. The enemy was clearly intent on finishing the job. Fortunately for Evertsen, the wind had dropped during the night, and the surface of the water was stirred only by the gentle currents below. Neither English nor Dutch moved in the dead calm that cloaked São Tiago Bay. For the first time, Evertsen had the opportunity to examine his opponents unhurriedly in the clear light of day. The British flagship appeared to be a frigate of from 56 to 60 guns; another mounted from 42 to 44 guns; and the two remaining ships-of-war each carried 38 to 40 guns. There was also a fireship or two obviously preparing to stir things up at the first hint of a breeze. Against this force Evertsen's two men-of-war and ketch were at a serious disadvantage. And still there was no trace of *Schaeckerloo*.[14]

The morning was occupied with bellicose posturing but no fighting as the two squadrons drifted aimlessly upon the windless, placid waters. Toward midday, Captain Munden dispatched his sloop (probably under oars), bearing a white flag, to *Swaenenburgh*. Evertsen quickly sent out Lieutenant Becker in his own sloop to see what the English wanted. Munden's terms were simple. Asking the Dutch to concede the decision in lieu of a bloody fight, the outcome of which was certain, the Englishman pointed out that it was obvious that there could be no escape. Moreover, he was not only aware of the capabilities of their ships, both of which were English-built vessels taken during the last war, but he knew their plans as well. The captain of *Assistance* boldly demanded that the Zeelanders surrender their two warships, in return for which they would be permitted to keep their third—for they also knew *Schaeckerloo* was at São Tiago—and would be permitted to go on their way. If they refused the offer, Becker was informed, a fireship would be sent into their midst to burn them out.[15]

The lieutenant dutifully returned to *Swaenenburgh* with the English terms. Evertsen did not mull over his answer, but dispatched him back with a terse reply. The brash young Zeelander informed the English that "we were resolved to defend our ships to the last man, and that they could do whatever they thought best."[16]

The English response to Evertsen's defiance was soon obvious to the men watching from the becalmed ships. His majesty's ships were making all sail, hoping to pick up even a slight midday breeze before their prey. As both squadrons slowly drifted in the currents around a point of land at the bay's edge, *Swaenenburgh* and *Suriname* felt the first welcome breath of air, which soon turned to a sail-filling breeze, even as the English canvas hung limp. Within minutes, the Dutchmen were leaving a respectable wake. And still the English remained becalmed in the lee of the headland. After achieving a three-mile head start, the Zeelanders observed that the English warships had finally caught the wind. But, as the race seemed to be developing, the English suddenly shortened sail and hauled off. Again the coming of evening intervened. Munden, with bigger game to stalk in the waters of St. Helena, willingly conceded the contest and turned his ships for São Tiago, for he, too, was obliged to take on wood and water.[17]

With the greatest possible combination of sailing ability and good fortune, the little Dutch squadron had been saved from almost certain defeat or capture. Evertsen maintained an anxious lookout for *Schaeckerloo*, *Zeehond*, and the hoecker. Not long after the English had given up the race, *Zeehond* was sighted downwind, and the squadron changed course, coming upon her at dark. Captain Thijssen's report that there was no salt to be had on Boa Vista lost some of its urgency as Evertsen informed him of the attack by, and narrow escape from, the English squadron. His concern for *Schaeckerloo* had by now undoubtedly increased tenfold, lest she fall in with the enemy[18]

Intent on finding *Schaeckerloo*, Evertsen ordered his squadron to heave to for the night, for on the morrow he would attempt to tack above the island against the incessant harmatten to search the west side. Fortunately, with the morning there was no sign of the English, and the squadron methodically commenced the arduous labor of sailing almost into the African winds. The difficulty of the task was compounded by the need to tack far enough upwind from the point of the island to avoid being dashed to pieces on its rocky shoals but close enough to remain in sight of the shore. To sail the easy way around the island to the south, however, was impossible, for the English were most certainly awaiting them downwind.

For two long days, the Zeelanders suffered very wet and difficult weather as they beat back and forth in an endless series of short tacks, searching for the elusive De Witte. Driving obliquely against wind and waves, their already battered hulls pounded by walls of water, the Dutch measured progress in yards rather than miles. The strain on the crews and their ships, spars, and standing and running rigging was fearsome and soon began to exact its toll. At 10:00 A.M. on Tuesday, February 11, Cornelis Eewoutsen, commander of *Sint Joris*, ran up the *chouw* (emergency signal) and quickly furled his foresail. Evertsen sailed for him immediately. He was soon informed that the fireship was not only leaking badly from a shot she had taken between wind and water during the recent engagement, but worse, her bowsprit was completely loose, threatening the loss of a mast. Repairs were imperative, even on the open seas, and Evertsen did not hesitate to order the squadron to heave to until Eewoutsen could complete them. Shortly after midday, the flotilla was again under sail, but was still well below the northwest point of the island they had been diligently attempting to round.[19]

On the following morning, *Suriname* let her own chouw fly and also furled her foresail. Again Evertsen sailed over to investigate the cause of the problem. Again, more damage was reported. The warship's bowsprit and gallion were loose, and her foremast was in danger of going overboard. Once more the squadron was forced to come up into the wind. *Suriname*'s problems, however, were far more serious than even *Sint Joris*'s had been. Her gallion was in imminent danger of falling off. The crew worked desperately, but efficiently, in the open waters to secure the gallion to the hull with a makeshift arrangement of cable run through the hawseholes and drawn up tight against the bow. Toward midday the Zeelanders, having finally effected repairs, again made sail. By nightfall they were near but still below the northwest point of São Tiago. Frustrated by the failure of every effort to round the tip of the island, Evertsen resolved to return the way he had come—undoubtedly to gain more sea room to make wider tacks. At

3:00 A.M. he ordered the squadron to come about on an easterly course and then to sail back.[20]

The following day the Zeelanders made yet another attempt and by midday they had managed to bring *Swaenenburgh, Suriname,* and *Zeehond* just above the point of the island. Yet, try as she might, *Sint Joris* remained stuck in the lee of the land, unable to get upwind. Unwilling to leave the vulnerable ketch behind, Evertsen ordered the squadron to alter course to the northeast, and then to the east. By sundown the little fleet was well offshore, not far from where it had been the day before. Fortunately, the fruitless effort to circumvent the island in search of De Witte would soon be called off, for De Witte would find the squadron instead.[21]

At 9:00 A.M. on Friday, February 4, after frustrating days of trying to work upwind of the island, a lone sail was sighted to the east. As the range closed, it was readily recognized as *Schaeckerloo.* Captain Passchier de Witte undoubtedly had more than a little explaining to do regarding his long absence. He must have accounted for his actions to Evertsen's satisfaction, for the commander failed to record any suspicion he may have had of the possibility of cowardice or intentional avoidance of duty. The thought, however, must have crossed his mind more than once during the frantic efforts to escape the English squadron, and may have influenced a fatal decision that would be made a full year later. De Witte's report, however, proved quite important. On February 8, he informed his commander, he had received word of the danger to the squadron from the boats left behind in São Tiago Bay. He had immediately weighed anchor and run to the east with the boats and sloop from the ketch under tow. At the end of the dogwatch that night, nine lights were sighted between São Tiago and the Isle of Maio. Suspecting them to be the enemy, he ordered on all possible canvas and sailed in the opposite direction, directly for Maio. Arriving at the island on the 11th, De Witte dispatched Evertsen's skipper in his boat back to São Tiago to quietly collect intelligence on the English and on the whereabouts of the Dutch. Two days later, upon his return, the skipper reported that he was informed by the governor that an additional nine English vessels, including two ships-of-war, had come into the harbor on Sunday, February 9. They promptly raised the anchors the Dutch had cut and departed that night with them, leaving behind in the bay the five warships that had fought the Dutch. The skipper also reported that he had learned from the governor that the English had suffered a number of dead and wounded as a result of the recent engagement. Unfortunately, their ultimate destination remained a mystery.[22]

Because the enemy had finally moved on and De Witte's report had been accepted, a council of war agreed upon the squadron's next course. Though still in great need of wood and water, they could not hazard São Tiago Bay, for Munden's squadron was still there. It was thus resolved to run to the Isle of Maio in hopes of answering their needs. Upon arriving at Maio, a boat would be dispatched back to São Tiago to keep watch on the enemy and, it was hoped, gather intelligence concerning their plans. About midday the following day, the squadron came to anchor in a sandy ground in 16 fathoms at Maio, only to discover that there was no fresh water to be had. That night, during the dogwatch, Evertsen quietly dispatched his skipper and ten well-armed men in a boat back to São Tiago, as planned, to gather intelligence on the enemy.[23]

The following day, a Sunday, the governor of Maio, a mulatto, came aboard the flagship and informed Evertsen that he was welcome to take water and firewood but that the location for that operation was near a roadstead two miles distant, which was generally considered inhospitable to heavy ships, and it would require a bit of tacking to reach the spot. Evertsen was well aware of the strain experienced during the recent effort to circumvent São Tiago against adverse winds, and decided, perhaps wisely, to await the return of the boat from that island. The squadron's crews were kept busy bringing aboard a number of cattle purchased at Maio, and salt from the island salt pans. Shortly after midday on February 7, the boat expedition returned from São Tiago with the welcome report that the English warships that had attacked them four days earlier had finally sailed. The nine ships *Schaeckerloo* had sighted coming into the bay and that had raised the Dutch anchors were also gone. Relieved at the enemy's departure, Evertsen resolved to return to São Tiago to secure water and wood where it might be had with relative ease—assuming the governor there agreed to permit the reprovisioning.[24]

On February 18 the squadron arrived at São Tiago Bay. This time, having been once stung by tactical indiscretion, Evertsen waited at anchor outside the bay while Lieutenant Becker was sent ashore to secure permission to take on water and further intelligence about the two English squadrons. This time, the lieutenant returned with the governor's approval to water, but, of even greater importance to the future of the Zeelanders' mission, he brought new information on the destination of the Munden squadron. The news was more than a little disturbing, for the enemy was bound for St. Helena. Although the young Zeelander did not learn of their specific objective, the capture of the Dutch East Indies ships, the very strong possibility of encountering

the more powerful enemy force again undoubtedly gave him just reason
to reflect on his mission and on his chances of success. As for the other
nine ships sighted by *Schaeckerloo*, two of which were warships and
the rest merchantmen, it was learned that they were bound for the
West Indies.[25]

While the Zeeland commanders pondered a resolution to their new
dilemma, the seamen of the squadron were busily occupied in taking
water onboard the ships, despite a stiff wind that only served to multi-
ply the difficulties normally inherent in such a task. For some, São
Tiago Bay must have appeared jinxed, for difficulties seemed to plague
the squadron. When the cable of *Swaenenburgh*'s main starboard anchor (plicht) parted one afternoon, Evertsen was obliged to order a
party out to fish it up, a laborious job, which took the better part of an
evening. That night the wind began to blow so hard that several vessels
dragged their anchors and *Schaeckerloo*'s boat drifted out of the bay.[26]

While the watering operation continued, Evertsen, taking advantage
of the imminent departure of a neutral Spanish bark from São Tiago,
prepared a report of the squadron's motions for the Zeeland Council in
Middleburg. Describing the encounter with the powerful English
squadron, which had ended more happily than the Zeelanders might
have initially expected, he explained that the mission to St. Helena, a
voyage of at least four weeks, would have to be aborted, and he would
be obliged to drop the first set of the Zeeland government's secret instructions. Simply put, it would be foolhardy to attack St. Helena,
where the English, who were apparently already apprised of the Dutch
objectives, were also bound and would, in all likelihood, be waiting.
Since the English had already sailed, it was quite likely that they would
arrive well enough ahead of Evertsen to alert the garrison of a possible
attack. The element of surprise would be lost, and the chances against
both the garrison and Munden's squadron were remote at best.[27]

Although empowered to continue in command until June 1673,
Evertsen realized that his principal objective was no longer possible. To
press on to the Indian Ocean without stopping at St. Helena would be
foolish, yet to sail home virtually empty-handed after the expense of
mounting such an expedition might well result not only in disgrace, but
in recriminations and probably dismissal by the Admiralty. It was readily apparent that the encounter with the English heavily influenced the
Zeelanders' decisions to forego St. Helena. There was little to do but
turn to the Council of Zeeland's final set of secret instructions. Evertsen's decision to do so, however, was destined to be debated and discussed in Middleburg for months to come, especially as the letter sent

from São Tiago, and another from the Dutch colony of Suriname somewhat later, were to be the last news the Fatherland would receive from Evertsen's own hand until he had completed his conquests in America almost a year later—for it was now America to which he would turn his undivided attention.

The wind dropped enough during the following days to permit watering to continue, albeit with regular pauses for afternoon storms. Finally on Friday evening, February 24, the squadron sailed from the bay that had very nearly been the scene of its destruction. The following day, in the presence of the officers assembled onboard *Swaenenburgh*, Evertsen opened the last set of the Council's secret instructions. The record of this significant council of war, one that would influence the course of history for much of English America, is curiously vague. Evertsen's log reports only that the squadron officers agreed to the orders their commander read. The instructions, written in cipher, included eight articles, and, as in the other sets of secret orders, left little room for interpretation.[28]

The first articles of the instructions were predicated on the assumption that the squadron had completed the voyage to St. Helena and was on the next leg of its expedition. The first article, indeed, directed that "on their return from St. Helena," the squadron was to set a course for Cape Orange, located to the east of French-held Cayenne, on "the wild coast," also known as Guiana, on the South American mainland. By the anticipated time of the squadron's arrival there, Evertsen was informed, a dispatch yacht with further orders would be awaiting him, accompanied by a reinforcement of men (if affairs in the Fatherland permitted). Upon the squadron's arrival at Cape Orange, a secret council of war was to be convened to insure that the ships of the fleet and their prizes be provided "with every refreshment, and thus be rendered the more fit for the further voyage."

If the attack on St. Helena was a success, and if it was followed by the capture of either English or French East India merchantships and their rich booty, the Dutch fleet was to attempt no further actions. Instead, they were to insure that "all proper care and vigilance shall be used to safeguard the captured ships." After 10 to 12 days' rest and refreshment at Cape Orange, they were to again put to sea and reconnoiter at the mouth or in the Suriname River to determine whether the tiny Dutch colony there remained in friendly hands. If the colony had not been captured by the enemy, the squadron was to supply the fort there with ammunition and "as many other necessaries as the Squadron shall be able to spare" without causing a scarcity in the fleet. While at Suriname, a small vessel was to be dispatched to reconnoiter the adjoining Dutch colony of Essequibo to determine conditions there and find out if the squadron could render some small assistance. If the fort and colony of Suriname had been captured by the enemy, the Zeelanders were to attempt to capture or ruin enemy shipping found in the river, but only if the opportunity was favorable. There were no specific directions, however, concerning the recapture of the colony. The instructions were quite explicit in stating that no risks should be taken that might jeopardize the safety of the rich booty, "which it is hoped shall have been captured at the Island of St. Helena." With this concern in mind, the Zeelanders were ordered to completely avoid the islands of the Caribbean owing to the danger of hurricanes, which were prevalent during the season the fleet was expected to be in the region.

Not until Article Five were the possibilities of a failed expedition to St. Helena or the capture of but "a middling booty" addressed. In such circumstances, the squadron was directed to seek out whatever advantage might be had against the French colony of Cayenne, on the Wild Coast of Guiana. If the fort and colony of Suriname had fallen to the foe, the Zeelanders, with no booty to protect, were authorized to employ all land and sea forces available to retake it. Failing in this, every effort was to be made to utterly ruin the colony, "and to take away from there whatever it shall be possible to do so, and subsequently to dispose, to the greatest advantage somewhere else of the captured slaves." The squadron was then to sail to the West Indies, hurricanes or no, to "see what advantages may be gained against any hostile ships about the Barbadoes and other French and English Islands."

Article Six expanded the permissible scope of the raid against enemy holdings in the Western Hemisphere even more dramatically:

> Their Noble Mightinesses are further considering the Island of the Bermudas, in order, as has been mentioned in the previous article, should the attempt against the Island of St. Helena fail, then to attack, to ransack or even occupy the said Island of Bermuda, as shall be considered best and also feasible. And further that a Cruise shall be undertaken before and along the coasts of Virginia, New Netherland, without forgetting New Foundland, subsequently capturing and ruining there whatever shall be possible; so that, should the design against the Island of St. Helena have miscarried, which is not surmised, to acquire through this [cruise] so much booty, that the expenses of this equipment shall be generously defrayed through the same.

The Raden had developed second thoughts at the eleventh hour while writing out the instructions, however, and thus included a contradictory note directing that Bermuda not be attacked, but that the squadron was to endeavor "to capture and ruin everything possible at Newfoundland and to dispatch most prizes from there to Spain" where they might be sold for the benefit of the country.

In the event that Evertsen did not encounter a dispatch boat at Cape Orange or thereabouts, the squadron was to sail for Fayal in the Azores. If a dispatch boat was not found waiting there, they were to immediately press on, setting a course for Hitland, to the north of England, to find out if any further orders from the Fatherland had been sent. In the event that no dispatch boat was found there either, the squadron was to make directly for the Fatherland and the harbors of Zeeland. The Raden specifically ordered that there were to be no stops in Norway, and the choice of routes, whether along the Scottish coast and the north of England or otherwise, was to be determined on the basis of which route was considered safest.

With the opening of the final set of secret instructions, Cornelis Evertsen had already reached a decision to give up the mission against St. Helena. But now, there was an entirely new schedule of objectives set before him. The Wild Coast (Guiana) of South America, the sugar islands of the Caribbean, the tobacco coast of Virginia, the former Dutch colony of New Netherland, and the bountiful fisheries of Newfoundland were now offered as fit objectives for Dutch attack. With little to show for their efforts thus far, the assembled captains of the Zeeland squadron had no difficulty in determining their next course of actions, and "it was agreed to follow orders." With a strong wind blowing northeast to north, Evertsen ordered a course set for the west-southwest. His objective now was to conduct a raid on America—a raid that would temporarily upset the balance of power in the Western Hemisphere.

6

THE WILD COAST

The vast, largely unexplored land of Guiana, the coast of which the Zeeland squadron had fixed as its next destination, was a place of both dream and legend dating from the days of the Spanish conquistadores. Many were the tales of this fabled region, cloaked by thick, impenetrable jungles, and surrounded by mysterious mountains and rivers, uncounted miles from the wretched European outposts on its Atlantic coast. There were such titillating stories as that of Lake Parmina, upon the shores of which stood fabulous Manoa, city of gold, in which dwelled a lost race of Incas, refugees from the Spanish conquerors of Peru, who were ruled by El Dorado, the golden king. Lake Parmina was a paradise surrounded by rich and populous cities, hidden in a land abounding with mines of gold and silver. For nearly 80 years, adventurers searching for Manoa had been drawn into Guiana's often fatal grasp.[1]

Those few bold seekers who ventured into its steamy fastnesses, lured by visions of wealth and paradise, faced, in reality, only vexation, poverty, and often death. Lying on the northeast shoulder of South America, roughly between the Orinoco River on the west and the northern border of Brazil on the east, the Guianas were anything but a land of dreams. The Dutch name, Wild Coast, was quite apropos. A land of devilishly hot and humid climates, tropical jungles, swamps, savannahs, alligators, ringworms, mosquitoes, and hostile natives, the Guianas all but frustrated even the stoutest of explorers.

Sighted by Columbus in 1499, the region was only skirted by those who followed. Ultimately, however, gold-seeking explorers began to penetrate the trackless wilderness; Gonzalo Pizzaro in 1539, Francisco d'Orellana in 1541, Walter Raleigh in 1595, and Laurence Keyms in

1598. Not until 1604, however, did the French launch the first colonizing expedition, sponsored by the Compagnie Royale des Indes Occiden-
tales (Royal Company of the West Indies), which founded the first
settlement at Cayenne, off the Cayenne River. A second settlement was
established five years later on the Oyapock River, and in 1633, the
French again fostered a number of plantation establishments through
the Norman Companies. The Dutch were not recalcitrant in securing a
foothold on the Wild Coast, and established a settlement there in
1621.[2] The coastal plain gave into civilization only grudgingly. In 1634,
the British, under the direction of Captain Marshall, erected the first
settlement in what was to become the colony of Suriname. Though
Marshall built a number of dwellings surrounded by a pallisaded fort
and diligently employed himself in the cultivation of tobacco, his settlement was doomed to failure. Six years later, the French also laid claim
to Suriname, "but finding it unhealthy, on account of the woods and
marshes, they presently abandoned it."[3]

The English quickly profited from the departure of the French and
moved to make themselves masters of the region. In 1650, Lord Francis
Willoughby established an alliance with the Indians on the Suriname
River—another colony was founded. Its capital, Paramaribo, was established a few miles up from the sea. In 1662, Willoughby and Laurence Hyde, son of the Earl of Clarendon, secured formal letters of
patent on Suriname. By 1665, the colony had grown to 4,000 inhabitants and supported 40 to 50 sugar plantations situated along a 30-mile
stretch of the Suriname River. The regency then consisted of a governor
and his council, who submitted to the general laws of England.

The competition between the Dutch and the English was as strong in
the outpost colonies of South America as on the North Sea, and with
the outbreak of the Second Anglo-Dutch War in Europe, fighting soon
erupted along the Guiana Coast. The English moved first, seizing the
Dutch river colonies of Poumaron and Essequibo in 1666, but they
failed to take Berbice. The Dutch retaliated from Berbice, retaking
Essequibo in 1667. Not until February 1667, however, did a Dutch
force from Europe assail the English in Guiana. It was then that Commander Abraham Crijnssen of the Admiralty of Zeeland led a squadron
into the Suriname River to attack the small English garrison defending
the approach to Paramaribo. The small pentagonal fort was in a poor
state of readiness and stood little chance against a Dutch assault. The
defenses were surrendered without a fight by Acting Governor William
Byam, and the flag of the Prince of Orange was raised in the fort as a
signal of conquest. By the terms of capitulation the English planters
were offered the privilege of keeping their property if they took an oath

of allegiance to the State of Zeeland. The colony was soon formally relinquished to The Netherlands by the Treaty of Breda.

Before the news of peace had reached the Americas, however, an expedition from Jamaica, under the command of Sir John Harman, viciously fell upon and sacked Cayenne, and then assaulted Suriname. Fort Zeelandia, on the Suriname River, was taken after a savage battle. Harman then proceeded to decimate the entire colony, destroying approximately 30 mills, worked by 500 inhabitants, the majority of whom were, ironically, English and Jews.

Soon after learning of the peace, Willoughby submitted to the treaty terms and dispatched his son Henry, with a warship and three merchantmen, to Suriname to persuade the English settlers to quit the colony, which had been restored to The Netherlands. In June 1669, by order of the court in London, 1,200 inhabitants were scheduled to be resettled (though some resisted) to Jamaica. Disputes continued, however, and not until 1671 was the last group of colonists, numbering 517 souls under Major James Banister, shipped off.

With the outbreak of hostilities in 1672, the Raden of Zeeland suspected, as implied by several articles in Evertsen's last set of secret instructions, that Suriname may have been retaken by the enemy, and thus issued the directives for the squadron to call upon and supply the colony with provisions and munitions. Yet it was almost an afterthought, for Zeeland had done precious little to maintain its new charge in the years preceding the third war. Beset by financial difficulties at home, the State had almost blatantly ignored its responsibility. Suriname, an adopted dependent, had become sickly, expensive to maintain, and was, it seemed, more trouble than it was worth. By the onset of the third war with England and France, the colony and its tiny garrison were near collapse.

In September 1672, Suriname's military governor, Lieutenant Pieter Versterre, had outlined in pathetic detail the conditions of Suriname and of his own forces. Virtually cut off from contact with civilization, with the exception of the few English and Dutch planters, the colony was dangerously flanked by the French in Cayenne on the east and the English to the northwest. Yet the feeling of isolation, and the air of desperation and abandonment that accompanied it, was not solely a sentiment of the Dutch on the Guiana coast. The few English planters in the region who had not been evacuated but who swore allegiance to Zeeland openly doubted that they would receive any support from England. Versterre and the few healthy Dutchmen at Paramaribo prayed they were right. Fevers, pestilential climate, and starvation had reduced the Dutch population of the colony to 200 men, including planters, merchants, and mariners. Fifty to 60 men were sick, eight had died, and many more were expected to follow as a result of scurvy and other diseases of malnutrition. Recuperation for the colony's sick was all but hopeless, since the surgeon had received virtually no medical supplies from Zeeland in years. The imminent departure of three merchantmen and their crews threatened to further depopulate the colony. There was little food for either civilian or soldier. What food was available was usually rotten bacon, peas, and groats. The officers of the garrison complained of the lack of wine, bread, butter, and edible pork and meat. By late summer 1672, rations had dwindled to a six-week supply of pork. Jungle humidity had spoiled 6,000 pounds of cassaire bread, and there was barely a three-week supply left. Though the sugar plantation owners were apparently getting by, the slave population on their farms had been reduced to living off of greens plucked from the fields. Bread, Versterre reported, was to be had from the Indians living upon neighboring rivers, but there were no trade goods left with which to barter. Painting a grim picture of a potential breakdown of authority, the governor noted that his garrison was faced with the specter of starvation, and in consequence he had been driven to order the seizure of all private stores of provisions. It was an unfortunate action, and he was soon forced to rethink his decision when a mass demonstration resulted. To maintain law and order, he was obliged to rescind the edict.[4]

Despite the grave scarcity of provisions, there were some positive aspects to the situation at Paramaribo. A strong new Fort Zeelandia had been completed below the settlement and was readily defensible—assuming there were healthy men to mount its walls. The labor charges for the construction had been paid in scrip, which the workers exchanged for provisions from one of the merchant captains in the river. Versterre warned the Zeeland government in advance that the captain upon whose good will the project had depended, Jacob Soeteling, had bills for Their Lordships the Raden of Zeeland amounting to 400 guilders, and another for 150 guilders for calico, train oil, and brandy for the Public Magazine. There had been no alternative. Despite the rampant starvation, he noted with some cynicism, the sugar plantations were producing well, and the departing merchantmen had their holds filled with the sweet gold. Versterre ended his report with a plea that he be removed from duty in Suriname and granted a good job at home in consideration of his service to the Fatherland.[5] The letter was not without effect; it was thus decided by an embarrassed Raden to attach the reprovisioning clause to Evertsen's instructions.

When Kees the Devil approached the South American mainland in mid-March 1673, he carried with him an undoubtedly painful personal burden—the body of his brother, Evert Evertsen Cornelis' Zoon. The loss, however, did not affect his decisionmaking capabilities in the least, for the true tests of his new mission were only beginning. The squadron was again in need of many services. Several of the ships were leaking badly, *Swaenenburgh* required work on her crosstrees, damaged during a storm on the open Atlantic, and her rigging was in want of repairs. And, of course, the squadron was again destitute of firewood and water. A call at Paramaribo (or Para, as the Dutch called it) would be welcomed by all. But first there was the important business of investigating the plausibility of a raid on Cayenne.[6]

On Saturday, March 8, Evertsen estimated his position to be 54 miles east of Rio Cassapoure (Cachiour or Cassipore), near Cape Orange. Exercising all due caution, he ordered that several soundings be taken the following day. The water was growing noticeably shallower. A midday sounding of 60 fathoms had decreased to 52 fathoms by nightfall. Maintaining course under shortened sails, though land had yet to be sighted, he dispatched the snaauw *Zeehond* ahead of the squadron to sound and signal when she reached shallow water. Then, on the 9th,

> In the 5th glass of the dogwatch [2:30 A.M.] he signalled that he had found shallow waters; we came about into the wind easterly and held position to daylight; [we] were in 14 fathoms water.[7]

Evertsen's caution was not unfounded, for the Guiana coast was notoriously treacherous, swept by tremendously powerful currents, which were traversed only on favorable tides and in full daylight. Reliable charts of the region were almost nonexistent, and owing to the confusing monotony of the low-slung coast, it was difficult for even the most experienced mariners to visually determine exactly where they were.[8]

At 8:00 A.M. on Monday, March 10, the landmass of South America was finally sighted after a voyage of 16 days from São Tiago. The water shoaled rapidly to barely six fathoms, and although the land was very low and no fixed position on a landmark could be made, Evertsen was confident, from the subtle changes of terrain, that he was south of Cape Orange.[9] In fact, superb navigation had brought the Dutch flota quite close to its goal. For many in the squadron, the sighting of the mystical coast was their first. The words of a later visitor to these parts might well describe the excited initial impressions harbored by many of those aboard:

> Large forests of trees extend along the coast even to the beach which appeared to consist of mud, with but a few intervals of sand. This prospect . . . . was not the most flattering, but it being the end of my journey, and the first land I had seen for several weeks, I belied it with glad eyes and really thought it a most delightful place.[10]

Evertsen sailed with the wind along the coast, taking a fix at midday, estimating the Rio Cassapoure at twelve to thirteen miles northwest. At sundown the squadron came to anchor in six fathoms only a few miles distant from the river. The anchorage proved alarmingly unsettled, as would many encountered during their visit to the Wild Coast. First the tide ran with great force to the west, and then, in the night, it turned north, running so hard that for several hours the ships were swung against the wind by the force of the flow.[11]

The squadron was now in enemy territory, for the French settlement of Cayenne lay immediately ahead, and Evertsen exercised unusual caution in proceeding forward. On the evening of the 11th, the fleet came to anchor in eleven fathoms a mile off several large black rocky islets known to the Dutch as Point Constabel and to the English as the Constables. Cayenne was close. The following morning, at daylight, the squadron pressed on, keeping well outside a pair of islands known to the Dutch as Vaer en de Moer, or Father and Mother. It was here, near an island northwest of these forbidding rocks, that the French settlement lay. Again Evertsen sent *Zeehond* in to sound the depths, this time behind the islands.[12]

An attack on the unsuspecting French at Cayenne would necessitate, at the very least, securing shelter from the open sea in the lee of the islands to disembark landing forces. Evertsen remained patiently at anchor to the west of the islands and about three miles from the mainland while Captain Thijssen conducted his reconnaissance. At about midday, the snaauw returned and Thijssen presented his report to the commander aboard *Swaenenburgh*. There were barely 19 or 20 feet of water ahead where, it had been reported, there had once been four fathoms. Although the big warships might venture into the Cayenne River, barely slipping their deep hulls across the shoals, to do so in unfavorable circumstances was risky. Evertsen decided to investigate other options and to examine the territory personally. Boarding the snaauw with Captain Anthony Colve, commander of the marines, Evertsen decided "to see how close a small craft could come to the shore." If a boat could press in close enough to Cayenne without serious jeopardy from the surf or shoals in a short time, a landing might still be possible. "About a good half mile from the shore," he later noted in his log,

> found no more than 12 feet of water, whereon the snaauw anchored and sent the sloop to see if it could get closer. At a long cannon shot from the shore found no more than 9 feet of water and a strong tide to the west, so that it took a good 2 hours to come back to the snaauw. It was then

agreed not to land there since it was impossible to put the crew ashore in groups no larger than 100 and relieve them within 2 hours.[13]

Evertsen, having reconnoitered, determined now that a landing against Cayenne simply presented too many risks for the slender results that might be achieved. The effort would have to be aborted. It was thus resolved to sail onward to the Suriname River.[14]

The Dutch were careful to sail only during the daylight along the alien and inhospitable coast, but with their usual efficiency they managed to utilize every minute of light. Each day the squadron upped anchors in the gray of dawn, and dropped them again in the afterglow of sundown. On the 14th the Maroni River [Marrewijne], which formed the boundary between Suriname and Cayenne, was sighted.[15] The river's reputation preceded it, for it was frequently—often fatally—mistaken by mariners for the Suriname River.[16] "Those who have the misfortune to enter," wrote the French chronicler Philippe Fermin nearly a century later, "rarely come out again, on account of the great number of sandbanks, and various rocks, there to be met with."[17] Evertsen, however, apparently experienced little difficulty in recognizing the river, for he maintained a healthy distance between himself and the coast about its mouth.

Though the squadron was now out of enemy territory, the approach to the mouth of the Suriname was undertaken with particular caution. If a ship's position were not precisely known there, the vessel "would undoubtedly be carried past the entrance and be unable to return on account of the rapidity of the current,"[18] requiring a wide sweep to be made on the open sea for a second effort. Thus, *Zeehond* was again kept busy sounding out the waters ahead. Slowly the little flotilla picked its way along the coast, occasionally hauling off into deeper waters when the snaauw reported shoals ahead.

In the late afternoon of March 15, the lookout spied a sail in the offing. Evertsen sailed directly for it, and much to his delight discovered it to be a Dutch caper commanded by one Captain Claes Reijniersen. The caper, it was soon learned, had been cruising the coast in search of the Zeeland squadron, which was apparently expected at Paramaribo. In *Swaenenburgh's* great cabin, Reijniersen's intelligence was consumed with relish by the assembled commanders of the flotilla. They were relieved to hear that the few English still in Suriname knew nothing of the Zeelander's plans or presence, and that everything at Fort Zeelandia was normal. The food shortage in the colony, however, was still a problem, particularly on the plantations, because the plantings had rotted in the ground. But, the caper noted cheerfully, things were improving. Reijniersen's offer to lead the squadron to the river was accepted with alacrity.[19]

That evening, just at nightfall, the Zeelanders dropped anchor in four fathoms of water three miles off the Suriname. The caper captain was dispatched ahead, apparently in *Zeehond*, with letters for Governor Versterre. As off the Cassapoure, the anchorage was turbulent, with strong currents running from the river obliging the squadron to remain some distance out until news arrived from the fort. At about midday on Sunday, March 16, Lieutenant Potteij of *Suriname* returned to inform Evertsen that the governor was sick. The garrison, as expected, was in desperate need of provisions. Evertsen acted promptly, ordering Captain Eewoutsen to maneuver *Sint Joris*, which was to carry the supplies destined for the garrison, close inshore. Potteij was sent back to the fort, probably to arrange for immediate land transport of the provisions. On Monday, a dismal, soaking rain braced by a stiff wind began. It lasted for days, preventing their immediately entering the river.[20]

As the rain beat upon *Swaenenburgh*'s decks, Evertsen mulled over his next move. The fleet, after its Atlantic crossing, was in urgent need of repair. The crosstrees of *Swaenenburgh*'s mainmast and foremast were by now virtually in pieces. For the carpenters to repair them the masts had to be stripped bare, a task that was all but impossible on the rolling seas. Moreover, both *Suriname* and the flagship were leaking badly and required immediate attention, possibly even careening, as soon as possible. Despite the sickness that was prevalent in the colony, the commander resolved to bring the squadron into the river and proceed as far as Fort Zeelandia to effect the needed repairs.[21]

On the morning of the 20th, the squadron shifted to a more favorable anchorage from which it might enter the river, and on the following day it prepared to sail. Again Evertsen dispatched *Zeehond*, along with two boats, upriver to take soundings. He was pleased to learn, upon their return, that there was no less than 20 feet of water in the river, just enough for the squadron to swim in. But there were dangers.[22]

To bring an entire squadron of deep-draft warships under sail into a muddy, narrow channel, laced with shifting shoals of unknown character, against an unusually swift current without major mishap was a true test of the abilities of the commander and his officers and crews. Equipped with sounding leads, experience, skill, disciplined teamwork, and a healthy dose of instinct, however, the Zeelanders excelled at such challenges, for they had been bred to these conditions, which were common in the waters of the Fatherland. Nevertheless, the operation

was not taken lightly. On March 22, Evertsen ordered all of the small
craft in the area to ground themselves on the shores of the channel to
make sailing room for the larger ships. At slack tide the fleet weighed
anchor and began the slow, careful ascent up the river, with a leads-
man in the lead ship loudly sounding out the passage along the way.
Mile after mile the ships pushed on until, finally, as evening descended,
the low shape of Fort Zeelandia appeared ahead in a clearing on the
western bank. Soon they had come to anchor in six fathoms, and everyone breathed a sigh of relief.[23]

Sunday was a well-deserved day of rest.

The newly-arrived Zeelanders, not yet desiccated by the tropical
malaise that eventually poisoned both inhabitants and visitors to the
colony, fell to work on *Swaenenburgh* and *Suriname* with apparent
zeal. Work crews immediately began to strip the flagship's masts and
rebuild the crosstrees, while others searched for leaks in *Suriname*.
With repairs finally underway, Cornelis Evertsen permitted himself a
few solemn hours to attend to the interment of his late brother Evert
Evertsen Cornelis' Zoon. On March 25, the body was laid to rest in a
secluded corner of the Oraenje Battery of Fort Zeelandia, in Dutch soil
an ocean away from his homeland.[24]

When Evertsen returned his attentions to the squadron, he found
that work on *Suriname* was proceeding with difficulty. The incessant
leakage in the ship's hull could not be located, and the rather active
waters at the anchorage off the fort compounded the difficulties of
repair work. It was thus decided to bring the ship even further upriver
to continue repairs in the calmer waters off Paramaribo. *Schaeckerloo*,
no stranger to these waters (having served there as recently as 1671 to
oversee the evacuation of the English settlers), would follow to take on
wood and water.[25]

On March 30, repairs to *Swaenenburgh*'s masts were finally completed, and Evertsen ordered work begun to convert the ketch *Sint Joris*
into a fireship. On the following day, *Suriname*'s leak was, it was
thought, finally located and closed for good. That night, the ship's hull
began to seep water as badly as it had before, if not worse. There now
seemed nothing left to do but beach and careen her to end the problem
once and for all.[26]

Careening was a labor-intensive effort, for it first required the offloading of everything onboard, including guns, ammunition, and provisions. The actual operation of heaving the ship down on one side was
usually undertaken after first beaching her at high water and address-
ing a strong purchase to her masts. The masts had to be properly sup-

ported for the occasion to prevent snapping under the unusual strain. When hove down, one side of the hull was brought almost parallel with the surface of the water, while the other was elevated and dry, permitting repairs and cleaning, or breaming, as it was usually called.[27]

After six days of labor, the leak was again believed repaired. *Suriname* was reloaded and brought down to the fort for Evertsen's inspection. As the ship was getting underway, however, yet another serious and bedeviling leak spouted. There was nothing to do but careen her once again. On April 8, after almost two weeks of fruitless labor, the ship was again unloaded, beached, and hove down. This time, the troublesome spot was located quickly. Once the source of the problem was pinpointed in the bow, the crews were taken off the heaving cables and set to work closing up the leak. The following day, cannon, ball, powder, and provisions were reloaded for the third and last time. For the next seven days, though minor refitting was carried out throughout the squadron, the crews entertained themselves as best they could at Fort Zeelandia. It was destined to be their last serious frolic ashore for some time to come, and for a few among them, the last ever.[28]

As the Zeelanders busily employed themselves upriver in *Suriname*, a small 20-ton, six-gun English privateer called *Little Kitt*, Captain Peter Wroth commanding, arrived on the coast unnoticed. Wroth was a diligent commander intent, as were most privateersmen, on plunder, and he sought out information concerning the Dutch from every possible source. Upon his arrival on the Wild Coast, he learned from friendly Indians that a party of Dutchmen and Englishmen of Suriname had been turtling together at a place called Three Creeks, near the Suriname River. Wroth quickly resolved to surprise them and, undoubtedly, rob them of their turtles, the meat of which was highly prized by mariners of the West Indies. Unhappily for the captain and his 30 crewmen, the turtlers had been warned of his arrival by the owner of Quomoka Plantation in Suriname, one Luis Dias of Martinique. To prevent Wroth from plundering their turtle pens, they had completely blocked up the dirty little waterway leading to their turtling grounds, thereby frustrating his efforts.[29]

Wroth's visit, however, was not entirely without profit, for he had learned from several local colonists, undoubtedly disgruntled Englishmen, that a small Dutch naval squadron was in the river. The former English man-of-war *St. Patrick*, they said, and two other warships of 30 and 24 guns, along with a victualler and a fireship, were at that very moment upriver. He discovered, further, that they planned to sail for Virginia with the next spring tide "to do what mischief they could."

Raid on America

In the meantime, however, they had brought 100 men to reinforce the garrison at Fort Zeelandia, along with two months' rations, ammunition, and pay. As for conditions in the colony, the local turtlers reported that the Dutch and English inhabitants were understandably divided along national lines over the issue of which nation should rule them. The colony was decidedly weak. Only 300 Dutchmen who could bear arms and most of the English who had not been shipped off in 1671 were now confined to the fort.[30]

Wroth was apparently cognizant of the importance of his discovery and sailed immediately to Isakebe on the Demarara coast, where he was apparently ambushed and lost several men. After taking on certain provisions supplied by Carib Indians on the Amecouza River, he proceeded with his report and a single prisoner, a 15-year-old lad named John Madder from Suriname, to Barbados.[31] Wroth's intelligence, attained after no small effort, provided the island colonies of the West Indies and the Atlantic seaboard of North America with the first hint of the storm that was about to beset them.

For the seamen and marines of the Evertsen expedition, the week ashore at Fort Zeelandia was to be their last opportunity for rest and relaxation for some time to come. For many it was undoubtedly an opportunity to partake in the escapades that sailors on shore leave have indulged in from the earliest times, even in the rude jungle frontier environment of Suriname. When the squadron finally weighed anchor to sail on the next leg of the expedition on April 18, their conditions were soon manifested in the operation of their ships. Several vessels were promptly run ashore on the riverbank below the fort, where they would remain until the rising of the tide.[32]

Finally freed, the squadron made sail at slack water, sliding across the shoalest of bars at high tide. By nightfall they had arrived at an anchorage half a mile below Boeteman's Plantation, the first such establishment on the river encountered from the sea. Here anchors were dropped in five fathoms and the Zeelanders slept off the last vestiges of their revels ashore. Not until midday on the 19th did the squadron again hoist anchor and sail. With the outflowing tidal current it proceeded only as far as a point between the Commewyne River, which flows into the Suriname from the east, and the Sandpunt, which marked the eastern lip of the main river entrance. Here the squadron again anchored to await flood tide.[33]

The position in which the squadron had come to rest was an unfortunate one. Evertsen was dismayed to discover that the low tide, when it came, was far lower than he had expected, and *Swaenenburgh* was grounded to two feet below her waterline, as were the other ships in the flotilla. The strandings at this particular point in the river, however, were doubly serious, for there was an extremely fast and strong ebb, and the crews were hard-pressed to keep their ships on an even keel as the bottom began to scour away beneath them, permitting the ships to settle into the sand. That was only the beginning of the Zeelanders' problems. Evertsen had intended to sail with the morning light of Sunday, April 20, but discovered that the powerful currents in the river's mouth had been busy all night. The anchors were now buried deeply in the bottom, and were only retrieved late in the afternoon, after hours of toil. It was about half flood when the squadron again sailed, doggedly now, against the tide. When the recently-arrived Dutch merchantman *Goude Poort*, bound upriver, was sighted by the squadron, she was passed without so much as a hail. Still, every yard of progress had to be earned. There was scarcely 18 feet of water, and *Swaenenburgh* touched bottom at least three or four times before coming to anchor at sundown two miles from shore.[34]

Once the entire squadron was safely across the shoals, Evertsen ordered it to begin the laborious process of taking on water. To have done so while in the river, though certainly more convenient, would have added greatly to each ship's draft; the already difficult passage out of the river would have been all but impossible. For more than ten days the watering continued, with the snaauw *Zeehond* and every shallow-draft vessel available serving as a veritable waterborne bucket brigade for the squadron. On May 1, while watering continued unabated, the merchantman *Goude Poort* sailed out of the river and came to anchor near the squadron to exchange news with the officers. The ship, it was learned, had only gone inside to revictual, and taken on wood and water. Her master, Zeelander Maerten Jansse Vonck, of Middelburg, exchanged a few pleasantries and some information with his countrymen and then put out to sea. He was unaware that he would soon cross paths with the squadron again, but under far more disagreeable circumstances.[35]

The watering continued well into May and not until the 9th, almost two months after arriving on the Wild Coast, was the Zeeland squadron finally prepared to sail. By the midday fix on the 10th, the Suriname River was more than 20 miles behind. Evertsen again scanned the last line of article five in his instructions: "And further they will see what advantages may be gained against any hostile ships about the Barbadoes and the other French and English Islands."[36]

With all sails set, Evertsen prepared for the first dramatic phase of his raid on America.

7

IN FACE OF THE WHIRLWINDS

The Zeeland squadron was 31 miles northwest of the Suriname River on Sunday, May 11, sailing through warm, open seas, and bound for the first of many targets, the rich British-held island of Barbados. Four days later, Evertsen estimated the squadron to be only 50 miles due east of its objective and entering well-traveled waters, frequented by ships of many nations but dominated by those of England, France, and Spain. Toward midday on the 15th, Maerten Andriessen's hoecker *De Eendracht* broke off from the flota, her victualling mission completed. As the fleet fell off to the west, the tubby little supply ship maintained a northerly course, riding the currents, bound for home. It would not be a short trip; Andriessen would not arrive at his destination for five months, and then only after an arduous voyage via Spain, dodging enemy cruisers, and riding out innumerable storms at sea.

Evertsen spread his flotilla out in a wide arc as he neared Barbados, the easternmost island of the West Indies, in an effort to sweep all shipping before him and reconnoiter the largest area possible. The pear-shaped island he sought was small and, with the slightest miscalculation, could be easily missed on the open ocean. And the coral reefs about it posed a threat to navigation not to be ignored. At 3:00 A.M. on May 16, the squadron, an estimated 30 miles from Barbados, heaved to into the wind and drifted with its bows to the south until the following dawn.[1]

On Saturday, May 17, the Zeeland squadron sighted Barbados, which loomed out of the early morning gray barely five miles to the west. Evertsen again ordered the ships spread in a wide arc and set a southerly course under shortened sail to maintain a position upwind of the island until he could determine his exact position and decide the next course of action. He was well aware of the havoc he might inflict upon the enemy by his unexpected arrival and did not wish to lose the element of surprise. He was equally aware of the dangers of acting prematurely without sufficient intelligence. No one in the squadron knew the extent of the island's defensive capabilities, but all were aware that for such a wealthy colony, they were certain to be formidable.

Upon the outbreak of the Third Anglo-Dutch War, William Lord Willoughby, governor of Barbados, had been in England on an extended visit for more than a year. Willoughby was an experienced authority on American and West Indian affairs, and he was a military man whose reputation for getting things done was impeccable. And with the onslaught of the new war, he aggressively presented the king with a number of well-thought-out suggestions for the defense of the British Leeward Islands and Barbados. In a memorandum of April 8, 1672, the governor outlined for the crown the problems of naval defense for the rich and strategically located chain of islands in the West Indies, as well as a solution. During the second war with The Netherlands, he pointed out, a few Dutch capers cruising in the latitude of Barbados had taken no less than 20 or 30 English ships as prizes, causing great injury to the island's mercantile trade. To prevent repetition of such costly incursions, he suggested that a "good sailing fifth rate frigate" be dispatched to patrol there, along with a second man-of-war to guard the Leeward Islands to the northwest. The expense of fielding the two warships might be absorbed by prize money generated from the sale of Dutch merchantmen that the frigates would capture while on duty. As communications among Barbados and the French and English Leewards was imperative, Willoughby requested an additional two small ships to serve as dispatch boats for that purpose. More telling about the vulnerable isolation of his island, however, was his strong case for the suspension of the Act of Navigation for the duration of the war so that Barbados might be adequately provisioned. Since the colony was far from self-sufficient, relying upon imported food, clothing, and tools, it was certain to suffer enormous deprivation if the act were continued in force. Indeed, it was imperative that the island be allowed freely to import food and clothing, since "the bringing of which to them from England, will undoubtedly be very difficult if not totally hindered by the Warr." Barbados was not alone in its vulnerability, for the British-owned islands of Antigua and Montserrat were woefully unprepared to defend themselves. Willoughby estimated that no fewer than 20 great guns, 1,000 firelocks, 1,000 swords, and adequate ammunition, which could be paid for out of customs duties, must be sent to insure their protection.[2]

The governor's pleas for the defense of distant pinpricks in the West Indies met with little favor or support from a government concerned with a war lapping at its doorstep. On May 10, 1672, though the Privy Council granted a wartime dispensation that permitted English merchants to employ foreign nationals and vessels, it refused to agree to Willoughby's request for a special-case suspension of the Act of Navigation.[3] The governor's request for additional arms was deflected by a counter-request for an inventory of those already available. Given the long delays caused by the vast distance between the West Indies and England, many months might pass before positive action at rearmament might be initiated. English ships, Willoughby was assured by those most unfamiliar with the realities of the West Indies, could easily sail in convoy from the Leeward Islands under the protection of the more numerous French. There were five French frigates reportedly at Martinique, and France was, after all, an ally![4] Eventually, however, two frigates, H.M.S. *St. David* and *Garland*, were dispatched to Barbados, the former to escort the Barbadian and West Indian merchant fleets homeward and the latter to patrol the Leewards. King Charles was in an aggressive mood, and caustically noted to Willoughby that in wartime a governor's proper place was at the head of the colony he governed. On June 13 he ordered Willoughby to embark at once at Portsmouth for Barbados.[5]

Willoughby's concerns that the Dutch intended to pay particular attention to his island and its merchant marine was not surprising, for it was one of the richest and most productive English colonies in the West Indies, enjoying a prosperity for which the Dutch were largely responsible. First occupied by settlers in 1627, the island was held by various English proprietors under grants from the Crown until 1652, when proprietary rule was eliminated.

Ironically, it was the small Dutch population of the island, driven from Brazil by the Portuguese, that had proven the key to wealth and prosperity, for they led the way by teaching the inhabitants the techniques of sugar cultivation and manufacture. By 1667, many hundreds of large plantations, averaging 300 acres or more per estate, were intensively farming the land and, fired by an enormous slave population, producing sugar in unprecedented quantities. Plate, jewels, and household goods alone on the island were estimated to be worth £500,000. As one observer wrote, "Their buildings [are] very fair and beautiful, and their houses like castles, their sugar houses and Negroes' hut show themselves from the sea like so many towns, each defended by its castle."[6]

In 1661, the island trade employed 400 ships a year, and exports to England were valued at £350,000. By 1670, the Barbadian planters had grown rich and powerful enough to maintain a regular lobby in London to protect their interests.[7] At the outbreak of the third war with the Dutch, it was reported that "50 great and good ships at anchor almost all the year round" could be found in the principal anchorage of Carlisle Bay.[8]

When William Lord Willoughby again set foot on Barbadian soil on October 17, 1672, he found the island in a formidable state of defense, primarily at and about Carlisle Bay, where a complex of forts and batteries had been erected. He had already appointed Sir Tobias Bridge, a soldier and collector of customs, to command all the forces on the island, and despite the complaints from planters and traders that the troops were long on officers and short on soldiers, Sir Tobias had done his job well. All dismounted guns on the island were remounted in carriages, and all gun platforms were paved with stone. Troops were exercised and readied for combat.[9]

Willoughby, however, was not content with merely passive defense. He had resolved soon after his return to carry the war to the enemy by capturing the Dutch-held island of Tobago. Strategically located off the coast of the Spanish main and adjacent to the island of Trinidad, Tobago possessed a fine harbor, which during wartime posed a constant menace to Barbados as a base for enemy warships and during times of peace as a base for serious commercial rivalry. The expedition against Tobago incorporated a regiment of 600 soldiers under the command of Sir Tobias Bridge and Captain William Poole, commander of H.M.S. *St. David*, a fourth-rate 54-gun frigate. On December 15, 1672, Bridge sailed, arrived at his destination three days later, and on the 19th subjected the Dutch defenders to a terrible bombardment. The island was surrendered on December 23, and the Dutch governor and many of the inhabitants were shipped off to Curaçao. The remainder, including a number of French, were taken back to Barbados. The island was stripped of all habitations, and the property that was not destroyed was hauled off as booty. Tobago was left entirely uninhabited by Europeans.[10] The attack on the island, however, had the beneficial effect of improving the defenses on Barbados. Willoughby ordered that an inventory of all guns captured during the expedition be taken, and the artillery added to the defenses of his own island. He had entertained hopes that the planters of Barbados might be willing to settle and colonize Tobago, filling the void left by the Dutch, and graciously offered the island to them as a present. Though grateful for the gesture, the planters, owing to the war and the weight of defense expenditures they were obliged to bear, lacked sufficient capital (and incentive) for such

an undertaking. When Willoughby suddenly fell ill and appointed
Sir Peter Colleton, member of a prominent Barbadian family, as deputy governor on April 6, the issue was all but forgotten. It was
totally extinguished three days later with the governor's death.[11]

In the days that followed Willoughby's demise, it was decided that
his body would be returned to England aboard *St. David*, which was
to sail as escort for the great Barbados and West Indian homeward-
bound convoy, even then assembling in Carlisle roads. In the meantime, H.M.S. *Garland*, a 19-year-old, 260-ton, 30-gun fifth-rater
assigned to patrol the Leewards, began taking on a month's provisions,
powder, shot, and ball preparatory to her assignment.[12] However, by
mid-May, her somewhat overbearing commander, Captain John Wyborne, had yet to sail. Finally, on May 14, amid reports that a strange
ship was apparently conducting a reconnaissance of the island's ports,
the Barbados Council requested action. With the *St. David* convoy
preparing to sail, they could ill afford to take chances, and Wyborne
finally put out to sea.[13]

When the Zeeland squadron approached Barbados on the morning
of Saturday, May 17, Commander Cornelis Evertsen was probably unaware of the fall of Tobago, the death of Willoughby, the recent departure of *Garland*, or the presence of the great convoy assembled in
Carlisle Bay. On the following day, however, the information void was
filled when a sail was sighted, chased, and captured by *Schaeckerloo*.
The prize was a large vessel, possibly a yawl, distinguished by a "fin"
sail carried aft the flagstaff, and was but a day out of Barbados. She
had been bound for the English colony of Maryland, and was laden
with a typically Barbadian cargo—*kilduijvel*, or Kill Devil rum, and
molasses. When questioned, the merchant captain provided his captors
with exciting information. Fifty merchantmen lay in the harbor, protected only by the king's ship *St. David*. Unhappily, the convoy would
not sail before mid-July, as many of the ships had not yet taken on their
lading. With a harbor undoubtedly well-fortified by shore batteries
and defended by a large man-of-war, Evertsen realized, a cutting-out
expedition was probably out of the question. Yet he was undoubtedly
aware that there were always a few English seacaptains willing to sail
unescorted, chancing capture, to reach England ahead of the pack to
obtain the best prices for their cargoes. He thus resolved to cruise for a
few days off the island to await the departure of those few impatient
merchantmen.[14] He could not have foreseen that the next ship to be
sighted would be that of a more recent acquaintance, Captain Maerten
Vonck's caper *Goude Poort*.

Vonck had last parted company with the Zeeland squadron 17 days earlier at the mouth of the Suriname River, but when he boarded *Swaenenburgh* on May 1, he informed Evertsen that he had been cruising about Barbados for some time. Indeed, it was probably his ship the *Garland* had been sent out to intercept. Though undoubtedly interested in whatever intelligence the caper captain had to relate, Evertsen was more concerned about the captain's role in the desertion of two soldiers from Suriname, who were reported to have been carried off onboard *Goude Poort*.

Vonck denied any knowledge of the deserters. If they were onboard his ship, he said, then most certainly his skipper (master), mate, and bosun would know about it. The three were promptly summoned to *Swaenenburgh* but also denied any knowledge of such men in their crew. Evertsen asked Vonck if he would care to swear under oath that he had never seen the two men in his ship. At that the caper swallowed hard, and admitted "that he had seen them but once."[15]

Resolved to put an end to the issue once and for all, Evertsen dispatched a boarding party in the flagship's sloop to *Goude Poort* to bring off the deserters. The boarding party, however, "couldn't find them, as they had hidden themselves among the caper's crew," and returned to the flagship empty-handed. The Zeelanders were angry over the shallow deception and threatened Vonck and his officers: if they refused to turn over the two deserters, they would themselves be held prisoner aboard the flagship. Captain Vonck, realizing the seriousness of his predicament—that of aiding and abetting military desertion—caved in. He requested that Evertsen's sloop again be sent to the privateer, this time with his bosun bearing a note ordering the mate to turn over the deserters. When the sloop reached the caper, the *Goude Poort*'s crew refused to turn over the two men, knowing full well that they might be executed for desertion. Instead, they seized *Swaenenburgh*'s skipper, who had come in the sloop. The agile officer managed to break free, and in a desperate escape jumped from the caper's half-deck into the sloop, leaving four of his oarsmen behind.[16]

In a panic, the caper's crew immediately "made as much sail as possible and sailed on," leaving their own captain a prisoner aboard *Swaenenburgh*. The incensed Zeelanders quickly took up the chase, but the heavy warships were no match for the faster, better-rigged privateer. *Goude Poort*'s escape was clean, but the situation of her commander was far from enviable. Vonck, however, was apparently an ingratiating sort, whose abilities as a mariner might prove useful to the expedition. Within a month or so, he had effectively worked his way into the peripheral trust of the persons he had sought to dupe. He would eventually be given command of a most important mission upon which the fate of an entire colony would hang.[17]

Evertsen continued cruising about the coast of Barbados for several days, but was disappointed by the unexpectedly poor showing of enemy merchantmen. The squadron's ardor was further dampened by several successive days of rain squalls. The division of the Kill Devil rum, taken a few days earlier, among the ships of the squadron may have lifted spirits somewhat, but it was a poor substitute for the rich sugar prizes lying at anchor in Carlisle Bay.

Finally, on the afternoon of May 21, after four days of rain, squalls, and fruitless hunting, Evertsen ordered the cruise off Barbados abandoned, and all sails set for the French-held island of Martinique.[18]

First discovered by Columbus on his fourth voyage in 1502, the island of Martinique was not settled by Europeans until 1635, when the French Compagnie des Isles d'Amerique established a base there. After quickly exterminating the native Carib Indians, the French made the island, situated between St. Lucia to the south and Dominica to the north, the linchpin of their possessions in the Leeward group. Thirty-four miles long and 18 miles wide, Martinique was steeply mountained almost to the water's edge. Though numerous bays indented the coast and provided excellent anchorages, approach from the sea could be hazardous. There were three principal harbors on the island, the most important of which was Cul-de-Sac Bay on the southwest coast. All of the harbors were normally defended by well-placed batteries and forts. Though none was very strong in terms of numbers of guns, the usually well-elevated positions of the works allowed them to offer a deadly fire to approaching hostile ships below. The fort commanding Cul-de-Sac, it was reported, had as many as 20 cannons protecting the shallow-water approach to the harbor. Combined with the French habit of scuttling vessels at strategic locations in the channels, such defenses made naval assault exceptionally difficult, if not impossible, by heavy ships-of-war. The island's rugged upland terrain, dominated on the north and south by clusters of volcanic mountains joined by a backbone of hills, was cut by ravines and valleys that made overland attack from the rear equally hazardous.[19]

Dutch intelligence concerning the naval and land defenses of Martinique, as at Barbados, was minimal at best. At Barbados it was said by the English that the French had five warships, one of 66 guns, stationed at the French-held island, which were capable of great deeds, even if "one hears of no feats they have done." It was unlikely that Evertsen was aware of such potentially powerful opposition, for he pressed on, sighting the island at dusk on May 21.[20]

In the Face of the Whirlwinds

Admiral Jacob Benckes by Nicolaes Maes.
Courtesy Metropolitan Museum of Art, Gift of
J. Pierpont Morgan, 1911.

Evertsen initially sought to sail around the southern tip of Martinique, known as Pointe d'Enfer, to take the most direct, southerly approach to Cul-de-Sac Bay, but wind and weather conspired against him, forcing him to proceed around the north end and double back down the west coast. At about midday on May 22, after the squadron had successfully rounded the north end and was approaching its objective, six sail of ships were sighted outside the bay. The unidentified ships, all wearing French flags at their mastheads, immediately sailed for the oncoming Zeelanders. Evertsen ordered his ships cleared for action, and raised the flag of the Prince of Orange-Nassau. Suddenly, a flicker of recognition: the six ships lowered their French colors and raised those of the prince. Evertsen had encountered quite by accident another Dutch squadron.

The force that the Zeelanders encountered off Cul-de-Sac on that fateful afternoon, it was soon learned, had been fielded by the Admiralty of Amsterdam, and was commanded by a naval officer of exceptional fighting ability, Commander Jacob Benckes. The Friesian-born Benckes, and his captains, Hanske Fokkes, Nicholas Boes, and Abraham van Zijl, had all been comrades in arms, and possibly even acquaintances, of the Zeelanders during many of the North Sea campaigns of this and the previous war. Yet the meeting of the two squadrons in hostile waters thousands of miles from home was entirely without plan, and certainly a coincidence of golden opportunity.

Upon conferring with Commander Benckes, Evertsen found that the four-ship Amsterdam squadron had sailed from Texel on December 8, 1672, to escort the rich Spanish "silver fleet" home from the Americas into Cadiz. It was not an unusual thing for either Holland or Zeeland to contract out state vessels to the service of other nations when feasible in return for financial or trade benefits. And with Spain having recently concluded a war with France, which was threatening to resume at any time, Holland consciously sought to stroke her former enemy whenever possible. Upon the successful completion of the escort duty, the Amsterdammers had been ordered to the West Indies to raid and injure the enemy as much as possible before the next season of combat in the North Sea resumed.

Benckes, who had arrived off Martinique only a few days earlier, had as yet secured only two prizes. The first had been a French *tartaen*, taken en route, and the second, a small partially laden ship, had been captured that very morning in the roadstead of Martinique. Of greater interest to the Zeelanders, however, was news that the Amsterdammers had observed a large warship, wearing the flag of a French rear admiral, and seven or eight merchantmen, lying at the quay in the harbor. Nearby was an English frigate.[21]

Evertsen studied Benckes with interest as the Friesian-born commander spoke. He noticed the most dominant feature about him was his large, heavy-lidded eyes, shaded by light, expressive brows that usually appeared furrowed as if in deep thought. His nose was long and thin, and his lips slightly bowed. Though the bone structure of his face was narrow and quite pronounced, the beginning of a second chin suggested the onset of middle-age. His whole face was accentuated by long flowing shoulder-length hair, parted in the center of his pate. His overall appearance was more of the dour, stoic burgomaster of a Hals painting than a sagacious seadog. Yet he was a naval commander of proven ability, intelligence, and courage.

Jacob Benckes had served the republic well as a general officer during the Second Anglo-Dutch War, participating in the Two Day Battle off Dunkirk in 1666 and in the daring raid on the Medway the following year. At the outbreak of the third war, he sailed again for the Admiralty of Amsterdam, first in command of the 70-gun *Woerden*, a line-of-battle ship carrying 270 crewmen and 70 marines in which he participated in the monumental Battle of Solebay. In mid-June 1672, he saw more action off West Kapellen while in command of *Groot*

Hollandia, but on July 21 he was returned to the command of *Woerden*. In September, with Vice Admiral Volkert Schram, Rear Admiral David Vlug, and Captains Henrick Brouwer and Adriaan van Kruinmger of Zeeland, Jacob Benckes was unjustly accused of having fled the Battle of Solebay. Fortunately, all five men were soon found not guilty and the charges dismissed by a court martial.[22]

Soon after the court martial, Benckes rejoined Admiral De Ruyter at Texel. With the threat of British naval invasion put to rest, however, and as the French showed no signs of initiating aggressive naval action, the Admiralty of Amsterdam, like that of Zeeland, had found ready duty for a small winter squadron. Benckes was given the opportunity to prove himself again, and received command of the 46-gun frigate *Noordhollandt*. She was a new ship, built in 1670 and manned by a crew of 210. She was to serve as flagship of the small four-ship squadron. Her primary mission had been to escort the Spanish silver fleet safely into Cadiz, but her secondary mission, to conduct a raid on the Leewards, was intended to provide revenue to the bleeding treasury of Amsterdam.[23]

The captains of the ships in the Amsterdam squadron, like Benckes, were all seasoned veterans. Hanske Fokkes had served on convoy duty during the last war and had participated in a 1666 attack on the Elbe River against a 17-ship English merchant fleet. During the 1672 North Sea campaign he had commanded *Amsterdam*, a 60-gun ship with a crew of 230 seamen and 15 to 50 soldiers. In 1673, though his ship had been damaged in fighting and he was assigned to the North Sea theater, Fokkes was re-rated to a smaller vessel and ordered to participate in the Benckes expedition to the West Indies. Captain Nicholas Boes had sailed with Lieutenant Admiral van Nes' fleet in command of the man-of-war *Jaarsveldt*. At Solebay, he too had seen trial by fire and had been in the thick of it, with his ship's mainmast shot away and his foremast shattered. And finally, there was Captain Abraham van Zijl, veteran of such victorious combats as the Four Day Battle and such defeats as the Two Day Battle. On September 13, 1672, he had been given command of *De Dolphyn*, which was undoubtedly the ship in which he sailed to the West Indies.[24]

Both Evertsen and Benckes were well aware that together they formed perhaps the most formidable naval force in the Leewards, and possibly even in the Americas. Even the two warships in Cul-de-Sac Bay, which might have successfully opposed either of the two squadrons individually, stood little chance against a combined attack—if the Dutch could enter the harbor. The two commanders thus resolved to attack in concert, and on the evening after their meeting set about tacking into the bay. This time, however, the weather was on the side of the enemy.

Throughout the night, the eight-ship joint squadron worked back and forth against adverse winds to penetrate the bay, but were frustrated at every tack. The final entry of the day in Evertsen's journal suggests the frustrations they encountered.

> Did our best during the whole night to tack into the bay; had hard rain squalls, so that we couldn't advance much in the face of the whirlwinds which came continually off the land.[25]

The following morning was little better, with variable winds and many squalls. Still, the joint squadron did its best to tack upwind. By 2:00 P.M. it had reached a position approximately half a mile from the enemy ships. Now both Evertsen and Benckes could plainly see the enemy warships moored close against the wharf with guns at the ready on their seaward sides. One of the warships was Captain John Wyborne's frigate *Garland*, which, having sighted the Dutch approach while on patrol between St. Lucia and Martinique, had fled into the roadstead seeking protection from the shore fortifications. Evertsen estimated her at 36 guns, but she was formally rated at 30. Like the French admiral in the harbor, which appeared to be carrying 60 guns, Wyborne had moored his ship "right under the most northern fort, and moored in such a way that it was impossible to sail between her and the shore." There was also a fleet of no less than ten merchantmen, most of which appeared, judging from their elevated waterlines, to be empty, probably having been offloaded upon first word of the Dutch approach.[26]

A close perusal with a good glass of the shores about the harbor revealed a minor bustle of activity in several areas, especially where batteries had been erected and others were even now being hastily constructed.[27] In addition to what appeared to be a formidable complex of defense-works, there were "such whirlwinds" blowing down off the shore that it was soon deemed "impossible to attack these ships in good order without great danger and, to all appearances, without chance of getting much booty, as most ships were empty."[28]

With an undoubtedly heavy heart, Evertsen and Benckes resolved to abandon the effort against Martinique. For the Zeelanders, the decision was probably doubly difficult, for it was the second foiled attempt against the enemy in as many weeks in perhaps the richest hunting grounds of the West Indies. Ironically, the appearance of strength had been somewhat deceiving, for Captain Wyborne reported to the Council of Barbados on May 27 that there were only 12 guns actually mounted in the batteries, and not more than 150 defenders to man them. With some exaggeration, he claimed that no less than eight Dutch men-of-war, each of which mounted at least 48 guns, had obviously not been in the West Indies long, and had recently arrived from Cadiz, for their hulls were still clean.[29]

The anxious Council of Barbados, which had on May 23 seen to it that the body of the late Lord Willoughby be conveyed aboard *St. David* with appropriate pomp and ceremony, muffled drums, and draped regimental colors, was shocked by Wyborne's report. Indeed, they had been entirely unaware of the menace that had recently been cruising off their coast. Belatedly, they resolved to contract with the owners of the sloop *Speedwell*, which was bound for Martinique, to scout out the Dutch fleet suspected to be cruising over the horizon, and probably lying in wait for the *St. David* convoy. As was normal in such cases, the owner of the sloop was to be compensated for the loss of his vessel should she be taken by the enemy. But for all their efforts, the council was too late. Evertsen and Benckes were already well en route to more profitable targets, reinforced by a new agreement of singular purpose between them.[30]

Having jointly decided that it was not wise to attack the enemy shipping at Martinique, it was agreed on the night of May 23 to sail north, bypassing the island of Dominica, to strike at the next richest colony in the Leewards, the island of Guadeloupe. Before departing Martinique roads, however, Cornelis Evertsen and Jacob Benckes formally agreed that their two squadrons would remain together "for as long as we should be in the Caribbean islands, judge that thereby we should do the Enemy the most damage and best secure the Country's interest." The following day, as the combined squadrons drifted below the islands of Dominica, a formal accord, joining the two commands into one, was drawn up and signed.[31] The agreement was to prove a most winning combination.

8

AS FAR AS THE EYE CAN SEE

The decision to bypass Dominica and press on for richer hunting grounds farther north in the Leeward chain was an easy one for the Dutch commanders to make. Though the island was even then being contemplated by the French as a place "to set down," to settle upon, largely because of reports of gold having been found there, Dominica was still "inhabited only by savages" and was of little interest to the raiders.[1] Instead, the order was given to sail for the French-held islands of Guadeloupe, next in the Leeward archipelago. Actually composed of two major islands—Basse Terre (or Guadeloupe proper) on the west, and Grande Terre on the east—divided by a narrow channel called the Riviere Salée, Guadeloupe formed a unique butterfly shape on the charts. And with a landmass of 656 square miles, it was clearly the largest in the Leewards in terms of area. The imperfect near-juncture of the two islands, the wings of the Guadeloupe butterfly, formed two large, shallow-water embayments, Grande Cul de Sac on the north and Petit Cul de Sac on the south. The dominant geographic feature of the islands was the rugged, volcanic peak of La Soufriere, a cone nearly 5,000 feet tall, which rose above the southern end of Basse Terre. The beaches of Basse Terre, unlike the white and rose-colored shores of Grande Terre, are composed of blackened volcanic sands. With rich volcanic soil to nuture it, the island's luxuriant vegetation—bamboo, ferns, mangroves, and palms—provided a vista that has come to be associated with tropical paradise.

Like most of the Leewards, Guadeloupe was discovered by Columbus in 1493, but was not occupied by Europeans until 1635, when French settlers arrived. The islands were not easily subdued and had seen the arrival of irregular and occasionally large influxes of settlers, refugees, and adventurers of various nationalities. In 1654, with the expulsion of the Jews from Brazil, one such group of nearly 1,000 Dutch arrived to attempt settlement, bringing with them and depositing their sugar refining technology before moving on.[2]

When Evertsen and Benckes reached Guadeloupe, the island's defenses were in a questionable state. Estimates varied as to the number of inhabitants in the sparsely populated colony, since many settlers had emigrated to other islands and climes. One account suggested that there were as many as 2,200 men on Guadeloupe and 800 more on tiny Marie-Galante,[3] a small islet of the Guadeloupe group. Sir Charles Wheeler, former governor general of the British Leewards, estimated that there were but 800 men on Guadeloupe fit to bear arms,

> 100 or 200 being Irish, whom [the French] would fain be quit of, for they live much as they do at home, in little huts, planting potatoes, tobacco, and as much indigo as will buy them canvas and brandy, and never advance so far as a sugar plantation.[4]

With such a small population, barely a quarter of the mountainous island was under cultivation, and defensive capabilities were limited at best. There were approximately 30 cannons for the defense of the coast, and most of them had been placed in a castle fort erected above the town of Basse Terre, on the southwest coast of Basse Terre island, and beneath the shadow of La Soufriere. The castle, noted Wheeler in a definitive analysis of the military establishments of the Leewards in early 1672, "is as well an ornament as a fortress," and was commanded by a veteran of several spirited actions in Flanders, one Monsieur de Lion, or de Lyon.[5]

On Sunday, May 25, with the wind at east northeast, the two Dutch squadrons had drifted well to the lee of Basse Terre Island and were obliged to tack upwind to reach the roads off the town of Basse Terre, where it was supposed that enemy merchant shipping might be concentrated. Upon arrival, it was observed that the roads were devoid of enemy warships, but two fat armed merchantmen were sighted lying at anchor. Instantly the Dutch swung into action. *Noordhollandt's* sloop was sent out after one ship, which proved to be the four-gun pinnace *St. Joseph*, laden with 280 barrels of sugar. Captain van Zijl was dispatched to cut out the second, more formidable vessel, a 14-gun merchantman called *La Francoyse*, which was partially laden with 220 barrels of sugar. Both vessels were easily taken, apparently without incident or casualty.[6] The feeble defensive fire from the fort above the town was poorly managed, and overall resistance to the surprise cutting-out expedition was less than effective.[7]

As evening fell, the breezes died and the two squadrons drifted on a placid sea. At about 10:00 P.M., a small pinnace sailed downwind of the flotilla. Evertsen immediately ordered Captain Daniel Thijssen's snaauw *Zeehond* to break off and take up pursuit. Within a short time, the pinnace *Nova France*, Captain Jan Doens, laden with provisions for Monsieur de Bas, governor of the French Leewards, was taken. The provisions were quickly distributed to the crews of the two Dutch squadrons.[8]

Evertsen and Benckes may have enjoyed a certain satisfaction in the capture of *Nova France*, for De Bas had only recently failed in an attempted reduction of the Dutch colony of Curaçao. In February, the governor had set sail with five French men-of-war, three merchantmen, 14 shallops, and 1,200 soldiers, expecting to be joined by an additional 600 buccaneers from Hispaniola, to attack the enemy colony. From the very outset, his campaign had been one of continuous misfortune. En route from Hispaniola, the 44-gun warship *Grand Infant*, commanded by the governor of Tortuga, Monsieur Bertram Ogeron, and carrying 300 to 500 buccaneers, was lost during a storm. When the main task force arrived at Curaçao, the remainder of his troops were landed but failed to take their main objective, Fort Amsterdam. The English later reported rather gleefully that the French army had simply "run away and lost of the design shamefully." De Bas had little alternative but to depart, sailing for Hispaniola, then Martinique, and finally for France.[9]

Throughout the night, the Dutch squadron led by *Swaenenburgh* drifted northwest, 34 miles across the Guadeloupe Passage, toward the tiny volcanic island of Montserrat. Barely eleven miles long and seven miles wide, this forest-clad island speck on the Caribbean had been colonized by Irish settlers from the island of St. Christophers (modern St. Kitts) in 1632. During the Second Anglo-Dutch War, it had been assaulted by the French and was bravely defended until the English commander was killed and his Irish troops gave up the fight.[10] When it was returned to English control, restoration of its defenses was undertaken with great acumen. In December 1672, Sir Charles Wheeler deemed Montserrat "a small island, but the securest of all the Caribbees." Not only were there between 800 and 1,000 Irish inhabitants, though few or no English, there were also 523 slaves. Wheeler was less than positive of the fighting abilities of the Catholic Irish who formed the defensive backbone, considering them "men of no great courage or discipline."[11] Yet the physical defenses of this small rock were substantial for its size. In July 1672, Wheeler's successor, Sir William Stapleton, drew 20 pieces of ordnance to replace those carried off during the French occupation between 1664 and 1668, as well as firearms and ammunition for both. Under his administration the island's militia was well-organized and could formally count on a regiment well in excess of that noted by Wheeler, including 10 companies of foot, numbering 1,171 men (700 of whom were armed), a troop of horse numbering 50 men, 7 guns, and 12 barrels of powder.[12] Stapleton, destined to serve as governor of the Leewards until 1686, addressed the improvements of the island's defenses with vigor. On February 24, 1673, for instance, an Act was passed "for the speedy making of a platform in the new Fort [at Plymouth] for the guns to be planted there,"[13] suggesting that work at refortifying the island and building forts against Dutch attack was well underway when the flotilla of Evertsen and Benckes arrived.

The dawn of May 26 found the two Dutch squadrons spread out well over a 20-mile stretch of the Guadeloupe Passage. Aboard *Swaenenburgh*, leading the van, Cornelis Evertsen noted the sight with understated awe: "Saw our ships as far as the eye could see," he had written in the flagship's journal. Indeed, some vessels, such as *Sint Joris*, were well beyond the horizon and were not visible at all.[14] It was an imposing sight, this flotilla of warships and their prizes strung out across an ocean. And it did not go unseen by the lookouts on Montserrat.

The approach of the enemy squadron was observed by the island's defenders at about daybreak, and the alarm was immediately sounded. Hundreds of musketeers rushed to their posts, and battery gunners prepared their cannons for the coming fight. The men defending the seven-gun fort overlooking the main roads and a three-gun battery guarding the tiny bay off Plymouth rushed to their work, for below, exposed to the oncoming armada, lay at least five merchantmen riding at anchor, oblivious to the onrushing danger.

Swaenenburgh spotted four of the five merchantmen as she approached the roads and immediately made directly for them, obliging Evertsen to bring his ship to within a pistol-shot of the enemy fortifications. Her guns loaded and ready, the frigate opened upon the enemy fort as she passed with "full load" broadside, and received the same in return. The battle had begun. Despite the strong opposition, Evertsen ordered out his boat and sloop "well manned" to cut out the enemy merchantmen. The first prize was taken quickly. She proved to be a small Irish bus, *Michael* (or *St. Michiel*) of Galway, laden with 136 tons of Irish meat. Governor Stapleton later claimed that the capture was effected because the master of the merchantman would not haul his vessel to within range of small-shot covering fire from the shore, although he had managed to haul her sails ashore before she was taken.[15]

Encouraged by its first success, the cutting-out expedition pressed on, but now under heavy fire from a force of 400 musketeers entrenched on the heights above the shore. One of the raiders was killed and six more wounded in an almost continuous hail of musket fire. Observing that two of the merchantmen were empty, the raiders moved to attack a third, a ketch that lay heavy with cargo in the water. However, as soon as the intended victim's master saw his ship drawing the attention of the Dutch, he cut her anchor cables and ran ashore. Protected by "the many musketeers and battery of 3 guns in the bay," the raiders soon determined that their chances to secure additional prizes were diminishing by the minute. The Dutch commander wisely recalled his boat parties to await the arrival of the remainder of the flotilla.[16]

Throughout the morning, a staccato of fire continued between the two sides, to little effect. By afternoon, the Zeeland flagship was finally joined by the entire allied squadron. Again *Swaenenburgh* passed the French fortifications, this time leading a grand parade of warships, each releasing its own barrage of fire on the enemy as she passed. The response from the defenders was resolute and this time quite devastating. From the guns of the fort, which were well served and able to fire down upon the passing ships, shot after shot struck with deadly effect. *Swaenenburgh* received one shot below her waterline, and had her main topmast "shot to pieces" and her cables and lines torn apart; undoubtedly the rest of the fleet suffered similar damage. A number of enemy shot had passed completely through the ship; one took a seaman's arm cleanly off. Worse, the objective of the attack, the capture of the enemy merchantmen, clearly had to be reconsidered, since all had been hauled up on the shore or beneath the guns of forts, which were certainly anything but impotent.[17]

At 5:00 P.M., after almost 12 hours of fighting, the Dutch command ordered firing to cease. Soon afterward, the flotilla was directed to heave to out of range for the night "to see whether we could land another day and walk over the island" to attack the enemy forts by land. Both Evertsen and Benckes realized that the enemy's resistance was stout, their fire unerring, and their works obviously strong. They were, in fact, far stronger than Kees the Devil had expected. Although Dutch records are silent on the point, Stapleton reported that the defenders had suffered but a single casualty, a gunner's boy who was blown up while loading a gun, while the Dutch had suffered at least 25 dead and wounded.[18] Despite the drubbing, the Dutch command, chastened but wiser, determined that the only means of silencing the forts would have to be by land assault. Thus it was resolved that a landing would be made the following day.[19]

On the morning of May 27, Evertsen discovered, much to his dismay, that the flotilla's numerous prizes had drifted out of sight during the night; he nevertheless resolved to attempt a landing as planned. Not until 3:00 P.M., however, could the joint squadron be formed into a line of battle and brought close enough to the shore to provide effective covering fire for the landing parties. With only a few hours of sunlight left, and many of the troops and seamen undoubtedly dispirited over the previous day's efforts and the prospect of stiff opposition ahead, the Dutch command wisely reconsidered their plans. Even if a landing were successfully made, the troops, with evening coming on, would be insupportable until the following morning, and would be pitted against an enemy of unknown strength but proven determination. Every hour of delay also permitted the unprotected prize ships to drift farther away. Thus it "was decided to forget about landing lest we lose the prizes, and to keep sailing."[20]

Licking its wounds, the Dutch flotilla now sailed slowly and unhindered in a northwesterly direction toward the fulcrum of British authority in the Lesser Antilles. This was the tiny but rich island of Nevis, termed by Sir Charles Wheeler "the whole strength of the Leeward Islands."[21]

Nevis was almost circular in shape and barely 36 square miles in extent. Like many others in the archipelago, it was dominated by a symmetrical, eternally cloud-covered volcanic cone, Nevis Peak, over 3,200 feet in height, and several subsidiary pinnacles, including Round Hill in the north and Saddle Hill in the south, both over 1,000 feet in elevation.[22] Settled in 1628 by a party of Englishmen led by Anthony Hilton, the island had miraculously escaped the ravages of the many wars of the previous 45 years. As a consequence of the peace and tranquility enjoyed by its colonizers, Nevis achieved a position of "opulence and importance" realized by few other islands in the West Indies. In 1672, it had been selected by the Royal African Company as its slave depot for supplying all of the Leewards. As a sugar producer and transshipment point for European products in the Lesser Antilles, Nevis insured its preeminent position as the hub of British administration in the region.[23] Though the island possessed no natural harbor, the roads under Charlestown, its principal town on the western lee, were considered adequate for the needs of commerce and trade. Ships riding at anchor here were protected from the prevailing winds out of the east, as was often the case in all of the Lesser Antilles, and by a strong fort.

When Sir William Stapleton assumed command of the Leeward Islands from Sir Charles Wheeler in 1672, the defenses of Nevis were substantial. A total of 1,200 men in arms, in 12 companies (a fifth of whom were Irish), and a troop of 60 horse "well mounted" could be quickly mustered. An additional 200 men were fit and ready to bear arms if the need arose.[24] During the previous war, the lee of Nevis, where "ships may ride so as to land their men in boats without much danger," had been entirely vulnerable to attack. Thus, the inhabitants had run a continuous, five-mile line of shallow defenses along the coast, with redoubts erected at various points along the way. Before the onset of the Third Anglo-Dutch War, Wheeler had vastly improved the defenses and batteries bristled at strategic points along the entire lee.[25]

> From Pelican's Point to Musketi Bay, about 5 miles, is all the leeward side of the island, for defense of which there are 30 pieces of cannon on the platforms of Pelican's Point, the Old Rock, the Old Fort, Duke's Sconce, and Morton's Bay.[26]

When Wheeler departed, plans for a sixth battery, at Musketi Bay, protecting the north coast from any attack that might come from the direction of the French-held southern tip of the island of St. Christophers, two miles away, were well under way.[27]

Wheeler's replacement, Sir William Stapleton, assumed command in the summer of 1672. An Irish soldier of fortune who had come to the West Indies during the previous war, Stapleton had first settled at Montserrat, and in 1668 he was appointed lieutenant-governor of that island. Efficient, intelligent, and married into the family of the largest plantation owner on Nevis, Stapleton was a man whose star was obviously on the rise.[28]

In June 1672, upon his appointment as governor general, Stapleton moved his residence to Nevis, thus conferring upon that island recognition as English headquarters of all the British Leewards. Soon after his arrival, the Nevis Council ordered the ship *James* and two sloops to sail to the Dutch-held islands of St. Eustatius, Saba, and Tortola and subjugate them to England, a feat that was successfully completed a month later.[29]

Stapleton was aware that from St. Eustatius and Saba, close neighbors to the British and French island of St. Christophers, buccaneers had operated against his majesty's dominions during the last war. Yet he, like Wheeler before him, never lost sight of France, England's other great rival in the Lesser Antilles, and was well aware of the tenuous balance of power. "All of the Leeward Islands [are] very weak,"

Wheeler had written in his final report, "comparatively to the French, having not one harbour so well secured as to defend ships or prevent the landing of an enemy."[30] Yet the raid by the Dutch fleets of Evertsen and Benckes, of which Stapleton was still unaware, had already put his new government's defenses to the test at Montserrat, and they had been found adequate. Now the Dutch had arrived at the very seat of the crown's authority in the Leewards.

Fortunately for William Stapleton and the merchantmen lying in the roads off Charlestown, the arrival of the Dutch flotilla on May 28 was preceded by ample warning, and mobilization of the island's defenses was carried out with great effect. At the governor's orders, the shipping then in the roads, consisting of at least two ketches and a large ship, were warped close to the quay beneath the fort at Charlestown. Cannons and muskets were primed and ready for the raider's attack. When the Dutch finally appeared, unmindful of the defenses, they "manned seven pinnaces to fetch off some vessels."[31] The cutting-out expedition, however, was, as at Montserrat, met with a heavy fire. The raiders persisted, but when boarding parties finally hauled up on the three potential prizes at the quay and found them empty of cargo, it was decided that they were not worth the effort of hauling off under fire. After cutting down their sails, the frustrated raiders returned to their ships, and Stapleton no doubt breathed a momentary sigh of relief.[32]

The skirmish at Nevis, unlike the engagement at Montserrat, was apparently without casualties on either side, and had been terminated before extensive damage was incurred. Indeed, it seems likely that the main squadron failed to even halt more than briefly to attend to the foray. Neither Evertsen nor Benckes, it was now clear, were willing to suffer the irreplaceable resource and manpower losses that a pitched fight such as that on May 26 might cause. Their mission was to harass the enemy and take prizes. If it could be accomplished with minimal losses, then such efforts would be undertaken; but if the cost proved excessive, they were quite content to sail on to their next target. Thus it was determined to abandon the effort against Nevis and push on to the next in the Leeward chain, the island of St. Christophers.

Separated from Nevis by a shallow channel called The Narrows, which was barely two miles wide at its narrowest point, the island of St. Christophers had in 1624 been the first island settled by the English in the Caribbean, and thus earned the distinction of being the Mother Colony of the British West Indies. Unlike Nevis, St. Christophers had been ravaged by intermittent warfare almost from its first settlement.[33]

Raid on America

By the outbreak of the Second Anglo-Dutch War, it was jointly occupied by both English and French, the former occupying the central portion of the 68-square-mile island, and the latter the northern and southern ends. In 1667, the English had attacked the French, but were themselves defeated and routed in bloody fighting. The French devastated their sugar plantations, plundered property, captured 400 slaves, and drove between 5,000 and 8,000 English settlers from the island. Indeed, the destruction had been so widespread that in 1669, after its return had been ordained by treaty, the Council of Trade and Plantations seriously questioned the wisdom of resettlement.[34]

Not until July 1671, four years after the Peace of Breda, was England actually able to regain control of its portion of the island. But it was proving extremely difficult, in practice, to reclaim the property of the English planters, both land and slaves, from the French governor or to induce Englishmen to return to the island. Nor were the French inclined to turn over the former English defenses. Before the French had taken the island in its entirety there had been three English forts: Charles, at the Old Road, armed with seven sackers; Stone's Fort, to the east, mounting six culverin, which were the most powerful defenses against attack from the sea; and Sand Point Fort, to the west, with seven great guns and three brass field pieces. These forts had been built mostly of stone found close at hand and lime taken from Brimstone Hill or from local salt ponds. There were also three small sconces at Permita Point, one at Brimstone Hill, and a single gun platform at the Old Road.[35]

In December 1672 Wheeler had completely evaluated the island's defense, both English and French. "St. Christopher's," he wrote,

> is divided into four quarters, as rudely set out in the map. In the French quarter of Basseterre are about 800 musketeers and 100 horse; in the town one platform commanding the road with 12 cannons; 2 miles inland the castle, so well built of brick and stone as to resist all hurricanes, and not to be taken without cannon . . . . In the other French quarter of Sandy Point are 600 to 700 musketeers, and towards 100 horsemen; a fort out of repair, whence they may shoot into the King's fort, yet not do any execution; under it a little village of merchant's storehouses, where they drive a good trade with leave from the English, all the strand being English; a quarter of a mile above it is Capt. Sperance's house, which gave the repulse to the English who attacked it, and consequently was the loss of the island in the first war, but is of no strength; in the fort are six cannon and a file of soldiers, and on the other side of the quarter has been another fort, now useless, without guns, and with a guard of a file of soldiers. The English quarter to Leeward has three companies of foot,

each a parish company, Palmetto Point, Capt. Benningfield, Middle Island, Capt. Treman, and Sandy Point, Capt. Eddrington; in the three companies are 120 English and Irish, the greater part Irish, and not above 20 substantial planters, and about 50 or 60 Dutch and French who have sworn fidelity to the King; at Stones Point are mounted six guns, and at Sandy Point 14, and on each hand of the fort are encamped the two companies of foot in little huts, and a fair street begins to be built leading to the fort or storehouses for merchants under the cannon of the fort; and at Old Road also are begun storehouses in expectation that the old fort may be repaired and cannon mounted.[36]

Wheeler noted that in the English quarter of the windward side of the island there were also three companies of foot, each containing 60 soldiers—English, Irish, Dutch, and French. It was expected that the two regular infantry companies of the king on the island would be offset by the arrival of an equal force with the new French governor of Martinique. At any rate, Wheeler had little faith in the king's companies since they were two-third Irish, for "there is great difference between them and the English in trust and valour."[37]

Before he had been cashiered, Wheeler had moved 20 cannon to the island, 16 of which were part of the stores of the Office of Ordnance. He had hoped to get 500 men under arms before he was recalled. By April 1672, London was still largely in the dark over how many Englishmen were actually on St. Christophers, but when war with The Netherlands became a certainty the island's little English community moved to its own defense. An act was passed in June, under which every person capable of bearing arms was to be furnished with good firearms, a pound of powder, and a proportional amount of bullets. In July, an inventory of the island's English strength revealed that there were only 496 Englishmen capable of bearing arms, of whom 437 were actually armed. There were as many as 19 great guns with powder, shot, and appropriate accoutrements available for service.[38] Governor Stapleton moved to improve the defenses in March 1673 by bringing additional big guns from the island of Anguilla and landing them at or near Cleverleys Hill. The French defense was estimated at approximately 1,500 men. No one, however, could determine just where enemy raiders might strike. Or, indeed, if they would strike at all.

On the afternoon of May 28, their guns already warmed by the brief foray against Nevis earlier in the day, the Dutch fleet arrived off the western shore of St. Christophers. Sailing past the main roads of the island, they found the anchorage abandoned. Word of their imminent arrival had undoubtedly preceded them. But upon rounding Sandy

Point, they sighted two small ships lying at anchor. With scant attention to the two forts guarding the anchorage, the Dutch sailed directly for them. Several sloops from the van of the fleet were immediately deployed. In the meantime, the flotilla's warships commenced a bombardment upon the two fortifications, one of which was the out-of-repair French works and the other the lightly-armed English works. Unlike the defenders of Montserrat, the enemy at Sandy Point could provide little in the way of return artillery fire, though "there was heavy musketeering upon the boats and sloops," from the detachment of 700 French musketeers.[39]

The defenders' musket fire continued hot as *Noordhollandt*'s boat closed with one of the merchantmen. Within a short time, the vessel was boarded and captured. She proved to be the French fluit *D'Indiaen*, half-filled with sugar. The boarders discovered, much to their dismay, however, that their new prize had been stripped of her sails and mainyard, which had been taken ashore. Nonetheless, they persisted in towing her away. Another effort was made against the second merchantman amid the deadly sputtering of musket fire, but she was found to be firmly stuck two feet into the bottom and could not be moved. The intensity of the shore musketry was by now becoming more than a nuisance. Before the boats and sloops had returned to their respective ships, 13 to 14 men had been wounded and four more killed, including the skipper of *Suriname* and a quartermaster. Casualties from the Dutch bombardment among the defenders, Governor Stapleton later reported, included one soldier, a woman, a child, one black boy, and two French killed.[40]

The prize had been a costly one for the Dutch and for little gain. With their dead and wounded aboard, they drifted with the current, tending to that grim business that must be addressed after every battle. Ahead, barely six miles away, lay the former Dutch colony of St. Eustatius, taken almost a year before by the English. It, like the several islands to the south before it, would soon become the target of yet another attack. But this time Cornelis Evertsen's motivation was more than military.

9

TREACHEROUSLY DESERTED

Late on Wednesday, May 29, 1673, the dual squadron of the Admiralties of Zeeland and Amsterdam made sail, coming about again and again in the warm Caribbean waters so as not to drift in the currents below their next objective, the tiny island of St. Eustatius.[1]

To the uninitiated eye, the three mile by six mile island might have appeared an improbable target. Desiccating in the Caribbean's stiff trade winds and harsh sun, 90 miles east of the Virgin Islands of St. Croix and St. Thomas, St. Eustatius had long appeared a forelorn and nearly empty volcanic rock of the Leeward Islands. Its history has been written by pirates, smugglers, forgers of bills of lading, and dealers in human flesh and foibles. It has been assumed by some that European discovery of the island occurred on November 13, 1493, when Columbus may have sighted its tall volcanic cone on his second voyage to the New World. If so, he was not compelled to stop and explore.[2]

Small and unfertile, without water sources other than rain, it was an island unpopular even among the Carib Indians of the region, who had deserted it before the Zeelanders arrived to set up their plantations. Despite its diminutive size, St. Eustatius nonetheless quickly rose in the priorities of European power and politics, commerce and trade. Far from the control of their patrons, its businessmen found magic ways to increase money and goods. Theirs was truly the "Golden Rock."[3]

In 1627, at the onset of the West Indies sugar era, the Duke of Carlisle received an English royal patent for a number of West Indies islands, including St. Eustatius, which he neglected to occupy. Two years later, a brief French occupation under the direction of François de Rotondy, Sieur de Cahusac, was reported. In April 1636, the Dutch arrived and ensconced themselves intending to remain. Under the leadership of Pieter van Corselles, a colonizing effort by Zeelanders erected a rudimentary fort on Orange Bay and brought the island under the patroonschap of Jan Snouck of Vlissingen, with partners Abraham van Pere the Elder and Pieter van Rhee. The patroonschap was under the nominal authority of the Netherlands West Indies Company, or WIC, which had been founded fifteen years earlier. Calling his settlement Nieuw Zeelandt, Corselles promised profits from tobacco which he believed might be raised on the island. In July 1638, the first shipment of Statian tobacco, grown by the tiny population of Zeelanders, Walloons, and Flemings, was landed at Vlissingen, Zeeland.[4]

Under its 1621 Patent, the first West Indies Company was divided into five chambers: Amsterdam, which provided 4/9ths of the capital; Zeeland, providing 2/9ths; the Maas (Rotterdam), providing 1/9th; Noordholland, providing 1/9th; and Friesland with Groningen, providing 1/9th. The WIC was pyramidal in structure. Each chamber received exclusive territory, and within that territory, the right to sell patroonschaps to entrepreneurs. The patroons fitted out expeditions and colonists, sent them out to occupy land under their respective chamber's control, and expected the profits to flow up from the colonists through the patroon, to the chamber, and eventually to the WIC. For several decades the system worked and profits rolled in. Unfortunately, in increasingly reckless pursuit of short-term profits the WIC paid out enormous dividends to investors and retained little capital for reinvestment in the business or support for the colonists. By 1648, the WIC had incurred heavy losses, and colonists, such as those on St. Eustatius, commenced illicit trading within the company's monopoly for their own accounts. Evasion of taxes, duties and convoy fees; profit skimming, and double bookkeeping; unreported trade and plain and fancy cheating kept the WIC's potential profits, once enormous, at the bottom of the pyramid. In St. Eustatius, the money and profits were recycled into entrepreneural operations that benefitted only those closely involved.

Given the prime motivational factor, profiteering, St. Eustatius's governors devoted little money or effort to the defenses of the island. Foreigners were their best friends. French and Spanish sugar found its way to the island, where it was transformed into English sugar, and sold on the legal, and frequently illegal markets. In less than thirty years of settlement, the island's reputation as an entrepôt of illicit but profitable trade increased geometrically. Thus, in times of war, it became an attractive source of plunder for those powerful enough to extract it. In 1663, the English provocateur, Sir Robert Holmes, ransacked the island, but did not bother to occupy it.

When the English privateer and filibuster, Henry Morgan, plundered the island two years later on July 23, 1665, he is recorded as having carried off 50,000 pounds of cotton. Jamaica Governor Thomas Modyford related his subordinate's tale in a report of August 23, 1669. Having

> notice of the [Second] Dutch war by Lord Arlington's dispatch of 12th November 1664, [I] persuaded all in or near this harbour to undertake against the Dutch at Curaçao, giving them suitable commissions and Col Ed. Morgan, [my] Deputy governor, for their general; they went cheerfully without putting the King to one penny charge, and took Statia and Saba.[5]

And as there was a war in progress, Morgan raised the king's flag and claimed the island's 330 Europeans and 840 Negro and Indian slaves for England—after deducting a share of booty for his troubles.[6]

Two years later, on November 17, 1666, the French captured St. Eustatius from the English and brought in Dutchman Jan Symonsen de Buck, former governor of the nearby island of St. Martin, as governor of their new property, now under nominal French rule. But French domination was equally short-lived. In mid-1668, the daring Zeeland captain, Abraham Crijnssen, during a raid on the "Wild Coast" of the Guianas and the Caribbean, retook the island for the Zeeland Chamber.

These captures and recaptures were part of the acceptable fortunes of war. What brought Evertsen's squadron and wrath into Orange Bay in late May 1673, however, was not only motivated by military reasons, but by a desire to inflict punishment for treasonous actions.

Following the model of the WIC's policy, the Zeeland Chamber had sought every opportunity to milk their colonies. If the colony requested a load of lumber and building materials, or even a cannon for its defense, the patroon in Vlissingen, with a watchful eye on profits and expenditures, was inclined to consider it only after the request had been halved. If a cannon were supplied, gunpowder and balls might turn up missing, or vice versa. Both colonists and patroons were chronically tight-fisted and suspicious of each other. Cheating on accounts was expected. Indeed, the guns of St. Eustatius were seldom fired in defense of the island on the grounds that a sharp defense would only bring ruinous reprisal on all their heads and business would suffer.[7]

When word of the outbreak of the Third Anglo-Dutch War reached the businessmen of St. Eustatius in June 1672, in the form of English and French expeditionary forces off Fort Oranje they voted, under duress but without even a symbolic act of defense for Zeeland's interests, for the English. Pitted against the French and English, whose attack seemed inevitable, it would have required an act of divine intervention to save them. Thus, the leading men of St. Eustatius quickly seized their first ripe opportunity, revolted against their patroons, Van Rhee and Van Pere, and the WIC's Zeeland Chamber, and permitted the English from St. Christophers to take over their island. On July 19, 1672, Colonel Stapleton, English governor of the Leeward Islands, informed Secretary of State Arlington that he had effectively "reduced" St. Eustatius, Saba, and Tortola.

For Cornelis Evertsen, this blatant act of treason was reason enough to disregard the secret instructions issued to him so many months before, and to undertake an expedition of reprisal. The inhabitants of St. Eustatius, who had exhibited an unwillingness to stand against their national foes, would now be obliged to stand against their own people, and all were aware of the probable consequences of defeat.

Stapleton had not left St. Eustatius undefended. Indeed, he had provided a defense force of three companies of troops, each consisting of 40 men, under the command of Deputy Governor Captain John Pogson, and Council members Captain William Mussedine and John Hansell. An additional company of 40 men had been dispatched to nearby Saba under the command of one Andrusin. The principal defense of St. Eustatius was a battery later known as Fort Oranje, built on a hundred-foot tall cliff overlooking the main island anchorage in the lee of the island. In theory, it could, with the few cannons on hand, command and control access to the island, for the fort could also monitor ships approaching from Saba, ten miles away, whose own dramatic, cloud-draped volcanic cone is always visible from the cliff. Down below, at the water's edge, were the rows of rich warehouses where sugar, tobacco, and cotton were stored alongside high value trade goods such as glass, wine, rum, and cloth. From the water, the fort and its environs looked formidable indeed.[8]

On May 29 the Dutch armada came to anchor off the island of St. Eustatius in ten fathoms of water. Evertsen promptly dispatched two trumpeters with a letter to its English commander, "whereby the fort and the island was demanded in the name of their High Mightinesses and the Prince of Orange." The fleet, anchored in the bay off the fort, awaited the reply even as preparation for the inevitable landing, necessary to subdue the rebellious islanders, was being carried out. "Yet the Commander," Evertsen recorded in *Swaenenburgh*'s journal, sent back to us a letter in answer that the island was not intending to surrender but rather to defend the same. Whereupon immediately the boats and sloops, which lay ready, were sent manned to the shore, their strength being 600 men, both soldiers and sailors, and began to cannonade the fort with the ship's cannons. To which at first a few shots were returned, but it did not last long as the crew all disembarked there. The Commander, seeing our people landing and marching upon the fort, requested quarter, the sauvegarde, which was granted him, after which the island was surrendered. Found there [the] Dutch nation under arms, so that on the island some 200 men were under arms, and found in the fort 12 guns and at various places another 7, making together 19 guns.[9]

The short battle for St. Eustatius claimed at least one distinguished victim. Captain Hanske Fokkes of the Amsterdam squadron, veteran commander of campaigns in the North Sea and English Channel, died quite suddenly upon landing, possibly a victim of the murderous climate in which he had been fighting for weeks. His remains, and those of the skipper of *Suriname*, were interred in the middle of the fort.[10]

Evertsen and Benckes, anxious to attend to the traitors who had taken up arms against them, made their first order of business the interrogation of St. Eustatius's Dutch inhabitants. On the day following the capture, all of the Netherlanders were examined. Each was questioned about the abandonment of their governor and the handing over of the island to the English. The inhabitants admitted to having taken up arms against their own nation

first because they had not been supported according to the promises of Mr. van Ree, and also because they feared that the English would otherwise shoot them dead. Yet they were just as strong as were the English, and the English Commander declared in their presence when they saw us coming that if they did not want to take up arms against their nation they should go to their homes and all keep themselves still; to this they knew not what to say, but had to admit that the same was true.[11]

The culpability of the inhabitants seemed clear to Evertsen, and their punishment would begin by the confiscation of all of their slaves and sugar stocks by Court Martial for the States General.[12]

Losing no time for the business at hand, namely booty, Evertsen and Benckes employed their men the next day in loading sugar from the storehouses into the prizes. On Sunday, June 1, the English commander of the island and all of the English population, "some 160 souls strong, both men and women," were embarked and sent to St. Christophers with a warship and the snaauw *Zeehond*.[13]

For Evertsen, the problem of the recent English occupation of the Dutch island was thus concluded. But there still remained the issue of retribution to be meted out to the Dutch inhabitants for their treason.

Seventeenth century military justice was swift and brutal, and the traitors were permitted a frightening view of what might lie ahead for them when a soldier who had broken the sauvegarde was ordered keel-hauled and then "condemned to be dragged up on the land at some island or another as a rogue." Many among the Netherlanders who had resisted his reassertion of Zeeland's authority expected little better from Evertsen.[14] They were more fortunate than they could know.

On Tuesday, June 3, the Dutch crews were kept busy emptying one of the prizes to make room in its hold to transport the traitors back to Curaçao. Evertsen also found time for an auction that day. Thinning out his flock of prizes, he managed to sell *De Prosperis*, the fin-boat laden with Kill Devil rum taken off Barbados on May 18th, for 12,000 pounds of sugar. The fluit *D'Indiaen*, taken at St. Christopher's Roads on May 29, was disposed of for 25,000 pounds of sugar. All sugar and slaves on the island, with the exception of property belonging to the former governor, Lucas Jacobsen, were seized for The Netherlands. The island, its guns, and all upon it were once again Zeeland's.[15] But Evertsen had come to extract retribution, not to regain Zeeland's lost colony, and his future actions were destined to be so directed.

As the Dutch busied themselves ashore, they managed to keep a watchful eye upon the sea. Evertsen continued to capitalize on every opportunity offered to inflict damage upon the commerce of the enemy. When a sail was sighted in the lee of the island on June 5, Captains Boes and Evert Evertsen were sent to investigate. That evening Boes returned to report that the sail had been a loaded fluit that had, unfortunately, reached the sanctuary of the roads at St. Christophers. Though the two Dutch ships had hoped to cut her out, their prey had moored hard against the quay to defend herself. Her crew had set up a battery on the beach, and stripped her of her sails. There was little the Dutch could do without the possibility of enduring some loss, and wisely did not bother.[16]

There were, of course, other equally important and immediate concerns to be dealt with by the victors at St. Eustatius. One of these was the showy court martial of three sailors accused of murdering Jan Symonsen De Buck, the Dutch governor brought over to the island by the French in 1666. Though little information concerning the actual crime has surfaced, it seems apparent that de Buck was murdered soon after the capitulation of the island. The accused sailors, Claes Kuijnder, Pieter Tastemelck, and Antonio Angulo, were quickly found guilty. Their sentence, not an uncommon one, was undoubtedly calculated to impress their shipmates with the magnitude and futility of such crimes. The condemned were ordered to draw lots to determine which of the three would be lucky enough to be hanged. The two losing the draw were, in fact, the less fortunate, for their punishment began where that of the first ended. The two losers were forced to stand on the gallows next to their condemned mate with ropes about their necks. When the condemned man was hanged, the two unfortunates next to him were ordered keelhauled and afterwards whipped with the *laars*, a one-yard length of unravelled four inch rope tipped with felt, until they were nearly senseless. Whatever remained of the two sailors after these punishments was to be dragged upon the shore as a rogue.[17]

Claes Kuijnder drew the short lot and was hanged on Saturday the 7th. After standing next to him on the gallows with the prescribed ropes around their necks, losers Tastemelck and Angulo were hoisted by their wrists up to the end of the mainyard. A weighted line was tied to their feet. The other end of the line was dropped into the water and taken under the hull to the opposite side of the ship and run up the other end of the yardarm. After an oil-soaked rag was tied around their mouths and noses to prevent immediate drowning, each man was dropped from the end of the yardarm into the sea, and pulled by their comrades down under the hull and, upside down, up to the opposite end of the yardarm. This exercise was repeated twice again. If there was enough slack in the rope, the victims might be spared the agony of being drawn against the razor sharp barnacles encrusting the outside of the hull and having their bodies sliced open. But if there was too much slack, and it took too long to haul them up, a victim could easily drown.[18]

It is unlikely that anyone was around to care for whatever remained of the carcasses that were hauled up at the end of a line onto the rocky beach of St. Eustatius and left there. For after witnessing this edifying punishment, the Netherlanders of the island were put aboard a ship and sent to Curaçao. Their 204 slaves were divided as prizes among the ships of the squadron. Having thus effectively reduced the population to but a handful, and fully aware that upon his departure either the English or the French from nearby islands would rush to claim that which was again, albeit briefly, a colony of Zeeland, Evertsen resolved to leave little of use behind. As evening settled over the island, the raiders set about demolishing the fort. The night sky grew red from the blaze of the burning works. As dessert, on the Sabbath, June 8, the retiring Dutchmen set fire to all about the ruined and smouldering fort, as well as to the warehouses on the beach below. At dark, the fleet quietly weighed anchor and sailed away.[19]

The blazing fires were a welcome beacon to the English, who immediately rushed from St. Christophers to reoccupy St. Eustatius. In a letter of June 18, 1673, Governor Stapleton wrote to the Council for Trade and Plantations in London with news of his own easy reduction of the island. Owing to a lack of first hand intelligence, his picture of the events that had transpired varied somewhat from those of the Dutch, but was accurate enough. He informed the council that Governor Pogson claimed that "he and his men were beaten by great shot," and that the Dutch had remained on the island for 14 days (though Evertsen's log indicated only eleven), "and did little prejudice." Then, in a repetition of the race for the island the year before, he reported that "as soon as [the Dutch] went away the French governor [of St. Christophers] sent to take it for his master; the English governor sent four hours before him. Most of [the Dutch] soldiers are his Majesty's subjects, who treacherously deserted their colors in Flanders." But his forces, he noted without reporting that there was absolutely no opposition, reduced it again.[20]

As the English forces from St. Christophers raced their French allies to fill the vacuum at St. Eustatius, the Dutch squadron was already sailing north by west between Sombrero and the treacherous reefs of Anageda in the Lesser Antilles. About midday on June 9, they sighted the neutral Danish boat *Fero*, Hans Erasmussen Monck commanding, eight days out of St. Thomas bound for St. Christophers with bacon and meat; observing her neutrality, they let her pass. When it was certain they had slipped by Anageda, and were safe from prying English or French eyes on that island, the squadron altered course to the west.[21]

At 9:00 A.M., June 10, they sighted the Virgin Islands, and proceeded to hold a southwest course to sail close by them. Somewhat after midday, a sail was sighted dead ahead and the Dutch took up the chase. As they gradually closed, it became apparent that they were pursuing another Danish vessel. Nevertheless, Benckes continued after the ship, even as the rest of the squadron took chase of yet a third vessel that had come from the shore. Closer observation of this last craft revealed her to be a caper flying the prince's flag. As it was now late in the day, there was little chance of overtaking her and they soon came about. The Dane, it was discovered shortly afterwards, had sailed out that morning from St. Thomas bound for Copenhagen, and had agreed to carry a letter to their High Mightinesses, the States General in the Hague.[22]

Evertsen and Benckes now turned their prows towards Puerto Rico. The squadrons carried aboard hundreds of slaves who, the two pragmatic commanders knew, had to be sold soon, both for their cash value and to eliminate the overhead of maintaining them. On Wednesday, June 11, the fleet was scudding along about two miles off the Puerto Rican coast when Evertsen ordered up a white flag to summon the squadron's commanding officers to a council of war onboard *Swaenenburgh*. They were nearing one of the strongest harbors in the Caribbean, San Juan, which was jealously guarded by Spain, and stoutly defended against all comers. Though the Spanish were not belligerents, their relationship with the Dutch in the West Indies was frequently less than cordial. Thus, Evertsen dispatched Lieutenant Joan Becker ahead in *Zeehond*. Becker's entreé would be the delivery of a letter from the Spanish Duke de Veraguas to the governor of Puerto Rico, "with a request that he grant his gracious permission to allow our ships to come in to take on water."[23]

About an hour after sundown, the squadron came close under the fort that guarded the harbor, Castillo San Marcos. Evertsen's and Benckes's reception at the 150-year-old city and port of San Juan, with its well defended fort overlooking the entrance to the wide, hospitable and sheltered bay, was not as they had hoped. Rather than a loose salute, which they had expected, the fort fired an aimed shot to acknowledge their arrival. They immediately anchored in 14 fathoms of water *outside* the mouth of San Juan Bay.[24]

Lieutenant Becker returned aboard early on the morning of June 12, reporting that the governor refused to permit more than three ships in the harbor at the same time. The governor, he said, was also sending two officers to verify that the fleet that had arrived before his city were indeed Hollanders, as he little trusted the English and French. Evertsen, undoubtedly irate, but obliged to observe protocol, sent Becker back to the governor to again request that all the ships of the squadron might enter the harbor at one time as the bad anchorage they presently maintained made it impossible for them to hold in the mouth of the bay. The lieutenant's mission proved fruitless. The governor refused to yield. Adding further insult, he decided to retract permission for three ships to enter, saying now that even if they had been the king of Spain's own ships, no more than two would be permitted inside at one time. He promised, however, to dispatch one of his officers to show the Dutch another place where they might take on good water.[25]

Evertsen was undoubtedly growing more irate at each hour of delay. The water pretext was getting them no closer to selling their slaves. It was soon apparent that the governor was signalling for a bribe. Becker was again sent ashore with the offer of "an honorarium of a few slaves" to allow all of the ships into the harbor. The governor again refused. Evertsen and Benckes had little choice but to accept the governor's offer of a watering area elsewhere, and soon weighed anchor and sailed to the designated location.[26]

The watering place was far from acceptable, and less substantial than the governor had indicated. As a consequence, a chain of mishaps occurred that only served to increase Dutch frustrations with their unwilling host. Both Commander Benckes and Captain van Zijl lost their anchors in a reef. A prize of the late Captain Hanske Fokkes, still under sail, collided with Captain Boes's ship, knocking his gallion off and shuddering his bowsprit loose. All were forced to come to anchor to await repairs to the prize. Toward evening, the prize again made sails and under shortened canvas the squadron made its way along the shore, carefully avoiding the fangs of unseen reefs. At nightfall, rather than press through uncertain territory, the squadron heaved to and held the wind in the sail throughout the evening to stay upwind of the watering place.[27]

The following evening, the fleet finally came to anchor in a clean sandy bay on the northwest coast of Puerto Rico in ten fathoms of water and on good holding ground. This anchorage may have been the present Bahia de Aguadilla, and proved a welcomed respite for the Dutch crews, although there was much work ahead. Here they found three fine and easily reached watering places and good firewood. For two days the squadron busied itself in taking on water. On the third day, Monday, June 16, the ships were careened and their bottoms scraped to remove the weeds and barnacles that had grown during their short stay in the tropics. While work progressed on the hulls, Evertsen and Benckes convened a council of war with their captains to decide their next move. As it seemed unlikely that they would succeed in divesting themselves of the slaves in Puerto Rico, it was decided that they should be sent to the market at Curaçao on the frigate *America*.[28]

America had been taken by the Amsterdam squadron in the Caribbean before meeting up with the Zeelanders off Barbados. Aside from the sugar she had carried as cargo, which Benckes claimed for Amsterdam, her lading now consisted of prize goods, apparently carried aboard at St. Eustatius, which were jointly shared by both commanders. Evertsen traded the small pinnace, *La Francoyse*, taken on May 26, for *America*, and then placed one Jan Moensen in command, with Goossen Janssen (or Jansen) as his lieutenant. Moensen was directed to arrange for the sale of at least 42 slaves at Curaçao, for the highest price possible, for the benefit of Zeeland. *America* was ordered not only to deliver the slaves to the mart at Curaçao, but also to attack and, if possible, capture any French or English merchantmen encountered en route.[29]

After removing her masts, sails, and anything else of use, the prize pinnace *Nova France*, taken on May 25 by Captain Thijssen, was set afire and abandoned. The goods aboard were distributed around the fleet. At daylight, June 20, the squadron sailed out of the bay, and soon after broke off with the frigate *America*. Captain Moensen and Lieutenant Janssen would eventually deliver their cargo of slaves safely to the Curaçao vendue master on behalf of Cornelis Evertsen, Evert Evertsen, and Passchier de Witte, along with substantial quantities of ammunition and powder, a compass rose, and 1,801 pieces of eight for the account of the Staten of Zeeland.[30]

At what point Commander Jacob Benckes resolved to cast his lot with Cornelis Evertsen for the duration of the campaign in America is uncertain. With both squadrons united as a single force, there seemed little that might stand in their way. With Evertsen's next target, as directed in his instructions, being the rich tobacco colony of Virginia at precisely the time the annual tobacco convoys were preparing to sail for England, the allure of a joint expedition certainly held much promise for Benckes. The two commanders had worked well together in the short time since their meeting, and neither seemed to foster either jealousy or animosity toward the other. Both officers' willingness to cooperate was soon manifested in an agreement of shared command. The perplexed English failed to comprehend how two rivals such as Zeeland and Holland could work together in the field, with both field commanders alternating as commander in chief. As one New Englander later remarked with incredulity, "one wears the flag eight days, then the other wears it eight days," and without apparent detriment to efficiency.[31]

On June 21, 1673, as the joint squadron sailed north on the next leg of its raid on America, the war in Europe was being prosecuted with intense vigor by both sides. Admiral de Ruyter had already inflicted a stunning naval defeat over the British at the Battle of Schoneveld on May 29, and again, at the same place on June 13. He would do so a third time at the Battle of Kijkduin, off Scheveningen in August. As England was growing weaker by the week in home waters, the strategic emphasis of the war for The Netherlands was shifting dramatically. Indeed, as Evertsen and Benckes pressed northward, the very complexion of the war in Europe was changing. For the moment, the two squadrons had been all but forgotten as the States General began to consider a land offensive against France.

An ocean away from the main European theater of conflict, nine ships-of-war and a gaggle of prizes, their bows turned northward, prepared for a descent upon the flourishing colonial outposts of the British empire. Their target was the Chesapeake Bay. Their main objective was to effect nothing less than the capture or destruction of the entire Maryland and Virginia tobacco fleet.

10

FORTS IN THE MOST CONVENIENT PLACES

Virginia Governor Sir William Berkeley, paunchy and jowly in his 67th year, must have experienced a sense of déjà vu in May 1673 when he learned of the imminent arrival of a powerful English frigate on the James River, and again on June 20, when a second ship of nearly equal strength came in. The two vessels, his majesty's Hired Ships-of-War *Barnaby* and *Augustine*, he knew, had come to escort the valuable Virginia and Maryland tobacco fleet, which was gathering in the York, the James, and other rivers of the Chesapeake Bay, home to England. The warships were overdue and Virginia merchants undoubtedly breathed a collective sigh of relief at their tardy arrivals. Berkeley, however, may have involuntarily grimmaced as he considered the potential difficulties and danger in getting the convoy safely off. Recent intelligence had arrived informing him of a possible Dutch naval raid on the gathering tobacco flotilla, and he was well aware of just how vulnerable it was, with or without the big warships. He had been through it all once before.

Berkeley did not need to recall the tragic episode of the last war with the Dutch, in which another tobacco fleet gathering in the James had been annihilated by a masterful Dutch ruse carried out by the daring Zeelander, Abraham Crijnssen. But he remembered. Indeed, he need not have mused over what seemed an unending series of crises that had wracked his administration over the last decade. But he did.

Sir William Berkeley, brother of the powerful Sir John Berkeley of Stratton, who was a member of his majesty's Privy Council and a proprietor of New Jersey and Delaware, had, by 1673, been governor of

Raid on America

Virginia for 23 of the colony's 66 years of existence. A cavalier of the first order, he had been born in the year of the colony's inception. In 1642, at the tumultuous onset of the English Civil War, Berkeley had assumed command of the colony and, as an ardent supporter of the king, had ridden the whirlwind. Vigorously defying the ascension of Cromwell and Parliament after the execution of Charles I, he had, in 1649, boldly proclaimed his fealty to Prince Charles II, then in exile in Holland, when most others were shirking their support of the monarchy. Despite his efforts, the colony of Virginia was eventually obliged to submit to the Commonwealth. When a parliamentary force arrived on the Chesapeake in 1652 and prevailed upon the colony to capitulate peacefully, Berkeley, though willing to fight on, was forced to resign. Retiring to his estate at Green Spring on the James River, the embittered former governor undoubtedly watched with interest as a succession of chief executives rose to power and stepped down, even as the chronically broke interregnum was played out.

With the restoration of the monarchy in 1660, William Berkeley, who had been one of Virginia's most popular leaders, against his will and by general and royal acclaim, again became governor. Unfortunately, the next dozen years of his regime were destined to be as stormy as his first tenure, rife with both war and depression. Virginia was growing and changing rapidly, despite efforts to maintain the status quo. Slavery was legalized in 1661: within a decade the colony population exceeded 40,000, of whom 2,000 were black slaves and 6,000 were indentured whites.[1] And Virginia was becoming increasingly dependent—indeed, a slave itself—to a single master: tobacco. In 1660, when Charles II reconfirmed the 1651 Navigation Act, which had brought on the First Anglo-Dutch War and prophesized the second such conflict, Virginia found itself in economic irons. Through the imposition of duties on the golden leaf, ostensibly "for the support of the Government . . . . and the advancement of manufacture and divers other good designs for the advantage of his majesties colony," Virginia had become the most important of all sources of colonial American revenue for the crown. By royal instruction dated September 2, 1662, the two-shilling-per-hogshead duty was generating, within a decade, revenues of £150,000 annually.[2] Berkeley was directed by the crown to stem the surreptitious trade many Virginians carried on with the Dutch. By the middle years of the governor's second administration, the colony was irrevocably shackled to the fortunes of the leaf.

Like any single-crop economy, Virginia's could be driven from boom to bust almost overnight; tobacco prices were subject to dramatic fluctuations. In 1665, with the adoption of Charles II's even more rash legislation to control trade, the depression in the tobacco marketplace was insured. Both Maryland and Virginia were now effectively denied their European markets. By law, since 1611, neither colony had been permitted to sell the leaf to any market other than England, a prohibition that was largely ignored. Now war with one of Virginia's principal foreign outlets, The Netherlands, only compounded the problems.

Though an ardent supporter of the monarchy, Berkeley may have recalled with mixed feelings the instructions he had received on June 3, 1665. The orders, issued by the king on January 27, 1664, directed him to put the colony "into the best posture of defense he could." Seventeen days later, Berkeley convened the Virginia Council of State to plan for the colony defense against foreign invasion.[3]

The governor may have recalled that then, as now, the colony had been woefully unprepared for war, and arms and ammunition were in short supply. Though 1,500 dragoons, 2,500 "able men with snaphances," and a reserve force of 3,000 to 4,000 militiamen could be fielded, both he and the Council had been well aware that it would be nearly impossible to guard both the shipping and the hundreds of miles of coastal and estuarine shoreline. Thus, they had ordered all ships to anchor in four designated anchorages where protective batteries could be erected—at Jamestown, at Tindalls Point (modern Gloucester) on the York River, in Corotoman Creek, and at Pungoteague on the Eastern Shore. As few pieces of artillery were available in Virginia to protect the anchorages, Berkeley directed all ships visiting the colony to donate two guns apiece for the common defense during their stay, as well as powder to use them. A fort erected at Point Comfort in 1640, at the mouth of the James, but now considered too expensive and unsuitable for defense, was ordered stripped of its 14 guns, all of which were to be brought up the river for the defense of the capital's anchorage.[4]

Though initial measures for Virginia's defenses were undertaken with some zeal, the elderly governor recalled, and his own optimism had been considerable, little attention had been paid to the security of the large number of tobacco ships once they had departed the Chesapeake. The consequences were diasterous, and many ships sailing alone or without protection quickly fell victim to roving Dutch capers. Finally, on November 5, 1665, the Crown issued instructions establishing an embargo that forbade any vessels from sailing from the Chesapeake until April 15 of the coming year, and then only in company with other ships.[5]

The initial measures for defense of shipping while in Virginia soon became a bone of contention between Berkeley and the crown. their differences centered on the abandonment of the Point Comfort fort in lieu of the four river batteries. The king and Privy Council insisted that the Point Comfort works should not only be reoccupied but strengthened. Berkeley and his own council insisted that Point Comfort was

> the only place on the mouth of this river where we conceive it to be of no defence at all because ships cannot hale on shore but they will be exposed to the violence of all the winds of three quarters of the compass and the place so remote from all assistance that it cannot be defended.[6]

They argued that the entrance of the river at that point was so wide that any enemy ship could ride secure from all possible danger, even from the greatest cannon in the world.[7] Berkeley later wrote that a fort at Point Comfort was entirely useless.

> because it being A direct Channell and A great Tide, A Shipp may ride in Safety in the Bay till it hath A Good Wind and upon A Tide may runn by A better Fort, than all the Wealth and Skill of this Countrey can build, Especially Considering the distance they may goe from it, which were it but halfe A Mile would be to farr for us to depend Certainly on its defence.[8]

Despite the long and detailed arguments of the governor and council of Virginia, the king and Privy Council's instructions to refortify the site prevailed. The construction, which would ultimately claim several lives and an enormous expenditure of time, money, and energy, was begun. On January 4, 1667, Francis Moryson, a member of the Board of Trade and Plantations, petitioned the Privy Council on behalf of Virginia that "twenty great Gunns, Culverin, Demi-Culverin and Sakers," with powder and shot, and 100 horse arms be sent for the defense and security of the colony. A fort without guns, after all, was useless. In response to a request of the Virginia Council of July 10, 1666, Moryson also petitioned "That a Frigate may be appointed to Sayle from hence by the midst of February next, and to Ride in Chesapeake Bay to secure the Shipps Trading thither." Berkeley had been willing to accept the Point Comfort fort, which he was confident would provide little protection, in exchange for the services of a Royal Navy frigate, which he hoped would.[9]

The governor undoubtedly recalled, with some satisfaction, that the admiralty took only seven days from the time of Moryson's petition to instruct H.M.S. *Elizabeth*, a 20-year-old, 46-gun, 474-ton frigate, to embark for Virginia. The Atlantic crossing had been horrible for the ship and her crew. Berkeley's Secretary, Thomas Ludwell, confessed to being "extreamly joyd" at the news that a frigate was en route to Virginia, but when she limped into the James, he was appalled: "when I saw the condition shee came in I heartyly wished her safe att home againe." The battered warship was immediately dispatched three leagues up the James to be repaired and refitted.[10]

Though a lone privateer had already terrorized shipping early on in this second Dutch war and caused the full mobilization of the colony, it was not until June 1667 that Virginia faced its first true test of military preparedness. On the first day of that month a Dutch squadron of four men of war and an eight-gun dogger, arrived off the Chesapeake, seized a small Carolina-bound shallop and a merchantman, and prepared for a descent on the gathering tobacco fleet. The hostile squadron was under the command of Commander Abraham Crijnssen (or Crimson, as the English called him), who had recently captured the English colony of Suriname in South America. Crijnssen, in a ruse remarkable for its simplicity, ordered his ships to raise English flags and, following the captured shallop past Point Comfort, pressed slowly up the James. The Dutch cleverly had English crewmen call out the soundings and hail passing vessels in English, deceiving everyone on the river. Several miles up river they encountered *Elizabeth*, still undergoing repairs and unguarded except for a 30-man skeleton crew. Crijnssen's squadron now revealed its true identity as guns were run out and blistering broadsides smashed the stunned English warship. *Elizabeth* was taken by boarding after firing a single cannon shot in her own defense. Unable to haul the lame ship off, the Dutch burned her where she lay, and, falling back downriver, began snapping up every merchantman in their path.[11]

Berkeley had been mortified by the news of the audacious Dutch attack. Nevertheless, he coolly mobilized a defense, arming nine merchantmen in the York and three more in the upper James, at Jamestown, with cannons taken from smaller vessels at those places. It had been his hope that a concentrated movement by the two forces might trap the raider in the jaws of a pincer movement. Unfortunately, the merchant captains whose ships had been armed and who, at first, had been eager for battle, now demurred. Their delay permitted the Dutch admiral to burn five or six of the tobacco fleet ships and to man a dozen or more as prizes. Crijnssen sailed away from Virginia on June 11, 1667, unmolested.[12]

It had mattered little to Berkeley, in the weeks and months that followed that grim occasion, that an ocean away, another Dutch squadron under the famed Michiel de Ruyter, in a single bold stroke, had entered the Thames estuary and captured an entire Royal Navy battle fleet. Virginia had indeed been humiliated. Fortunately, the catastrophe in England and the signing of the Treaty of Breda soon after distracted London from distributing the blame that might have been expected.

From the mid-1660s onward, the colony had reeled from one disaster to another. In April 1667, prior to the Dutch raid, "a most prodigeous

Storme of haile, many of them as bigg as Turkey Eggs . . . destroyed most of our younge Mast and Cattell." Then came Crijnssen. He had barely departed when the rains came and continued for 40 days straight, spoiling most of the grain spared by the April storm. On August 27 Virginia was hit by "the most Dreadful Hurry Cane that ever the colony groaned under," which

> carried all the foundation of the fort at point Comfort into the River and most of our Timber which was very chargably brought thither to perfect it. Had it been finished and a garison in it, they had been Stormed by such an enemy as noe power but Gods can restraine . . . . [13]

Ships were blown about like so much flotsam and at least 10,000 houses were levelled. The corn crop was flattened in the fields and the tobacco crop destroyed, as were the warehouses in which it was stored. Fences were ripped from the earth, and hogs and cattle wandered about at will, devouring the little the storm had left. [14]

Virginia had belatedly learned of the end of the war with the Dutch, but had, in the interim, struggled to improve its defenses in accordance with the dictates of king and council. It was, however, a matter of making do with the resources at hand. Soon after the departure of the Dutch and before the hurricane, the colony Council ordered one Colonel Leonard Yeo to press as many men and all materials necessary to mount eight guns upon the walls of the Point Comfort fort. Gowing Dunbar was appointed chief gunner at the installation. The guns he was to command were to be salvaged from the charred remains of *Elizabeth* by one Christopher Gould and carried down to the fort in his sloop. Twelve more of the ship's guns were to be mounted for the defense of Jamestown. Unfortunately, when the pieces were raised and tested, not one endured the trial. Some of the vessels burned or scuttled by the Dutch, which might have provided additional materials, had been plundered by a party of Virginians, including one justice of the peace from Pagan Creek. The whole ordeal of refortification, in fact, had become a painful exercise in futility, for when the August hurricane struck, the Point Comfort fort ceased to exist. [15]

Berkeley and Ludwell had been of a like opinion as to how the defense of Virginia should have been conducted. A fort offered no security for shipping unless vessels could be hauled close ashore beneath the protection of its guns or the difficulty of the adjacent channel hindered an enemy's approach long enough to permit the fort's gunfire to be effective. Ludwell expressed his hope that the king and Privy Council would direct all shipping to come to Jamestown rather than order a fortification erected, at great expense and difficulty, "in a place w'ch can be of noe certaine security to them" such as at Point Comfort. [16]

Following the Crijnssen raid, there were still only 14 cannon in all Virginia, "and many of them very small and believed unserviceable by being much scald and honeycombed." Ludwell expressed an open concern that if all efforts in the colony were directed toward the reestablishment of the Point Comfort works, the remainder of the colony anchorages, at which many ships called to take on tobacco and offload trade goods, would be open to attack. Thus, all shipping would be forced to ride in the James for their own protection, making "the fraight of all the remoter [places] to be soe deare that at the rate it now beares in the world will not repay it."[17] As a result, those parts of the colony would go begging for supplies, their tobacco would not be shipped, and the king would lose his custom. It was not attack by land that distressed the colony leaders so much as the vulnerability of shipping. Indeed, if an enemy attempted a land invasion, Ludwell boasted, "wee shall undoubtedly make them buy whatever they get from us att toe deare a rate to sell it again to any profit.[18]

With the end of the Second Anglo-Dutch War, Virginia's defense efforts were permitted to slide, and the fortification of Point Comfort was quietly forgotten. Berkeley continued to grow in power, almost to despotic proportions, and the once-most popular leader in colony history became the most feared and hated. He and his hand-picked council, controlling the Burgesses and Assembly with ruthless abandon, asserted "full power to impose any taxes and impositions upon the said territories [of Virginia] and the inhabitants thereof for the public defense."[19]

War clouds had not dispersed over Europe, however, and Berkeley was sorely aware that Virginia was still incapable of defending its shipping with the resources at hand. He had written in exasperation to the Privy Council at the close of the last great war that there was still a great want of powder and ammunition for the defense of the plantation "which cannot otherwise by supplyed, then by the Merchants which trade thither." The Privy Council responded in March 1668 by ordering that his majesty's Customs send for "the most considerable Merchants trading to Virginia" and "treat" with them about causing every ship sent to the colony to carry powder and ammunition. After all, Berkeley had promised not only just payment, but considerable profits to the traders to boot.[20] The merchants were apparently unresponsive, for in June 1669 Ludwell suggested to Secretary Arlington that, though the colony was in "a very peaceable condition," it was still in great want of at least 40 or 50 culverine cannon and shot with which to defend itself. France, it was said, was arming for another war, and peace, as everyone knew, was but an ephemeral thing.[21]

Virginia, having quietly shelved the Point Comfort project, proceeded slowly with its own program of fortification of key anchorages. Berkeley justified the program to the crown by noting that as the average loading time for ships calling in every river of the colony was between five and six months, "We thought it best to build Forts in the Most Convenient places for their defence, during their Stay, Rather than at Point Comfort, which at best Could but Secure James River."[22] For once, the crown thankfully remained quiet on the matter, and Berkeley proceeded on his own. The works at Jamestown were to be improved, albeit at considerable cost, and the forts at Tindalls Point and on Corotoman Creek enlarged. Though the defense works at Pungoteague on the Eastern Shore were apparently abandoned, two additional earthenworks, at Nansemond on the tributary of the same name running into the James, and at Yeocomico on the Potomac, were begun. The five forts were to be defended by a minimum of eight guns apiece. Composed of earth, their ten-foot-high, ten-foot-thick walls were to contain "a court of guard and a convenient place to preserve the magazine."[23] Construction, to be paid for by the counties bordering the rivers to be defended, went slowly. By June 1671, Berkeley had grown exasperated over the progress. The works were eroding faster than they could be repaired, and the cost for their restoration was increasingly despised by those obliged to foot the bill. Worse, neither skill nor ability to insure their maintainence was to be found in the colony: Virginia lacked even a single competent engineer to supervise the work.[24]

Not only were the forts in miserable shape, but munitions and supplies were still practically nonexistent. In February 1672, when Thomas Grantham, one of the commissioners for trade, departed Virginia for London, he noted that "there was not powder enough at Tindall's Point upon York River to charge a piece." Indeed, the colony was in such want of munitions on the eve of the Third Anglo-Dutch War that it was unable to defend itself. Grantham recommended that by a speedy effort, a surprise attack (as in the last war) might be aborted. "If his Majesty will give him protection for a ship and men," he volunteered, "he will carry ammunition of all sorts and dispatches the King wishes to send without charge."[25]

Secretly preparing its declaration of war, the crown responded on March 10 by ordering that all ships sailing from Virginia, New York, and Boston would only be allowed to depart at specific intervals—March 24, June 24, and September 24—and were to "use their utmost endeavours to keep company and defend each other during the voyage."[26] But there was not one word on the supplying of ordnance or munitions.

When news of the declaration of war with The Netherlands arrived in Virginia, the state of the colony's defense network was atrocious. Though the Council had been directed by the king "to doe our best to putt the People of the Colony of Virg^a into the best posture wee Can for the Defense of it and the shipps trading to it," little was actually accomplished.[27] The Virginia Assembly found the existing fortifications in such poor condition that it was determined that they were unable to resist any attack. Most of the materials employed in their construction had "suffered an utter demolition," while others were in a ruinous state.[28] Orders were issued to restore the works, and the various counties in which they had been erected were authorized to institute new taxes to pay from them. Despite vigorous efforts, several forts were never completed, and the artillery eventually mounted in them was destined to end up "buried in sand and spoyled with rust for want of care."[29]

On March 25, 1673, Berkeley informed the Committee for Trade and Plantations of the colony's continuing woes. Few ships had come in, and those that did had brought less than a fifth of the goods and tools necessary for the colony's survival. Clearly, the depredations of enemy cruisers and capers in home waters were having a telling effect. And of course there was the matter of ammunition. The governor begged the commissioners to intercede with the king for at least a small supply. Moreover, the spectre of famine loomed large, for an unexpectedly hard winter had destroyed more than half of the cattle in the colony, one of the inhabitant's mainstays of personal wealth. The situation, in fact, was even darker than Berkeley had indicated. An epidemic during the winter, compounded by an extremely cold season, had destroyed at least 50,000 cattle. In a desperate effort to save their livestock, the owners had fed them all their corn, and as a consequence brought starvation upon themselves.[30]

The bleak outlook for the citizenry aside, the military aspect for the defense of shipping and shore seemed insoluable. Though "all that Land which now bares the name of Virginia," Berkeley wrote in midsummer, "be Reduced to little more than Sixty Miles in breadth towards the Sea, yet that Small tract is intersected by Soe many Vast Rivers as makes more Miles to defend, then wee have men of trust to Defend them." There were now as many indentured servants, besides slaves, as there were freemen to defend the shores; and at their backs, on the western frontier, there were the Indians. Slave insurrection and Indian attack were twin spectres that weighed heavily on many a Virginian's thoughts. "Both," reminded Berkeley, "which gives men fearfull apprehentions of the danger they Leave Estates and Families in, While they are drawne from their houses to defend the Borders." At least a third of the single freemen, whose labors were barely able to sustain them, and debtors who were in equally dire straits, might be expected to revolt if the enemy prevailed in some quarters, in hopes of securing plunder.[31]

The logistical problems of keeping troops together were severe, for the ability to stockpile provisions was nonexistent. The hot and humid Virginia spring and summer climate, and the vermin that thrived in it, had long defeated efforts to establish public "Magazines of provisions" of corn and other necessaries to maintain garrison forces for any extended period of time. And as for the Virginia fighting man, though great care had been taken to exercise him, he had for many years been unacquainted with military duty or battle. Thus, Berkeley concluded, "We cannot with much Confidence rely on their Courage against an Enemy Better practized in the hazards of Warr."[32]

When, in April 1673, word arrived "that severall the Shipps of Warr belonging to the States Gen^{ll} are designed Against this Place," Virginia accelerated efforts to mobilize "Against any Attempts which may be made on it" or its shipping. On April 22, though Berkeley was absent, the Council of State, led by Secretary Thomas Ludwell and including colonels Thomas Swann and Nathaniel Bacon, Lieutenant Colonel Daniel Parke and Edward Diggs, took immediately action. The commanders of the colony militia were directed to draw their respective regiments together to march at the first summons of the governor. Since arms were at a premium, the commanders were instructed to "take Care what Armes shall bee in any Howse more then the people Listed Can use be secured for those who shall be found wanting Armes." Weapons in disrepair were to be speedily repaired. All powder and shot, both in public stores and private homes, were to be inventoried and made available for the public defense. Those who refused to comply would suffer the consequences.[33]

The council further instructed that, "Because the Enemies shipps may come on the Soddane and Attacque the shipps with[in] our Harbours, Notwithstanding the Resistance of these forts wee have been yett able to Build," at the first alarm, local militia commanders were to raise 50 men from each of their companies for every ship in their respective harbors. Each 50-man unit was to board a specified ship "with their Armes to serve as a smale shott to defend the said shipps till further Order can be taken for their Better Defense."[34]

The fort at Tindalls Point, despite previous orders for its repair, was in no condition for defense. The Council thus directed "that by Cannon Basketts or otherwise the Gunns there be soe Couvred as to Offend the

Enemy and to secure the men who shall Defend them." Each fort in Virginia's river defense system was to receive and be defended by appropriate foot soldiers from the respective counties in which they lay.[35]

The Council then turned its attention to the defense of the important Jamestown anchorage. The government had previously entered into a contract with Major Theodore Stone, William Drommond, and one Matthew (or Mathias) Page for the construction of a 250-foot-long brick fort at Jamestown. Page had since died, and the two remaining contractors had failed to carry out any work whatsoever. The Council, which had cast a blind eye to such contractual shenanigans in the past, could no longer permit such affairs to slide. With Virginia threatened, Jamestown undefended, and "that Pt of the Country . . . Exposed to the Attempts of the Enemies," the Council threatened the contractors with severe punishment, and then authorized them to complete the job and to build new gun carriages for the artillery in the town—or else. They were sternly warned that failure or the least neglect would result in state proceedings against them "According to the greatness of their offence with All Severity,"[36]

Work on the fort progressed at a snail's pace; by May 27, the contractors had accomplished little more than the manufacture of a few bricks and other materials for the construction. The bricks were, unfortunately, "reported to be very bad and altogether Insufficient for the said Worke." Berkeley and the Council ordered the bricks and timbers examined on June 6 to judge their value, "and in all things see and Comand that the Said Fort be forthwith Erected and built according to the dimencons and Rules in the said Agreem^t." Again the contractors were chastised, and this time told that they would not be paid until the job was completed.[37]

It was becoming obvious that Jamestown was unlikely to be fortified before the end of summer at the earliest, yet the town and its anchorage, as was all of Virginia, was in immediate danger of attack. The Council procrastinated, and decided to put off a decision until June 9 "to treat Consult and Examine what is done and what is to be Done for the Speedy Erecting A Fort" at Jamestown.[38]

And even as the Council deliberated, a fleet of battle-hardened Dutch warships was making its way with all due speed directly toward the Chesapeake.

The danger that history might repeat itself, if not uppermost in Governor Berkeley's mind, was undoubtedly considered as a strong possibility as he viewed the arrival of the hired warships *Barnaby* and *Augustine*. Yet the presence of the two ships must have heartened the captains of the scores of merchantmen assembling in the roads for the convoy home, as sailing unprotected from the Chesapeake was a bleak prospect indeed. As recently as May, a Dutch caper of 18 guns cruising off the coast had snapped up several inbound ships with ease. Who was to say that the far richer outward-bound ships might not also fall victim to such a fate? And with rumors and reports of eight Dutch men-of-war intending to pay a visit to the Tidewater, no one felt secure.[39]

Though both *Augustine* and *Barnaby* were, in fact, not regular Royal Navy vessels, but hired merchantmen fitted out as ships-of-war, the tobacco ship captains could take some consolation in knowing that the warships' commanders, captains Edward Cotterell and Thomas Gardiner, were seasoned naval officers. Since 1661, Cotterell had commanded five of his majesty's ships and served as a junior officer on two others. Commissioned by Prince Rupert, he had been in command of *Augustine* from late 1672 on.[40] H.M. Hired Ship *Barnaby* was Gardiner's first senior command, although he had been appointed by the Duke of Albermarle as lieutenant on at least three of his majesty's ships during and after the last war with the Dutch, and was no stranger to hard naval duty.[41]

The record concerning the vessels commanded by Cotterell and Gardiner is, unfortunately, only partially complete, yet quite representative of the lengths the Royal Navy was obliged to go to in its effort to achieve naval superiority while providing sufficient protection for the merchant marine. From what survives it is apparent that their principal mission was to convoy England's commercial shipping. Their ability to perform such missions was frequently far from adequate. Both vessels assigned to protect the important summer Virginia convoy had been hired by the English government in late 1671 or early 1672 from independent shipowners as a desperate, last-minute effort by the crown to reinforce the Royal Navy before the actual declaration of war. Yet it was also a form of mobilization of naval resources that had been employed since the days of Henry VIII.

Frequently, little attention was paid to a ship's condition or sailing qualities when she was hired by navy agents, and wrangling over such issues as who would pay for alterations, repairs, or victualling while on line caused unending delays in getting such vessels to sea. As early as January 3, 1672, the Navy Victualling Office, attempting to secure provisions for *Barnaby* (which had already been earmarked for convoy duty to the West Indies and Virginia), had been directed by the crown to negotiate with Virginia merchants on the most expeditious way of victualling the ship *on credit*. It was a necessity born of insolvency; government coffers, even then, were practically empty.[42]

Barnaby, like many vessels acquired on short notice, was unable to sail, and indeed it was not until mid-May that she was even graved.[43] Appointed to her command, Captain Gardiner was, from the onset, irate and outspoken over the inordinate delay in getting his ship prepared for sea duty. Though finally certified on June 13, 1672, work by the contractors in outfitting her had progressed so slowly that the captain, in disgust, requested another command, "Desiring to serve his Majesty in one of his own ships, as the owners [of *Barnaby*] are so backward in performing and providing what is necessary." He begged that the contract for payment of the work not be signed "until he satisfies his own honour of their better performance."[44] The contractors were lacking in the masterful art of converting a fat, worn-out merchantman into a 50-gun ship-of-war, for when *Barnaby* put to sea it was noted that she was "an extreme ill sailer, and steers bad." One Royal Navy officer even suggested that she was unfit for the simple voyage to the Canary Islands.[45]

Getting his ship to sea was one thing, manning her was another; like most Royal Navy commanders, Gardiner was faced with the manpower shortage that plagued all of his majesty's forces and obliged to impress men into service aboard his ship. It was a harsh measure hated by the general public, but one seemingly born of necessity. The absence of a national draft and the extreme, ongoing competition for skilled or unskilled mariners made the press gang a feared but common sight at every naval port in England. In mid-July, *Barnaby*'s press gangs were ranging up and down the banks of the Thames, forcibly inducting every able-bodied working-class man encountered. Sir John Bramston, writing from Chelmsford, complained of the abuses heaped upon the local population by Gardiner's roving "recruiters." "All servants and workmen in the marshes," he wrote, "are continually taken away on board unless they redeem themselves with money, so they can get no men to work there [in the marshes]."[46]

Even those employed to repair, outfit, and rig his majesty's ships were not exempt from being pressed. In May 1672, the civilian captain of *Augustine*, Zachary Taylor, charged with readying the ship for naval service, was obliged to request warrants to protect the ship's civilian master, boatswain, and 15 or 16 riggers working under him from being pressed by other ships.[47]

When *Barnaby* was finally prepared for sea duty later in the year and awaiting her first convoy assignment near the mouth of the Thames, like the rest of the convoy fleet of hired ships, her crew of only five-score men was far too few to manage her at sea. Three weeks later, Gardiner was vigorously requesting the assistance of a fishing smack for securing what pressed men he shall get at London, or that he may be sent to sea for a week or fortnight, for all the colliers and merchantmen are so ransacked before they come to them, that there is not a man worth taking.[48]

More often than not, vessels such as *Barnaby* and *Augustine*, hired for naval duty, were in a miserable state of repair when the navy obtained them. In April, *Augustine* was little more than a hulk sitting on the bottom of the Thames at the navy yard. In mid-May she was still there, and the navy was growing increasingly upset over the delay in getting her afloat. "I was this morn on board the Augustine hired as a man of war," wrote one navy commissioner sent to inspect the work supposedly underway on her, but unwilling to take matters into his own hands,

and found none of her owner [John Thornbush], or her master, who promised me to be there on board. If she does not float this tide, it will be a great hindrance to the other [hired] ships, for she lies at the gate, so that not one can be got out till she is out. Last tide there were 13 feet of water outside the gates. If the master is not here, & she floats, I will haul her half her length into the dock to make room for getting out the others next tide.[49]

Augustine required considerable alteration before she could be put to sea, and even more before she could undertake a long ocean voyage. Yet the Admiralty, in its desperate press for armed ships, was eager to get her off as soon as possible, as her crew was apparently one of the fuller complements. Indeed, it was imperative to send her out, as the jealous captains of other hired ships were "all but meanly provided with men and have obtained these few with great difficulty." *Augustine*, however, would be limited in her cruising range, for the room allocated for her provisions, principally the bread, was insufficient. Though specified to carry enough bread for 168 men for six months, she could stow only half that amount. The contractors had refused to cooperate in enlarging the storage area, and with 10,000 weight of bread arriving, her then-captain, James Watkins, was in a quandry.[50]

Such problems abounded, not only for *Barnaby* and *Augustine*, but for the navy at large. By the end of July 1672, however, both ships had put out and received sailing orders, and with five other hired vessels and two navy fireships, dropped down the Thames to the Hope to await their convoys. Over the following months, both vessels would be employed in arduous and dangerous duty, escorting large convoys as far as Gottenburg, and to exposed English coastal ports such as Hull, on the River Humber.[51]

By early January 1673, a massive armada of merchantmen began to swell in the Downs, eventually numbering 140 ships, bound for all parts of the globe, from the East Indies to Virginia. With them gathered the warships assigned to shepherd them to their destinations and back. By January 16, several hired ships-of-war, including *Barnaby*, had received orders to escort the Virginia-bound convoy across the Atlantic. But for want of adequate victuals, the warships were obliged to let the merchantmen sail ahead. Frustration mounted, and not until February was Gardiner able to sail. On February 14, he reached Plymouth, and three days later arrived at Falmouth in company with the ship *Hercules*, also bound for Virginia. Adverse winds locked the two ships in port until sometime after February 26, when they were finally able to sail for Ireland to rendezvous with other Virginia-bound ships.[52]

By the first of March several of the Virginia-bound fleet had departed from Pendennis. *Barnaby* and *Hercules* followed on the 2nd, and arrived in the Chesapeake in late April or early May. The date of *Barnaby's* arrival is only speculative, based upon word brought to England by the ship *Providence*, which had departed Maryland in May and apparently stopped in Virginia long enough to learn of the imposition of an embargo by the governor and of the arrival of eight ships from London, possibly the *Barnaby* flota. *Providence* also noted that a convoy was already assembling under *Barnaby*.[53]

Delayed by myriad accidents, shortages, alterations, and repairs, *Augustine* was not able to sail from the Downs, having also received orders for Virginia, until after April 29. The delays, though at the time necessary, were to ultimately prove catastrophic.[54]

On or about June 20, when *Augustine* arrived in the Chesapeake, she discovered the tobacco vessels of the Tidewater feverishly preparing for the assigned June 24 departure date. The resourceful Captain Gardiner was already well along in organizing the details of the convoy, which promised to be exceptionally large. The tobacco crop had been very good, though, it was said, not the usual quality. Unfortunately, Cotterell's ship, after a voyage of at least six to eight weeks was in dire need of wood, water, and other necessities before she could hazard the return trip.[55]

Several days after his arrival, Cotterell presented his situation to governor Berkeley and the Virginia Council, in the presence of the masters of all of the ships thus far assembled. He informed them that he could not possibly sail in less than three weeks. It was, perhaps, not an unreasonable request, for the masters of the ships loading in York River noted that they too would be unready to sail until that date. The Maryland

fleet had yet to appear, five ships were still loading in the Rappahan-
nock River, and two more were doing likewise farther up the bay. In
all, a known total of 22 merchantmen would be unable to sail by the
appointed deadline. In any event, sentinels had been stationed along
the coast to provide an early warning of the arrival of any hostile ships.
Thus, it was agreed by all, the departure date would be pushed back to
July 15.[56] For many in the Virginia and Maryland tobacco fleets, the
delay would prove fatal.

11

COURAGE AND CONDUCT

On the morning of July 10, the approaching Dutch fleet at first appeared to Governor Berkeley's coastwatchers as little more than pinpricks dancing on the edge of an ill-defined southern horizon. As the hours passed, the shapes that shimmered in the growing heat of day grew in both size and number. Slowly their true identities as ships of great force became clear. By midday there was little question as to their nationality and where they were bound.

The sentinels at Cape Henry dispatched an urgent express to the James River to inform Captains Thomas Gardiner and Edward Cotterell that there were at hand, or rapidly coming up, 4 sail of Hollanders, from 30 to 44 guns in strength, 4 Flushing men-of-war, 3 of which were from 30 to 46 guns and 1 that had 6 guns, and a single fireship.[1]

Aboard the approaching Dutch flagship *Swaenenburgh*, as his impending arrival was being reported up the James, Commander Evertsen studied with interest the unfamiliar maw of the noble estuary ahead. He scanned the horizon between the low-slung shoulders of the Chesapeake at capes Henry and Charles. Here, he knew, Commander Crijnssen had wrought hell and havoc on enemy shipping during the last war, departing with many valuable prizes. And here, Kees the Devil, for Zeeland's glory and profit, intended to do the same. If he acted with speed and resolution, nothing could escape his dragnet. The combined Dutch fleet, soon to be spread across the entrance of this majestic bay, were the keys to unlock and plunder the wealth of British North America's richest and most important colony, Virginia.

Evertsen undoubtedly expected little resistance in the Chesapeake, beyond, perhaps, the few small guardships that may have been assigned to convoy the tobacco fleets to Europe. The greatest deterrent to his surprise strike was the bay itself, a dangerous and shoally body of water. Despite the experiences provided by the Crijnssen raid seven years earlier, the Dutch carried neither maps nor pilots familiar with the ever-shifting bottom of the estuary and were thus obliged to move up slowly and cautiously.

As the fleet crept closer to the gaping entrance to the Chesapeake, its watch observed a pair of small sails heading down. Spotting the squadron, the oncoming vessels abruptly altered course; one came about sharply and fled back up the bay. The other, a small ketch nearest to the fleet, also displayed her heels, but sought sanctuary amidst the Smith Island flats near Cape Charles where deep draft warships might not follow. Despite the danger, Evertsen decided to take the chase: the little ketch might be worthless, but judging from its course, it doubtless carried an experienced bay pilot. *Swaenenburgh* was quickly brought about and pressed after the boat. The chase proved frustratingly brief. Evertsen soon learned that the deep-draft frigate could not penetrate the shifting, uncharted Middle Ground shoals, let alone the Smith Island flats. He wisely broke off and ordered his flagship to rejoin the squadron.[2]

Fickle coastal breezes also played a delaying role in the face of the Dutch attack plans. Not until the evening of July 11 did six of the largest ships of the combined Zeeland-Amsterdam squadron, having been forced to tack laboriously against adverse winds throughout the day, finally drop anchor off Princess Anne County, just inside Lynnhaven Bay. Three of the remaining warships, including *Schaeckerloo* and the gaggle of prizes captured in the West Indies, were still strung out and had yet to come up. Cornelis Evertsen and Jacob Benckes, however, were undoubtedly pleased with the prospect presented to them. By sunset they could plainly see in the distance a substantial fleet of heavily laden tobacco ships assembled in the roads ahead, seemingly unaware of the destruction about to befall them.[3]

Unknown to the Dutch commanders, they had long since lost the element of both tactical and strategic surprise. Word of their arrival had already reached the banks of the James. Captains Gardiner and Cotterell had immediately been apprised of the Dutch presence, and were painfully aware that they were outnumbered by at least four to one. They acted, nevertheless, with a certain boldness, perhaps born of desperation. Given their limited resources and manpower, they needed time to get the large merchant fleet in the river upstream to the shelter of defensible narrows and shoals. They needed time to permit Governor Berkeley to mobilize the Virginia Militia to oppose a Dutch landing in force. And most importantly, they needed time to organize naval resistance. Gardiner and Cotterell immediately commanded "Several Masters of the abler Merchant Shipps in James River on Board, and order'd them to Cleare their Shipps for Fight." Press gangs, hated by all common seamen, but deemed the most convenient expedient to flesh out the ad hoc battle fleet's manpower needs, were sent to round up sailors from many of the weaker ships in port. This cruel and unpopular means of recruitment was destined to work unexpectedly to the advantage of the Dutch.[4]

By the following morning, Gardiner and Cotterell had made remarkable headway in their efforts to field a fleet of armed merchantmen to accompany *Barnaby* and *Augustine* into battle. As long as the Dutch remained quietly at anchor in Lynnhaven Bay awaiting the remainder of their squadron, Virginia might still have time to prepare her defenses. Abruptly, however, the calm was broken when a third group of ships, between eight and eleven in number, was observed coming down the bay. For the English naval force assembling on the James, the arrival of the long-delayed Maryland tobacco fleet—as yet ignorant of the crisis into which it was blundering—could not have been more inopportune. For the Dutch, it was an invitation to action.[5] Employing a time-tested deception, Commander Evertsen ordered his ships to fly English flags and to hold position until the last minute when they would up anchor and swoop down upon the unsuspecting merchantmen.[6]

On the James, Captains Gardiner and Cotterell were cognizant that, unwarned, the Maryland fleet would sail serenely into range of the waiting Dutch unless their ships took immediate action. They quickly resolved to sail at once with the few forces ready for action. Their principal objective, a brave one, was to draw the Dutch from the Maryland fleet by throwing themselves in harm's way. Within a few hours, *Barnaby* and *Augustine* had raised anchor and set off with six hastily armed merchantmen to do battle with a squadron of The Netherland's finest.[7]

The Royal Navy's task was far from simple. Aside from the more obvious disparity in men-of-war, their most serious tactical problem was that the Dutch fleet lay anchored astride the most strategic position in the lower Chesapeake Bay. The ships commanded not only the north-south access to the mouth of the bay, but also the main channel approach to the James River. To reach the safety of the James, the Maryland tobacco fleet would first have to negotiate the treacherous channel around the southern tip, or "Tail" of the Horseshoe Shoals, an ever-migrating sandbar that projected many miles southward from the York River Peninsula. This dangerous shoal formed a rough V-shaped wedge at the point where the James River and the main bay channels converged. It was at that precise point that the Dutch fleet had come to anchor. Gardiner and Cotterell not only would have to draw them off in such a way as to permit the tobacco ships maneuvering room to turn the Tail of the Horseshoe and enter the James without running aground or into Dutch cannons.[8]

Onboard *Swaenenburgh*, the two approaching fleets, the Marylanders from up the bay and the English battle fleet from the James, only served to confirm the belief that everyone had been duped by Evertsen's false flags. The commander noted the approach of the two king's ships with "various others," concluded that "they took us for English ships," and ordered the squadron to remain at anchor until the last minute. Both he and Benckes believed they could afford to play a waiting game.[9]

The English battle fleet was beset by problems almost from the moment they set sail. They had to struggle against the winds simply to come up with the foe. And then there were the auxiliary ships. Four of the armed merchantmen, their pressed crews perhaps unwilling to hazard battle, were run aground before a shot had been fired. A fifth turned about in utter panic and fled back toward the James. Before the first whiff of smoke drifted across the Chesapeake, the English defenders had been reduced to two hired frigates and a single stout merchantman commanded by a resolute captain named Grove.[10]

Still the defenders pressed on and closed rapidly to within a quarter mile of the Dutch fleet as evening approached. Then, in an instant, "they came about by the wind and retired up the James." This was the maneuver Gardiner had hoped would lure the Dutch away from the Maryland ships. Evertsen, sensing the game had come to an end, ordered anchors weighed and an immediate pursuit of the king's ships.[11] Within minutes, the well practiced labors of getting underway having been completed, the five foremost Dutch vessels took up the chase with spirit. As the leading Dutch ship began to close to within firing range, the English guns opened. Amid the ensuing smoke and pandemonium, Captain Grove's ship ran aground, although, according to later reports, only after having given a good account of herself. Evertsen ignored the stranded merchantman and continued in hot pursuit of *Barnaby* and *Augustine*. The big armed merchantman could wait. For the moment, the overriding imperative was either to defeat or neutralize the king's surprisingly powerful men-of-war. With them out of the way, the Chesapeake Bay would become a Dutch lake. Neither Evertsen nor Benckes could forsee, however, just how difficult the achievement of that end could be.[12]

For three hours, the two elusive British warships managed to stay ahead of the pursuing Dutch, continuing the contest "with Great resolucon," while drawing the foe ever farther from the Maryland tobacco fleet.[13] Shortly after 7:00 P.M., however, Gardiner and Cotterell found themselves on the proverbial horns of a dilemma. Having seduced the main Dutch fleet away from the Maryland tobacco ships, they discovered that they had, in so doing, drawn the foe's attention and ships toward the mouth of the James. Simultaneously, they observed that Captain Grove's stranded ship, now apparently well to the rear of the Dutch line, appeared to have been refloated. With twilight coming on, Gardiner employed a tactical maneuver, the suddenness of which caught the Netherlanders completely by surprise.[14]

Hoping to rescue Grove and judging "that the Enemy (if he Checkt them not) would be in with our Merchant Shipps Rideing in the James before they could Gett from [the Dutch]," Gardiner suddenly tacked sharply and brought *Barnaby* directly across the line of enemy ships. With cool, adroit seamanship the English had executed the classic maneuver of "crossing the T," a tactic designed to bring one's full broadside to bear on the bow of a temporarily defenseless foe. For some unknown reason, Cotterell apparently failed to follow but continued toward the James. Evertsen, aware of the consequences of *Barnaby's* maneuver, immediately followed suit, tenaciously attempting to hang on to his elusive opponent. "They seeing that we began to overtake them," the Zeeland commander later wrote in *Swaenenburgh's* log, "one of their large ships broke away from the group, and fearing that he would reach the sea, we followed him." The Netherlanders "came up hard on him," firing as opportunity permitted.[15]

For the better part of an hour, Gardiner maintained a brave (albeit costly) defense against the entire Dutch squadron. His great mainmast and foretop were shattered, and his rigging was shot to tatters, yet he clung to a steadfast course for Grove's ship. Upon reaching her, he was not a little chagrined to discover her still aground and perfectly helpless. There was little to be done; Gardiner's only recourse now was to beat a retreat. Thus, about 8:15 P.M., he again succeeded in outmaneuvering his closest pursuer, *Swaenenburgh*. With "Courage and Conduct," as Governor Berkeley would later write in his praise, and beyond all hopes or expectations of those watching the fight from afar, Gardiner again successfully brought his ship hard about in the face of the pursuing fleet. This time he passed so close to the Zeeland flagship as to cut her wind and momentarily stall her progress. With this brief, slim advantage, Gardiner was able to disengage—and none too soon—his ship had been terribly savaged and was incapable of maintaining the fight any longer.[16]

Despite *Barnaby's* adroit maneuvers, diversionary tactics, and successful disengagement, the Dutch were by no means deterred from their original goal. They quickly came about, regained lost momentum, and pressed on toward the James. They again opened fire on the fleeing Englishmen, yet "due to the darkness, [but] mostly due to the shooting, and to the shallows of the bay, could not come alongside."[17]

By now, Captain de Witte had arrived with *Schaeckerloo* and the snaauw. Evertsen and Benckes could now afford to briefly shift their attention to mopping up the stranded armed merchantmen that dotted the Chesapeake before concentrating on the ships in the James. Twenty men were transferred to De Witte's ship and the snaauw, and sent in the growing darkness to secure three of the grounded merchantmen. Benckes, whose ship apparently occupied a forward position in the flotilla, also took advantage of the night to seize a prize. Masquerading as the Vice Admiral of the English fleet, he brought his ship alongside after two unsuccessful passes and stormed and captured a large enemy pinnace with little difficulty. Benckes then anchored in 18 feet of water near the shore.[18]

Concerned that "the enemy was still firing heavily upon us," even though night had fallen, Evertsen sought to come up with Benckes to discuss the situation. Ignorant of the shoally nature of the waters in which his fellow commander had anchored, or of his close proximity to shore, Evertsen sailed recklessly on toward the Amsterdammer. Suddenly, the *Swaenenburgh* shuddered, lurched, and ground to a halt on a sandbar. The Battle of Lynnhaven Bay had finally come to an end.[19]

For Virginia, the ordeal of invasion had only begun. The English might have counted the day's events as something of a victory if the portents for the immediate future had not appeared so bleak. On the positive side, a total of nearly 40 sail, from both the Virginia and Maryland tobacco fleets, had escaped "almost a Tide Way before the Enemy," and by nightfall had managed to remain out of the invader's hands.[20] The sacrifice, however, had been high: four armed merchantmen from the James had been captured; one of the Maryland fleet had been abandoned and left to drift on the Chesapeake. But most significantly, *Barnaby* and *Augustine* had been so badly mauled that they could no longer fight and were barely able to run. Indeed, they had been spared their deathblows only by the onset of darkness.[21]

Commander Evertsen and his men labored throughout the night to free *Swaenenburgh* from her imprisonment. With so many rich English merchantmen lying nearby, there was little time for leisure for men whose hearts and minds were fixed upon the spoils of war. Finally, their toils were rewarded when, with the "greatest difficulty," the ship was refloated. With the coming of morning, *Swaenenburgh* was once more ready for battle, and awaited only the floodtide to resume pursuit of the British ships on the James.[22]

While awaiting the tide, the Dutch were not idle. Sighting a large vessel adrift on the bay, and apparently unmanned, Evertsen ordered the snaauw to bring her in. The prize proved to be the tobacco pinnace *Pearl*, heavily laden with 600 hogsheads of the leaf. Shortly afterward, Captain Boes's sloop captured a large boat belonging to one Mr. Custis, who, "knowing no better than we were English," had sent her down to post letters for England with the outward-bound convoy.[23]

The Dutch set sail at 11:00 A.M. with the floodtide. Soon they "drew hard upon the King's Ships, so that it appeared that within a half hour we would be alongside, which was also noted [by the Englishmen] (as she could not sail above us)." Suddenly, the fleet was stalled by a dead calm. Dutch and English canvas alike hung limp and useless. But the ever-aggressive Cornelis Evertsen saw this as an opportunity to close the distance between himself and his prey. He ordered Boes's sloop and *Swaenenburgh*'s boat to put out oars and tow the flagship with cables up to the enemy. Before the English realized what was afoot, the enterprising Zeelander was already closing the distance between them with celerity. The alarmed English "did their best to get quit of us," Evertsen's log reports, and their best was good enough—but barely.[24]

Gardiner and Cotterell, at the end of the previous day's contest, had anchored near the mouth of the Elizabeth River. This stream was a moderate-sized tributary flowing from the south bank of the James near its mouth. Apparently Cotterell preferred flight to the fleet's protection and "deserted her merchantship." Gardiner, again faced with overwhelming odds, could do little but follow suit. Now both *Barnaby* and *Augustine* were forced to scurry into the Elizabeth and, probably like *Swaenenburgh*, towed by small boats under oars. Fate had chosen their refuge well, for the river was "very narrow and full of oyster banks," a waterway into which the Dutch, still without a local pilot, dared not venture. Moreover, the site was also a convenient location where the two hired warships could "Refitt wth Roapes & Sailes" in relative security.[25] On the other hand, the two vessels charged with the safety of the rich tobacco fleets were now entirely cut off from the James and their charges.

Raid on America

With their own unwitting assistance, Evertsen and Benckes had finally neutralized the only viable naval defense force on the Chesapeake. They had yet to win the cooperation of wind and tide. For, as the two Dutch commanders returned their attention to the pursuit of prizes on the James, contrary winds conspired against them. The difficulty was aggravated by the lack of local pilots: progress was now measured in yards rather than leagues. Toward evening, as the squadron picked its way upstream and approached the mouth of the Nansemond River (the second major waterway feeding into the James from the southern shore), misfortune again befell the fleet. Four ships ran aground almost simultaneously: Cornelis Evertsen's, Benckes's, Van Zijl's, and the ship of the late Hanske Fokkes. Though Evertsen's and Fokkes's ship were soon pulled off, the other two remained hard aground. Again the joint squadron was obliged to break off the hunt and come to anchor.[26]

As they prepared for another long night of labor to free their ships, the Dutch watched in disgust as eleven or twelve fat merchantmen slipped unhindered into the sanctuary of the Nansemond, "a very narrow and dangerous river running at full banks." Only a short distance upstream the ships came to anchor under the walls of an imposing earthen fort. For the moment, it made little difference that the Netherlanders were unaware that the fort was almost defenseless, being both poorly manned and badly armed, if, indeed, there were any cannon at all. Without pilots the raiders dared not enter the river even under the best conditions. The need for reliable local intelligence was underscored a short time later as they watched still more ships escape up the James, equally unharmed.[27]

Ironically, their enforced stay near the Nansemond was not without its benefits for the Dutch. During the evening, while efforts were underway to refloat the two stranded warships, a number of English prisoners taken from the recently captured merchantmen were interrogated. Much to Evertsen's and Benckes's delight two of the captives were familiar with the local waters and were willing to serve as pilots for the Dutch invaders. Thus, on the following morning, the two Netherlander commanders, having resolved to continue the pursuit by any means, set in motion an effort to hound the enemy tobacco fleet on the James "as high up as possible." Captain Boes of Amsterdam and De Witte of Zeeland were ordered to sail their shallow draft vessels upstream after the enemy while the rest of the Dutch squadron remained behind to assist and protect the still grounded warships.[28] Soon the cluster of anchored and stranded ships began to attract a steady stream of English deserters, many of whom had either been impressed into service against their wills, or opposed the Berkeley regime and its increasingly autocratic rule.

Among the first to arrive were several apprentice seamen who reported that among the men aboard the king's ships and their auxiliaries were many who had been pressed and that various vessels in the merchant fleet were being stripped for battle. On the following day, more deserters confirmed the story, adding that the English impressments were on a massive scale and that the "largest merchant ships were being unloaded to take on crews and guns, intending to come out after [the Dutch]."[29]

The intelligence brought in by the English deserters began to outline the somewhat ticklish position the invaders were now in. Boes and De Witte were upriver stalking merchant prizes. Two warships were still stranded and helpless. The bulk of the squadron was at anchor nearby, assisting the grounded ships and blockading the reach between the Nansemond and Elizabeth rivers. The Dutch had taken the precaution of positioning a lookout boat just below the Elizabeth to keep a watch on *Barnaby* and *Augustine*, which were presumably still up the river licking their wounds, and to protect the covey of prize ships at anchor or still aground farther down the bay. The Dutch forces were divided and fragmented. And while they little feared the English naval forces, both Evertsen and Benckes were aware that should Governor Berkeley be able to coordinate an attack from upriver by a fleet of armed merchantmen and an assault from the Elizabeth River on the Dutch rear, their position could prove precarious.

On Tuesday, July 15, the Dutch learned how vulnerable their lightly defended rear was when two English sloops attacked and captured the picket boat. Fortunately for the Dutch, the English failed to reach the fleet of prize vessels farther down before a response could be made. Informed of the attack, Evertsen and Benckes immediately agreed to dispatch the 25-gun *Suriname* down to protect the prizes and to assist several of the grounded vessels off should a rapid retreat prove necessary. Evertsen learned that the English were also quite capable of making good use of the element of surprise: "a good guard was not kept [aboard the picket boat] and the sloops were upon them before danger was sensed."[30]

The English sortie, combined with repeated intelligence and warnings of enemy preparations for a counter-attack, was not taken lightly by the Dutch command. Cognizant of Admiralty orders regarding the safety of the squadron, and sensible to the growing danger, Evertsen and Benckes decided to play safe. They dispatched orders upstream to Boes and De Witte to return to the main fleet anchorage with as many prizes as had already been taken. Prizes that may have run aground and could not readily be refloated were to be destroyed.[31]

Boes and De Witte were, in great measure unintentionally assisted in their mission of destruction by the English themselves. Although many ships managed to escape up the James, some as far as Jamestown, a number were far less fortunate. One large fluit had run aground during the helter-skelter of retreat and was set afire by her crew to prevent capture. Five others also stranded in the chase were abandoned so hastily that their crews could not destroy them; these awaited only the denouement. When orders reached Boes and De Witte, they were already hard at work refloating the largest of the grounded ships, the heavily-laden pinnace *Madras*. The prospect of prize money slipping through their fingers was apparently too much. The two Dutch captains sent the snaauw back down the James with news of the golden opportunity lying before them. As commanders of the expedition, Evertsen and Benckes would have received a healthy share of the prize money, but as officers responsible for the safety of the entire squadron, they wisely countered Boes's and De Witte's suggestion. The snaauw was sent back up the James with orders to assist in the refloating of only *Madras* and no others. The rest were to be burned.[32]

On Thursday, July 17, when Boes and De Witte returned with *Madras* in company, they were pleased to find Benckes's and Van Zijl's ships afloat. They reported that they had been unable to pull the other four merchantmen off, even though they had thrown an enormous quantity of tobacco overboard to lighten the ships. All had been burned as ordered. From prisoners taken during that operation it was learned that the English had destroyed five more of their own ships to prevent capture. Thus the toll of English shipping taken or destroyed on the James alone numbered eleven ships. Evertsen initially estimated that between 3,600 and 3,700 hogsheads of tobacco had been destroyed as a consequence, but later reduced the total to 3,050. There was undoubtedly a great deal more unreported that the British had destroyed. And though the Dutch returned with only one prize, she was a worthy exchange for the picket boat lost on July 15, for *Madras* was a London ship carrying 1,050 hogsheads of the leafy Tidewater gold—the richest vessel captured to date.[33]

With the Dutch squadron finally reunited and free to move at will, Evertsen and Benckes considered a preemptive strike against the king's ships in the Elizabeth or a raid on the merchantmen ensconced in the

Nansemond. The two English pilots who had successfully navigated Boes and De Witte up the James and back were again consulted. They were specifically asked whether "they saw any chance to bring our lightest ships into the Elizabeth River" to attack *Barnaby* and *Augustine*. The pilots replied that they were unfamiliar with the Elizabeth and that if the Dutch ran aground while going in, "there would be great danger of losing the ships." As for the Nansemond, they suggested that the river was simply too shallow for the Dutch warships, even the lightest among them, to enter. There were only thirteen feet of water over the bar at the mouth of the river, and the passage was barely two ship's lengths wide.[34]

After this disappointing conference, Evertsen met with another Englishman, a deserter who had just come in. From him he learned that while the fleet had been occupied on the James in refloating the two stranded warships, the Nansemond defenders had been busy felling trees and pushing them into the river to form a barrier against possible Dutch attack. If this was not sufficient discouragement, Evertsen was then told that a post had been sent to the York River, where a number of large merchantmen lay at anchor. They had been instructed to offload their cargoes and make ready for combat.[35] If that group were armed and sailed out of the York before the Dutch could reach the strategic Tail of the Horseshoe, there was the distinct possibility that Cornelis Evertsen and Jacob Benckes might find themselves cut off from retreat, or worse, locked within the James and assailable from all sides. The Netherlanders had long since spent their main asset, surprise, and would soon be in need of water; the British could draw at leisure on endless time and geography for their defeat.

If the Dutch hoped to escape with their winnings intact, it was clear that retreat from the Chesapeake was worthy of consideration. But it was to be a decision made from the vantage point of victory rather than defeat. No stigma would mark the raiders should they choose to depart, for they had achieved every objective outlined in their instructions, even though the Admiralty of Zeeland had not forseen their raids penetrating so deeply into Virginia. They had captured seven ships and thousands of hogsheads of tobacco, caused the destruction of ten more ships, and defeated and humiliated the Royal Navy in open battle. They had driven both the Virginia and Maryland tobacco fleets into hiding beneath empty defenses at Jamestown and on the Nansemond while operating among the intricate shoals of the Chesapeake Tidewater, handicapped by lack of knowledgeable pilots. And all of that was at a cost of three dead and twenty wounded. No, there could be no stigma attached to any decision to withdraw. Their mission had been accomplished in Virginia: all that remained was to determine their next objective and depart from Chesapeake Bay.

The following day, Friday, July 18, after having considered recent intelligence reports, Evertsen recorded in his log that "it was agreed and resolved to sail down the river with the prizes which had been taken, which lay in the mouth of the river. Then weighed and came to anchor within a mile of the prize."[36] There, while the squadron waited out the ebb tide and the coming of fair winds, the next hammer blow against English America began to gestate.

As it turned out, Evertsen's vantage point to the northwest of the prize flotilla was most fortuitously chosen, especially as the game of flying false colors continued to draw unwary English merchantmen into their hands. *Suriname* played it with great success while maintaining patrol below the prize ship anchorage. When one English vessel, *Benjamin* of London, Robert Cocdas master, sailed up the bay from the open sea, she was quickly snapped up by *Suriname* and taken prize along with her 500 hogsheads of tobacco. When Cocdas was questioned, he replied that he had not attempted to run as "he knew no better but that we were English."[37] Another ship was picked up soon afterwards in the James. After her master, a flinty Swede named Sander Sanderse, refused to cooperate with an interrogation, both he and his ship, a Swedish vessel from Staden, were held under suspicion of smuggling Dutch goods in exchange for 400 hogsheads of English tobacco.[38]

For all their promise of prize money, the capture of such vessels paled in comparison to the day's best catch, a vessel of neither size and force nor rich cargo. It was little more than a small ketch, or yawl carrying a few victuals and necessaries and about fifty hogsheads of tobacco. The little vessel was commanded by a resourceful commander named Samuel Davis. She did, however, count among her passengers several persons of great importance whose capture would directly influence the course of the Dutch campaign in America. The yawl had been bound from New York for the Chesapeake, where her passengers had hoped to join the homeward-bound convoy to England. Among their number was Captain James Carteret, bastard son of New Jersey Proprietor and Member of the Admiralty Sir George Carteret, and rebellious "president of the Country" of East Jersey. With him were his young bride of three months, Frances Delavall, daughter of the rich and powerful Thomas Delavall, New York Auditor General to the Duke of York, and Samuel Hopkins of Elizabethtown, New Jersey, professor, confidant, supporter, and co-conspirator in the rebellion of James Carteret.[39]

Had The Netherlands contrived to collect a party more inimical to the extant structure of England's colonial establishment in America, or more likely to benefit Evertsen's and Bencke's objectives, they could hardly have done any better. For upon the information supplied by a single member of this small party would hang the fate of England's control of the mid-Atlantic seaboard of North America.

12

ALL THEYR CRY WAS FOR NEW YORKE

The dramatic sequence of events that swept James Carteret and his accomplice Samuel Hopkins into the hands of their nation's mortal enemy began more than six years earlier when the seed of revolt against the Lords Proprietors of the infant colony of New Jersey sprouted. That growing hostility was rooted in classic, bitter conflicts over land, political representation, and taxation—all curiously similar antecedents to a revolution that would engulf the colony a century later. Dissension first erupted in the newly settled region known as the Monmouth Patents, which included such key settlements as Middletown and Shrewsbury. The settlers of this region, many of whom had migrated from Connecticut shortly after the English capture of New Amsterdam in 1664, had secured their patents not from the Lords Proprietors of New Jersey, with whom legal claim to the area could lay, but from the first English governor of neighboring New York, Richard Nicholls. By right of Nicholl's patents, offered in the wake of the expulsion of the Dutch colonial administration in New Amsterdam (renamed New York), the settlers were authorized to pass their own laws and were to be free of government taxation for a period of seven years. As early as 1667, they convened their own assembly at Portland Point (later called the Highlands), at which they refused to publish or to fully acknowledge the laws of the duly authorized New Jersey General Assembly or to swear allegiance to the Lords Proprietors of that colony. They were at first, however, anxious to assure the colony governor, Philip Carteret, cousin to Sir George, and his Council that they meant no willful contempt by their independent actions. Yet conflict seemed inevitable. When the

General Assembly appointed commissioners to collect assessed taxes and to determine the true positions of the settlers in such places as Middletown and Monmouth, the dissidents denied them every assistance. The settlers then renounced their earlier determination to remain aloof from all such governmental claims to taxation. In response, and wishing to set an example, the General Assembly declared at a session held in November 1671 that the two sinks of resistance, Middletown and Shrewsbury, were to be held guilty of contempt of the lawful authority of the province.[1]

The village of Elizabethtown soon became a hotbed of opposition to the proprietary and a center of open resistance to the payment of quit rents. Governor Carteret steadfastly refused to negotiate and found himself facing potential anarchy and rapidly withering support for his proprietary authority. On March 26, 1672, an assembly of largely unauthorized deputies from every major settlement in the colony convened to address the situation, but the governor and his council refused to recognize its validity and suppressed its records. The crisis intensified, and in May another assembly was convened "without the knowledge, approbation or consent" of Governor Carteret or the Council. Though the convention representatives from Elizabethtown, Newark, Woodbridge, Piscataway, and Bergen, failed in their efforts to chart a unified course of action, the flames of revolt were fanned. And nothing served better to widen the schism between government and governed than the delegates' election of their own chief executive, who was promptly given the grandiose title of President of the Country. That individual was Captain James Carteret, illegitimate son of the proprietor.[2]

At first blush James Carteret's credentials appeared considerable. Aside from his personal lineage, which, it was hoped by the dissidents, would soften the proprietor's and governor's stance, Carteret had been a captain in both the public and private marines of England. Only the year before he had been appointed Landgrave at Carolina. He was intelligent, had studied "the moralities," and was a man of obvious breeding. Under different circumstances he might have risen to a position of considerable import. Unfortunately, young Carteret was a man of little principle and responsibility and even less character. He was deemed by some to be "very profligate," enchanted with the virtues of demon rum, and had undoubtedly achieved his Carolina appointment through his father's influence as proprietor of that colony. And Carteret had a way of drawing men of a similar ilk to him—men such as "professor" Samuel Hopkins, a strong, opportunistic proponent of the antiproprietary movement in New Jersey.

Raid on America

James Carteret arrived in New Jersey during the chaotic summer of 1671. Within a short time he was being flattered and courted by colony dissidents, and his support of their cause in New Jersey blossomed. On May 14, 1672, when the dissident colonial convention failed to achieve an accord with Governor Carteret over quit rents, James Carteret found himself elected "President" of the colony. Though the move had been an obvious attempt to secure influence with the established authority by the convention members, Captain Carteret was neither shy nor slow in asserting his newfound powers—especially for personal gain. He immediately began to lay claim and title to lands allegedly granted to him by his father, without offering proof of his assertions. To insure his ownership, he imprisoned his father's officers who were sent to repudiate his claims, and then confiscated their property. The role that Samuel Hopkins may have played in these affairs is uncertain, but he soon took up residence with Carteret in Elizabethtown and supported the dissident faction in New Jersey with zest.[3]

As the schism deepened, the governor's Council advised Philip Carteret to sail for England, resecure confirmation of his authority, and muster whatever support he could to strike back. On July 1, 1672, he embarked for London, leaving as deputy governor one John Berry, who was himself a recent immigrant in the colony, having arrived from Connecticut in 1669. Berry was barely able to muster even feeble support from his hometown of Bergen, much less maintain control of a chaotic colony.[4] While in England, however, Carteret, with the support of Berry and the Council at home in America, easily secured confirmation of his authority among the Lord Proprietors and the Duke of York. York immediately informed Nicholl's successor, Governor Francis Lovelace, that the insurgent claims based on Nicholl's patents would not be received with favor and should no longer be supported. Thus, all claims by settlers to lands in the Monmouth Patents were now without foundation. King Charles II placed the final nail in the coffin lid of rebellion by directing Deputy Governor Berry to publish the terms of the proprietary government with which he was temporarily entrusted, and directed that universal obedience to the Proprietors be observed. Berry ordered the terms published in May 1673, and the long, bloodless insurrection that brought New Jersey to the brink of anarchy evaporated overnight.[5]

James Carteret's heady flirtation with power, and those of his associate Samuel Hopkins, were at an end. Cognizant of young Carteret's family ties, Berry elected to evict the erstwhile "President" from the colony rather than imprison him. That the exile fled to New York where he might find refuge in his father-in-law's house came as no

surprise to anyone. Thomas Delavall, the Duke of York's Auditor, however, apparently did not approve of the embarrassing presence of his
new son-in-law. By early July, Captain Carteret's welcome in New York
was also at an end,[6] and with his wife and loyal supporter Samuel
Hopkins (who was equally unwelcome in New Jersey and New York),
he embarked for the Chesapeake, some said to secure passage to the
Carolinas and others to join the convoy to England.[7]

For the colony of New York, the exile of the dissidents was to prove
most unfortunate, for one of the two proved to be a veritable Judas.

When the Dutch took Captain Davis's vessel and her notorious passengers on Chesapeake Bay on July 18, they apparently overlooked the
importance of both Carteret and Hopkins. Despite later testimony that
at least one of the pair turned traitor immediately and pointed the
raiders toward New York, Dutch records suggest otherwise. Evertsen's
log clearly details the capture of James Carteret, but mentions nothing
to suggest an immediate appreciation for the importance of the prisoners. Yet the taking of the son, even an illegitimate one, of so highly
placed an Englishman as George Carteret, would certainly not have
been ignored. Indeed, his detention would almost certainly have been
assured, if not noted in records and communications. Whatever revelations the former "President" of East Jersey may have made will probably never be known, but subsequent events suggest that he made good
use of his charm while concealing his identity. On July 21, Carteret
and his wife were set ashore in Virginia. Samuel Hopkins, however,
was detained aboard the fleet—or, perhaps, elected to remain.[8]

Whatever his shortcomings as a leader, Carteret may have proved
useful to the Dutch in opening communication with Berkeley's forces
ashore to begin a prisoner exchange. On the evening of his release, the
boat that had ferried him ashore returned with seven Dutch sailors,
five of whom were wounded. All had been taken during the July 15
English sortie against the guard boat. Also aboard was an English major who had come to arrange for the prisoner transfer. Although the
evidence is circumstantial at best that Carteret assisted in establishing
communications between the two contending forces, the sequence of
events suggest he may have been instrumental. The Dutch informed the
major, however, that the English prisoners would be released only after
the remainder of the guard boat's crew, still ashore, was released. The
seamen were freed and rowed out to *Swaenenburgh* the following day.
Less than forty-eight hours later, as the Dutch fleet prepared to depart,
the majority of the English prisoners aboard were sent ashore in Colonel Custis's boat, that vessel being deemed of no further use.[9]

Raid on America

Before the Netherlanders could depart the Chesapeake, there were myriad details to attend to—the prizes had to be put in order, crews were transferred, and repairs made. Typical of the work carried out was the extensive carpentry necessary to repair the prize pinnace *Pearl*, which had lost her rudder and loosened a number of rudder braces as a result of grounding during the recent battle. There were also practical decisions to be made, such as what was to be done with the Swedish Captain Sanderse and his ship. After much consultation, Evertsen and Benckes decided that, as "there was insufficient good evidence to convict him of smuggling, he was released on his oath . . . that neither his ship, nor any of the same loaded cargo belonged either to the English or to the Netherlanders but only to Stade and the owners there."[10]

Notwithstanding all such considerations, on July 21 the Dutch fleet raised anchor to allow "the ships to drift a piece to get out of the straits" of the lower James. Though final departure was temporarily stymied by a driving rain squall, on July 22 the squadron and its covey of prizes sailed triumphantly out of the river, sweeping along with it a small tobacco-laden ship from the upper Chesapeake that had blundered headlong into the squadron's progress. On Thursday, July 24, the train reached the entrance of the bay, rounded the treacherous shoals of Cape Charles, and "took a northeast course under shortened sail" toward the Delaware. Trailing along in the prize fleet was Captain Davis's sloop with James Carteret's cohort, Samuel Hopkins, still aboard and undoubtedly seething over his recent string of bad luck.[11]

Owing to the overwhelming strength of Governor Berkeley's land forces, neither Evertsen nor Benckes had been foolish enough to hazard a landing on Virginia shores for water during the recent raid. Indeed, the fact that they had confined their depredations to Virginia's waters had been the singular saving grace in Berkeley's otherwise grim report to the crown. But fresh water was now of paramount importance and played heavily in the Netherlanders' subsequent course of action. A visit to the Delaware River was next on the agenda, "should it be possible." The two commanders were wary of the Delaware, however, for the lack of knowledgeable pilots made that estuary no less treacherous or difficult to navigate than the Chesapeake.[12]

With favorable breezes, the Dutch squadron and its train of prizes arrived off Cape Henlopen on the evening of July 25, and by midday of the 26th was fully abreast of Delaware Bay. But as it

was understood from various people who had sailed before in the South [Delaware] River that it was very difficult to get water there, and that the ships would have to travel a good distance, and that the river was full of shoals and sand banks, it was resolved to continue on to New Nether-

land [New York] and the Staten Island, where, it is said, water was good
and easily got.[13]

Propelled by weak southerly winds and always within sight of the
New Jersey coast, the fleet pressed on until the evening of July 28,
when the entrance to New York Bay was sighted. By the following
evening the squadron had come to snug anchor in 13 fathoms of unfamiliar water off Sandy Hook, New Jersey, a low, sandy peninsula near
the entrance to the bay.[14]

The presence of the Dutch fleet on the shores of a former Netherlands colony quickly aroused the long-smouldering fires of patriotism
and support in the hearts of many former Dutch citizens of New Netherland. That night, several farmers from the town of New Utrecht on
Long Island and from Staten Island made their way out to the fleet and
boarded the Zeeland flagship *Swaenenburgh*. Commander Evertsen
listened attentively as his former countrymen "complained bitterly
about the hard rule of the English." They were tired and fed up "with
the oppression of such as ruled the town and trade," and spoke long-
ingly of their wish to again be governed by the States General. He
listened even more closely when they reported that the governor of New
York, Francis Lovelace, was not in the fort that guarded the town. In
fact, the fort was so poorly garrisoned and its guns so "badly postured
on the battery" that it might well be taken by storm.[15]

The interest of the two Dutch squadron commanders was piqued. It
was one thing to listen to the well-intentioned pleas of simple farmers
who had probably never been admitted to the fort, but cold, hard
intelligence was another matter. It was apparently at this point that
Evertsen summoned Captain Davis and Samuel Hopkins into his cabin
for a long-delayed interrogation. The commander demanded that Davis, who had recently been at New York, "tell them the true state of the
place."[16] He promised that if the captain told the truth, he would return
his vessel and all that was in it. As Davis began to speak, an English
prisoner who had not been cartelled, one Nathan Gould by name,
stood near the cabin door, eavesdropping. Despite the promises made to
him, the captain, aware that the fate of New York hung in the balance,
attempted to mislead the Dutch by informing them that in the space of
three hours the city's governor could raise 5,000 men and 150 pieces of
ordnance "mounted fit for seruice upon the wall."[17] He coolly pointed
out that the city, having recently received a substantial supply of arms
and ammunition from the Duke of York, along with intelligence concerning Dutch designs against New York, was indeed in a "very good
condicôn" to withstand an assault.[18]

Unconvinced by Davis' patriotic but less than masterful effort to dissuade them, the Netherlanders turned their attentions and questions to Samuel Hopkins. Embittered by the recent turn of events in New Jersey that had obliged him to depart with Carteret, he "did voluntarily declare to ye Dutch that what the said Dauis had informed was altogether false." New York, stated the traitor with unvarnished resolution, was in no condition to defend itself against the Dutch. The fort contained barely 60 to 80 men, and it would take at least three or four days to raise even 300 to 400 men. There were only 30 to 36 pieces of ordnance mounted upon the fort walls, and, he added, "a shot or two would shake them out of their Carriages." Indeed, it was later reported, that "ye carriages of their great gunns [were] out of repaire, & rotten & [there were] noe plattforms to play ye gunns upon." The Dutch farmers had been quite correct in noting that Governor Lovelace was not in the fort. In fact, declared Hopkins, he was not even in the province, but on a visit to Governor Winthrop, the chief executive of the neighboring colony of Connecticut. The effects of the traitor's detailed revelations were dramatic. No longer would Dutch objectives be simply to water and conduct a bit of raiding and foraging. Now, "all theyr cry was for New Yorke."[19]

A council of war was immediately convened to weigh the virtues and dangers of conducting a direct attack. Despite the alleged weaknesses in English manpower and artillery and the promised support, or at worst neutrality, of the Dutch population, the former Dutch entrepôt posed some tactically serious and potentially difficult obstacles to the invaders. Situated at the extreme southern tip of Manhattan and flanked on the east by the East River and on the west by the North River, New York had grown considerably since its streets were first laid out seventeen years earlier under Dutch control, and so had its defenses. In 1656 the town comprised 120 houses, a thousand inhabitants, and a large garrison. By 1673, it contained more than 300 buildings, over 2,500 citizens, mostly Dutch, and a very respectable defense complex.[20]

In many respects, New Amsterdam, as it was called prior to its subjugation by the English, was a picturesque little port that had failed to degenerate in charm as it expanded in size. Its houses were still handsomely constructed of plain and glazed brick or red stone. Their roofs were still predominantly sharp-peaked and covered with black and red tiles. "Its aspect," remarked one antiquarian musing over its quaint appearance, "was diversified by hill and dale. Its eminences were clustered with buildings, and the whole formed a delightful perspective from the water."[21]

The fulcrum of its defenses was Fort James, a work originally erected in 1635 by Governor Van Zwiller. Neglected by his successor, Governor Kieft, the works were repaired and surrounded by a strong wall during the Stuyvesant administration. Situated on high ground at the southernmost point of Manhattan Island, the heavy stone fortification was square in shape, with four large bastions projecting from each corner. It possessed two gates, the main being near the northeast bastion, and its walls normally mounted 42 cannons.[22]

Within the confines of the fort, several stone buildings of some import had been erected. Principal among these was the Reformed Dutch Church (Gereformeerde Kerk), begun by Governor Kieft in 1642 and completed five years later. It was, in fact, the first church established in the New Netherland colony. From its bell tower, which was visible above the walls (and consequently presented a superb range marker or target), the bell could ring the summons to church—or to arms—with astonishing resonance. Adjacent to the church was the "corps de garde," or barracks for the garrison. And beside that was the gaol. Also within the walls was one of the nerve centers of the colony, the governor's house, a large stone building 100 feet long, 50 feet wide, and 24 feet high, with two broad walks on either side. The colony secretary's office was also within the fort near the north gate, at the northeast bastion. The weekly post rider was dispatched to Hartford, Boston, and other points along the way from this office with mails, government dispatches, and the latest news.[23]

To the east of the fort were the public wharf and harbor, built by the burghers of the city in 1658. Here coursed the life blood of trade as vessels were loaded and unloaded, paid their duties, and gave the town its reason for being. The harbor, one of the first of its kind in America, had been constructed specifically to accommodate and protect vessels and small craft of all types against the elements, and to facilitate their loading and unloading. During winter weather, barks were occasionally stationed there to secure the sanctuary from floating ice packs, for which service the larger vessels paid an annual fee of "one beaver . . . small in proportion."[24] Immediately to the rear of the harbor were situated the magazine and public store houses, in earlier times the Pack-huysen, or warehouses, of the Dutch West India Company, the "lords patroons" of the city.[25]

To the north of the public store houses was situated the Great Dyke, a canal that divided the upper town from the lower town. Immediately north of this canal, and overlooking the East River, was the State House, or City Hall, the second nerve center of the town. Originally constructed at the expense of the West India Company by Governor

Kieft in 1642 as a tavern, the building was granted to the city as a municipal center. Here were to be found the symbols and artifacts of judicial administration, the town stocks, the whipping post, and the wooden horse, tools for the punishment of major and minor transgressions of the law. And here too, every day at half an hour before sunset, the town drummer beat out his summons to the guard to assemble before City Hall. In a well-established ceremony, the guard then proceeded to the north end of town to officially lock the city gate at sunset. It would be opened at first light the next morning, but without the same ritual.[26]

The State House was fronted on its water side by a strong, half-moon-shaped redoubt, or *rondeel*, projecting over the water and armed with several cannon. A second rondeel lay some distance north of the first, and a third north of that. All were built of stone specifically for the defense of the East River approach to the town, and all were connected by a curtain of stone. The curtain was designed to defend the town not only against the depredations of man, but against the tides and sea as well. Near the northernmost rondeel, the city wall began. Constructed of earth thrown up from a moat dug in 1653 and running across the island from the East River to the North River, the works were anchored on both ends by strong wooden blockhouses. The moat was four to five feet deep and ten or eleven feet wide at its base, and somewhat sloping at the bottom. On its lip was constructed a closely connected line of pallisades extending alongside the wall and also running from river to river. The city gate perforated the center. From here the Broad Way ran south to the fort, and north into the countryside. Another road ran alongside the southern base of the moat-wall and pallisades, intersecting the Broad Way at the city gate. This path became known simply as the Wall Street.[27]

In sum, the physical defenses of New York appeared imposing. Unfortunately for its English defenders, appearances cruelly belied reality, for the city was far from prepared to meet a major assault. And the man charged with its defensive preparedness, Governor Francis Lovelace, was absent and unaware of the menace to his city and colony.

The Dutch war council was convinced, given the correctness of Hopkins' report, that a successful effort against Fort James could be made. Therefore, they resolved to attack the fort the next day, and if possible to capture it. The Netherlanders' objectives were, in that single meeting, irrevocably altered. They no longer intended to merely raid, plunder, and ruin. They meant to conquer, regain, and again rule their North American colonies.[28]

The first move necessary before they could implement their plans was to allay the fears of the Dutch population by securing their trust and favor. It was imperative that they wean away from the English any support that might be forthcoming. They hoped for their assistance, but the council of war would be content with their simple neutrality in the battle that would soon be joined. Thus, it was decided that Evertsen and Benckes send a letter to the citizenry of the town. It began,

> To the good residents of the City of New York, Their High Mightinesses, the lords of the States General of the United Netherlands, and his Serene Highness, the lord Prince of Orange, etc., having sent this group of ships of war (which you see lying within sight of the city of New Amsterdam and its related fort), in order to wreck damage upon the enemies of the aforementioned High Mightiness; Thus it is by this means we wish to make known to you how we plan as quickly as possible to become master of the fort, presently called James and the city of New York, but before we proceed thus most rigorously we wish to inform the reader that we do not intend to bring harm to anyone who voluntarily submits to the aforementioned High Mightinesses, under whom, before this, you lived so peacefully, but to the refusal to do so we shall make use of such means as we shall judge best. Please do not think that we see any difficulty in overmastering the fort at short notice, but due to the affection we have for many devout residents whom we would not wish to harm, so have we desired to make our views known to them so that they can protect themselves from harm, because if we are obliged to strike the land with our crews, it is to be feared that this will be done to the disadvantage of many good residents, who are, to this end, kindly requested to persuade the Governor to turn over the fort and city to us forthwith, to which end we shall send a letter to the Governor tomorrow.[29]

The letter was dispatched early the next morning and entrusted to the hands of a simple farmer from Long Island. All that remained was to administer the coup de grâce.[30]

13

STUCK IN THE MUZZLE OF THE CANNON

Francis Lovelace was an affable, good-natured fellow, moderate in his politics; he was a generous High Church Anglican, noble of mind and tolerant of most religious creeds. As the governor of New York, however, he was, as one chronicler aptly put it, "a follower in beaten paths, rather than a trail blazer." And as a military commander, he was totally incompetent.[1] By the summer of 1673, Lovelace had been chief executive of the former Dutch city of New Amsterdam, and the colony it dominated, for five years, but during that time his accomplishments were as limited as his leadership was insipid. To his credit, Lovelace had been a supporter of shipbuilding and the colony's maritime trade and had tried to secure a printer and press for the benefit of the province. Both efforts had failed miserably. When major issues of substance arose, he was but a shuffler content to fall back on established political protocol and the tactics of procrastination—especially when it came to military preparedness.

In 1669, his first crisis in office erupted among the English towns of Long Island over many of the same issues that had caused upheaval in New Jersey. The most serious problem arose when various townships asserted in unison that they possessed the right to annually elect their own legislators. Some even challenged the very commission by which Lovelace held his office. As in New Jersey, the issues of taxation, representation, and land ownership formed the core of conflict. In 1670, that contention was nearly brought to a head by a tax levied to pay for the needed repair of Fort James. Lovelace was soon fending off serious opposition from such towns as Jamaica, Flushing, and Hempstead, which had declared the assizes to be in direct conflict with British law and the citizenry's right to elected representation. By 1672, and the outbreak of war with the United Provinces of the Netherlands, the fort still lacked the necessary repairs. The governor, who had begged off meeting the dissension head on, was again moved to secure funds. This time, however, he compromised and requested not a tax, but a voluntary contribution from each town to pay for the needed work. The English settlers of Long Island were disgruntled that their monies were to be used almost entirely for the improvement of the defenses for the city of New York, whose population was primarily Dutch and who did little to support the war effort. Predictably, their response was negative.[2]

Dissension among the English colonists continued to increase. The towns of Long Island complained that they were taxed more heavily than those of New England—and without benefit of representation in court by deputies. Many claimed that they were forced to comply with unfair laws imposed by officials who insulted and threatened them. Some towns even sought to be transferred to the jurisdiction of neighboring Connecticut or to be made free corporations.[3] And throughout the maelstrom of discontent, Francis Lovelace and the English citizenry of the colony of New York, wrapped up in their own bickering, failed to tend to their defenses.

The Declaration of War against the United Provinces was not published in English America until May 26, 1672, and New York would not learn of the outbreak until June. On the 27th of that month, Governor Lovelace published a proclamation in accordance with an edict issued by the king prohibiting the departure of ships from New York unless they sailed in company, and then only on specified dates. Worried, perhaps, about the effect the news might elicit from the Dutch population of New York City, he delayed posting the declaration of war at City Hall and on the main gate of Fort James. For the next six months the colony continued on as normal: no Dutch army or navy appeared to wrest control of the colony from England, and a false sense of security enveloped the office of the chief executive. Efforts to improve the state of military preparedness were paid lip service, but nothing more.[4]

Then, on January 22, 1673, on the occasion of the official opening of weekly postal service between New York City and Boston—one of the few bright accomplishments of his administration—Lovelace informed Governor Winthrop of Connecticut that reports from Virginia had come in stating that the Dutch had dispatched upwards of 40 well-fitted ships to the West Indies. If such information was to be relied on, he suggested, "it will be high time for us to buckle on our armor." Unfortunately, both Lovelace and his council were obliged to flounder about in the dark for specific information on enemy motions, for, owing to the war, no ship had arrived in his colony from England in a year, though 7 or 8 had reached Boston, and 50 or 60 had arrived in Virginia. Thus, New York was obliged to rely on second hand, stale intelligence.[5] It scarcely mattered, however, for despite his manful talk, Lovelace still did little to improve defenses.

Throughout the early months of 1673, the colony suffered from frequent invasion scares. In March, while visiting Westchester, Lovelace was summoned back to New York City because of a rumor then current suggesting impending attack by a hostile battle squadron. Captain John Manning, smuggler and English spy in New Amsterdam during the Dutch rule and now Sheriff of New York, had been left in command of Fort James in the governor's absence. Manning was apparently made nervous by the rumors and half-truths that floated about the city, and his occasional alarm was heartily scoffed at. When Lovelace returned to the city in haste from Westchester, he determined the cause to be "one of Manning's 'larrums.'"[6]

Invasion scares filtered down from the north as well. When Thomas Delavall visited the colony outpost on the upper Hudson River at Albany (where he owned considerable property), he sent a messenger to Manhattan. The fellow arrived with wild tales of impending French invasion from the Canadian frontier. With everyone apparently forgetting that, in this war, the French were England's allies, the tales spread rapidly. One particular rumor caused panic among many "credulous women," who were restrained from flight only by their governor's presence and calm demeanor.[7] Though he displayed fear of neither French or Dutch, Lovelace prudently summoned to New York 350 English troops stationed at outposts on both the North River and on the Delaware—only to dispose of them when the purported crisis was over. Fort James was now garrisoned with only 80 soldiers.[8]

Lovelace's confidence in the colony's safety was undoubtedly bolstered by the failure of the frequent alarms to materialize into actual attacks: perhaps he sincerely doubted that there was any danger at all. Whatever his reasons may have been not to move aggressively on behalf of the colony's defense, the governor was obviously not worried about the remote possibility of attack. Nor did he see any harm in leaving the colony to visit with his neighboring governor of Connecticut, John Winthrop. In late July 1673, he set off for Hartford, accompanied by the colony secretary and three servants, to confer with Winthrop on business related to the recently established postal route between New

York and Massachusetts Bay. He could not have picked a more inappropriate time to leave the colony, for it was precisely at that moment, when New York was without its chief executive, that Cornelis Evertsen and Jacob Benckes appeared off Sandy Hook.[9]

The approach of the Dutch fleet was discovered on July 28, well before it had come to anchor off Staten Island. Indeed, it was Thomas Lovelace, the governor's brother, who had scurried "against tide, through a swelling sea" in a log canoe to bring the terrible news to Fort James. There he found, in his brother's absence, Captain Manning in charge as acting governor, seconded by Captains Dudley Lovelace and John Carr. The latter had, until recently been in charge of the defense of the Delaware region, but had stayed on in New York when his troops were returned after the last alarm. Thomas Lovelace's report was sketchy but frightening. Half a dozen large ships—more than had been seen at one time in these waters in years—had been sighted from Sandy Hook. And there was every reason to suspect that more were coming up.[10]

The arrival of the enemy, to whom it was immediately supposed the ships belonged, caught Manning at a particularly bad moment: "there was neither Bedd, Spade, Handspike or other material" to be had in the fort. Many of the heavy guns mounted on the walls were pointed toward land, not the sea, and "the platformes and carriages were alsoe Badd, either the carriages broke or they could not bring them to pass againe."[11] Beyond perhaps half a dozen guns, effective firepower was almost nonexistent.

To his credit, Manning did his utmost to make the best of a bad situation. A pinnace was immediately dispatched toward Sandy Hook to substantiate the intelligence brought in by Thomas Lovelace. All available troops in New York City, approximately 90 in number, were ordered into the fort. All seamen in port were directed to board their ships in the harbor. Provisions, beer, liquor, and "other necessarys" to withstand a siege were brought in. Warrants were issued to Lieutenant Willet and Coronet Doughty to draw up their troops to the town of Utrecht and along the coast "to make discovery or give resistance, and to send down an officer to the [Long Island] ferry to attend orders." Though Manning was perfectly aware of the unsympathetic views of the large Dutch population of the city, and of the dissatisfaction and animosity of the English settlers on Long Island toward the Lovelace administration, he sought to raise whatever reinforcements he could in the countryside. Warrants were issued to the officers of the various militia units on Long Island "to get their companies together and immediately repair to the garrison." At the same time another order was dispatched to one Disborough of Mamoroneck "to press Horse and man to go to Hartford" to inform Governor Lovelace of the situation.[12] If the governor could be warned and the neighboring province of Connecticut stirred to come to New York's assistance there might be a fair chance of holding out.

Late on the evening of July 28, it was reported that the Dutch fleet now numbered nineteen ships. Morale in the garrison plummeted. The degenerating situation, one defender later reported, "did so bereave our men of their wonted liveliness and vigor that in all that night there was little or nothing done in the way of preparation for an enemy." By the following morning, a total of 21 sail could be counted in the lower bay.[13]

Manning again dispatched a call for reinforcements, but his efforts were largely in vain, as only ten or twelve "town livers" joined the garrison. He continued to bring in provisions, and to carry in all ladders found in the town to deny the enemy a ready means of storming the walls by land. It was obvious to all of the defenders that the Dutch citizens of New York would remain "neuter," but many still nourished hope of reinforcements from Long Island. Oddly, Manning apparently made no attempt, even now, to man his guns, carriages, or platforms.[14]

On the afternoon of July 29, when several giant frigates glided through the Narrows and came to anchor under Staten Island, the entire town stood enthralled "in a strange hurly-burly" by the waterside. Few citizens or soldiers slept well that evening. Some townsfolk spent the time in moving their goods out of the city, while many English citizens thought "no place so safe for their storage as the fort." A strong guard was set at the fort and beacons were fired to warn those still unaware of the impending danger. Apparently, Manning failed to attend to the protection of other areas of the city defenses, preferring to reserve his limited manpower for the walls of Fort James. That night, a party of Dutch saboteurs from the city spiked the guns in the rondeel near City Hall.[15]

On Wednesday morning, the garrison at Fort James prepared "for a brush" with the enemy, though the fleet spread before them under the red, white, and blue "Prince" flag of the United Provinces was the largest ever seen in the harbor. Rumors had been freely circulating about the fort, but by far the most chilling story was that there were as many as 3,000 men aboard the warships. Not a few of the defenders must have wondered to themselves when Governor Lovelace and the hoped-for reinforcements from Long Island would arrive—or indeed whether they would arrive at all.[16]

Stuck in the Muzzle of the Cannon

Across the waters, the Dutch fleet patiently awaited the flood tide to carry it within firing range of the fort. Aboard each ship, the principal activity focused upon preparations for the assault on Manhattan Island. The 600 troopers selected for the landing, a mixture of Dutch and expatriot English marines, were well-seasoned and capable of working efficiently together. Their commander, Captain of Marines Anthony Colve, was equal to the quality of his men. He was a soldier of considerable experience on both land and sea, and well-chosen for the task ahead.[17]

The delay caused by the tides provided the expedition commanders with an appropriate moment to formally extend the official demand for surrender to the governor of Fort James. Thus, Evertsen and Benckes dispatched a sloop with a trumpeter to the fort to call for English capitulation.

"My Lord," read the demand,

> The ships of war, which presently lay within sight of Your Excellency, have been sent by their High Mightinesses the Lords of the States General of the United Netherlands and his Serene Highness the lord Prince of Orange, etc., to wreck damage upon their enemies; to that end we send Your Excellency this missive, as well as our trumpeter, to the end that You on sight of this shall hand over this fort, presently called James, promising good quarter, and in absence of same that we shall be required to take immediate action on both water and on land as we shall judge to be of best service to their aforementioned High Mightinesses.
> —Cornelis Evertsen the Younger. Jacob Benckes.[18]

Even as the Dutch flag of truce pushed off for Fort James with the surrender demand, Captain Manning was launching a campaign of obfuscation designed to forestall the enemy until Governor Lovelace or the hoped-for reinforcements arrived. He dispatched his own flag of truce to the enemy fleet. About midday, Ensign Thomas Lovelace, Captain John Carr, and John Sharpe, the English envoys from the fort, boarded *Swaenenburgh*.

"What ship are you and by whose order have you come into the river that belongs to the Duke of York?" they demanded.

"You can see very well from the flags and ships who we are," replied the Dutch commander with severity. "We have come to bring the country back under obedience to their High Mightinesses the Lords States General, and his Serene Highness the lord Prince of Orange under whose government this once was."[19]

It became immediately apparent to the three Englishmen that these were not simply Dutch capers, as they first believed, but were "commissioned by the State to make spoil where they could." The war had, indeed, come to New York. The envoys stiffly asked to see Evertsen's commission.[20]

Perhaps insulted by the insinuation that he was little more than a privateer, Cornelis Evertsen replied haughtily that his commission "was stuck in the muzzle of the cannon, which they would quickly learn if the fort was not handed over." Even as he spoke, the envoys noted with consternation, *Swaenenburgh* weighed anchor and set sail with the entire fleet, bound directly for Fort James.[21]

Ashore, Captain Manning received the Dutch trumpeter with hospitality, treating him with "meat, drink, and wine, and such accommodations" as would delay for two or three hours either his departure or the enemy's approach. Only then was he given the captain's reply and permission to return to the fleet.[22] When the trumpeter finally boarded *Swaenenburgh* some time later, Evertsen perused the captain's communique with some disdain. Manning would not answer the Dutch surrender demand until Lovelace, Carr, and Sharpe had been safely set ashore. Evertsen was not amused by the blatant effort at procrastination. He showed the letter to the three envoys and then informed them—as if they could not already see—that he was bringing the squadron "close under the fort." With the tide being fair, his intentions were painfully obvious. Unnerved, the Englishmen begged the commander to refrain from using hostile force until they could bring a letter from Manning.[23] Evertsen grudgingly agreed to the request, but warned them that they must return within half an hour, "or we should, in absence of same, begin to act as we judged best." To emphasize his meaning, he turned the hourglass up. Lovelace, Carr, and Sharpe retired to their boat with celerity.[24]

The English troops in Fort James could not help but be intimidated by the powerful armada drawn up before them. When the Dutch fleet had drawn up close to Nooten Island some time earlier, they had cried: "Let us fire! Let us fire!" but had been restrained.[25] Now, as the squadron closed in and dropped anchor in a half-moon formation "not a Musquet Shot before the fort," the defenders were presented with a brief but golden opportunity to wreak great havoc upon the Zeeland flagship.[26] *Swaenenburgh*, it seemed, had come to anchor in a severe eddy, somewhat behind the crescent line of warships. For some time she struggled to hold herself steady abeam, but despite all measures was practically powerless to keep from turning dizzily about in circles. Fortunately for Evertsen, Manning was not a man of quick decision, and the guns of the fort remained quiet. For the Dutch, however, the incident was disconcerting. Evertsen himself later admitted that had the enemy guns opened fire, they would have inflicted great damage upon his ship. But the error in anchorage was rectified and *Swaenenburgh* was warped off a bit into the steady tidal currents, where she joined the other vessels in formation.[27]

Captain Manning continued his efforts to forestall the inevitable. Before the half-hour deadline was up, John Sharpe was again dispatched to *Swaenenburgh* with a letter requesting that hostilities be delayed until the following day "as there would be talks with the Lord Mayor and aldermen of the city to determine what way they could deal with us."[28] Evertsen and Benckes were now firmly convinced that Manning was playing for time so that reinforcements might be brought up. Sharpe was curtly informed that the fort must be surrendered within another half-hour or it would be violently assaulted by land and sea. Not only would the works fall by evening, Evertsen confidently promised the envoy, but every vessel lying before it would be sent to the bottom. Again he turned the hourglass on end. And again Sharpe departed in great haste.[29]

Immediately, the Dutch began to clear their decks for action and began the disembarkation of the 600 marines for the final assault. Ashore, the five-score defenders of Fort James locked the gates and prepared "to stand upon their defence."[30] With perhaps only half a dozen dilapidated cannon mounted against nine powerful men-of-war and a landing force six times their own number, theirs was a forlorn hope at best.[31]

The half-hour passed without incident. Then two guns were fired to leeward as warning shots to announce that the grace period was over. Suddenly, "the General [Evertsen] fired his broadside and the rest after him."[32] The cannonade was instantly returned in kind by the fort. Amid the choking smoke of gunfire, Nathan Gould, the English prisoner aboard *Swaenenburgh*, watched in awe as Colve's landing boats picked their way across the river like so many bugs upon the water. Of the 600 men in the force, he later reported, "he thought they had not above four hundred men, some hand pistolls, some swordes, [and] some halfe Pickes."[33]

As the exchange of fire continued, it became apparent that the fort's guns were not well-served, even though after the initial broadside they had managed, by one report, to shoot *Swaenenburgh* "through and through."[34] Dutch casualties throughout the entire fleet were later counted at no more than two or three wounded, and damage to the ships, overall, was apparently minimal. Indeed, one detractor of Cap-

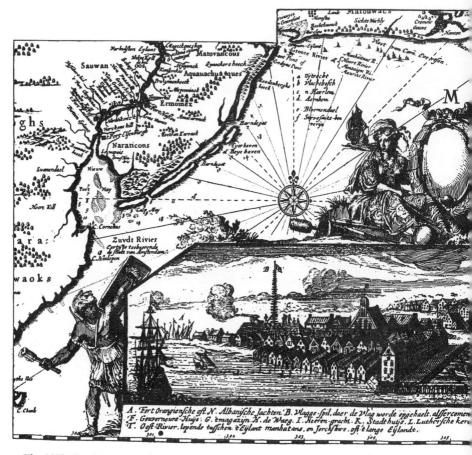

The 1673 "Restitutio" inset by Hugo Allard, depicting the Evertsen-Benckes capture of New York, appears in the *Atlas maior* published by Reinero Ottens. *Courtesy Library of Congress.*

Key:

A. Fort Orange or Albany sloops (on horizon), *Suriname* (left), and *Zeehond* and city lighters (right)

B. The flagstaff whereon the flag was hoisted upon the arrival of vessels in the harbor.

C. Fort Amsterdam, otherwise called Fort James by the English and officially renamed Fort Willem Hendrick by Evertsen and Benckes in 1673.

D. The city gaol.

E. The Reformed Dutch Church.

F. The Governor's House.

G. The *Pack-huysen*, or public store houses.

H. The city weight, or balance.

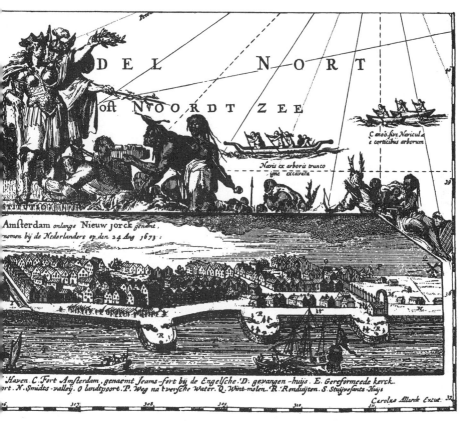

I. The Great Dyke, or canal. In 1676 this moat was filled with earth.

K. The State House (or City Hall).

L. The Lutheran Church.

M. The Water Port, or Gate, sometimes called the East River Gate, was connected with the blockhouse at the east end of the city wall.

N. Smidt's Valley, a salt marsh on the East River.

O. The Land Port, or City Gate, was in the Broadway.

P. The "way to the fresh water."

Q. The windmill, erected by the West Indies Company during the former Dutch rule.

R. The Rondeels, or half-moon redoubts.

S. The Stuyvesant House, erected by Governor Peter Stuyvesant ca. 1660.

T. The East River.

tain Manning's conduct later wrote that "ye ffort fired but 4 gunns att the shippe all ye Tyme."[35] For an hour, however, both sides continued the fight, though one by one Manning's guns collapsed on their platforms. Undoubtedly, many of the fort's defenders began to consider their position hopeless, although a few maintained a staunch determination to resist to the end. One brave soldier, flourishing his sword in defiance, leaped upon the wall by the English flag, fully exposing himself to the heavy Dutch fire, promptly had his head shot off and collapsed into a bloody heap. Outgunned, outmanned, and perhaps fearful of an uprising of the Dutch burghers of New York, Manning ordered up the flag of truce and "beat a parley." It was said, the Dutch had expended 2,000 rounds against the fortress before the fight was through. As Manning raised the white flag, Captain Carr, terrified by the gunfire and eager for the fight to end, instantly jumped forward to pull down the fluttering Royal Ensign.[36]

In the meantime, Colve's hardened veterans bumped ashore on the banks of the North River, just above Governor Lovelace's gardens and orchards near Trinity Church. The noted chronicler of New York history, Cadwallader Colden would write warmly, almost a century later, of their immediate reception by the town's Dutch citizenry who allegedly flocked to the river's edge "to welcome them with all the demonstrations of joy they could make." As the troops marched down the Broad Way, they were encouraged to storm the fort by no less than 400 ebullient burghers, many of whom were themselves armed and eager to join in the fray.[37]

Though the white flag of truce fluttered above the fort, the bombardment by the fleet did not stop for some time, possibly because the flag could not be seen through the smoke and haze of battle. Finally, the signal to cease fire was given and a dull silence swept over the waters and lands of lower Manhattan. At that moment, Captain Colve paused on his march toward the fort and dispatched a trumpeter to the wall to demand that an officer be sent out to negotiate a surrender. None appeared. Then, after some anxious moments, Manning dispatched Carr, Lovelace, and a certain Captain Gibbs, all of whom had been given less-than-precise instructions with which to secure for the defenders the best possible terms of surrender. Irate over the vagueness of their instructions, Colve informed the envoys that they were now prisoners of war and that if they had anything to say they must speak up immediately. After some discourse, Lovelace and Gibbs were detained, and timid Captain Carr was sent back to the fort to inform Manning that he had no more than fifteen minutes to submit a definite surrender proposal. The ultimatum was simple and the alternative obvious, but as the minutes ticked by no proposal was forthcoming. More than half an hour elapsed, and still no proposal. This time, ironically, the delay was not Manning's. Unknown to both sides until later, Captain Carr had deserted. Before his act of cowardice could be discovered, Carr was well on his way to the wilds of the Delaware. As one participant of the episode, John Sharpe, later noted: "like a traitor he had turned another way and was never since seen!" Unaware of Carr's desertion, Colve was enraged by the delay. Believing the delay due to Manning's bag of duplicities, he promptly marched his troops toward the fort.[38]

At the appearance of the powerful enemy land force beneath his walls on one side, and with the already-proven devastating power of the Dutch fleet on the other, Manning had little choice. He quickly ordered John Sharpe out to discuss specific articles of surrender. Sharpe requested in writing that the garrison be accorded the right to march out with the honors of war, and that all persons belonging to either the town or the garrison who were still inside the fort be permitted to proceed unmolested, with their "goods, bag and baggage," wherever they pleased.[39] Colve politely promised the envoy that, upon his word of honor as a gentleman and a soldier, these requests would be honored. However, he added, there was no time left to write down such an accord. As Manning had already recklessly squandered the moment for negotiation, with the haughty superiority of a commander confident of unconditional surrender, Colve informed the Englishman that "it would be appreciated if the British militia would come out with their armes and to surrender the same in front of the fort and then to remain Prisoners of War."[40] As Evertsen noted in his journal on this important day, "without making any other capitulation," the surrender of Fort James, and consequently the city of New York, had been secured.[41]

Captain Manning and the fort surgeon, Doctor Tayler, personally threw open the gates and let the Dutch in. In so doing, the captain provoked an uproar of bitter criticism and universal condemnation of his character among the peoples of the English colonies of America. One typical critic, appalled at the easy surrender of Fort James, wrote that "at home the Souldiers would have fired [on the Dutch entering the fort] but they were ordered to the contrary."[42]

As soon as the gates swung open, the English troops marched forth with their arms and colors flying, formed into a ring, and laid them down. Colve then commanded the prisoners to return to the fort, where they were to be temporarily incarcerated in the Dutch Reformed Church. He graciously allowed the officers the privilege of remaining in their own lodgings. Manning was even permitted to retain his sword.

The following day, the prisoners were transferred to more secure quarters aboard the fleet.[43]

Evertsen and Benckes now had the leisure to survey their conquest and assess their position. They had taken from the fort some 100 prisoners, all under the command of Captain Manning. Though only a few mounted cannons had been found, a total of 38 mostly unmounted guns had been discovered lying at various places about the fort, mute testimony to Governor Francis Lovelace's inability "to buckle on" his armor. Cannons, goods, and other properties within the works were promptly confiscated in the name of the States General and the Prince of Orange, as were two English ships lying in the harbor. One of these vessels was 500 tons burthen and mounted no less than 35 guns; the other was of 100 tons burthen. Both were heavily laden and both were taken without opposition.[44]

Despite orders to the contrary, the excitement of such an easy, almost bloodless victory was overwhelming for many of the Dutch troops, who celebrated by plundering several properties. Before order could be reestablished, they had looted the homes of Governor Lovelace, Captain Manning, Thomas Delavall, and the estate of a certain Mr. Rider. The home of John Lawrence, the English Mayor of New York, was saved only through the timely intercession of the local Dutch burghers. Since neither Evertsen nor Benckes were of a mind to permit disorder, especially when the cooperation of the populace was likely to be necessary, they took immediate action. Retribution for the crime of plundering against orders was swift. At least one soldier was executed for his transgressions as an example. Looting stopped immediately.[45]

The two Dutch squadron commanders moved to consolidate their military control over New York, which was promptly renamed New Orange on July 31. Ninety soldiers and 60 sailors were detached from the fleet to garrison the fort, which was renamed Fort Willem Hendrick. The Dutch also organized efforts to identify what they considered property that would qualify for formal confiscation. When the two commanders learned of the flight of two merchantmen up the East River to Hell Gate, two sloops and 40 men were detached from the main squadron to bring them back. The expedition proved successful and the two merchantmen were taken without a struggle near the Two Brothers Islands. One of the prizes was a pinnace called *Batchelor* (*Batselaer*), partially laden with planks and staves, but also carrying various sugars, some tobacco, logwood and Brazil wood, and other freight goods. The other, a bus called *Expectation*, was filled with meat, bacon, bread, flour, fish oil, tobacco, wood, and hides intended for Barbados. All of the provisions would be heartily welcomed when distributed among the ships of the fleet.[46]

Though absorbed with occupying and taking control of a major colonial center of an enemy power, Evertsen did not lose sight of his instructions. Even as the garrisoning of Fort Willem Hendrick was carried out, he moved to prepare for another operation—the attack on the Newfoundland [Terre Neuf] fishing fleet, which Zeeland authorities had included in the secret instructions months before. Four ships, Boes's, Van Zijl's, De Witte's, and that of the late Hanske Fokkes, now under the command of Lieutenant Jan Richewijn, were immediately provisioned for the operation. Their mission was to intercept and destroy the annual sailing of the English Terre Neuf fleet. The remainder of the Dutch fleet at New Orange was to remain in port "until such time as everything is put in good order."[47]

As the days and weeks that followed would attest, Cornelis Evertsen and Jacob Benckes were increasingly viewed by the majority of Dutch inhabitants of New York, and even New Jersey and Delaware, as liberating heroes. Yet most citizens, true to their oaths of nine years earlier that they would bear no arms against any nation, had awaited the outcome of battle before making their sentiments known. That their oath of loyalty to England contained the clause "whilst I live in any of his Majesty's territories," however, permitted all to absolve themselves of charges of violations of good faith. New York, and soon New Jersey and Delaware, could no longer count themselves as belonging to his majesty's territories. Evertsen and Benckes were well aware that the Dutch citizenry's support would be imperative in the days to come if their conquest was to take hold. Should the States General decide to reestablish New Orange as a permanent base in America, then all the better.

As early as July 31, the day after the English surrender, Evertsen and Benckes began to discuss the implications of their success and the future fortunes of the lands they had, or soon would, return to Dutch control. They clearly realized that the total surrender of New York City held far greater consequences—and opportunities—than the secret instructions under which Evertsen sailed could address. Indeed, the instructions had indicated that only under certain conditions could New York be attacked and pillaged. No one had considered wholesale conquest, and there was nothing in the provisions stating what should be done if the colony was regained in its entirety, as now seemed possible. New Orange's value, militarily and as a bargaining chip in the inevitable peace talks, seemed inescapable. Evertsen noted in his log that the country was of such great import that he and Benckes had agreed on July 31 "to do everything to bring it under a good government and defense." Ultimately, because the States General of The Netherlands had not directly authorized the expedition, and Evertsen's instructions failed to address the issues at hand, it fell to the two commanders to establish a working provisional government. While this task was far in excess of what anyone could have envisioned when either the Zeeland or the Amsterdammer expeditions were launched, it was not beyond the capacity of either of the leaders to successfully institute a new government.[48]

The weeks following the surrender of Fort James and New York were filled with hectic activity for the Dutch victors who moved quickly and resolutely to consolidate their immediate gains. They were aware, however, that if they were to secure their flanks to the north, east, and west, they would be obliged to extend their activities and influence well beyond the confines of the city. The initial step would have to be political, beginning with the total dismemberment of the English administration of Francis Lovelace. To accomplish this, they required the allegiance—or at least the tacit neutrality—of the citizenry, first of New York and then of the surrounding areas. It is curious that the first move in this direction was inadvertently promulgated by Lovelace. It was an action that later served to arouse English charges against him of outright conspiracy and treason.

Lovelace had been at Mamaroneck, en route home from New Haven, when he learned of the Dutch advance on New York. But it was not until July 31, fully two days later, and at least twenty-four hours after he learned of the actual storming of the city, that he informed Governor Winthrop of Connecticut of the impending danger to his colony. If Lovelace's lethargy, self-interest, and incompetence had been a source of ridicule among his peers before the war, they were now a potential menace to others. Perhaps representative of his character is that what appeared to have galled him almost as much as the attack on his province was that the enemy had the audacity to have "breakfasted on all my sheep and Cattle at Staten Island." That he placed his personal interest above that of his country was evident. That it may have led to an effort to collaborate with the enemy is possible. Cloaked with bravado, Lovelace vowed to his fellow governor that he would hurry to Long Island to raise the militia.[49] Had that truly been his intention, he failed miserably in it. The unpopular governor apparently evoked little response or support upon his arrival on the island, and, indeed, may not have sought it. That he failed even to establish contact with many important townships or sources of potential English support is evident, for on August 4 the towns of Southampton, Easthampton, Southold,

Setauket, and Huntington reported "wee having noe Intelligence to this day ffrom o^r Govern^r: Fra^s Lovelace Esqui^r of whatt hath happened or w^t wee are to doe."[50] Indeed, on July 31, the very day that he vowed to Winthrop to raise the militia to oppose the invaders, he was establishing communications with the foe and requesting a pass to meet with their commanders!

Lovelace did, in fact, cross over to Long Island as soon as possible. Near Flushing he was met by one Matthias Nicholls. Nicholls had come from the city in one of the Dutch commander's barges, and fervently urged the governor not to place himself in harm's way by entering the city. Nicholls volunteered to return in his place. The governor, however, was counseled by a Dutch cleric to return to New York for three days. Lovelace's mission to New York has never been examined in light of his objectives; indeed, his goals were never fully revealed. Yet, thus persuaded by the Dutchman, he embarked on the barge, and on August 2, 1673, the governor of New York delivered himself into the hands of his country's sworn enemy.[51]

When Lovelace arrived in New York, he must have noticed that his home and property, as well as Manning's and Delavall's, had been looted, while that of the town's citizenry had been spared. Unfortunately, history records neither the governor's observations nor his motives for seeking a meeting with Evertsen. To some, particularly the New Englanders (who were by no means overly fond of their neighboring government and rival to the south), it appeared that he had been openly invited by the enemy "to come in . . . for protection from the deserved punishment" that would certainly be meted out to the governor for his ignominious loss of the city. Equally scandalous, some felt, was that by placing himself in the hands of the enemy, if in itself not an act of treason, Lovelace had left the inhabitants of Long Island "without commission or Commander to stand up for their defence."[52]

Governor John Leverett of Massachusetts was most critical of all. In a letter to English Secretary of State Arlington, he not only castigated his fellow governor for losing his capital, the largest city in English America, but documented the unceremonious treatment Lovelace received upon his entry into that place. "It is expected," he wrote,

> that Coll. Lovelace would haue kept himselfe out of the Enemies hands though he had not kept the fort, that thereby the country might have been emproved (who as I hear was ready to rise for the reduceing the place), but by one of their Dutch Domines hee was collogued with, whereby they got him in for three dayes, and before those were out, the Inhabitants laide Arrests upon him for debts due to them, soe that time

lapsed the Dutch Captains declared that hee had liberty (paying his debts) within six weekes to depart the Country, that haveing seized his Estate before, soe that they keepe him & it is said intend him for Holland.[53]

With Lovelace no longer a threat, Evertsen and Benckes pressed on with consolidation of their conquest and establishment of a provisional government. On the day after the governor established his initial communication with Evertsen, the two Dutch commanders, their confidence soaring, boldly resolved to restore not only New York to its founding masters, but indeed all of The Netherlands' former dominions on the Mid-Atlantic coast. Their first move was to dispatch a 70-man expedition under the command of Lieutenant Joan Becker, with the six-gun snaauw *Zeehond* and another small vessel, up the Hudson to Fort Albany. If the fort could be taken, the settlement there (Beverswyck during the former Dutch administration), and the "colony" of Rensselaerswyck, might again be returned to the fold, along with several other villages in the Esopus Highlands. Becker sailed on August 2 with orders to inform the tiny English garrison at the fort that New York had fallen, and then "to demand it[s surrender] and that not being granted, to force it to do so."[54]

Once the Becker expedition had been fitted out and dispatched, Evertsen and Benckes turned their attention to provisioning Captain Nicholas Boes's four-ship squadron for the raid on the Newfoundland fisheries. For three days, the ships took on water and provisions, and then 50 English prisoners, including Captain Manning, Dudley Lovelace, and his wife. On August 8, the squadron set sail with orders to attack and destroy not only the enemy's important fishing fleet but also his drying stations and habitations on the Newfoundland coast, and then to rendezvous with Evertsen and Benckes at Fayal, in the Azores.[55]

Despite its originally limited objectives, Evertsen's raid on America had become something far greater than anticipated. It had become, with the recapture of New York, and almost overnight, a mission of liberation from English rule.

14

CONSTABLE STAVES AND ENGLISH FLAGS

The establishment of a provisional Dutch government to replace the Lovelace regime in New York rapidly became the paramount goal of Evertsen's and Benckes's agenda during the first days of August. Though both commanders undoubtedly wished to relieve themselves of civil matters as quickly as possible, both were cognizant that if New Orange were to remain in Dutch hands, it would require a stable Dutch government. Thus, on August 2, the able Captain Anthony Colve was appointed military governor-general pro tem of the province and Fort Orange. The Council of War, which would actually govern during Evertsen's and Benckes's stay, moved quickly to re-establish the province's mainland boundaries as they had been defined by the English's Hartford Treaty of 1670 between Connecticut and New York. But now they boldly added to that claim all of Long Island as well as the proprietary of New Jersey and Delaware, which had formerly been part of The Netherlands' American holdings. Though his commission was not made public until more than a month later, Colve's authority was to extend from

> Cape Hinlopen, or the south side of Delaware bay, and fifteen miles more southerly, including said bay and South river, as they were formerly possessed by the Directors of the city of Amsterdam, and after by the English government, in the name and on the behalf of the Duke of York; and further from the said Cape Hinlopen along the Great Ocean to the east end of Long Island and Shelter Island; and thence westward to the middle of the channel, called the Sound, to a town called Greenwich, on the main, and so to run landward in, northerly; provided that such line shall not come within ten miles of the North river, conformably

to the provisional settlement of the boundary made in 1650 and afterwards ratified by the States-General, February 23, 1656, and January 23, 1664; with all the lands, islands, rivers, lakes, kills, creeks, fresh and salt waters, fortresses, cities, towns, and plantations therein comprehended.[1]

As Councillor of State, the Council of War appointed Cornelis Steenwyck, a former Burgomaster and one of the richest men in the colony. He was to assist Colve, as "an expert person," in "all cases relative to justice and police," military and naval matters, and in the promotion of the general welfare and prosperity of the country. Nicholas Bayard, former City Clerk during the years of the West Indies Company rule, was appointed as colony secretary, recorder of secrets [geheim schryver], auctioneer for the city [vendu meester], book keeper, and receiver general of revenues. Cornelis Eewoutsen, former commander of *Sint Joris*, was appointed "to superintend the gunners and ammunition of warr," and to manage the strengthening of the city fortifications and the laborers employed in such work. Tactfully, Evertsen and Benckes refrained from issuing an actual public commission until order and government had been fully established under the Council of War.[2]

The Council was methodical in its institution of a Dutch form of civil government in New Orange. One of the first orders of business was, of course, to dismantle the former regime. The old city magistrates and municipal officers were formally released from their oaths of allegiance to King Charles II and the Duke of York taken nine years earlier under duress of conquest. The city seal, mace, and magistrates' gowns were duly surrendered by Mayor John Lawrence. The following day, the Council ordered an election be held by the commonality of the town at City Hall on August 4 to choose a nominating committee for the selection of candidates for the offices of burgomasters (magistrates), schout (sheriff), and schepen (aldermen). By a plurality vote, six reputable citizens, five Dutchmen and one Englishman, were elected and directed "to confer with said commanders and Council of War."[3]

The committee then proceeded to nominate six individuals for the posts of burgomasters, and fifteen for schepen, but, as directed by the Council of War, only "from the wealthiest inhabitants and those only who are of the Reformed Christian Religion." From these candidates the Council would select the municipal government of New Orange for a term of one year. On August 6, each of the nominees swore an oath to administer law and justice, to promote the welfare of the city and its inhabitants, to maintain obedience to the government established by the Lords States General and "his Highness of Orange," and to defend "the upright and true Christian Religion agreeably to the Word of God and the order of the Synod of Dordrecht taught in the Netherland church." The following day, the Council, by proclamation, formally re-established the Dutch magistracy of New Orange "to its previous character of Schout, Burgomasters and Schepens, which exists in all the cities of our Fatherland." Johannes van Brugh, Johannes de Peyster (Pijster), and Egedius Luyck (Luijck) were chosen as burgomasters, Anthony de Milt was selected as schout, and William Beeckman, Jeronimus Ebbing, Jacob Kip, Laurens van der Spiegall, and Gelyn Verplank were chosen as schepen.[4]

The attentions of the Council were, of course, not entirely occupied with the establishment of Dutch government in New Orange. There were still the many towns surrounding Manhattan to the south, to the east on Long Island, across the North River to the west, and on the mainland to the north to be dealt with. Staten Island, the settlements of New Jersey, and those on the Delaware had to be attended to as well, lest a nucleus of opposition be formed to challenge the renewed Dutch presence on the North American mainland. The five Dutch towns on Long Island—New Utrecht, Brooklyn, Bushwick Inlet, Amersfoort, and Midwout—and the single English town of Gravesend, had welcomed the conquerors of New York almost from the moment of their arrival. These six places were directed immediately to nominate three persons for schout, three for secretary, and six for schepen for each town. The English towns of Flushing, Hempstead, Jamaica, Newtown, Oyster Bay, Southampton, Easthampton, Setauket, Huntington, and Southold on Long Island, West Chester and East Chester on the mainland to the north, and Staten Island to the southwest, were another matter. Having deprived them of a leader around which resistance might rally, the Council of War ordered these places to send two deputies each, together with their Constables' staves and English flags, to tender submission to The Netherlands and to exchange their national colors for the flag of the Prince of Orange. Each of the deputations from these enclaves of potential resistance, particularly from the towns to the east of Oyster Bay, were then directed to nominate, by general election in their respective towns, three candidates for schout, three for secretary, and six for schepen, from which the Council would make the final selection. By August 29, even the most recalcitrant English village, Southampton, which had pleaded in vain with New England for help, had delivered up its constables' staves and English flag and submitted, albeit grudgingly, nominations for the prescribed offices.[5]

Dutch authority was imposed over the flanking English colony of New Jersey with equal aplomb and remarkable celerity. Only two days after the capitulation of Fort James, on August 2, Evertsen and Benckes convened the Council of War in City Hall and received the first voluntary deputations from several of the key settlements of New Jersey. These had come unsolicited to request permission to treat for the peaceful surrender of the towns of Newark, Elizabethtown, Woodbridge, and Piscattaway. In the absence of New Jersey Governor Philip Carteret, and in the wake of the bloodless but debilitating antiproprietary revolt of 1671–1672, the colony government under Acting Governor John Berry was far from strong. During his short administration, Berry had accomplished little more than to put a cap on dissension in the colony. Thus it was not surprising that the first urban centers in the colony to offer voluntary submission to the Dutch were those that had been hotbeds of antiproprietary sentiment. Not wishing to be outmaneuvered in the surrender process by Berry, lest some harm be done or hoped-for privileges be endangered, the delegates were quick to request that New Jersey's unpopular acting governor not be granted an audience "before and until the same be granted to the said Delegates."[6]

Spurred by the ready submission of these four towns, the Council quickly moved to demand that the towns of Bergen, Middlesex, and Shrewsbury also send delegates to treat for surrender. Six days later, the Council wisely sought to pursue a deliberate policy of moderation to those in New Jersey who readily offered obedience. By Council decree, it was agreed to grant the inhabitants of the seven townships of that colony "the same Privileges and Freedoms as will be accorded the nature born subjects and Dutch towns." Furthermore, in times of hostility with their native homeland, no Englishmen would "be impressed against their nation on condition that they comport themselves quietly and peaceably," although their ships and boats might be drafted into service by Dutch forces for the war effort. Should anyone not wish to submit to Dutch authority or swear allegiance and seek to leave the country with his property, he would be at liberty to do so, provided he departed within the six month period following the decree. No new immigrant, however, would be permitted to settle within the government without specific permission from the new governor, Anthony Colve. And finally, the towns were "granted and accorded Freedom of conscience as the same is permitted in The Netherlands."[7]

As if to confirm acceptance of the provisional government's pacific intentions towards all inhabitants of its newly gained dominions, New Jersey's former acting governor, Captain John Berry, and three prominent citizens of that colony were finally allowed to appear before the Council to beg "that they and their plantations may be confirmed in the privileges which they obtained from their previous Patroons and that they retain possession of their houses, lands, goods, and enjoy privileges accorded other inhabitants of New Jersey." The Council immediately concurred. Four days later, the rights and privileges guaranteed to New Jersey were also accorded Flushing, Hempstead, Jamaica, Middleboro, and Oyster Bay on Long Island and West Chester on the mainland, and eventually all of the towns lying within the now substantial Dutch orbit. They too were obliged to accept allegiance to The Netherlands and to nominate a slate of schouts, schepen, and burgomasters.[8]

On September 2, a deputation from the Delaware, or South River, region presented its credentials to the Council and readily offered submission. With an eye on The Netherlands' chief attraction to the colonies, the Council again accepted and agreed to permit the continuance of free trade and commerce with both Christians and Indians. They ordered appointment of a military commander of the region, who was to enlist ten or twelve men on the account of the Council. Every sixth inhabitant along the South River was to be summoned to assist in the erection of a fort "in the most suitable place . . . for the defense of said river." All inhabitants, be they Swedes, Finns, or English, were to be permitted the same privileges as all other subjects of New Netherland (although only the English seemed to have been required to swear allegiance). All were to be permitted to retain their homes, lands, and goods, but all debts due the former English government were to be collected by the Dutch commandant and turned over to the provisional government. The inhabitants were to be allowed "Freedom of Conscience" and religion. However, recent emigrants from Maryland (which had for years laid claim to the South River territory) would be permitted to remain only on the condition that they apply to the provisional Dutch government for confirmation of their patents. This particularly applied to the settlement at Hoeren Kill (modern Lewes), which had recently been captured by Maryland by force of arms from New York. And, as in the remainder of the areas that had submitted, magistrates were to be nominated and selected and courts of justice established. These were to be erected at New Amstel (New Castle), Upland (later Chester), and Hoeren Kill (later Lewes).[9]

Throughout this entire region, termed "the naval" of English America, Evertsen and Benckes oversaw an almost flawless and orderly transition from its former administration to civil government in a traditional Dutch form, and without a drop of blood being shed. Everything, of course, in this remarkable feat was undertaken subject to the approval or revision of the governments of Zeeland and Holland.

The Council of War, of course, refused to extend its good will or largess to the kings of England and France, or to their subjects who continued to "injure, spoil, damage and inflict all possible loss and obstructions" upon the subjects of the Prince of Orange and the Lords States General. They were to be treated with an iron fist and, from the Dutch point of view, justifiably so. Reparations and satisfaction for losses incurred in the transfer of government from the Stuyvesant administration nine years before, had long been sought, but in vain. Utilizing this excuse, the Council of War, undoubtedly hoping to set an example as well as to fill its coffers with money and goods and possibly to legitimize the looting that had been carried out immediately following the fall of Fort James, deemed it necessary to arrest and seize all estates, goods, effects, and outstanding debts of the English "remaining and belonging within this government." Such actions, overall, appear to have been minimal at the outset, and were limited for the most part to the direct property of the English Crown or that belonging to its chief agents or representatives.[10] Governor Lovelace suffered terribly, as did Thomas Delavall and his son-in-law William Dervall. In a letter to Governor Winthrop, in which he attempted to explain that *digitus Dei* had decreed the capitulation of New York and not any fault of his own, Lovelace seemed more upset over the loss of his own estate than that of an entire province.

"Would you be curious to know what my losses amount to?" he queried Winthrop. "I can in short resolve you. It was my all which ever I had been collecting: too great to miss in this wilderness."[11]

But it was Captain Thomas Delavall who suffered perhaps the greatest loss. As principal landholder in New Haerlem, he possessed property at Albany and owned several islands in the East River as well as a warehouse at Kingston. After the 1664 capitulation by Stuyvesant to the English, he had been granted the lucrative post of Collector of Customs, and later that of Auditor General of the Duke of York's revenues.[12] He had become one of the wealthiest Englishmen in the colony. Now, Delavall stood accused by his foes, at great convenience to the Dutch conquerors, of theft and numerous other technical and real violations of the 1664 articles of capitulation.[13]

Delavall's vast property holdings in New Haerlem were ordered confiscated on August 30, and that lying near Fort Albany on September 5. Nothing seemed to escape the Council's eye. Even an old ketch, *Rebecca and Sarah*, owned by Delavall and sunk in Westchester Creek (possibly to prevent confiscation) was declared a lawful prize. The vessel was promptly sold to one Jonathan Slick, the informant who had notified the Council of its existence. Slick paid the Council the sum of 60 beaverskins, "thirty in cash, and the value of the balance in cattle."[14]

When Delavall requested permission for his daughter, Margaret, and his brother-in-law, Edward Dyer, to leave New Orange for Setauket in his sloop *Planter*, the agreement was approved only on the condition that he provide sufficient security for the "restoration" of the vessel in three weeks. With all of his fortunes confiscated or being held, it seems likely that the former auditor general would have indeed been hard-pressed to send his daughter away.[15]

William Dervall, Delavall's son-in-law in Boston, bitterly claimed that the actual justification for the confiscation of his father-in-law's possessions and estates was simpler than the contrived charges levelled against him: it was only because he had served as auditor general for The Netherlands' most rabid opponent, the Duke of York. Dervall suffered considerably at the hands of the Dutch, a fact he attributed to his living in Massachusetts at the time of attack, and he bore the invaders no small enmity. His relationship to Delavall no doubt contributed greatly to the attractions his rich holdings held for the Dutch. Dervall estimated his losses at 160 hogsheads of tobacco, 30 tons of logwood, 14 tons of Brazeletta (Brazil wood), and 70 tons of oil, in all valued at £2,000. He complained that "most English lost all only some few that take their Oathes" to the Netherlanders and the Prince of Orange being excepted.[16]

Not all confiscations were quite as fortright. On August 18 the Council ordered the seizure of Shelter Island on the east end of Long Island. The island was, at the time of the conquest, occupied by Nathaniel Sylvester, but owned by Constant Sylvester and Thomas Middletowne. As the latter were residents of England and Barbados, the Council deemed their property, like that of Dervall's, subject to confiscation. Though Nathaniel Sylvester had willingly submitted himself to the new order, the island and all the houses, goods, and effects upon it technically became the property of the Dutch government. As a consequence of his submission to the new government, however, Nathaniel was permitted to retain all of his "personal goods, effects and furniture, [and] negroes." The day following the official act of confiscation, the Council agreed to sell the island and all upon it to him for £500 sterling. As part of the agreement, the new owner and proprietor of Shelter Island would be exempted from all taxes, could not be cited in any court actions except in the Supreme Court, and was exempt from the normally obligatory requirement of a proprietor for the outfitting of soldiers from among his tenant population, "save only what he shall voluntarily do for the defence of said island and government" in the event of foreign invasion or Indian attack.[17] It was a quick and expedient means for Evertsen and Benckes to convert real estate into ready, portable cash—and certainly one of the major objectives of their expedition to America.

Though the Council of War had nominally sequestered all property of the English crown and its subjects, principally that belonging to either Charles II or the Duke of York, according to John Sharpe, who sought permission to leave New Netherland, English residents of New Orange were soon suffering "hard imposures and molestations." It was a charge, while not without some foundation, made with bias, for Sharpe was among those expelled. Understandably concerned about the dangers of infiltrators and spies from neighboring colonies and a core of English settlers quietly loyal to the crown, the Dutch authorities were obliged to close the access to Manhattan Island from the north, and to expel most if not all non-Dutch subjects who were not residents or had refused to swear allegiance. Those English residents who refused to take the oath were among the body of individuals not permitted to remain, inducing a situation, recalled Sharpe, which "cannot but draw tears from all tender-hearted Christians."[18] Despite Sharpe's charges, those actually exiled were few, and a mass exodus of citizens of any national origin failed to materialize.

Lieutenant Becker returned in *Zeehond* in triumph from Fort Albany on August 19. Nine days before, the fort "had given itself up on the same condition as the other [Fort James]." With the only major defense work in the region again in Dutch hands, the entire upper Hudson submitted to Dutch authority with barely a quiver. Becker had appointed Andries Draejer, an officer in the squadron, to command the fort in his stead. The defenses were renamed Fort Nassau, and after leaving a dozen soldiers and an equal number of seamen to hold the place, Becker returned to New Orange to report on his mission's success. When the lieutenant departed, he was apparently accompanied or followed by delegates from Albany, now renamed Willemstadt, Schenectady, Horley, and Marbletowne, situated in the Esopus Highlands, and Jeremias van Rensselaer, master of the vast wilderness "colony" of Rensselaerswyck. The deputation came to submit themselves and their towns and property formally to the authority of the new government.[19]

The delegation from the upper Hudson was received by the Council of War on August 22 and offered the same terms as the towns of New York and New Jersey. Willemstadt was ordered to nominate officers for the posts of burgomasters and secretary. Unlike those who came before, its delegates were deeply concerned over the issues of defense—not against the return of the English, but hostile Indians and Frenchmen— and petitioned the Council for "a reasonable garrison," and powder and lead for Fort Nassau "as the place is badly provided therewith."

Four cannon were requested for the defense of Willemstadt. The Council, its resources already stretched to the limit, could only agree to provide the town with a garrison, ammunition, and cannon at "the first opportunity." Trade with friendly Indians by the town of Willemstadt would be permitted as it had been during former Dutch administrations. However, Schenectady, whose citizens had been granted their lands by the late Governor Stuyvesant on the express condition that they confine themselves to agricultural pursuits, were forbidden such trade. The great landholder Van Rensselaer was permitted to retain his previous privileges for one year but was sternly ordered to cause the nomination of three burgomasters to govern for the following year. Only by so doing would he be permitted to retain his personal privileges, and even then only on a year by year basis subject to review.[20]

On the same day that Willemstadt and the other towns of the upper Hudson formally submitted to Dutch rule, the schout and secretary nominated through elections by the villages of New Jersey and selected by the Council were sworn into office. John Ogden was installed as schout and was charged with enforcing the will of the burgomasters in managing the civil affairs of New Jersey, which was now being called by its former Dutch name of Achter Col. Ogden was authorized by the Council to enforce the will of the government "according to the Laws of the United Belgicq Provinces" on the explicit instruction of the governor-general of New Netherland. Of greater interest, however, was the installation of Samuel Hopkins, co-conspirator with Captain James Carteret in the short-lived rebellion against Governor Philip Carteret. It is not surprising that the first order of business for the two new officeholders was to inventory Philip Carteret's estate, of which they were to provide a complete report to the Council of War, undoubtedly in preparation for confiscation. The opportunity for sweet revenge for his exile at the hands of the Carteret government must have seemed a welcomed bonus to the new Secretary of Achter Col.[21]

Both Ogden and Hopkins were eager to assert their newfound authority. They quickly visited the estate of Philip Carteret only to discover that the governor's goods had already been removed by Robert Lapriere, late surveyor general of New Jersey and loyal member of the colony's former Council of State. When summarily ordered by Ogden to produce the goods, Lapriere not only refused, "but moreover stating with threats that the Duke of York had an interest in Fort James, and that there would be another change within half a year." Outraged, Hopkins and Ogden requested the Council of War's permission to arrest the obstinate loyalist. Soldiers were promptly dispatched, Lapriere was arrested and ordered to turn over the goods, and "as an example to others" was summarily banished from the country.[22]

Another Carteret loyalist, former colony Secretary James Bollen, was directed by Ogden and Hopkins to deliver Carteret's official records and papers to them or face confiscation of his own property by the new government. Captain Berry and fellow Bergen County landowner William Sanford immediately discerned the danger to all New Jersey landowners, especially those who remained silently loyal to England and the former government of the colony if the state papers, patent certificates, and other documents were turned over to the likes of Hopkins. They moved quickly to appeal the order by petitioning the Council of War. All they asked was that the papers be transferred to the authority of the honest secretary of New Netherland, Nicholas Bayard. The Council, though "provisionally" agreeing, failed to act until three days later, when Berry, Bollen, and others once again petitioned. They requested that the books and papers "concerning the province called New Yarsie" be delivered into Bayard's hands in lieu of the clutches of the Secretary of Achter Col, "as they have great reason to suspect said Hopkins of having made away with some of them." The Council, undoubtedly wishing to extinguish any form of opposition and to stifle the roots of discord, finally agreed.[23]

Some adamant Carteret loyalists were merely reprimanded with a fine for being troublesome. Continued insubordination was another matter. One such case was that of John Singletary, who refused one of Ogden's orders, and then sent the new sheriff a "rude" letter when called to task. Singletary was let off with a fine of £5 for his rebellion, but was ordered closely watched thereafter. At the first complaint of trouble, Ogden was authorized to have Singletary punished "as a mutineer," a charge that implied a penalty of exile, and possibly death.[24]

Though some Englishmen who refused the oath of allegiance were forced to leave their homes and farms, a few who fled before the invaders came back. One such was Captain John Carr, the deserter who had run away at the surrender of Fort James. Carr, through his wife (and possibly without his knowledge), petitioned the Council for permission to "settle under this government," and was readmitted to the colony—at least on the records—no doubt much to the chagrin of those such as John Sharpe who surrendered and were obliged to leave.[25]

The conquest of New York created considerable consternation in all of the neighboring colonies to the north. But in nearby Connecticut, the concern was borne not so much out of fear of attack as for the loss of territory that Governor Winthrop had been laboring to annex to his own colony. For quite some time he had nurtured hopes of securing a toehold on the eastern end of Long Island, where long smouldering dissension against the Lovelace administration had all but exploded in open rebellion even before the Dutch invasion. Winthrop had gone so far as to conduct discussions on the matter with numerous key figures, and towns such as Southampton were inclined to support his efforts. Now, he realized, if the invaders successfully extended their authority over the whole of Long Island, under treaty terms at the end of the war it might revert back to the crown and the Duke of York. With the weak Lovelace regime certain to be replaced, any hopes of annexing, or receiving the region through intercolonial or proprietary treaty, would likely evaporate.[26]

On August 17 Winthrop summoned his government into an emergency session at Hartford. The governor's best intelligence estimates, supplied by his son Fitz-John Winthrop, suggested that "the Dutch had landed 3000 men upon Manhatas Island."[27] Such estimates, although far from accurate, nevertheless greatly influenced Connecticut's attitude in dealing with the foe. As nervous assemblymen filed into the meeting chamber at Hartford, all were probably aware that the colony could not hope single-handedly to confront such a powerful enemy on such short notice. Connecticut needed time to organize and time to secure assistance from her more powerful and populous neighbor to the northeast, the Massachusetts Bay Colony. Thus, Winthrop's strategy was one of preparing for war while winning time in the name of peace. A Grand Committee was appointed with powers to recruit troops and requisition ships, animals, or other means of transport.[28] Simultaneously, the Assembly dispatched two deputies, James Richards and William Roswell, to New Orange to lodge official protests with the invaders on behalf of the "united colonyes of New England," and to assure the invaders that peace was their only desire.[29]

Significantly, one of the major thrusts of the unilateral protest—though it was not couched as such—did not concern the conquest of New York at all, since "the chiefe trust of those parts reside in other hands," but the submission of the lands east of Oyster Bay. The principal occasion for discussion was provided by a minor protest concerning the Dutch seizure of a vessel belonging to a Connecticut citizen close to one of that colony's harbors.[30] It was intended, however, only as an excuse for Connecticut to assume the mantle of an injured party in the negotiations that followed.

Richards and Roswell arrived late on August 13 at Fort Willem Hendrick, but were immediately given an audience with Evertsen and Benckes. Dutifully they presented Connecticut's formal letter of protest

drafted by colony Secretary John Allyn. But, as the delegates had trav-
elled far, and "as they were quite weary from the journey, and had not
thought that they would gain audience so quickly," they requested
another meeting the following day.[31] Their request was instantly
approved.

The next day, Evertsen and Benckes were undoubtedly stunned by
the presentation of the two delegates from Connecticut. Surprisingly,
the two men had been directed by Winthrop to deliver a verbal message to the Council—a message of apparent conciliation and peace.
They informed

> the Commanders that, as they [Connecticut] had remained at peace in
> the time of the previous Dutch government, even in a season of war, they,
> on their side were equally disposed thus to continue without molesting
> this Province, or making use of any act of hostility against it. On condi-
> tion that nothing be undertaken to the prejudice of their Colony from
> this side [New Orange], it certainly will not first attempt anything hos-
> tile; in case such should be committed against them by this Province,
> they thus protest themselves guiltless of the blood that may be shed in
> consequence.[32]

Incredible as it may have seemed, the colony of Connecticut appeared to be offering the peace of a neutral state, unilaterally and
without consulting the crown, with The Netherlands. New Jersey and
Delaware, were one thing, for they had more or less been under Dutch
domination before and substantial portions of their populations were of
Dutch nationality. But Connecticut was another matter, though it now
appeared on the surface of it all that she wished only to be left alone.

Whatever their first reactions may have been to the olive branch
offered them by the Connecticut delegates, Evertsen and Benckes were
masters of formality. They were also astute enough in the subtle arts of
negotiation not to accept things as they first appeared. Without pursuing the issue further, they requested that the men of Connecticut put
their peace proposals down on paper. Then and only then, noted the
ever cautious Dutchmen, would they provide an answer in like manner.
Richards and Roswell refused, saying that they were not authorized by
their government to do so, and, in any event, "such written negotiations might be turned to the worst use by any disaffected person of their
colony." The Council countered that argument with one of language: as
they could not readily understand English they were therefore obliged
to request the terms in writing. There simply could be no verbal agreement, they stated blandly, because the sense of any agreement could be
changed in translation or by the simple misplacement, intentional or
otherwise, of a single word. Confronted with the Dutchmen's answer,

Richards and Roswell frostily requested an hour or two to deliberate over the demand. The meeting that had started so positively came suddenly to an end. Several hours later, the two delegates declined to meet with the Council and sent, in their stead, a servant to inform the Dutch "that they [the delegates] were not qualified to make any propositions in writing." The negotiations were over.[33]

On the following day, the delegates were given a short and uncompromising reply drafted by Secretary Bayard to be carried to Hartford. Evertsen and Benckes, the terse note read, were authorized by the States General of the United Netherlands and the Prince of Orange "to doe all manner of damage" to their enemies on land and sea. For this purpose they had come into the Hudson and subjugated the king's lands and forts. Long Island belonged to The Netherlands and would thus revert to Dutch administration. As for the matter of the villages of that island, which lay east of Oyster Bay, they had been directed to take a loyalty oath "to prevent certain unpleasantries." Those failing to do so would be subjected to force of arms, as would those (such as Connecticut it was implied) who "urged" them to do so. As for the vessel taken near Connecticut, she was considered an enemy craft and thus a fair prize.[34]

The warning to Connecticut was clear. On Friday, August 15, the two delegates departed for Hartford, their mission an unmitigated failure.[35]

Though constantly occupied with the details of establishing civil law and order "as was practiced under the Dutch before this, solely and only by the West India Company," Evertsen and Benckes worked tirelessly to bring New Orange into a state of defensive readiness. In mid-August, Evertsen penned a detailed report to the Zeeland government of the complex sequence of events that had transpired since departing the West Indies. He paid particular attention to the work underway to improve New Orange's defenses.

> We are daily busy strengthening the Fort as we are to bring all residents which we have summoned from all sides, under oaths of loyalty. The Fort is reasonably provided with cannon, but deserves another dozen heavy pieces to make a battery on the waterside.[36]

With the departure of the Terra Neuf squadron, there were four warships, a fireship and a snaauw left at New Orange: Benckes' Amsterdam flagship *Noordhollandt,* and the Zeelander's *Swaenenburgh, Suriname, Sint Joris* and *Zeehond.* Evertsen informed his government that it was his intention to remain only until the fort was in an advanced state of readiness, after which he and Benckes would sail to rendezvous with Captain Boes at Fayal. There he hoped to find orders from the government awaiting him that would direct his subsequent actions.[37]

On August 22, the small pinnace *St. Joseph*, the sugar prize taken in Guadeloupe Roads, was dispatched for Europe with Evertsen's report and a list of arms and materials needed for the fort and the defense of the colony. He dutifully promised to send more information in a few days.[38]

Exactly how word was leaked to the public is unclear. That rumors of the impending departure began to circulate after the sailing of *St. Joseph*, however, is certain. By late August many in the city were increasingly disturbed over the prospect of abandonment. On August 27, the burgomasters and schepen of New Orange met with the two commanders at Fort Willem Hendrick. They came to the point of their visit quickly but diplomatically. They noted that while they were thankful for the unexpected reduction of the former government and the establishment of the Dutch form of administration after the old style, there were only 6,000 Dutch souls in all of New Netherland. Most had reason to believe that they would soon be left to the untender mercies of the enemies who surrounded them. They were "informed and unexpectedly heard" that Evertsen and Benckes were preparing to depart without leaving, "as we had hoped, some ships of War or one of the three superior officers." Thus, they felt it incumbent upon themselves, on behalf of the citizens of New Orange, to remind the commanders of the dire straits in which their departure would leave the country.[39]

"Before you, Valiant gentlemen, arrived here," they began,

all was peace and quietness; the entire coast from Virginia unto Nova Scotia far beyond New England being occupied by thousands of English, Canada on the other side occupied by some thousands of French, all of whom can, in a few days' journey come and on all sides attack us who are scattered in this government, in the centre of these English and French, in divers corners, some here, some up at Fort Orange, now called Willemstadt, some at the South river, others in various towns on Long Island who all together when compared with those of New England can scarcely amount to one in 15, even though we could come together, which is indeed impossible on account of the distance of the places. All these English and French round about, in consequence of their High Mightinesses, with whom they are at war, are become now our enemies by whom we, as already stated, are encompassed round about on all sides withersoever we face or turn.[40]

Though these enemies were for the moment quiet, it was certain they would attempt to reduce New Orange for England as soon as the squadron departed. The weaknesses of the Dutch of New Netherland were well known to their neighbors and former masters who had controlled them for the past nine years. "Besides," noted the burgomasters, "they will not want instruments to promote this work, several great lords being themselves as much interested as the Duke of York, Lord Berkeley and Carteret." There were, indeed, those who said the king of England would never permit the Dutch to remain in the heart of his American dominions, and many expected that a concerted attempt to retake it would be mounted before Christmas. It seemed inevitable to many that New Orange might expect a visit "from our malevolent neighbors of old, now our bitter enemies unless prevented, under God, by your valiant prowess and accompanying force." In concluding, the petitioners humbly begged Evertsen and Benckes to leave behind at least one of the superior officers and two ships to winter at New Orange.[41]

Though they did not say as much, both commanders were in complete agreement with them, and were well aware of the vulnerable state in which they would leave New Netherland. The fort and surrounding countryside were encompassed by powerful—albeit constantly bickering and disorganized—enemies, and by Evertsen's own admission, "could scarcely withstand an attack with so few people, to wit: 120 men, of which 20 [are] at Fort Nassau."[42] And many of the English inhabitants, though they had sworn allegiance, were not to be trusted. As early as August 10, Evertsen had indicated that it was his intention to leave the capable Lieutenant Becker behind "in the character of Captain, as Governor," with six score men from the squadron. The lieutenant, he thought, could recruit another 180 men in the colony "and so to this and diverse officers both Holland, and Zeeland will remain." With equal representation from the forces of both states left behind, the touchy question as to which state would ultimately administer New Netherland, and which would bear the expense or profit, would be left for the states themselves to work out.[43]

Evertsen and Benckes assured the petitioners that it was their first intention to protect them against invasion. This, they stated for public benefit, could be sufficiently effected with the garrison they had intended on leaving behind. However, owing to the deep concern voiced by the inhabitants, the two commanders also agreed to leave Captain Colve behind as commander, and the 25-gun ship *Suriname* and the snaauw *Zeehond* until help arrived "either from the Fatherland or by the ships already sailed hence."[44]

The burgomasters of New Orange, despite the commanders' assurances and protection afforded by the warships, were still skittish, aware they were only a temporary expedient. Thus, on August 29, they composed a lengthy letter to the government of Zeeland.

The address was penned in the name of the burgomasters, schepen, and shout of New Orange. The letter began with a note of appreciation for the recovery of New Netherland and the three cities and thirty villages therein. The thrust of the appeal, however, was composed in such a way as to detail the importance and value of the colony to the Fatherland and its dependencies. It noted that in the present state of war, the many families disenfranchised by the recent invasion of the French and the subsequent flooding of the water defenses "could in this land very easily recover themselves, if only they are offered the helpful hand." New Netherland, it was pointed out, lacked in nothing for the support of those who wished to carry on farming or plantation life. Indeed, with such immigrant industry in the colony, should it be provided, it would not be long "before it could serve the Fatherland as granary and storehouse of many necessaries" that were ordinarily obtained in the Baltic trade. In fact, the three tiny villages in the remote Esopus Highland alone had been so productive that they could afford to export 25,000 bushels of grain. Thus, given enough immigrant manpower, such Dutch dependencies as Suriname and Curaçao could be adequately supplied with provisions with ease, and a whole new commerce developed. The colony was also ideally situated as a base for cruisers in time of war. It was a perfect place for the disposal of prize vessels and for the provisioning of Dutch men-of-war. And in "a lengthy war an eye can be kept upon the actions of the King of England in this land." Yet, if England were permitted to continue its domination over the whole length of North America's Atlantic Seaboard, they warned, it could well serve as a base from which surprise attacks could be launched against The Netherlands and its colonies at any time without warning. As for natural resources, the beaver and peltry trade alone would insure the maintenance of the important commerce with Muscovy. And, of course, there was the rich tobacco trade to think about. For details, they suggested that the bearer of the letter, Cornelis van Ruijven, former collector and receiver general of the Duke of York's revenue, and a man who "has occupied many considerable functions," would be quite competent to answer any questions that the government might have.[45]

That New Netherland was well worth protecting was obvious. The burgomasters and schepen then discussed the dangers ahead, and the necessity of "speedy aid." Having pointed out the colony's virtues to justify their position and request, the burgomasters noted grimly that the colony could not survive, as it had already been pointed out to Evertsen and Benckes, against its many enemies on all sides "who shall doubtless bend all power to take their revenge." Unless assistance was not immediately sent, the six thousand Dutch souls in New Netherland "have nothing else to expect except a total ruin and destruction."[46]

As the twin objectives of improving the colony defenses and preparations for the fleet's departure moved forward, Evertsen, Benckes, and Colve continued to deal with the day-to-day government issues of state. On September 3, the sachems and chiefs of the Hackinsack Indians, accompanied by a score of braves, requested an audience with the Council of War at the fort. They had, they said, been sent by their tribe "to request that as they heretofore had lived in peace with the Dutch, they may continue in future." The Indians, as a token of friendship, presented the council with deer and beaver skins and a string of wampum. The Council graciously accepted the offer of continued peace and sealed the agreement with a ceremonial present of linens, woolens, and a small quantity of gunpowder. Two days later, the sachems and chiefs of the powerful Mohawk nation arrived to see for themselves "the naval force of the Commanders and to make a report thereon" to their people—no doubt to confirm stories that the Dutch were once again in control of New Netherland. They too, awed by the tiny but imposing fleet of warships, departed in friendship, bearing gifts of cloth, woolens, powder, and several muskets.[47]

On the same day that the Hackinsacks had called upon the Council, Evertsen penned a second report to the government of Zeeland. He informed his masters, among other things, of the concern expressed by the inhabitants for the colony's safety, and of the Council's actions in this regard. He also sought to head off the inevitable criticism of the Zeeland Raden for the expenditures necessitated by his actions by explaining the military situation in detail, as well as his methodology for calculating the cost-sharing approach between Zeeland and Holland that he and Benckes had taken the liberty of instituting. Though he did not state as much, he was certainly aware that both states would wish to benefit from the joint reconquest, but neither was likely to willingly accept its economic burden. In fact, it was more likely that each would attempt to pass on the expenses of the operations and maintenance of the colony to the other.[48]

The second dispatch and the letter from the burgomasters of New Netherland, as well as copies of Evertsen's letter of August 10–12, were sent on September 2 aboard the prize bus *Expectation*. After being loaded with a prize cargo of hides and tobacco, confiscated in the name of Zeeland, the vessel set sail under the command of Captain Maerten Jansse Vonck, the caper commander from Middleburg. Making her way into the open seas, the heavily laden bus immediately began to wallow in the troughs and swells, and soon was in imminent danger of sinking. Captain Vonck quickly transferred numerous barrels of tobacco and a few hides to a pilot boat that had been sent to escort his vessel out to sea, and then pressed boldly onward.[49]

It had been an ill omen indeed, for neither *Expectation* nor her predecessor *St. Joseph* were destined to reach their intended objectives. The critical messages they carried, informing The Netherlands of the incredible stroke of good fortune—the reconquest of her former colony and the upset of the balance of power in America—never arrived in Zeeland.

On September 8, Evertsen and Benckes attended to the last few details of administration before turning their complete attentions to their impending departure. Formal decrees were issued, officially appointing Colve Governor General of the Province of New Netherland, and Steenwyck as his Councillor. Captain Eewoutsen was appointed to the command of *Zeehond*, and commissioned to superintend the colony's guns and ammunition. On the 9th, *Swaenenburgh* and most of the prizes were sailed to Staten Island to top off their wood and water supplies. That evening, the local village magistrates on the island were officially "brought under the loyalty oath." Evertsen, who had remained in the city until the last minute arranging the final transition of government, soon joined his ship. Two days later, *Noordhollandt* sailed, taking with her the former English Governor of New York. Soon, the entire fleet would follow.[50] Governor Colve and New Netherland were on their own.

15

IT IS THEIRS WHO ARE
STRONGEST AT SEA

Evertsen's and Benckes's decision to dispatch a strong force to attack England's Newfoundland fisheries was a natural extension of their string of successes against the English colonial establishment in America. The action was also one explicitly ordained by Evertsen's instructions from the Zeeland government. Indeed, the hapless fisheries practically invited attack. The rocky, barren coast of Newfoundland was sparsely occupied by both England and France, who cared more for the defense of their home waters than those populated by simple codfishermen. Yet such a raid, if successful, would strike a major psychological blow against the English, whose West Country mariners dominated the British share of these vast international fisheries. In recent months, the West Countrymen had borne the brunt of The Netherland's war on English commerce, suffering repeated and vigorous privateering attacks in home waters and abroad. Their losses had been so great, in fact, that they were among the first and loudest to clamor for peace. A raid against them now could not help but exacerbate internal dissension in England and increase pressure to end the war.

Newfoundland and its vast fishery potential was first discovered by Captain John Cabot in 1497. Upon his return to England, Cabot reported that "the sea there is swarming with fish, which can be taken not only with the net, but in baskets let down with a stone."[1] Within three years of his first visit, Basque and Portuguese mariners were busy harvesting the bounties of the Newfoundland Banks. They were soon followed by Frenchmen, Spaniards, and Englishmen eager to join in extracting the finned riches from the sea.[2] On August 5, 1583, when Sir

Raid on America

Humphrey Gilbert slipped into St. Johns Harbor to proclaim British sovereignty over the island, he was surprised to discover no fewer than 36 sail of fishermen (including 20 Spanish and Portuguese, and 16 French and English) riding at anchor there ahead of him.[3]

Though the European powers ignored Gilbert's claims, England and France rapidly achieved preeminent positions in the fisheries, while Spain's and Portugal's shares diminished commensurately. English mariners from the West Country counties of Somerset, Dorset, Devon, and Cornwall and Frenchmen from St. Malo and other French continental outports began to dominate the trade while at the same time gaining valuable experience in deep-ocean seamanship.[4] "The stormy, perilous voyage and the long summer fishing," wrote one historian of the bold West Countrymen who dared the waters, "afforded the most arduous training in seamanship in the world offered. Once the fishermen were dragooned into [naval] service, His Majesty was assured of tough, hardy seamen, inured to all sorts of seas and weather."[5] The same could be said for the French, who concentrated their operations on the bountiful but dangerous Grand Banks. Indeed, the Newfoundland fisheries provided nothing less than the finest nursery for seamen in the world, which benefited the commercial marine and national navies of both England and France during the next century.

By the onset of the seventeenth century, English fishermen had established a tiny settlement on the Newfoundland coast, principally as a station for drying codfish, and by 1605 as many as 250 vessels in the English fishing fleet sailed for the banks each year.[6] Additional drying stations, the nucleus of settlements at isolated but often superbly sheltered harbors such as St. Johns and Ferryland, were first seasonally inhabited and then permanently—if sparsely—occupied. By 1644, more than 270 English ships a year were employed directly in the fisheries, not including those that brought salt and carried the catch to European and Mediterranean markets. The Lords Commissioners for Trade and Plantations estimated the average ship size in the fishery at 80 tons, an estimated total of 21,600 tons of shipping, 2,160 boats, and 10,800 seamen. Each vessel accounted for a normal catch of 200 to 300 quintals of fish, which sold for eight shillings per quintal in England.[7] The French harvest, which was often larger than the English catch, was even more profitable.

Despite interruptions caused by the English Civil War and the subsequent stillborn era of Commonwealth and Protectorate, the administration of Charles II eagerly sought to support and improve England's Newfoundland operations. In 1660, salt and other materials used in the fisheries were exempted from duties and three years later the fisheries themselves were exempted from taxation.[8] Each year convoy guardships were sent out with the fisheries fleets to protect them from pirates and interlopers. And to insure that all benefits of the trade would flow to England and to its fishermen, no vessels were allowed to take passengers to settle in Newfoundland or to form syndicates to compete with the established operations.[9]

In 1662, King Louis XIV, eager to increase France's share of the lucrative trade and to help fulfill his nation's colonial ambitions, dispatched 150 men and women to establish a permanent settlement at Placentia, on a broad bay that penetrated the south coast of the Avalon Peninsula of eastern Newfoundland. Armed with a commission that claimed French sovereignty over the entire island, the governor of the new colony fortified Placentia with a battery of 18 guns and proceeded to eject all English settlers from the vicinity of his settlement. Within a year, the French had spread—albeit thinly—from Cape Race to Cape Ray.[10]

France did not forcefully attempt to assert control over the entire island, despite its avowed intentions, but left the east coast to the English. At the outset of the Second Anglo-Dutch War in 1665, the inhabitants of Newfoundland, both English and French, lived in an uneasy but peaceful state of co-existence. With war against the United Netherlands becoming a reality, England turned her attentions from a French menace in Newfoundland to the danger of direct assault on home waters by her Dutch antagonist. Thus, the English fisheries of Newfoundland were vulnerable everywhere. Enemy attack might be directed against either the lightly defended English drying stations and harbors or the exposed and unprotected fishing fleet. Though the eager French were occasionally known to arrive off the coast of Ferryland as early as February, the English fleets rarely stirred from home waters before March 1, and usually returned home no later than October. The most and best fishing, it was agreed by all, occurred only after the last of the winter ice had broken up, usually in May.[11] But it was when the heavily laden fleet was preparing for the homeward voyage to England or the European markets, having assembled in the various outport harbors of the island to take on the processed and salted fish, that it was the most vulnerable—and valuable.

The English stations, which at the outset of the Restoration were divided into six admiralties and "imposts," of which St. Johns and Ferryland were among the most important, were initially supposed to be defended by a total of 56 guns, most of which, however, were never transported over. Those that had reached Newfoundland were usually dismounted, disabled, or in such poor condition that they were useless.

It is not surprising, then, that English mariners placed considerably greater confidence in nature's defenses than in those of the Crown. "It is said," testified one English inhabitant of the island,

[that] Newfoundland is guarded after fish'g ships go suffuc'tly by foggs & ice till [the] arrival of English fishermen [It] therefore need no other guard to prevent invasion that it is theirs who are strongest at sea. St. John's & fferryland and other harbours are deemed by some men accustomed to war so strongly fortified by nature that some of them having one fort and necessaries for defence its hard for any ship though never so bravely furnished to enter and if they sh'd pass without burning or sinking or being cast ashore when entered they may stay there perhaps 14 days for a wind to go out [and in] the meantime fight rocks and fort.[12]

Captain Nicholas Boes, commander of the task force assigned to attack the fisheries, must have taken great satisfaction in the knowledge that the great De Ruyter had not ignored the strong natural defenses and enemy forts when he attacked the English at Newfoundland during the last great war. In 1665, the admiral had been dispatched by the Grand Pensioner to the east, where the English fleet under the command of Sir Robert Holmes, without declaration of war having been made, had attacked the Dutch African stations en route to the Indies. De Ruyter managed quickly to undo Holmes's handiwork and then track his opponent to the Americas where he wrought havoc and ruin to England's West Indian trade. Turning his prow toward Newfoundland, De Ruyter entered undefended St. Johns Harbor on June 6. The admiral, like Boes, had come to destroy the implements of the enemy's commerce, not to fight, and proceeded to level the houses and property of the settlers and destroy the equipment and facilities for drying, salting, and storing fish. He then struck at stations on the Bay of Butts and Petty Harbor before heading homeward. The devastating blow left the once lucrative English fisheries in near ruins.

Following the end of the war, a sizable number of London and Bristol merchants, eager to obtain control of the Newfoundland fisheries by displacing the West Countrymen's ad hoc monopoly over the trade, began a drive for the permanent colonization of the island and the establishment of their own processing and distribution facilities.[13] They cited as a principal reason for such an effort the increasing power and presence of the French on the island and their growing dominance of the fishery trade—and not without some justification. The French settlement and the almost impregnable fortifications at Placentia (later termed the Gibraltar of America) were well selected for both defense and as a marine sanctuary. Unlike the English harbors on the eastern side of the Avalon Peninsula, Placentia was free from field ice in the spring. Its admirable harbor provided security for the fishing fleet, drying room for the annual catch, and an abundance of herring for bait fish.[14] As for its defenses, the first fort was erected at the strategic entrance of the gut on the south shore of the harbor and was well described by a French soldier named Le Hontan who had been stationed there. "It stood," he wrote, "upon a point of land so close to the narrow entrance of the harbor that ships going in graze so to speake upon the angle of the bastion." To further reinforce the already strong position, a battery was also erected on the opposite shore.[15] The presence of the French stronghold considerably aided the London and Bristol merchants in arousing anti-French sentiments and pro-British nationalism in their efforts to secure support and promote their schemes.

Yet their colonizing effort was fiercely opposed in court by the West Countrymen who had enjoyed a veritable fishing monopoly for nearly a century and a half. It was noted with some skill during the debates for control over the fisheries that they accounted for an annual customs revenue of £40,000 a year. In 1668 and 1669, approximately 300 ships and 15,000 men were gainfully employed in the fisheries, the port of Dartmouth alone accounting for upwards of 60 ships in the trade. However, the London an Bristol merchants contended that the French were ahead in all aspects of the trade. Their operations employed over 400 vessels (120 of which were from the port of St. Mâlo) and 18,000 seamen.[16] The West Countrymen counterattacked by arguing that colonization would lead to the divorcing of England from the profits derived from the fisheries, and the rise of an indigenous industry similar to the despised fishing operations of New England, to the economic detriment of the nation. In 1670, the government finally subscribed to the West Countrymen's arguments. Rules were issued by the Board of Trade to regulate the fisheries and effectively prohibit settlement.[17] The judgment, though preserving the monopoly, unfortunately had the detrimental effect of preventing the growth of an English population on the island. Hence, there was little willingness by seasonal inhabitants to defend its various stations, warehouses, and harbors.

In early 1672, when the outbreak of war with The Netherlands had become a foregone conclusion, the English Crown moved to provide at least the trappings of concern for the defense of the fisheries. On February 4, the king ordered that all vessels sailing to the fisheries would be provided protection upon providing £250 security "on penalty of 250£. to each vessel of 100 tons, and so proportionably," to carry "all sorts of fit and necessary instruments" for fortifying St. Johns and other places, and each vessel was to carry 20 fire arms with ammunition. All vessels were to obey His Majesty's frigates appointed as their convoy, and were directed to carry no more men than their usual complements, lest the manpower pool of mariners in England be depleted.[18]

On April 25, the Duke of York issued instruction to Captain William Davis, commander of H.M.S. *Mary Rose*, to proceed to Newfoundland in company with H.M.S. *Richmond*,

> and remain there during the fishing season, using . . . best endeavours for the protection of his Majesty's subjects there; to muster the fishermen there and keep them in good order that they may be in readiness on any occasion for the defence of the country and ships, with power to mount ordnance in St. John's Bay if necessary. To convoy the fishing ships to the Strait [of Gibraltar] and Tangier [to market] and seize all the Dutch ships he can.[19]

By fall, when the first of the fleet reached its Spanish markets, word of a season of depressing results and catastrophes began to trickle into English outports. Few in the Newfoundland fleet had experienced a fruitful season and most boats had failed to take more than 100 to 120 quintals of fish. Many investors or shareholders would realize less than 40 shillings a share in the season's venture. In some areas, such as at Bonavista, the take had been good, but the weather, turning sour, had conspired against the fishermen and prohibited drying and curing of the catch.[20]

In early October, when four or five of the fishing ships arrived at Dartmouth, it was learned that three Newfoundlandmen from that port had been "cast away there by the great drifts of ice that came upon them." And those ships that had managed to survive the ice were obliged to run a deadly gauntlet of Dutch capers to reach their English and Spanish markets. On November 4 it was reported that ten to twenty privateers, of from 6 to 36 guns were in Mounts Bay, and had recently taken three or four Newfoundlandmen.[21] The following day, it was said at Plymouth, that a vessel recently arrived from Bilbao "reports that but one vessel of all those bound thither from Newfoundland is escaped in safe, and that it is reported there are 80 capers between the North Cape and the Lizard."[22]

Account after account told of ever greater depredations against the Newfoundlandmen: three ships from Topsham here, a pair from Plymouth there, or four Southamptonmen and a Poole ship en route from the market at Malaga. One of the most humiliating occurrences took place during December when ten Dartmouth ships were taken en masse.[23] Then, in February, an entire fleet from Newfoundland, under convoy of the *Ruby*, Captain Nicholas Nowell of Dartmouth, was captured. *Ruby* was a vessel of 200 tons and 20 guns, but lacked a master willing to fight. "This Ruby," it was later reported, undertook to be convoy to 14 or 16 other English merchant ships, small and great, all Newfoundlandmen, that had with him been at Alicante and Valencia with their fish and loaded with fruit [for] home. There were three privateers, and it's said they [the Newfoundlandmen] were all taken. This Capt. Nawell refused to make any resistance, though seamen were all willing to fight.[24]

Though the Newfoundland ships were repeatedly savaged in European waters, few could have anticipated the ruinous storm that the war would dash against the Newfoundland coast, or against the fishing fleet in its waters. By the end of 1672, the West Country maritime communities, hardest hit by the depredations of the Dutch capers, had begun to cry out for peace, "for we account our poor Newfoundland men that are gone to market in a very great jeopardy."[25]

And now, even as that great nursery of seamen prepared to send its graduates homeward with the annual catch in the fall of 1673, the Dutch squadron of Captain Nicholas Boes prepared for its descent.

Near the beginning of October, Boes's squadron, composed of three ships of 40 guns each and one of 36 guns, carrying 50 English prisoners taken at New York, arrived off the Avalon Peninsula. Boes apparently decided that the principal attacks should be made against the weakly defended English outposts rather than the strong French bastion of Placentia. He had, after all, come to destroy, not to fight. His first target was Ferryland Harbor. On or about October 4, the fleet gingerly picked its way into the harbor, cautiously watching for the sharp gray rocks lying just below the waters and the first puff of smoke above that would betray the presence of harbor defenses. Fortunately for the Dutch, the harbor, once moderately well fortified, was now devoid of such works. Only four guns were mounted in a battery, and all were out of repair and unfit to contest the arrival of the Netherlanders. Ferryland was taken without a fight.[26]

Boes ordered his men ashore immediately and commenced the plundering and destruction of all household goods and stores of the inhabitants. Their cattle were slaughtered and settlement laid out to complete ruin. Damages were later placed at no less than £2,000.[27]

Upon the arrival of the Dutch squadron, more than 30 vessels belonging to a West Countryman shipowner named Nix Nevill of Dartmouth were hopelessly trapped in the plantation harbor. On October 5, Boes ordered the vessels seized and burned. The Dutch lingered about Ferryland for several days, systematically plundering and destroying everything in sight. On October 9, in an exercise that was becoming typical, they descended upon the estate of one William Pollard, three miles distant from Ferryland, and looted the premises of its stores of fish, provisions, and household goods, amounting to £400 in value. There, they also discovered 40 more fishing vessels, warehouses, and other facilities, all of which, with the exception of several ketches taken as prizes, were promptly burned.[28]

After laying waste to all that stood, floated, or moved in and about Ferryland, Boes turned his attention to the next major British harbor in Newfoundland, the little outport of St. Johns, approximately 40 miles to the northward. St. Johns, however, was not to be subdued as easily as Ferryland, for it was commanded by an old West Country seacaptain of a rather feisty disposition, one Christopher Martin of Cockington, in Devon. For 17 years Martin had served as vice admiral of St. Johns, and once as admiral. In 1665, apparently shortly after De Ruyter's descent on that place, and again in 1667, he had personally landed guns and built a small earthen fort to protect the harbor from further enemy depredation, supplying the guns with his own ammunition. Now, having received good warning concerning the new attacks on the Newfoundland coast by the Dutch, Martin again rushed to prepare for the defense of his settlement.[29]

Captain Martin lacked a large battery of guns to protect St. Johns, for the government had not, apparently, seen fit to authorize such for the defense of Newfoundland in years. Thus, he was obliged to strip *Elias Andrews*, a lightly armed ship in the harbor, of her six pieces of ordinance, and with a defense force of barely 30 men, bravely prepared to meet the foe, though, he expected to be attacked by no less a personage than Cornelis Evertsen.[30]

When Boes arrived at the entrance to St. Johns, the reception was far more spirited than he had anticipated. Though the records are silent regarding the affair, it is likely that Martin fired several shots from his strategically situated battery at the mouth of the harbor, where concentrated fire would have the greatest effect. Boes, perhaps wisely judging that a victory might be granted only at a cost he could ill afford, chose to sail on to another target. It was not a question of gallantry, but of sound military judgment, for even De Ruyter had stated after his capture of St. Johns in 1665 that had the place been defended by six guns he too would not have hazarded an entry. Thus, the diligence and bravery of Captain Christopher Martin and his handful of West Countrymen had saved the only major harbor of English Newfoundland from destruction.[31]

Boes was undismayed and continued his raids on the Newfoundland fisheries with gusto, taking prizes and burning vessels at an incredible rate. Frequent forays ashore were made at various stations along the coast. Usually, great quantities of fish were discovered in warehouses awaiting shipment. That which could not be destroyed was left behind for lack of men and vessels to carry it off. Before all was said and done, at least 150 vessels, large quantities of fish oil, and innumerable facilities were destroyed. Eight vessels—four ketches, two small "frigates," a bark, and a pinnace, laden with fish, salt, oil, bacon, and meat—were taken as prizes. Boes's manpower was stretched to the limit to secure the prizes and captured cargoes. Two West Country ketches, in fact, were allowed to sail with the fleet as prizes under their own crews, simply because there were not enough men in the Dutch squadron to go around.[32] Thus, having captured or destroyed the entire Newfoundland fishing fleet (or at last the largest portion of it), most of the shore facilities for processing fish, and a sizeable segment of the habitations on the island, Boes turned his squadron to the southeast for a rendezvous with Evertsen and Benckes at Fayal, in the Azores. His mission had been accomplished beyond all expectation.[33]

16

BLOWN INTO A THOUSAND PIECES

The dawn of September 14 greeted the joint Zeeland-Amsterdam squadron anchored off Staten Island with a fair northwest wind and every prospect of a swift departure. By mid-morning, anchors were weighed and sails set. The fleet began to move, sluggishly at first, then with increasing speed, toward an open sea. Unfortunately, *Swaenenburgh*, "due to the clumsiness of the pilot," was run aground. Her commander boldly ordered that an effort be made to press her across the shoal by "force of sail alone," It was a tactic not without considerable hazard, for there was always the chance that the ship would be driven even harder aground than before, or that her timbers would be torn asunder in the effort. With luck, the maneuver enabled the vessel to reach her natural element, deep water, but not without cost, for she began leaking badly as a result of the impact. When one of the prizes also ran aground and could not be refloated until the evening flood tide freed her, the entire fleet was obliged to come to anchor.[1]

Frustration soon followed frustration, for, once refloated, the prize and her companions were then held hostage to contrary winds. Indeed, for the next two days, the wind blew hard directly from the east. Having already experienced the many exasperations inherent with any stranding and possessing little faith in his pilot's knowledge of the area, Cornelis Evertsen wisely refrained from taxing his luck by tacking his ship through the hazardous channel and out to sea. Finally, on the 17th, though the dawn had been hidden by an early morning fog, a northerly wind began to blow. By 9:00 A.M. the fog had disappeared and the fleet again got underway: two warships, a fireship, and nine prizes in all.[2] For the next month, the voyage across the Atlantic proceeded without major event or injury until October 16, when, Evertsen noted with classic understatement in *Swaenenburgh's* log, "it began to blow hard."[3]

On October 17 the gale grew in violence as the fleet struggled desperately to keep together. Such objectives were scarcely possible as the heavily laden prizes wallowed in the deep troughs, rapidly falling away from the swifter warships. *Swaenenburgh*, in imminent danger of losing her flock, was forced to run "under bare poles and the prizes couldn't keep up," but in vain. About midday the big warship intentionally came up into the wind to wait for the straggling fleet, but as evening came on she was obliged to make enough sail so that she might control her drift. The tempest was unrelenting in its violence, damaging many ships in the convoy. *Swaenenburgh's* foresail was ripped from its boltstraps and her mainsail shredded. Another mainsail was set and the foresail was repaired as the ship again ran under bare poles before the wind, with only a damaged rudder for control. Finally, about midnight, the weather calmed a bit and the foresail was reset, providing some degree of management.[4]

By the next morning, the weather had again degenerated. As Evertsen scanned the black, froth-tipped seas about him, he could no longer see Benckes's *Noordhollandt*, the fireship, or five of the nine prizes, and presumed that they had pressed well ahead during the night. By evening the storm had renewed its intensity, accentuated by lightning, thunder, and hard, pelting rains. Still, *Swaenenburgh* held her course, ever hopeful of coming up with her companions.[5]

The gale abated somewhat on October 19 and the distended fleet, spread about the Atlantic like so much flotsam and jetsam, slogged onward, attempting to make repairs as it proceeded. On October 22, the ships of the fleet, separated by this time for nearly a week by the gale, began to regroup. Damage, fortunately, was reparable, although the Zeeland flagship had suffered considerable injury to her rudder and chain. Then, on October 25, the lookout aboard *Swaenenburgh* shouted out the long awaited words, "Land ahead." The island of Flores, westernmost landfall in the Azores, had been sighted.[6]

Flores, and its nearby sister isle, Corve, lay, as one historian noted, "on the outer periphery of the Azorean consciousness." And as the Dutch had already learned, the two islands occupied perhaps the wildest and windiest stretch of ocean in the Azorean Archipelago, if not in the entire Atlantic Ocean. Landfall was a welcome sight nevertheless, for all aboard the fleet knew that they were now barely 120 miles from Fayal, where they hoped to join up with their comrades from the Terre Neuf Expedition. Here too, they could take on fresh water and make needed repairs in a relatively secure, neutral roadstead. At Horta, the principal town of Fayal, they could also drop off the French and English prisoners, thus relieving themselves of the danger of a potential prisoner uprising and a steady drain on their provisions.[7]

At daylight, October 27, Fayal, one of the four major islands of the central Azores, was finally sighted. By midday, *Swaenenburgh* was barely four miles southwest of the island's westernmost tip. But maneuvering into Fayal Channel, between the islands of Fayal on the west and Pico on the east, and then getting into the roads was another matter. Throughout the night and well into the afternoon of the following day the ships of the fleet tacked back and forth in a tedious effort to get into the roads. Finally, at 3:00 P.M. *Swaenenburgh* came to anchor in 22 fathoms in the roads. Soon, she was joined by the entire fleet,[8] with the notable exception of Benckes.

Evertsen was gratified to find safely anchored here the four ships of Captain Nicholas Boes's Terre Neuf squadron, along with six prizes taken by Captain Van Zijl and two ketches captured by Captain De Witte.[9] Though a few of his own prizes failed to maneuver into the roads during the day, the Zeeland commander was undoubtedly pleased to greet his countrymen, fresh and flush from their raid on the Newfoundland fisheries. He was also eager to learn of their exploits. "The Captains told us," he later wrote, "that they had found a great deal of fish on land in the warehouses, which for lack of ships was left there, and that they had ruined and burned at least 150 sloops and some containers of fish oil."[10]

Boes and his officers were modest in the extreme, for they had so injured the English fisheries at Newfoundland that it was impossible for the king's ministers to produce an annual account for the 1673 harvest, simply because it—along with the entire Newfoundland fleet—had been all but destroyed.[11]

The reunion of the two Dutch fleets at Fayal was undoubtedly an occasion for excitement and merriment for the seamen. And the roadstead in which they were anchored presented for them perhaps one of the most dramatic settings encountered on the entire voyage. To the immediate east, less than five miles away, lay the rugged, mountainous island of Pico, already famed for its wines, with its imposing, snow—capped volcanic peak. The peak, which still occasionally wisped smoke, was as famous as the island's wines, and rose over 17,000 feet above the ocean floor (of which 7,175 feet was above sea level). To the west, across the shallow Fayal Channel, lay the sister island of Fayal and the town of Horta, one of the most important victualling and fueling stations between North America and Europe. Fayal, like Pico, was a small volcanic island, dominated by a single cone, Pico Gordo, or Fat Peak, which rose heavenward over 3,400 feet. Though inferior in size to her sister, Fayal's terrain was every bit as rugged, and perhaps more dangerous. As recently as April 1672, a new volcano had erupted in a fiery birthing ordeal on the western end of the island, followed by a devastating earthquake. The combination of deadly ash falls and fire inflicted heavy damage on pasturelands, agricultural fields, and a few villages.[12]

The attraction for transatlantic travellers was the sanctuary offered by the Bay of Horta and the Fayal Channel. Not only was the scenery imposing, but the protection afforded from easterly and westerly gales by Pico on the east and the hills behind Horta on the west, was enormously important to mariners thirsting for a safe anchorage after weeks of being battered on the open ocean. The southerly and southwesterly winds, to which the shipping in the harbor and roads were frequently exposed, were moderated by cross-channel currents. The roads, with a fine sandy bottom, varied in depth from 18 to 25 fathoms, and provided an excellent holding ground for ships of all sizes. In addition to the main ship anchorage, a short volcanic protrusion jutting toward the channel at Porto Pim, just south of Horta, and another a bit to the north, at Praia de Almoxarife, provided modest but important shelters for small craft as well.[13]

Unfortunately, the roads at Fayal and those of the rest of the Azores such as at Angra, on Terceira, were not without a major flaw. If Flores was eternally cursed with the windiest weather in the Atlantic, the central island of the archipelago suffered the deadliest. Known as the *Carpinteiro*, or Carpenter Winds, this often fatal southeasterly gale sprang up without warning, forcing masters of ships to slip their cables and run for the open seas: if anchored too close to a southern shoreline, they faced a strong possibility of disaster. Shipwrecks were common in the Azores. Between 1550 and 1650 the Spanish documented no fewer than 53 of their ships as lost in the islands, usually as a result of storms. Two centuries later, five or six ships annually were lost in or near the port of Angra alone.[14] Unfortunately, the Dutch fleet anchored in Fayal Roads would soon add some of its own ships to the growing number of wrecks caused by the dreaded Carpinteiro.

By October 29, the entire fleet was finally drawn together, with the exception of *Noordhollandt*, and began the onerous task of taking on fresh water for the final leg of the voyage. The business of setting the English and French prisoners ashore (or at least a portion of them) was also begun. Few paid much attention to the weather in the harbor as the sky darkened and the breezes intensified. About midday the south-southeast wind began to blow harder and, though *Swaenenburgh's* cable snapped, her main starboard anchor was immediately dropped and held fast, preventing a stranding. The following day, with light, calm breezes, passed with little event and Evertsen spent no small time fishing for his lost anchor. He had already decided (and wisely so, as events would prove) to shift his anchorage into deeper water and farther from shore in case he needed to escape the roads in adverse weather. That night, almost imperceptibly, the winds began to creep around to the southeast again. And by the following morning, October 31, had commenced the first skirmishing rounds of a major engagement. The prize ship *Batchelor*, with only a single anchor to hold her, began to drift toward shore, and would certainly have been stranded without Evertsen's immediate assistance. The commander, seeing the prize drifting helplessly toward the rocks, quickly dispatched his own third port anchor for her to deploy, preventing certain disaster. The omen, however, had become even more menacing as the sky darkened again and the winds increased by the hour. That evening, the fatal Carpinteiro careened across Fayal Roads in all its natural fury.[15]

When the storm struck, there was little any ship could do but fight for its own survival. There could not, and would not be any help forthcoming from any other in the fleet. By midday, November 1, the tempest intensified. *Swaenenburgh* dropped her topmasts, but wisely kept her yards and a portion of her rigging up. In the event her cable snapped again, she could readily put on sail, maintain steerage way, and perhaps, if lucky, avoid being driven ashore and lost. Captain Van Zijl, whose ship was anchored aft the Zeeland flagship, quickly followed suit. With evening, the full wrath of the Carpinteiro was felt. "At night a full storm blew," Evertsen recorded in his ship's log, replete "with rain and lightning, which drove most of the ships ahead of it running great danger of being driven against the shore."[16]

The storm, despite every human effort to the contrary, claimed its victims. Two of the rich Virginia prizes, *Elias* of London and *Pearl* of Bristol, laden with approximately 1,300 hogsheads of tobacco, and the two ketches taken by Captain De Witte at Newfoundland, laden with fish, lost their anchors and were instantly doomed. "The ships," reported Evertsen, "were blown into a thousand pieces, except for a ketch, which had been driven up so high by the seas that with low water it was sitting mostly high and dry." Eighteen or 19 crewmen from these unfortunate vessels were drowned, and the remainder cast away on the beaches, some sustaining severe injuries. Another of the Newfoundland prizes lost her foremast and bowsprit, and one of the Virginia ships her rudder. By the middle of the dogwatch, about 2:00 A.M., the storm mercifully began to slacken. Had it continued, Evertsen remarked rather ruefully, "it would have been all over for us since if our cable had broken in the night there would have been no escape." Indeed, he entered into his log, if the tempest had sustained, "to all human judgment not a ship would have come out of it."[17]

Though morning brought better weather, it was still extremely unsettled, with abnormally high seas and, occasionally, driving rain squalls. After having survived the terrors of the night in treacherous proximity to the shore, *Swaenenburgh* and one of the prizes that had anchored farthest out, fearful of another storm, resolved to cut their anchors "no longer to wait the dangers which had beset us the previous night." This was not without hazard, for one mistake and the ships would have easily ended up on the beach, bilged and broken. A spring line was set on the anchor cable and hauled up to bring the ship's bow to face the open sea. A buoy was attached to the cable to locate the anchor for retrieval under more favorable circumstances and weather. Then both cable and spring lines were cut and the ship, sails on, passed into safer waters. Unfortunately, the remainder of the fleet had anchored so close to shore that such maneuvers were impossible for them. All that could be hoped for was a break in the weather, and a prayer that the Carpinteiro would not return.[18]

On November 3, *Swaenenburgh* attempted to return to the roads, but for two days the ship was hampered by adverse winds and dirty weather and could make no headway. Gradually, one by one, the fleet in the roads also began to escape the windy manacles that bound them and joined the flagship off the west end of the island. By November 6, a total of a dozen vessels came out despite the winds, calms, heavy rains, thunder, and lightning.[19]

The winds shifted to a favorable position on November 7, blowing from the north. Soon the fleet was joined by Captain Van Zijl who also fortunately managed to escape from Fayal Roads. Evertsen, eager for news concerning the disposition of the remainder of the fleet, pressed the captain for every bit of information he had. Van Zijl reported that *Schaeckerloo* had sailed from the roads the previous day with two of the Newfoundland prizes. Before he departed, however, De Witte managed to salvage the mast from one of the wrecked ketches and fashion it into a foremast for one of the prizes that had lost her own. Captain Richewijn, it seemed, was still in the roads with the Virginia ship, which had lost her rudder while a new one was being made.[20]

Van Zijl informed Evertsen of an unexpected danger facing the Virginia ship, even while under Richewijn's protection. The English and French prisoners who had been put ashore some time earlier, had vowed to overwhelm the tobacco prize if she remained much longer in the roads, a conspiracy that Evertsen and the captain took quite seriously. They agreed that prompt action was necessary. Van Zijl would return to the roads and bring the Virginia prize out, towing her if necessary, with or without a rudder. The captain was also directed to see if *Swaenenburgh's* anchor could be brought out. Evertsen, in the meantime, would escort the remainder of the fleet to the island of Terceira, to the east of Pico, where he would continue to take on water and await Van Zijl. Perhaps, he hoped, he would encounter Jacob Benckes as well.[21]

The flotilla sailed north and east, threading the islands of São Jorge and Graciosa on the night of November 7, and arriving at Terceira the following day. Originally dubbed, shortly after its discovery, Ilha Terceira do Nosso Senhor Jesus Cristo (The Third Island of Our Lord Jesus Christ), the island's name had been rapidly abbreviated to simply Terceira. Though of significance, strategically and economically, to Portugal, and of international importance as a mid-Atlantic waystation, the island could boast of only 16 small villages and few anchorages, most of them far inferior to those of neighboring Fayal. Its principal town, Angra do Herōismo, was situated on the tiny oval Bay of Angra, on the south side of the island, and at the base of the 585-foot-tall Monte Brasil volcano. Agra Bay, barely 700 yards wide at its mouth and 800 yards deep, was rarely employed as a principal anchorage. Vessels preferred to drop hook at its mouth or slightly outside, where there was a sandy bottom and good holding ground.[22] An alternative anchorage, but one often favored, lay over a mile seaward, exposed to winds and in 30 to 35 fathoms of water with an uncertain holding ground. But it was, at least, not as dangerous as the bay during a southeasterly gale. And over all loomed two intimidating fortresses, São João, with its massive 3,000 foot-long wall of stone, and São Sebatiāno across the harbor.[23]

Upon reaching Terceira on November 8, Evertsen was pleased to find that Captain De Witte and *Schaeckerloo* had arrived safely in company with the fireship *Sint Joris* and two prizes. As the wind was out of the northeast, the commander apparently preferred to secure his anchorage in deep water, well off Angra Bay, to await Richewijn and Van Zijl. It was only a matter of hours, however, before Richewijn appeared with the rudderless Virginiaman under tow.[24]

The following day was largely taken up with watering, repairing the injured Virginiaman, and making reports. On Tuesday, November 11,

Van Zijl came in from Fayal. There, he reported, he had entered the roads, apparently immediately after Richewijn's departure, and found them empty. Though he had not bothered to anchor, he learned from a lighter from shore that all of the shipping had departed from the harbor only a short time before. Before leaving the roads, he had dispatched an order to the acting Dutch consul there, a merchant named Abraham de Vogelaer, "to take charge of and secure for the State everything that might wash up on shore" or articles that might be "fished up" from the wrecked prizes lost in the recent storm. Finally, he informed Evertsen that he had not seen the buoy for *Swaenenburgh's* lost anchor and voiced an opinion "that the Portuguese had cut it."[25]

Cornelis Evertsen had been eager to reach the Azores, the oasis of the Atlantic, not only because of the respite and succor promised, but because he expected to find orders awaiting him there. He had, by now, remained in the islands for over three weeks and had received neither respite from the howling tempests nor orders. His fleet was in poor condition, and would undoubtedly continue to degenerate as the season progressed. Thus, in a later report to the Zeeland government, he explained the course of action he now took.

> This storm [of November 1] left our ships still more leaky and the rudder [of *Swaenenburgh*] quite loose since the rudder braces were worn through . . . our prizes, some of which were not very [water] tight, were very uncommoded, all this taken together decided me to sail with the Hollands Lands Ships to Cadiz, not daring to sail for the Fatherland with a leaky ship and prizes without full sets of sails and needing everything.[26]

It was a critically important decision born of caution rather than boldness, since Cadiz was an officially neutral but friendly port, and one in which the Dutch held considerable economic influence. Evertsen lost little time in getting underway. Signals were raised on *Swaenenburgh*, and all Dutch ships and their prizes lying before Angra were summoned to depart as quickly as possible.

The convoy sailed on the evening on November 11, approaching the island of São Miguel in the Eastern Azores group two days later. On the 14th, the fleet was becalmed and slowly drifted with the current between São Miguel on the north and the island of Santa Maria on the south. The following morning, a favorable breeze picked up, and the last of the Azores disappeared over the horizon.[27]

As expected, the voyage was rich with difficulties. The sluggish prize ships were constantly falling behind, obliging their shepherds to come up into the wind and wait for them. Again the storms struck, replete with sleet and rain, thunder and lightning. From November 20 through

25, the fleet was subjected to an almost continuous gale. By the third day of the storm, *Swaenenburgh* was "leaking so badly that it was as much as we could do to hold on with two pumps running." In the midst of the blow, *Schaeckerloo* and four of the smallest prizes disappeared. Though a sighting four days later to the leeward of the fleet was presumed to be the warship, no one could say for certain.[28] Indeed, it seemed as if the five ships had been swallowed up by the sea.

At last, on November 28, the coast of Spain was spotted, and on the next day, Lagos could be seen in the distance. But nature conspired, even now, to retard the voyagers. On the 30th, strong winds sprang up out of the east. The prize ship *Batchelor* lost her main topmast, and progress was minimal. Then followed two frustrating days of calm. Finally, on the night of December 2, a friendly breeze began to blow.[29]

At dawn, *Swaenenburgh*'s lookout, ever watchful now that they were in European waters, spotted a strange sail to leeward. Soon the chase was on. Within a short time, the big warship hove in sight of six more sail and pressed the pursuit with renewed vigor. About midday, Evertsen came up with the prey and found them to be friendly Vlissengen capers. They, and seven more of their comrades—a fleet of 14 in all—were but five or six days out of home port and had, they reported, been cruising off Cape St. Vincent in search of prizes. Though Evertsen was undoubtedly eager to learn of recent events at home, he could ill afford to tarry. After sailing a short time with the commander and his tattered fleet, the capers broke off on their own on the evening of December 3. Evertsen now steered a course of east northeast, directly for the Bay of Cadiz. By sundown of the following day, the noble and ancient city of Cadiz lay only three miles ahead.[30]

17

VERY ILL AND DANGEROUS
CONSEQUENCES

By the beginning of the summer of 1673, the new British Admiralty Secretary, Samuel Pepys, had grown deeply concerned over the fates of the lightly protected convoys due in from the East Indies, Barbados, and Virginia. His concerns were well founded, for the main enemy fleets of Cornelis Tromp and De Ruyter, which poised a constant menace to the English coast, had been spotted as recently as mid-June at the back of the Shipwash and in the Sledway. Their subsequent presence off Harwich and the mouth of the Thames caused some to even fear a possible attack on the main British squadron under Prince Rupert. Though battle had not been joined, and the Dutch eventually retired to their former positions in the shoals of Schoneveld on the Dutch coast, the hazard to convoys coming through the Downs and into the Thames estuary was still enormous.[1] Unhappily for the English, the danger was compounded by the presence of enemy capers that patrolled in large numbers along the western approaches to England and Ireland, and even in the Channel. Indeed, as recently as June 9, it had been reported that a number of Dutch privateers were cruising near Cape Clear, Ireland, specifically awaiting the arrival of the rich, tobacco-laden Virginiamen.[2] Pepys undoubtedly groaned over the necessity of stretching the Royal Navy's already over-extended resources even further to accommodate the incoming convoys with adequate protection on the last and most dangerous leg of their voyages. Unfortunately, such efforts had become central to the continued promulgation of the war.

For England, the organizational problems and the physical and economic limitations encountered in providing convoy protection in home waters were becoming monumental. No sooner had one convoy arrived or departed than planning and provisioning for the protection of the next began. It was a sophisticated system Pepys had helped develop and hone to a fine edge, but it had, unfortunately, a few rough spots still. With money, men, ships, and provisions in terribly short supply, the components for convoys were found and fielded with the utmost difficulty. And once they were at sea, they more often than not stayed at sea. No sooner did escort or patrol vessels return from a tour of duty than they were, of necessity, immediately ordered back to sea, often without adequate preparations, repairs, or provisioning. Wear and tear on ships and crews alike was telling, and losses through accidental strandings or founderings that stemmed from such stresses were common. Morale among crew members, many of whom went unpaid for months, was abysmal. Their food and drink, still often procured through favored and frequently crooked naval contractors, were usually putrid by the time the ships had left port, if not before. Yet Pepys, during his tenure as Clerk of the Acts and later as Admiralty Secretary, had made great strides, despite the corruptions of the system, in stemming corrosive procurement practices, in reorganizing and streamlining the contracting system, and providing the means that built and kept the navy afloat, armed, and fed.

Pepys understood the enormous financial import of the incoming convoys to the war effort, and in particular the Virginia fleet, which by itself produced between £120,000 and £140,000 in customs revenues for the Treasury annually.[3] Without such funds to fuel the sputtering English economy, the war might well be lost. In late May, the first word of potential danger to the Chesapeake trade reached Ireland with vague reports that 17 to 18 Dutch privateers were intending "to attempt something on Virginia."[4] In early July, Pepys received additional indications that the danger to Captain Gardiner's convoy lay not only in home waters, but in the Americas as well. Word arrived from Lyme on June 7 that a merchantman called the *Providence* had reached Plymouth two weeks earlier, having left the colony of Maryland in May. Her master brought both good and bad news, for when he sailed, a convoy was just forming under protection of Gardiner's *Barnaby*. Confirmation of Gardiner's safe arrival in the Tidewater was wholeheartedly welcomed. What was unexpected, though, and certainly most troubling, was word that the convoy was specifically targeted for attack by "8 Dutch men-of-war homeward bound from Guinea [Guiana?], which . . . intended to visit them, which put them on making the best provisions for their defence." Equally distressing were reports that caper activity on the western coast of England was on the increase, posing a threat not only to Gardiner, but to all incoming convoys from the west. Indeed, only a few days before, a Dutch privateer of 18 guns had, with bold impunity, snapped up 2 or 3 inward-bound ships directly off Plymouth. By July, it was being reported that the entire coast "is extremely infested with capers."[5]

Despite the mandatory concern for the convoys, the Admiralty was also up to its elbows preparing for a major allied naval offensive against Tromp and De Ruyter and an invasion of The Netherlands. As a consequence, unallocated resources, ships, and men, which might have been drawn upon for patrol and escort duty, were minimal. Thus, Pepys reacted expeditiously, but conservatively to the need for convoy protection. He was well aware that every spare ship and man was necessary for the next campaign—one that might just end the war. Only two fourth-rate men-of-war, *Adventure* and *Morning Star*, fresh in from several weeks of hard patrol duty in the west, could be spared to shepherd Gardiner in. Both ships were ordered back to sea immediately to meet and escort the expected Virginiamen.[6] King Charles II was apparently more apprehensive over the convoy's security and revenues than was Pepys, and he was not inclined to be stingy in the matter of convoy protection. He forcefully suggested, in a face-to-face meeting with the admiralty secretary, that the fifth-rate warship *Speedwell*, also just in from patrol, be immediately dispatched with or after the other two, to the Soundings, there to look carefully out for the Virginia fleet and convoy it out of danger. Then, second-guessing even himself, the king directed an additional five ships—*Norwich*, *Dragon*, and *Hunter* from the Thames and two frigates from Prince Rupert's fleet—to join the small squadron.[7]

Pepys, of course, endured far more than a second-guessing monarch. He frequently had problems in both motivating occasionally less-than-obedient or incompetent commanders to do their duty, and then in answering the complaints of the merchant community clamoring for more and better protection for their ships. The most common complaints lodged with the Admiralty, often by powerful and influential merchant syndicates, were that the commanders of the king's ships to the west "neglect their duties by lying in port, and so expose trade to the enemy's privateers." Under such pressures, Pepys more than once found it necessary to urge the governor of Plymouth, Colonel Hugh Piper, to report all captains who stayed longer in port than necessary. The secretary was often obliged to prod his captains to stay at sea as long as possible. When Captain Tyrwhitts, commander of the *Adventure* patrol, hurriedly put out from Kinsale, Ireland, to watch for the Virginia convoy, he was specifically directed to "keep the sea with his squadron as much as may be, to stop the complaints of the merchants."[8] Yet, with tact and skill, goading and blustering, Pepys somehow managed to hold things together while tending to the all-important planning for the Anglo-French naval offensive against Tromp and De Ruyter.

As the days and weeks slipped by, and escort patrols, came and went with regularity, anxieties over the fate of the overdue incoming convoys from the west continued to mount. Finally, in late summer, there was at least some relief. On August 5, Arthur Capel, Earl of Essex and Lord Lieutenant of Ireland, sent a dispatch from Dublin Castle informing Secretary of State Arlington that a combined fleet of no fewer than 40 East and West Indiamen from Barbados had safely arrived at Kinsale. They were under the convoy of a single warship, H.M.S. *St. David*, Captain Poole commanding.[9] The vulnerability of the fleet, with but a single guardship, was shocking to Essex, and he was quick to point out that "had four or five of the Dutch privateers on this coast met and had intelligence of them, they might have burnt and taken all these ships."[10] Delighted with the news of the convoy's safe arrival at Kinsale, but concerned over the now-hazardous final leg of its voyage into the Downs, Pepys reminded Colonel Piper on August 9 that the "value of the fleet is such that no means are to be neglected for bringing them safe into their ports; to which purpose the king's ships which they meet are to accompany them into the Downs."[11]

On August 11, the combined Anglo-French fleets of Prince Rupert and the Count d'Estree engaged Tromp and De Ruyter at the Battle of Schoneveld and were decidedly beaten. The invasion of Holland was indefinitely postponed. Within days, a resurgence of caper activity around the British Isles had commenced. By August 20, no fewer than 40 to 50 colliers had been chased on shore by Dutch privateers, unescorted merchantmen suffered commensurately, and the vital fisheries were seriously imperiled. With Prince Rupert's fleet obliged to retire to the Nore to refit, and the French having all but abandoned the Channel, the Lords of the Admiralty again grew anxious over the security of the East and West Indian fleet en route from Ireland, and even more so for the long-overdue Virginia fleet, which was daily expected. Pepys, no doubt pressured by both King and the Council of Trade and Plantations, again beseeched Rupert to send out five or six frigates to insure the fleet's safe arrival.[12] Soon, every available vessel on the coast was being ordered out as well.

When Captain Poole's convoy finally arrived in the Thames, much to the relief of all concerned, it brought not only the West India trade, but also new and extremely unsettling intelligence concerning Evertsen's marauding in American waters. From depositions taken in Barbados from Peter Wroth, captain of *Little Kitt*, the London government belatedly learned of the Dutch naval visit to the South American mainland.[13] Wroth reported the presence of at least several Dutch warships in the Suriname River, including two of 20 and 24 guns, a victualler, and a fireship "which next spring tide intended to go to Virginia to do what mischief they could." The warships, he reported, had landed 100 men and two months' provisions, ammunition, and pay for the Dutch garrison.[14] With sketchy accounts and rumors concerning Dutch warships and capers marauding about the West Indies beginning to come in as well, the Admiralty was finally beginning to piece together the mosaic of enemy intentions in the Americas. The threat to the rich Virginia flotilla was now all but confirmed. Even news of a successful British foray from Barbados against the weakly held Dutch island of Tobago failed to calm growing fears of a potential disaster in America.[15]

Fearful for the safety of the Virginia fleet, and still ignorant of the surrender of New York, a worried King Charles II and the Lords of the Admiralty fretted over the increasing tardiness of Captain Gardiner's convoy, as well as the paucity of ships available to protect it on its final leg home. By September 9, Pepys wrote, the king and Admiralty had become "so apprehensive of the want of ships in the Soundings to secure the Virginia fleet, now hourly expected in, that they have ordered the convoys with the Kinsale fleet [the warships that had escorted Captain Poole's fleet into the Downs] to return to their stations."[16] Two days later, the king ordered Rupert to send out all ships that had only recently been returned to him from the Western Station (or replacements if they were unfit) to watch for Gardiner.[17] As late as September 16, Pepys was still juggling with ships of the main battle fleet to provide protection for the homeward-bound convoy.[18]

Anticipatory rumors of the fleet's arrival at Kinsale began to circulate in Ireland in early September. Most were quashed by the Earl of Essex, lest there be some unfortunate repercussions. He informed Secretary Arlington that he had dispatched orders to that place

> to be ready for Captain Gardiner, in case he should arrive, and if any time should intervene before his coming thither, such as should give opportunity to any squadron of the Dutch, or a considerable number of their capers to appear on our coasts, I shall be watchful to give him early notice.[19]

The earl was quick to squelch unconfirmed reports, as was Pepys, who feared such false accounts of the fleet's arrival might promulgate unforeseen, even unfortunate, occurrences—such as a surprise enemy attack.[20]

Raid on America

Finally, on September 18, the long-awaited convoy appeared. Forty sail of Virginiamen limped into Plymouth under the protective wing of his majesty's Hired Ship *Barnaby*. Nine more were escorted into Bristol by Captain Cotterell, whose own vessel, *Augustine*, was in deplorable condition. Yet they were heartily welcomed by the Admiralty Office, the Board of Trade, the king's chambers, and every concerned merchant in England.[21] Unhappily it soon became all too apparent that their worst fears had been substantially realized. The Virginia fleet had been savaged by Dutch raiders in the Chesapeake, even before it had sailed. *Augustine* was in such bad condition that she required immediate and extensive repair and refitting. Her crew was composed of men more dead than alive, both from wounds suffered in battle and from sickness. And she had arrived seriously short of provisions, powder, and match. Gardiner recounted the grim events of the Chesapeake disaster first to Colonel Piper, and then to Pepys. The clash with Evertsen and Benckes had been a catastrophe, with five ships burned and at least seven more captured. The defeat was caused, it was said, "through the cowardice of Cotterell in running away,"[22] words that extinguished the captain's career in the Royal Navy. The official communiques from the government of Virginia, however, caused the greatest commotion within the Admiralty and Privy Council.

Exactly when Pepys, Arlington, and the king first examined the reports from Virginia is unclear. What is certain, however, is that official reaction was dismay. The letters from Governor Berkeley and his Council told a depressing tale of defeat and humiliation suffered on the Chesapeake. While praising the Royal Navy for its bravery and courage in battle against overwhelming odds, the Virginia government sought to excuse itself—and managed to do so convincingly—by presenting a long list of disadvantages and disabilities it had faced in attempting to place the colony on a full wartime footing.[23] Virginia Secretary Thomas Ludwell, in his own brief account of the affair, sought to smooth the waters of the tumult that was certain to arise when the official Council report was made known. Ludwell's letter was entrusted to Lieutenant Edward Price of *Augustine* who was directed to deliver it personally to Arlington, along with a plea for the Secretary of State's "assistance towards his Matie when our declaration shall be p^rsented to the Councill table." He begged

> the true state of our p^rsent condicõn being weighed and our inability to defend our selves [be] considered and the consequences of saveing so considerable a plantacõn, wch employes soe many shipps, spends soe much of the manufacture of England, and brings soe great a revenue to

the Crowne being duly valewed, His Matie may be graciously pleased to afford us that protection wch wee cannot give our selves.[24]

Hot on the heels of the Virginia disaster, even worse news concerning the Dutch depredations in the Americas arrived, leaving all that had gone before pale by comparison. On October 3, Whitehall received intelligence of the arrival of a French vessel called *St. Joseph*, retaken from the foe by a privateer. The Dutch prize crew aboard when the ship was retaken testified that Commander Evertsen had captured the vessel 18 weeks earlier in the West Indies. More shocking, however, was that only six weeks before her recapture and arrival in the Downs, Evertsen had sent her to Holland from New York, "where he then was with nine stout men-of-war and a fireship in possession of that place." That New York had fallen was distressing enough, but the most humiliating part of all was that the city had surrendered with barely a fight, it was said on the condition that not a house be plundered.[25] The English government was momentarily stunned as a flood of accounts began to arrive detailing the capitulation of the city. Letters and depositions of various witnesses to the event, sent by Governor Leverett of Massachusetts, told a depressing tale of treachery, cowardice, and subjugation.[26] When word of the raid on the Newfoundland fisheries began to trickle in from Boston, it seemed that affairs in America had become a shambles almost overnight.

By the middle of October, as more information concerning the state of affairs crossed the Atlantic, the English mercantile community began to clamor. On October 22, a memorial was presented to the Board of Trade urging, in the strongest terms, the recovery of New York. The document, which was read before the Board four days later, noted (incorrectly) that all or most of the enemy's forces were still in New York, permitting them, as they were so strategically central to New England and Maryland and Virginia, to threaten and infest those places at their pleasure. There could be no security in any of the Atlantic colonies until England regained New York and instituted full protection of the merchant marine by a "competent strength of ships & men of War." Without such naval protection, "both the Colonies and traders will probably suffer frequent losses, to their impoverishment, if not their utter ruine; and his Matie will loose a considerable part of his customes."[27] Indeed, recent secret intelligence reports from The Netherlands suggested that at least six men-of-war and enough troops to fortify themselves in those parts would soon be sent out to insure the establishment of a permanent Dutch stronghold in America. Unless a speedy course of action was undertaken, warned the memorialists, "it will in a short time be more difficult to reduce that place."[28]

Schemes for the recapture of New York sprang up on every hand. One of the first was presented to the government by one William Dyer (later destined to become New York's Collector of Customs). The colony, he pointed out, was the key to his majesty's dominions in America. Strategically, "it is as commodious in obedience and contrary when in the enemy's hands as Tangier to the Straits [of Gibraltar] or the Downs to the Channel of England." He reminded the government that New York possessed a most excellent harbor in which enemy shipping could not only anchor in safety, but be conveniently repaired and provisioned as well. From there, they might launch raids at will against any or all of His Majesty's colonies from the Caribbean to New England, "burning shipps, disturbing ye people, and so obstruct all commerce there." They could ultimately destroy or divert the entirety of the American trade to England's economic detriment at home and abroad.[29]

Dyer tinkered with several plans for New York's reduction. Aware that the crown could ill afford the diversion of a great number of warships or men to retake the colony, he suggested only

> a considerable fforce of ffrigotts with what ffire ships shall be necessary for the design, man'd sufficiently for defence till they arriue in New England where men may be had to supply his Maties occasions; who being acquainted with the Countrey and ffresh ffor seruice, one may be capable to perform as much as two Tyered wth a long Voyage.[30]

In a later revised plan he suggested that four ships of 30 to 40 guns be dispatched. After the reduction of the city, these would be sufficient to convoy the next Virginia fleet home in safety. As for the Dutch inhabitants of New York, at least those who failed to remain loyal to the English king would be expelled from the province. As to just how the city might be reduced, Dyer was not so precise. He suggested that a land force of about 2,000 men, both horse and foot, could be raised in the country. With the British blocking the harbor and the army cutting off supplies from the countryside, he concluded, the Dutch would be forced to surrender, or else they would "expose them selves to the inconvenience and Terrour of ffire and sword, wch must be executed by storming the Town, and Burning their ships in the Rhoad."[31]

Dyer was quick to point out that the loss of the £150,000 or so in annual customs duties provided by the king's plantations in America would certainly cause irreparable damage to England's economy. But there were other dangers, he reminded the government, in addition to the direct military threat of an enemy foothold on the North American continent. Principal among these was the economic or political dismemberment of the English colonial establishment in America. The recalcitrant and independent-minded inhabitants of New England, he noted with some justification, would not move without direct orders from the crown, and unless speedy relief was forthcoming, "they may be compelled to embrace terms of a very ill and dangerous consequence." Finally, he recommended, once New York was retaken and the Dutch expelled, their estates should be sold, the harbor refortified, and a governor "acquainted with the manners and constitution of the country" appointed. And who could lead such an expedition of reconquest? Why, Dyer suggested, he, himself, who "dares engage his life to raise men enough, if his Majesty give[s] commission."[32]

Though Dyer's services were not called upon, his plans were reflective of several that gained considerable favor in governmental circles. On October 29, a similar scheme was formally proposed by Sir John Knight to the Earl of Shaftsbury, Sir Anthony Cooper, who was then serving as Lord Chancellor of England and President of the Council of Trade and Plantations. Knight's plan, the first to be seriously considered by the Council of Trade, was presented with the assumption that Evertsen would winter his ships and men at New York. While there, it was supposed, he would make the best use of his time to "get what other plantations he can Lying neare to that place from His Majesty." To counter such an eventuality, Knight proposed that 10 warships be secretly dispatched with 500 soldiers and a store of arms and ammunition for his majesty's subjects living near New York to assist in the recovery effort before the Dutch had an opportunity to fully entrench themselves in the region. The individuals selected by the crown to command the operations should be given "full and sufficient power" to raise forces in New England and Virginia, as well as an adequate number of merchant ships "as are fitt for warr" at Virginia, to join the Royal Navy force sent there. Concerned that the Virginia planters might revolt and join the Dutch "if some better gouerment there then formerly be not kept over them," and to better defend the merchant fleet from the enemy, he revised the threadbare suggestion that forts be erected near the harbors and seacoasts of Virginia. Unfamiliar with the realities of the Tidewater, and critical of the Berkeley administration, Knight provided many reasons to justify such actions, some of which were similar to Dyer's. Not only were there no substantial fortifications in Virginia, he reminded the Earl, but the planters there had failed to offer the slightest resistance to the recent Dutch invasion. It was even stated that they had permitted the enemy to land (which they had not, except to accommodate a prisoner exchange) and allowed his men-of-war to lie in local waters for several days. But the ultimate threat posed by the perceived Dutch presence in North America, and one fed by independent attitudes among the colonists was

> that the planters there doe generally desire a trade with the Dutch and all other nations & would not be singly bound to the trade of England, and speake openly there that they are in the nature of slaues soe that the hearts of the greatest part of them are taken away from his Majesty.[33]

Knight, too, pointed out that with as much as £150,000 in customs on tobacco annually, and prospects for £250,000 in the future, Virginia was England's "best, greatest and richest plantation," and one that was "as [of] great importance to his Majesty, as the Spanish Indies are to Spaine." The colony engaged more ships and bred more seamen for his majesty's service than any other trade. And it was all, it seemed, in very great danger of falling into enemy hands—almost by default.[34]

Virginia certainly could not subsist without yearly relief by way of trade in materials to clothe and preserve the planters, for which they provided tobacco in exchange. In fact, Knight reminded the earl, two dozen ships were at that very moment preparing to sail for the colony from Bristol despite the recent turn of events, as were many more from London and elsewhere. If the fleets returned home safely they would enrich the Treasury by an additional £140,000. Given the present situation, however, Sir John was fatalistic about their chances. Yet without this trade, which would, at best, be nearly impossible to maintain under the present circumstances, the planters of Virginia, numbering some 130,000 widely dispersed operations, could not long survive. They thus might, without a fight, deliver up the entire colony to the foe.[35]

From the New Englanders, "though they be fractious," better might be expected. The Dutch at New York would certainly "be bad neighbors to New England and destroy their trade" if allowed to stay. But here, conditions were different. As many as 30,000 men might be raised to form an army that could fall upon New York by land, while the Royal Navy struck Evertsen by sea. Echoing Dyer's plan, he suggested that a fleet of ten ships, dispatched immediately, might not only meet and destroy the daring Zeelander, but also could preserve the rest of the colonies from harm. It might then return home with the Virginia fleet by April of the next year, bringing with it the all-important customs duties and seamen to help man the navy in the coming year.[36]

After an unaccountable delay, the Council of Trade and Plantations finally convened on November 3 to lay on the table and discuss a proper course. Almost a month of valuable time had been lost, despite pleas for immediate action. The Council, beset by equally important problems caused by the war throughout the realm, was often ponderous in its actions and not easily moved. However, having finally reviewed and digested the most recent intelligence concerning the Dutch forces at New York, the Council drafted its own memorial regarding what might be required to retake the city. Revising Dyer's and Knight's plans, they estimated that six ships of war "not under 40 guns apiece," one fireship, and six hired ships (to carry 500 soldiers who would remain in garrison after the city's reduction) would be necessary. The hired ships would each carry ten guns, which would be landed at New York for future defense. Upon termination of the expedition, "which will not be probably above 15 or 20 days after their arrival," they could then proceed to Virginia to take on a load of tobacco and then return home under convoy of the warships. The Council recommended that commissions be granted to the governors of Virginia and Maryland to raise a thousand men, in effect local militia, who, at the end of the campaign against New York, might return home in the same ships. Arms and munitions for these troops and an additional 1,000 arms for the supply of the volunteers from Long Island, New Jersey, and adjacent areas, as well as equippage for a troop of horse to be "easily raised on Long Island," would, after the successful conclusion of the expedition, remain at New York as a magazine.[37]

Lord Culpeper, Vice President of the Council, ruminating on the Council's memorial, proposed a modification on November 13. He suggested that a single third-rate, three fourth-rate, and one fifth-rate men-of-war, with four merchantmen, each carrying 40 guns, and three fireships be dispatched to New York, along with 600 landsmen. He proposed that a public convoy be sent separately, undoubtedly to reduce chances of discovery of the government's intentions by enemy spies, to rendezvous with the war fleet at Lands End. An embargo would be laid to prevent all private ventures from sailing for New York, again in an effort to maintain secrecy until the last possible moment. At sea, the flotilla's commander-in-chief would form all of the merchantmen into a squadron "and exercise such planters and servants as are sent to Virginia and Maryland, letting none go away till the expedition be over." Culpeper, aware that valuable time was being wasted, urged all possible speed. Directions, he added almost as an afterthought, would later be given "about disposing of the Dutch there."[38]

Two days after Lord Culpeper had voiced his proposal, and after having studied the various depositions and reports provided by Lord Arlington concerning New York and Virginia, the Council finally submitted its formal "Opinion and humble advice" to King Charles II. New York, they stated, was not only a very good harbor, it was the only one in all of English North America that was fortified, and would provide a superb base of operations and retreat for Dutch warships and capers preying upon Maryland and Virginia shipping. His majesty's Chesapeake trade stood in danger of total ruination since "the inhabitants by their scattered way of living in a country with many great rivers" were "utterly incapable of resisting sudden incursions." New England, albeit more capable of resistance, was more interested in its trade than in the public support of the English government. Indeed, if the Dutch were permitted to continue in quiet possession of New York, the Council advised, New England might even enter into commerce with them, diverting a great part of the English trade into The Netherlands, "and lay a foundation for such a union with Holland as would be very prejudicial to all his Majesty's plantations, if not terrible to England itself."[39] The Council was obviously well aware of the inclinations of such colonies as Connecticut, and would, no doubt, not have been shocked had the secret proposals suggested by Governor Winthrop to Evertsen and Benckes been known.

The Council incorrectly assumed that the English-dominated eastern end of Long Island had not yet submitted to the Dutch and, if a strong force was sent, would speedily join an expedition against New York. Failure to mount such an adventure could be disastrous. Not only would New England, Virginia, and Maryland be endangered or lost, but Barbados and the rest of the West Indies dependent upon the northern plantations would be reduced to extremities, "or else that trade [would] come into New England men's hands by connivance of the Dutch . . . [and] would be of as ill consequence."[40]

Modifying Culpeper's suggestion a bit, the Council recommended that one third-rate, one fourth-rate, two fifth-rate warships, three 40-gun merchantmen, three fireships, and 600 foot soldiers would be necessary for the reduction of New York. The three merchantmen would have their complements made up in good part from landsmen so that as few seamen as possible would be diverted from navy duty in other areas. Following Culpeper's plan, an embargo was to be laid on all ships preparing for America so that none would be permitted to sail before the convoy. Those permitted to sail afterwards would have to be strong vessels and operate under direct orders from the navy. Servants and passengers in these vessels would be trained and exercised for military duty along the way. The fleet would carry sufficient ammunition and provisions to supply the forts at New York and Albany after they were taken. To insure secrecy, "no more of his Majesty's ships [would] sail with the [next] Virginia fleet out of the Thames than would serve for an ordinary convoy," but at Plymouth or some other appropriate port in the west country they would be joined by the rest of the force and the soldiers. At the rendezvous point, the commander-in-chief would open his commission and instructions, but not before. The fleet would then sail directly for New York, taking care to dispatch, when near the American coast, small vessels to Rhode Island and the eastern end of Long Island with orders to raise forces in New England and on Long Island to assist in the campaign. Once the city had been taken, the Dutch inhabitants were to be removed to the north, at least as far as Albany, "their inhabiting New York having been a great cause of the loss of the town and castle [fort], of which there would be the like danger for the future."[41]

In the meantime, an ocean away, Captain Colve did his best to hold an entire province with 120 soldiers and two well-worn ships of war.

18

WE ARE NOW COME TO DEFEND YOU

The Governor General of New Netherland, Captain Anthony Colve, lost little time after being formally installed in office in pressing forward the programs initiated by Evertsen and Benckes and the reestablishment of Dutch government in the colony. He would have to pay considerable attention to areas left unattended by the two commanders, including those farthest from central authority, on the frontier extremities of the colony. On September 9 the first act of his administration was to appoint Peter Alricks (or Alrights), a former commissary in the Delaware country during the Stuyvesant administration, as commander and schout of Delaware, or South River, "both on the east and west banks to govern, rule and against all hostile invasions to protect as he shall find consistent with the best means in his power for the public service."[1]

Alricks swore his oath of allegiance on September 25, and was, in turn, directed to secure a similar oath from all inhabitants of South River "from Cape Hinlopen off unto the head of said river, both on the east and west banks." The following day, the new commander and schout of South River was authorized to enlist ten to twelve soldiers, including two corporals, on government account. On September 27 he received instructions from Colve, chief of which was that the "pure true Christian Religion, according to the Synod of Dort [recht]" should be taught and maintained. He was instructed to build a fort "in the most suitable place such as the Commandant shall judge necessary for the defense of said river." As a reward to the inhabitants who were to shoulder the expense, they were granted an exemption from all rent charges and excise taxes on beer, wine, and distilled liquors consumed on South River until May 1676. Alricks was "earnestly recommended" to keep his troops in good order and to close them in their fort each night. The government, he was informed, would allocate rations to each soldier, which would include six pounds of beef, three and a half pounds of pork, six pounds of bread, a half pound of butter or three stivers Hollands a week in addition to one skepel of peas per man per month, and a half barrel of beer for every seven men each week.[2]

An aggressive marine captain, Colve was concerned about the sea-borne approach to New Orange and the necessity of monitoring all maritime traffic in the region. He thus instructed the magistrates of the Achter Col towns near the coast at Neversink to publish "that they on the first arrival of any ships from sea shall give the governor the earliest possible information thereof." Schout Peter Biljou was sternly ordered to instantly inform the governor of "any ships coming from seas inside Sandy Hook."[3]

Directing his attentions toward the isolated garrison at Fort Nassau on the upper Hudson, Colve instructed its commandant, Andreas Draeyer, to insure and protect the teachings of the "pure, true Christian Religion." His men, who were also not permitted to leave the fort without proper consent, were to be called in every night to prevent the possibility of surprise by marauders such as Indians or Frenchmen. Draeyer was directed to maintain a regular correspondence with the commissaries of Willemstadt.[4] But most importantly, he was to do all possible to

> keep the Natives and Indians devoted to him, and according to his ability
> render the Dutch government agreeable to them, and obtain from them
> all the information he can respecting the trade and doing of the French.[5]

Draejer was also to prevent all native correspondence with the inhabitants of Willemstadt to frustrate unreported fur trading. Communications with the French, particularly the Jesuits, from Canada, was to be prohibited. The Dutch were painfully aware that there was a distinct danger that the energetic Jesuits, who were active among the Iroquois, and the dynamic governor of New France, Count Frontenac, would succeed in winning over the allegiance of the Indians and turning it against the Netherlanders. Aware that the commandant was certain to stand in need of money for the maintenance of the fort and its garrison, Colve saw to it that credit was made readily available to him.[6]

Fort Willem Hendrick, of course, was not ignored, and would become the focal point of a great deal of energy and expense. On September 21, Colve drafted a memorandum to Ensign Jan Sol, major of the garrison at the fort, for the regulation of the troops. It contained the usual rules regarding guard duty, gate closing hours, watch procedures, hours of reveille and tattoo, drinking on duty, passwords, walking rounds, and drill. But it made a particular point "that no Dutchman nor Englishman (the city magistrates excepted) come here into the Fort without permission, much less be suffered to go on the batteries."[7] There would be no repeat of the easy intelligence gathering that had led to the fort's downfall under the English.

After the departure of the fleet and the many months away from home for the men, maintenance of discipline among the garrison at Willem Hendrick was becoming an increasingly serious problem for Colve. By late September disorders were becoming more numerous with each passing day. Irate over the potential degeneration of order, the governor general determined that the only means "to prevent and obviate the same" from continuing was a rigid, unswerving adherence to the Articles of War. On September 24 he ordered the articles read to the troops "that no man shall plead ignorance." The standards were indeed strict. Seditious, mutinous, or disobedient conversation, indeed even unreported knowledge of such, was punishable by death. Venturing farther than a cannon shot from the garrison without an officer's consent would result in corporal punishment. Neglect of duty, particularly guard duty, was punishable by death. Whoever neglected his parade would be forced to being seated on the wooden horse for three hours, after which he would be obliged to stand guard—assuming he could stand at all. Sleeping at one's post while on sentry duty would result in flogging "without mercy." Absenting one's self from his guard house or being found outside the fort at night was worthy of corporal punishment. "Whosoever smites another," read one order, "with sheathed sword, stick, stone or otherwise and blood flows, shall suffer the loss of hand." Anyone issuing a challenge to fight would receive corporal punishment, as would any officer, sergeant, or corporal commanding guard who might know of it but did nothing to stop it. Interestingly, the rule that stated whoever "in a quarrel or fight shall call his comrade to help him, shall be hanged and strangled," suggested that personal combat was not entirely frowned upon, but gang fights were. A trooper who failed to obey the orders of his superiors, or orders communicated by drum, would suffer corporal punishment. He who "resists" his superiors might receive the death penalty. Drunkenness would result in being broken in rank and ejected from the company, and any evil or forbidden act committed while drunk was to be punished all the more severely. Any effort to obstruct an arrest by the provost or his men would result in corporal punishment. Growing increasingly concerned over the civilian sale of alcohol, Colve ordered that the inhabitants of the city be strictly prohibited from selling or even providing credit for strong drink to the soldiery.[8]

Godliness, cleanliness, and order were almost as important as military discipline. Blasphemy, for a first offense, was punishable by three days in prison on bread and water. A second time offender "shall have his tongue bored with a red hot iron" and be banished from New Netherland and the United Provinces as a villain. Cleanliness was to be strictly observed in all aspects of garrison living, from the barracks to the very walls of the fort. A special instruction in the garrison regulations stated that sentries "who happen to ease themselves or permit others to ease themselves on the ramparts or breastworks" were to be severely punished, as was the sentry near whom the waste was found, if he could not justify it.[9]

Colve was particularly concerned about fort security, and explicitly detailed how it must be insured. A guard was to be continually maintained and a watch kept at all times. During the night, the sentries were to be relieved every half hour, and during the day "according to circumstances." Arms were to be kept at the ready.[10]

The possibility of attack from New England or even England was undoubtedly uppermost in Colve's mind. Fort Willem Hendrick and the harbor batteries were in a forward state of repair thanks to the efforts of Evertsen and Benckes. However, there was far more to be done, including reconstruction of certain sections, and removal of obstructions from the fort's field of fire. Colve plunged ahead where the two commanders had left off. Contracts were let in mid-September for the purchase of pallisades for earthen constructions. On September 28, the governor and his chief civilian advisor, Cornelis Steenwyck, informed the burgomasters of the city of the necessity "of demolishing or removing some houses, gardens and orchards situate under the walls of this fortress Willem Hendrick, and the newly begun fortification of New Orange."[11]

The burgomasters concurred, but requested the governor and Council discuss the projected demolition personally with the citizenry to be affected. The need for the work was apparent to all. The city had grown rapidly between the Second and Third Anglo-Dutch Wars, so rapidly that the fortress walls were, in many places on the landward side, shoulder to shoulder with the town which obstructed the field of fire. The governor and Council proposed that the cost for removing or razing buildings, orchards, and gardens in the critical areas, as well as indemnification paid to the owners, could be raised from proceeds from "an extraordinary duty" on exported beaverskins and pelts, and on imported blankets, duffels, wines, brandies, distilled liquors, rum, powder, lead, and guns. On October 1, Colve appointed Steenwyck and three burgomasters to make the appraisals for indemnification of affected property. Soon afterwards, two carpenters were added to the

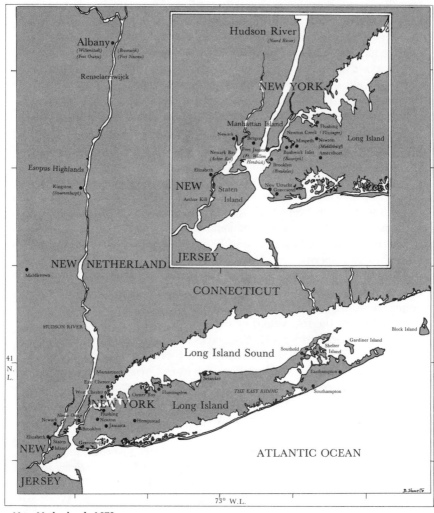

New Netherland, 1673.

committee.[12] Five days later, on October 6, the governor issued a public decree noting that Fort Willem Hendrick and the city defenses were

seriously encumbered and weakened by the houses, gardens and orchards which lie so close under the walls and bulwarks that it is impossible to defend it properly when occasion requires against its enemies, unless at least some of those houses, lots and orchards be demolished and removed.[13]

Twenty-one houses, gardens, and orchards, including the new Lutheran Church, were to be removed to other lots in the city or razed. Appointed to work with Colve's engineers, one Martin Creiger would superintend the demolition, as well as the repair and reconstruction of the walls. The town burghers and citizens would contribute the labor, in addition to manpower for three foot-companies and a troop of horse to assist in the construction and defending of the works.[14]

Colve could not long concentrate upon the improvement of the defenses of New Orange. Upon the departure of Evertsen and Benckes, several of the villages on the eastern end of Long Island, or the East Riding of Yorkshire as the region was then called, had begun to reassert their disdain for Dutch rule. Several displayed a marked disaffection for the New Orange administration, nurtured in no small measure by Connecticut in their increasingly rebellious attitudes. In late September, the governor received the first of a series of unwelcome intelligence reports concerning the East Riding towns, and several even closer to the central Dutch orbit. In the town of Hempstead, it was learned, a stranger had arrived "who Endeavoured to disturb yo[r] Pease, devulging that he was sent by some other authority." Colve soon discovered that the stranger was an agent provocateur sent from Connecticut with orders from that government "to raise men for theire acc[ts] in the s[d] towne, etz, and the Like Seditious Words tending to Meuteny." It was not surprising, perhaps, that most of the town's inhabitants had yet to take the oath of allegiance, despite their earlier avowed willingness to accept Dutch rule and nominate officials.[15]

The governor was irate over the incident and expressed his displeasure with the new magistrates of the town, instructing them not to overlook the presence of such obvious troublemakers. The magistrates offered, as an excuse for their nonintervention, that the meeting was held in a private house and ordinary, and that the stranger had departed before they had learned of the incident. Colve responded by ordering that an investigation be carried out and that the inhabitants of Hempstead take the oath within four days of the publication of his decree. Those who neglected or delayed in so doing, he warned, would be considered "disturbers & Publicq Enemijes off this Common Wealth," and proceedings against them and their estates would be carried out accordingly.[16]

The failure of many of the inhabitants of the East Riding towns to swear allegiance, and the proclivity of some to temporize, posed considerable danger to the Dutch administration. Disaffection and incitement to rebellion, sowed by Connecticut, might well result in appeals for intervention—appeals that could end in a military confrontation from which Colve stood less than even chances of emerging victorious. Thus, it was imperative that an end be brought to the growing dissension and refusals of allegiance. On September 21, the governor, having little trust in the ability or willingness of local magistrates to secure allegiance to The Netherlands, commissioned Captain Willem Knijff (Knyff), Lieutenant Antonij Malepart, and clerk Abraham Varlett to travel to the villages east of Oyster Bay, call town meetings at each place visited, and administer oaths of fidelity to the inhabitants. That there be no grounds for contention, provisional instructions were dispatched to the schout of the East Riding district and to each town's magistrates (not only on Long Island but throughout New Netherland). The instructions were to be posted and detailed the manner in which civil government was to be carried out.[17]

The ten part instructions dealt with such key issues as the maintenance of the Dutch Reformed Church, power of schout and police, criminal justice, voting rights, public works, posting of ordinances and laws, the acknowledgement by schouts and schepens of the sovereign authority of the Lords States General and the Prince of Orange, selection of civil office holders, duties of the schouts and manners of election, and so forth. Perhaps the most explosive issue, aside from the requirement of fealty, was that of the seizure of properties of both English and French subjects loyal to their respective sovereigns. Evertsen and Benckes had been lenient on the issue, but Colve intended to deal with the matter with an iron hand.[18]

On October 9, Knijff, Malepart, and Varlett returned to New Orange from the East Riding towns. For Colve, their report was depressing, if not unexpected. The commissioners visited all of the towns east of Oyster Bay as ordered, called for town meetings, and tried to administer the oaths of allegiance. But with the exception of Oyster Bay, where the oath was taken, and Huntington, where the inhabitants requested to be exempted from the oath but promised fidelity in writing, all of the towns refused to cooperate.[19]

Southampton, the seat of opposition, balked at Colve's instructions, declaring them to be in conflict with the original terms of surrender.

The inhabitants refused outright to acknowledge any sovereign but the king of England, but promised to live in peace "Soe long as wee are not Molested by them [the Dutch] nor any other from or vnder them Vnlesse Called thereunto by his Maties Power of England."[20] Southampton's stance was consistent. Soon after having been summoned by Evertsen and Benckes to submit to the new Dutch government, the town appealed to Hartford for aid. While Connecticut listened, Southampton "received no Incouragement to stand out of our-selves although they favored us so farr as to consider our Condition." The town then appealed to the Boston General Court in a message delivered by one John Cooper, "a resolute man," who proposed that with but 100 armed men, all of the towns of Long Island could be brought back into the English fold. The New Englanders "wholly refused to engage the country in the undertaking." Failing to garner support, the town issued a declaration, addressed to all of the English colonies, explaining their situation and why they were being forced to acquiesce to the Dutch.[21] But now, with a breath of support from Connecticut, Southampton had gained new resolve.

The citizens of Southold also refused to follow Colve's directives, claiming that they thought the oath was only intended for the schout of the East Riding and the magistrates of every town, and that for each of the inhabitants to be required to take it would deny them freedom of conscience. They were upset by the orders to seize all debts belonging to the subjects of the king of England. But of equal import, the town had been obliged to dismantle its former government as they had initially agreed to after the conquest, yet in the interval had not instituted a replacement and was without any form of protection. The town, claimed the inhabitants, was vulnerable "to the Invasion of those who threaten dayly wth ye spoiling our goods." They informed the commissioners that Southold was willing to submit "during the prevelince of your Power over us" only if a firm and peaceful government was permitted, which would provide protection from "ye Invasion of those wch Dayly threaten us."[22] Though the inhabitants of Southold did not identify just who might conduct such an invasion, it was undoubtedly apparent to Colve that they feared reprisals from Connecticut or their neighboring bastion of anti-Dutch sentiments, the town of Southampton.

Initial response from Easthampton was similar. The town also refused to accept Dutch authority, preferring to be "regulated by our fformer Lawes and that authority is resident amongst us." Though unwilling to recognize Dutch sovereignty over itself, this town too, requested to live only in peace. Like Southold, Easthampton feared reprisals should it enter the Dutch fold. The inhabitants informed the commissioners that they could not "but bee Sensable of the great danger wee are in boath from those that are neere home So well as those abroad of Our owne Nation." Indeed, the town's own security depended upon maintaining its former allegiance. Significantly, Colve learned soon after the receipt of Easthampton's official response that it had been sent to New Orange by a messenger who had passed through Southampton. There, the letter was intercepted, opened, and examined by opponents to the Dutch regime. The document was then read "wth severall Railing Expressions," whereupon the messenger suggested that another be sent in its place, which was done, and which Colve had accepted as the authentic reply. Late on the evening of September 23, having learned of the interception, Easthampton constable Thomas Dyment and Recorder Thomas Tallmage dispatched a second letter, informing the New Orange government that it was "not the first time wee have had our letters opened & stopt at Southampton and many threatning Expressions have proceeded from severall disaffected persons there wth Respect to our Submission to your governm^{t} that we have yeilded Unto."[23]

Setauket, belittling its own importance, but claiming a strong desire to live in peace, claimed that it was equally intimidated and could not "bear eup alone against the prevaling sense of Neighbouring Townes." Thus, at a town meeting held on September 27, the inhabitants voted to preserve their allegiance to the king of England, and humbly apologized to the Dutch commissioners "for their not takeing the Oath in this unexpected posture of destracion^{s}."[24]

Huntington's citizens requested that they be excused from taking the oath on the grounds that they had never been under the Duke of York's authority in the first place, had never sworn an oath to him, or, for that matter and with few exceptions, to the king of England. The Netherlanders had but two enemies, they said, England and France, "& against ye Frensch wee are Resolved . . . to defend our Selves against there tirrany." But if the English arrived, they would remain neutral "till forced to doe other waijes." The town asked for a trial period of one year of independence under their own laws. If in that time Colve saw "Cause and Cleer foult" in their peaceful relations, they would swear allegiance. They wished neither allegiance with their neighbors of the East Riding country, they stated, nor with the Dutch to the west, but sought only to "Stand of our Selves."[25]

Distraught, Colve called his Council to meet on October 10 to discuss the means by which the dissident towns might be brought to heel. He questioned "whether it would not be necessary to send a considerable force thither to punish them as rebels." But after much debate by the burgomasters and schepens, who were nervous over the potential repercussions, it was deemed inadvisable to employ force of arms. Such a move might, they feared, only afford them and the neighboring colonies an excuse to attack New Orange. The Council proposed that a second delegation be sent to the East Riding country to try one more time to secure the inhabitants' allegiance.[26]

Perceiving that the attitude of English Long Island ultimately could end in military confrontation, Colve sought to determine exactly where the government of New Netherland stood with the Dutch population there, most of whom lived quite close to his base of power. He summoned the schepens from Midwout, Bushwick Inlet, New Utrecht, Amersfoort, Brooklyn, and Gravesend. Would they observe the oath of allegiance which they had taken, asked the governor? Would their patriots be willing to come to Manhattan in case of attack to resist the common enemy? "They had no doubt," replied the schepens, "but it will be done by the entire people." Delighted with the response, Colve ordered that they be permitted to choose their own militia officers, and that a "double number" of names be submitted for the militia officers of each town.[27]

Acquiescing to the view of the Council, though it was not his own, Colve approved that a second delegation be sent to call upon the Long Island towns. On October 15, Captain Knijff and Ensign Vos were directed to visit the villages of Huntington and Setauket once more to try and secure the oath of allegiance from the inhabitants—or at least from those willing to observe it. Three days later they returned to New Orange in triumph, for both towns had reconsidered their positions and complied. Distant Southold, Easthampton, and Southampton, on the eastern extremity of Long Island, would be far more difficult. On October 20, Colve commissioned Councillor Cornelis Steenwyck, Captain of Marines Carel Epesteijn, and Lieutenant Carel Quirinssen to travel to the three towns and secure their obedience and allegiance, "to the End I may not be forced to use such meanes as would tend to the ruine & greatest Damage of some of them."[28]

This time the commissioners would employ *Zeehond* to make the trip swiftly, and, no doubt, to remind the settlers of the military force available to the Dutch at New Orange. *Zeehond's* commander, however, was strictly ordered not to molest any New England vessels lest cause for retaliation be provided. On the issue of allegiance, Colve was now prepared to bend slightly. If "great objections were made to the oath" the inhabitants of the three towns were to be permitted to merely promise obedience, although magistrates would be required to swear allegiance. In the event that there was obstinate refusal to both oath of allegiance or promise of obedience, the inhabitants were to be publically informed that "they will be the cause of their own ruin." The commissioners were advised to collect the names of the chief mutineers in writing and return without delay to New Orange.[29]

In the meantime, across Long Island Sound, Connecticut prepared to contest the Dutch efforts head on.

On October 21, the day following the Steenwyck Commission's appointment, the governor and General Court of Connecticut wrote Colve a scathing and accusatory letter that only served to deepen tensions between the two neighboring governments. The message, signed by Secretary John Allyn, was carried by one John Bancke. It was not, the Connecticut government haughtily wrote, "the manner of Christian and Civill nations to disturb ye poore people in Cottages & open Villages in times of warr or to impose oaths upon them." Having heard of late efforts in the East Riding country urging his majesty's subjects to take an oath contrary to their allegiance to their actual sovereign, and "to use many threatning Expressions towards them in case of the Refusall of such an oath," Connecticut expressed disbelief that Colve could have commissioned such actions. He could only have done so, they assumed, "to attaine some plausible pretence for Plundering & pillaging." If such were indeed to occur, they warned, they knew "verry well where they may be Easy Reparacon" amid the farms and villages of New Netherland. If Colve continued to pursue the issue of forcing allegiance on the Englishmen of Long Island, they threatened, the English colonies would "not make it their worke to tamper wth your peasants about sweareing but deale wth your head quarters."[30]

Colve indignantly returned a copy of the threatening letter to Winthrop on October 26, along with a note expressing disbelief "that such an impertinent and absurd writing" could have come from the governor and General Court of Connecticut. He later noted that the Long Island towns had first submitted to the new Dutch regime upon favorable conditions, surrendered the English colors and constable staves, and selected new magistrates. Had "evilly disposed" persons from Winthrop's colony not interceded, they would have peaceably taken the oath of allegiance. It was well known to everyone, he added scornfully, how much more gently the Dutch treated vanquished enemies than the English.[31]

Winthrop expressed astonishment that Colve would question the authenticity of his haughty letter. He retorted that it was indeed genuine, and commended it to the New Orange governor's serious consideration,

even though Colve's last communication—"I will not Call Impertinent, because it suits your owne fancy"—had aroused Connecticut's
hackles.[32]

Resolute in his objectives, Colve refused to be intimidated by the
Connecticut governor. The Steenwyck Commission set off to Southold,
Southampton, and Easthampton on schedule, the three commissioners
embarking aboard Captain Eewoutsen's *Zeehond* about noon, Tuesday,
October 21. Their mission would be neither easy nor without some
danger. Immediately after sailing, in fact, they were almost cast ashore
near Corlear's Hook, and then faced several days of delay from adverse
winds and tides in getting through Hell Gate and into Long Island
Sound. While awaiting a fair wind, they encountered the inbound
sloop *Eendragt*, Captain Luycas Andriesson commanding, from Boston, and learned the unwelcome news of the tragic fall of Maastricht to
the French. Difficulties multiplied. Two days later, during a violent
storm, *Zeehond* lost an anchor. Finally, on October 24, they were favored with a northerly wind, sailed through Hell Gate, and eventually
into the sound. The following day, while they scudded along south of
New Haven, the wind turned bitterly cold and violent. About 3:00
A.M., the little warship narrowly avoided running into the rocks of
Falcon's Island. For the voyagers there seemed no end to trouble as "the
storm sensibly increased, and about day-break it was a complete hurricane." Throughout the following day, *Zeehond* ran with reefed foresail,
battered by wind and sea, and all aboard, no doubt, believed that each
moment might be their last.[33]

At daybreak on the 27th, the storm having finally abated, *Zeehond's*
watch sighted Plum Gut, on the eastern end of Long Island. He also
sighted a sail to leeward. Supposing it to be a West Indiaman, and thus
fair game, Captain Eewoutsen raised English colors to mislead her, set
his courses, and hoisted his topsails. The tide being against the unidentified ship, she quickly came to anchor near Shelter Island. *Zeehond*
came to also, having cornered her prey in shoal water, lowered the
English flag and hoisted the Prince's colors, whereupon the second vessel instantly lowered her own in submission.[34]

It was soon discovered that the vessel had come from New London,
Connecticut, bearing none other than Governor Winthrop's own son,
Captain Fitz-John Winthrop, and one Samuel Willys. When the two
Englishmen boarded *Zeehond* as ordered, it was learned that they bore
commissions from the government of Connecticut, which they prom-
ised to later show the Dutch, and a letter addressed to Governor Colve.
Steenwyck, Epesteijn, and Quirinssen displayed their own commis-
sions, together with evidence of the initial petition and agreement be-

tween the East Riding towns and the Dutch government of New Orange.[35]

During this unexpected parlay, Winthrop and Willys argued that because a single article, regarding the freedom of the East Riding towns to procure weapons for the whaling industry, had been refused, all articles of the agreement between the Dutch provisional government and the Long Island towns "had been rendered null & void." It was apparent that the Connecticut commissioners were employing technicalities as an argument to rebut the agreement. The Dutch commissioners, frustrated, and "after having treated them to the best in our power," permitted their guests to depart. That evening, *Zeehond* anchored under Shelter Island and the Steenwyck Commission went ashore in a boat sent by Nathaniel Sylvester to spend an undoubtedly restless night.[36]

The following morning, October 29, Winthrop and Willys dispatched a copy of their commission, as promised, to the Dutch. It could not have failed to excite concern among the members of the Steenwyck Commission. "Whereas by divers Reports & Informations," it read,

> wee are given to Vnderstand that there are some forces Expected spedily from New Yorke at the Eastern End of Long Island to force and Constrayne the People there to take the oath of Obedience to the States generall & Prince of Orange; Wee have thought it Expedient to desire & Empower you Samuel Willis Esq[r] & Capt[n] John Winthrop or Either of you to take such necessary attendance as you Judge meet & forthwith to goe over to the Island or Shelter Island & treat wth such forces as there you shall meet & doe your Endeavour to divert them from using any hostility against the said People & from Imposing uppon them letting them know if they do proceed notwithstanding it will provoke us to a due Consideration what wee are Nextly obliged to doe.[37]

The letter for Colve was also delivered to the Dutch commissioners. In it, Connecticut requested that the Dutch abandon their voyage and all efforts to persuade the English of Southold, Easthampton, and Southampton to take the oath. The Dutch commissioners responded that they were duty bound to carry out their commission. Both Dutch and English commissioners would now vie directly for the support of the inhabitants of Southold.[38]

The Steenwyck Commission set off for Southold late in the morning, somewhat behind their English counterparts. The Connecticut men pressed ahead in a boat borrowed from Sylvester, with the king's Jack flying from the stern. They were closely followed by the Dutch, who, having lost their own boat in the recent hurricane, were also in a borrowed boat from Sylvester, with a prince's flag flying from their own stern. About 2:00 P.M. both boats neared the town. The Dutch commissioners, however, were undoubtedly dismayed to hear drum beats and a trumpet sound, and to observe a salute with muskets fired when Winthrop and Willys passed. Fearful of landing, but obliged to go ashore owing to low water and the turn of the tide, the Dutch discovered a troop of calvary riding back and forth along the beach in front of them. As their boat bumped ashore, four of the horsemen rode toward them and offered them mounts. The commissioners accepted and were soon met by Willys and Winthrop and a troop of 26 to 28 men on horseback. Together they rode toward Southold, passing, en route, a company of 60 menacingly armed men. Entering the village, they proceeded to the house of Thomas Moore, one of the magistrates approved by the New Orange government, but who was, as yet, unaware of his election to office. Steenwyck quickly called for a town meeting to inform the citizens of the reason for his visit and to present the commission from the Dutch government.[39]

When the inhabitants were all drawn together, Winthrop and Willys presented their case first, stating that the citizens of Southold were subjects of the king of England and had nothing to do with any orders or commissions of the Dutch. "Whosoever among you will not be faithful to his Majesty of England," they challenged, "your lawful Lord and King let him now speake."[40]

The Connecticut commissioner's challenge was answered by a wall of silence.

Steenwyck then spoke up, reminding the citizens that they were the subjects of the Lords States General and the Prince of Orange, as evidenced by their colors and constable staves, by the nomination of their magistrates presented to the governor, and the election of said magistrates afterwards by Colve. He called upon the two elected nominees for Southold to appear, but only one, Thomas Moore, did so. The second, Thomas Hudsingsen (Hudsisson) was not to be found. When Steenwyck informed Moore, in full view of the assemblage, that his election as magistrate had been approved by Colve, Moore refused to accept, saying "that he had nothing to do with it." When Isaack Aernouts, who had already been sworn in as schout of the East Riding was summoned, he informed the stunned Dutch commissioners that it was not in his power to execute the office, for he had resigned, "having been already threatened by the inhabitants that they would plunder his house." Steenwyck turned to the assemblage, and asked them directly if they would remain faithful to the States General and take the oath. Again, a dead silence pervaded the meeting.[41]

With little alternative, the commissioners directed that Colve's orders be read to them, that there be no mistaking the potential consequences of the course they were taking. Winthrop and Willys interceded, stating that the inhabitants were subjects of the king and had nothing to do with a commission from the Dutch. The Steenwyck Commission, it was quite clear, was faced with overwhelming and intractable opposition, skillfully led by the Connecticut Commissioners, and enforced by the fear of reprisals against those who dared support the Dutch. Nothing further could be done. After submitting a formal protest, the Dutchmen resolved to leave Southold and visit Southampton the next morning.[42]

As Steenwyck, Epesteijn, and Quirinssen prepared to depart, they were verbally accosted and intimidated by a group of English inhabitants of the East Riding country led by a firebrand named John Couper (possibly the same that had served as Southampton's emmissary to Boston). Couper warned Steenwyck, in no uncertain terms, that he "take care and not appear with that thing at Southampton."

What was meant by the word "Thing?" questioned Steenwyck.

"The Prince's Flag," spat Couper.

Did he speak for himself, or on behalf of the authority of the inhabitants of Southampton, asked the Dutchman.

"Rest satisfied," retorted the Englishman, "that I warn you and take care that you come not with that Flag within range of shot of our village."

What village *did* they intend to visit the next morning, queried the Connecticut Commissioners? It mattered little what answer was given, however, for Governor Winthrop's men quickly informed the Dutchmen that they would also be in attendance, "as they intended to be present at every place the Commissioners should visit."[43]

Intimidated by the show of military force upon their arrival, the rejection of Colve's commission by the inhabitants, and the obvious influence of the Connecticut Commissioners over the Long Islanders, the Steenwyck Commission shoved off toward Shelter Island. Dejected over their failure at Southold and the opposition arrayed against them, they resolved that a visit to either Easthampton or Southampton would prove fruitless, if not dangerous, "as we clearly perceived that we should be unable to effect anything, and rather do more harm than good." On the evening of October 31, they arrived at New Orange to report their transactions to Colve.[44]

Clearly the problems with Long Island and Connecticut were likely to intensify even further if prompt action was not undertaken. But, lacking offensive military muscle, and with little prospect of reinforcements in the near future, for the moment Colve could only temporize and continue strengthening his defenses. Unauthorized communication with the English colonies to the northeast was ordered to halt, and John Holt, the magistrate of East Chester, through which the overland road to those parts passed, was directed to prevent unofficial passage to and from New England.

Unhappily, the Colve administration of New Netherland faced serious opposition not only from New England, but also on the exposed, unprotected southern periphery of its jurisdiction. One of the most violent and cruel depredations against the new Dutch regime was destined to take place in the South River region. Ironically, the attack, which originated from the province of Maryland, had been engendered more out of the pre-war territorial claims of Lord Baltimore, proprietor of that colony, than as a blow intended against The Netherlands.

Lord Baltimore had long considered the vast Eastern Shore peninsula lying between the Chesapeake and Delaware bays as part of his dominion. As early as 1662 he had asserted a major claim to the region when, on June 19 of that year, he issued a warrant for the establishment of Worcester County, directing that the county's territory be composed of "the Sea Board side of the Eastern Shore the Whore Kill and Delaware Bay to the fortieth degree of Northerly Latitude," but south of New Castle. Seven years later, on October 22, 1669, Lord Baltimore dispatched in a set of instructions to his son, Charles Calvert, governor of Maryland, orders to physically occupy the region by attempting to seat settlers on the Eastern Shore, on the South River, and, specifically, at Hoeren Kill. A new county of Durham, including Hoeren Kill, was to be carved out of Worcester to extend northward as far as the fortieth parallel. Settlement was to be urged and promoted by the sheriffs of Baltimore, Talbot, and Dorchester counties, Maryland. Special incentives, in the form of low rents, would be offered to attract English and Irish settlers. He also directed that the surveyor general lay out at the Hoeren Kill and on the "Seaboard side" of the two proprietary counties two 6,000 acre manors for the proprietor.[45]

Soon afterwards, at the instigation of Governor Calvert, a claim was made by Maryland Surveyor General Jerome White, in a letter to Governor Lovelace of New York, which placed the South River town of New Castle, said by the surveyor to lie at thirty degrees thirty minutes latitude, well within Lord Baltimore's jurisdiction. Maryland Provincial Secretary William Talbot followed, on December 23, 1670, by appointing deputies, who were to provide rights to land and issue warrants, and a deputy surveyor. On June 20, 1672, Governor Calvert put muscle into his father's territorial claim by appointing one Thomas Jones of Worcester County to the captaincy of all military forces in the county. He also issued instructions to Captain Paul Marsh to assemble all Somerset County forces to join Jones. Together, the two commanders were directed to subdue "all Enemies that shall be shewed you by the said Captain [Jones] to encounter fight with Overcome and destroy or take Prisoners."[46]

The Lovelace administration in New York, under whose authority Delaware had been garrisoned for eight years, paid little heed to Maryland's aggressive actions, even when Francis Jenkins arrived at Hoeren Kill to survey land under Lord Baltimore's commission and threatened several inhabitants. Lovelace and his Council merely ordered the officers stationed on the South River to take care to insure that the interests of the Duke of York were not being infringed upon. In June 1672, when a party of settlers from Virginia, led by one Richard Perrot, came to settle on the Hoeren Kill after having applied for their land from Lovelace's deputies, they discovered that Lord Baltimore's agents had already surveyed the same lands. New York was finally moved, albeit lethargically, to defend the Duke of York's territory. New Castle's defenses were ordered strengthened. A sheriff and commissioners were appointed at Hoeren Kill.[47]

Before Francis Lovelace could act, however, Maryland began a course of armed aggression. Under Calvert's commission and directions, Captain Jones and a party of six or eight horsemen descended on Hoeren Kill, and through force of arms, methodically raided and plundered many settlers and carried off their goods. Jones, it was said, had not only tied up his victims and kept a guard over them, but held a cocked pistol to the breast of a magistrate, threatening his life if he failed to follow orders.[48]

Unaware that Jones held a commission from Governor Calvert, Lovelace failed to interpret his actions as anything but those of a brigand. But he did call the Maryland government to task and vigorously protested the incursion. He was particularly upset that Jones

who wth a Party as dissolute as himselfe took ye paines to ride to ye Whore-Kill, where in Derision and Contempt of the Dukes Authority, bound ye magistrates, and Inhabitants despitefully treated them, rifled & plunder'd them of their Goods.[49]

Barely was the ink dry upon the letter than Jones, this time with 30 or more horsemen, again struck against Hoeren Kill. The captain's depredations on behalf of Maryland against the largely Dutch settlement was preserved for posterity in a deposition given by the town's schout, Hermanius Wiltbanck, eleven years later. "In the Month of September following," recalled the schout,

> came up the said Capt. Jones with a Troop of Horse with force of Armes and made forcible Entry in this Place, and called a Court of their own Men, and made us come to their Court and Demanded the Oath of Allegiance wherein we were not willing, whereupon the Court did commit us to Prison and kept us untill the next Day without meat or Drink, and threatened to carry us for Maryland and confiscate our Estate, so that we were forced to take the Oath of Allegiance to be true to my Lord Baltimore.[50]

For Governor Lovelace, worse news followed. On September 27, the skittish Captain John Carr wrote from New Castle, which he commanded, that he had received intelligence that Maryland had mustered a strong force with the intention of seizing all of the settlements along the South River, including New Castle, up to the fortieth parallel.[51]

Lovelace ordered the New Castle garrison strengthened to defend the fort and town there by any and all means. Carr was, however, ordered to attempt to reason with the attackers, should they beset him, that the Duke of York, though holding no patent on the land (which he had also seized by force of arms), had, in fact, controlled it for the last eight years. While Carr saw to improving the defenses, Lovelace busied himself in preparing an appeal to the only authority he could. A courier was dispatched to London on the next ship to request directions of the Duke of York on what actions should be taken.[52]

When word of the outbreak of war between England and The Netherlands reached New York and the South River region, neither Governors Calvert nor Lovelace could have envisioned what lay ahead. The contest for control of Delaware, however, receded in importance—temporarily.

Shortly after the fall of Fort James, the new Dutch masters of New Orange had dispatched delegates to the South River region to demand submission to the new government. At Hoeren Kill, Lord Baltimore's commissioner, appointed to govern there, Colonel Francis Jenkins, received a copy of the Dutch demands and forwarded them to his master, but received no instructions in return. When pressed from New Orange for an answer, Jenkins pleaded that he had received no orders. Undoubtedly fearing for their lives, the commissioner and many of Lord Baltimore's men, on the pretense of going to Maryland to secure a reply from the colony government, fled, and did not return.[53]

Two months after Jenkin's departure, New Orange again pressed the town for an answer from Lord Baltimore's government, but "their being none that the Dutch possessed them selves of this place and sworn the Inhabitants to that Government."[54] Hoeren Kill swore allegiance to The Netherlands, but the young Colve administration was obliged to instruct the town to look to its own defenses, or to rely upon those of Commander Peter Alricks at New Castle.

Governor Calvert now saw an opportunity to reassert his father's claim to the entire region. The territory was undefended, and had sworn fielty to his nation's enemies. Invasion was now a justifiable duty. Thus, on October 1, 1673, he commissioned one Thomas Howell, a former burgess from Baltimore County, Maryland, to raise 40 men to retake Hoeren Kill from the Dutch. He was ordered, if resistance was encountered, "to fight and Overcome Kill Destroy and Vanquish as occasion shall Require" all enemies. Howell was authorized to press into service all such arms, ammunition, provisions, and horses as deemed necessary for his force. Once Hoeren Kill had been taken, he was "to keepe and Defend the said place by force or otherwise, against all p[er]sons until I shall signify my will & pleasure therein."[55]

When the captain and his 40 horsemen thundered into the undefended settlement in early December 1673 "with swords drawn," the sleepy village was taken by surprise. Howell "threatened and Terrified the Inhabitants" so thoroughly that the town was given up without a contest. Indeed, when called upon to surrender by the Marylanders, the settlers replied that they had already been Lord Baltimore's tenants once before and were, in any event, unable to defend themselves. Howell pompously informed the citizenry that "we are come now to Defend you, and if it cost the Province of Merry-Land a million in Tobacco we will protect you."[56] No one bothered to ask the settlers if they wanted protection.

The occupation of Hoeren Kill by Howell and his troopers, soldiers of less-than-gentle demeanor, was not to be at the expense of Lord Baltimore, but rather at that of the helpless townspeople. For two weeks the troops slaughtered cattle and livestock, quartered themselves in private homes, and survived off the limited provisions that the citizens had stockpiled for the winter. Plunder, however, was meager, and was gained, on occasion, through torture. One victim was Harman Cornellinson, a 32-year-old merchant and fur trader "of a Considerable Estate & Trade." Only the year before, on December 16, 1672, when the town was under the administration of Colonel Jenkins, Cornellinson had secured a commission from Lord Baltimore to trade with Indians and whites alike in Somerset, Dorchester, and Worcester counties in Maryland. As a consequence, he was undoubtedly known to have been successful at his occupation, and Howell pressed him to reveal the location of his valuable stock of pelts, furs, and property. The trader adamantly refused to divulge the information, but when a burning match was applied to his hand, the location spilled from his lips. Cornellinson was then robbed not only of his pelts and furs, but of valuable property in his personal chest. His business and livelihood was ruined.[57]

Having effectively severed the town's tenuous connections with the Dutch government at New Orange, and heedless of the handful of soldiers at New Castle, Howell began to worry over Hoeren Kill's ability to support the winter billeting of his troops. He resolved to return to Maryland to consult with his master and "to Aquaint him that the Inhabitants of this place was poor and not able to maintaine soe many souldgers."[58] When the captain reported to Calvert, informing him of the mean conditions at Hoeren Kill, the governor's response, though not recorded for posterity, was clear. The captain was directed to destroy the town and its surroundings to prevent the Dutch from settling there again.[59]

Howell returned to the Hoeren Kill about the third week of its occupation, his intentions and directions known only to himself, and, apparently, to a few of his troops. It was the Christmas season, raw and cold on the Delaware. On the day before Christmas Eve, one of Howell's men, perhaps in a slip of good cheer, informed one of the region's inhabitants, an Englishman named John Roads, Jr., that the town was to be destroyed. Fearing that he would be hung for his indiscretion if it were discovered by Howell, the trooper implored the settler to promise that he would not reveal the secret. Roads, whose farm was eight miles from the town, and who undoubtedly hoped his nationality and distance from Hoeren Kill Town would promote his own salvation, agreed.[60]

In order that his objective might be achieved with the utmost efficiency, and to prevent any possible organized resistance, Howell summoned all of the inhabitants of the town and surrounding countryside to muster at Hoeren Kill Town on Christmas Eve day. On the pretense that they were to undergo a military drill, he directed that they were to bring their arms and ammunition with them. At the appointed time, the town filled with the inhabitants. The ruse had been a success.[60] Then, presumably after having collected their arms and mounting a strong guard, the captain informed the settlers

> that he must tell them with Greife that his orders from the Lord Baltimore was that he must burne all their houses and that he must not Leave one stick standing; and that he Could not be Excused from soe doeing;

And that he was to give but one quarter of an hour warning before he did it.[62]

The stunned citizenry could barely comprehend what had been said before the Maryland troopers commenced the destruction of their town. Then, as their anger rose, several were restrained and placed under guard, even as the incendiaries proceeded with their work. The troopers moved quickly, pausing at each house only long enough to steal what pleased them before setting the building ablaze.[63]

Though the destruction of their town and the confiscation of their weapons would leave the inhabitants defenseless, destitute, and exposed to the full ravages of the freezing Delaware winter already upon them, and to attack by hostile Indians, the Marylanders carried out their orders with zeal. When several expectant mothers pleaded with the captain to spare at least one house, he solemnly promised that "if God would save them one they should have it and not Else."[64]

There was a thatched barn near the middle of the town adjacent to a wooden one belonging to Alexander Moultson that contained 200 bushels of unthreshed wheat. Several buildings and outbuildings stood nearby. Howell taunted the inhabitants that if the thatched barn near Moultson's did not burn, "it should be saft," knowing full well that the fires raging about the surrounding village could not fail to consume the miserable little structure. The flames of the burning Moultson barn and the nearby houses were soon sending acrid smoke heavenward, and sparks toward the thatched barn. Three times the structure was set afire—and three times the fire went out. Incredulous, Howell declared that "God had saft the Thatch Barn; and that he did not dare to meddle anymore with it."[65] It was to be the only building spared in Hoeren Kill.

The farms in the outlying countryside fared no better. About the same time Hoeren Kill was being burned to the ground, a party of soldiers had gone into the neighborhood to insure the destruction of all else within the area. No one, apparently, was spared, including the Englishman John Roads, Jr. His deposition, taken ten years later, detailed the methodical manner in which the Maryland incendiaries carried out their brutal assignments. On the morning of the destruction of the town,

> a party of the souldgers came to the said John Roads house & within one quarter of an Houer after they fired his Tobaco house which was seaventy Foot long & Twenty Foote wide full of Tobaco & consumed it all; & then they sett the dwelling house on fire; & whilst this deponent was beating down the Gaball [gable] end of the dwelling house to throw out his Corn, the Souldgers cutt the Meat with their swords as it was

roasting to the great Terror of the family; & that they might destroy the house ye sooner they took Wheat sheaves & carryed [them] up [to] the Chambers & sett them on Fier & by that Means quickly burnt the dwelling house, as allso one Milk house of fifteen foot long & another out house of the said John Roads, this deponent by the Lord Baltimores party did loose to the Vallue of two Hundred Pounds Sterl[ing].[66]

With the ashes of Hoeren Kill rapidly cooling in the freezing December winds, one inhabitant, Richard Pattee, still believing that some shred of mercy might be extracted from the Marylanders, pleaded for permission to erect a small thatched shed or cabin to shelter himself and his wife and infant child from the weather. He had lost three houses to the flames, two of which were warehouses filled with corn and tobacco. Before the arrival of Howell and his men, he had been "in a very good way to live happily." Howell refused, informing the pathetic settler that "it was death for any to build anything there." In anguish, Pattee suggested that they might as well "knock them on the Head & end there days," for they were already doomed. The captain replied sardonically "that his Commission did not reach so far."[67]

Having destroyed all that lay in and about Hoeren Kill, allegedly for its allegiance to The Netherlands, Captain Thomas Howell and his troopers departed. They took with them their meager plunder from the town, but more importantly all of the boats lying in the creek. The pitiful victims of the attack by those who had supposedly come to defend them, were 60 miles from the nearest relief. Facing the harshness of winter with no food, clothing, or arms, prospects for survival were grim. Starvation or slaughter at the hands of hostile savages were specters that loomed large. Thus, many of the settlers set out overland for New Orange. Others began the trek to New Castle or other places. A few, such as John Roads, Sr., who, like his son had suffered terribly, and his neighbor, Thomas Tilley, never made it to New Castle. They were murdered by Indians. Some of the unfortunates assembled on Murder Creek, on Delaware Bay, where they soon starved. A few families, with pregnant women among them, remained at Hoeren Kill, crowded in the little thatched barn to face the winter.[68]

Upon his return to Maryland, Captain Howell and his men were rewarded by Lord Baltimore for their sack of Hoeren Kill. In June 1674 they received for their efforts

2000 lbs of tobacco for 35 @ 400 lbs of tobacco p. man 14,000 pounds of tobacco—to the same Howell for his lieutenants 700 lbs of tobacco, for his ensign 600 lbs, for his sergeant 500 lbs—in all 1800 pounds to Howell for provisions and necessaries 776 pounds for his attendance upon a prisoner of warr.[69]

Raid on America

When the human debris from the destruction of Hoeren Kill arrived at New Orange in early January, Anthony Colve opened his heart and the meager city treasury. In a proclamation issued on January 4, 1674, he declared that since the destruction of the town had stripped many of its people of all means of subsistence, all exiles, "Dutch and English," who came into New Orange with certificates from Commander Peter Alricks stating that they were among the sufferers would be provided with means of support. Colve moved quickly to prevent a recurrence of the disaster and ordered all inhabitants on the Delaware to place themselves, upon the approach of any enemy, under Alrick's command, after which it would be determined how to counter the foe and inflict harm upon him.[70]

Considering the paucity of his forces and the enormous expanse and vulnerability of New Netherland, Colve's words were brave but empty.

19

THE NAVEL OF HIS
MAJESTY'S TERRITORY

With powerful enemies on every border, the atmosphere of crisis must have been pervasive in New Orange. It was kept in check only by the stern leadership of Governor Colve and the hope that reinforcements might soon arrive from the Fatherland. Unfortunately for the Colve administration this was only a hope, as it was battered and torn by a series of unfortunate accidents and incidents. The most pivotal was the stranding in enemy territory of Captain Vonck's bus *Expectation*, one of the two vessels sent out for home in the fall of 1673 with dispatches and appeals for help.[1] Indeed, the wreck of the ship not only caused Dutch morale in New Netherland to plummet, but also set in motion a chain of events that further threatened the security of New Orange.

The seeds of the new crisis were planted in early November 1673, when the city learned that the little vessel that had departed for the Fatherland on September 2 with Cornelis van Ruijven's and the magistrates' appeals for assistance, lay dismasted and helpless near Nantucket, Massachusetts. Colve immediately sent Captain Eewoutsen in *Zeehond* to aid the crippled bus. He returned on November 15 with disheartening news and four English prizes. The stranded *Expectation*, he reported, had been captured on November 3 by a Boston privateer brigantine of two to four guns and 14 to 20 men commanded by one Captain Thomas Dudson (or Diedson). The privateer, bearing a letter of marque from the king's government, was said to have been backed by Boston merchants, but had taken Captain Vonck's ship without the consent of the Boston government. Vonck and his crew were safe, having been temporarily lodged by the "governor" of Nantucket, Thomas Gardner, and then carried to Boston as prisoners aboard their own vessel, which had been refloated.[2]

In reprisal, Eewoutsen seized the first New England vessels that crossed his path and returned with them to New Orange. These included: the ketch *Providence*, Captain Richard Hollingsworth, owner and commander, taken near Block Island while en route from Boston to Virginia with tobacco; the ketch *Nightingale*, John Ingersol commanding, belonging to John Grafton of Salem and taken in Tarpaulin Cove with rum, salt, cloth, sugar, wool, and mackerel; the ketch *The Friend's Supply* of Boston, Thomas Bearch, captain and owner, with assorted goods; and the ketch *Neptune*, David Kalley, commander, Richard Cotts of Piscattaway, owner, with wine, rum, salt, and sugar.[3]

Expectation's loss, of course, "was no small disappointment to the Dutch Interest." The enemy's interdiction of the letters and the emissary she carried meant much to the potential survival or collapse of the colony. The English colonies were now informed of the state of Dutch morale, strength, and the condition of the colony.[4] Thus it is not surprising that the escalatory seizure of the four New England vessels met with the full approval of the New Netherland government. Colve released the four skippers and their crews almost immediately, and even provided an express boat to convey them home, along with the request that *Expectation*'s captain and crew be accorded the same civility. On November 20, however, the governor formally stated that the ketches "belong to subjects of England actually in open war against our state," whose subjects, under the command of Captain Thomas Dudson, had seized the Dutch bus *Expectation*. As such, he ordered, the ketches were to be declared subject to confiscation and forfeiture and would be disposed of to the best advantage of the government.[5]

Boston, which had hitherto remained aloof from the affairs of its new Dutch neighbors, and may have even been unaware of Dudson's actions, was stung by the seizures. The New Englanders had long been wary of the Dutch in New Orange, and upon the fall of the city had feared an attack on their own colony. The accidental destruction (by fire) of the "castle" fort in Boston harbor had rendered that city vulnerable to attack by water. The independent-minded citizens of Massachusetts Bay were understandably nervous. The New Englanders, undoubtedly hoping to avoid reprisals while a powerful Dutch fleet was on the coast, cautiously refrained from entering the fray when the town of Southampton requested armed assistance soon after the fall of New York.[6] Some prominent Bostonians, such as Richard Wharton, however, were from the beginning well aware of the danger if the

Dutch were permitted to remain unmolested and to flourish. He urged, early on, that an "expedition to unkennel the enemy" be undertaken. "New York," he stated, "being the navel of his Majesty's territory, and his subjects on both sides so familiarized to the Dutch trade and converse, that all will not believe they are their enemies."[7]

Boston had undoubtedly refrained from acting against the infant Dutch regime almost as much from hatred of the former Lovelace government as from fear. When Captain John Wyborne arrived in Boston from Barbados to refit and victual H.M.S. *Garland*, he quickly volunteered his ship to reduce New Netherland, providing the colony would supply a few soldiers, sailors, and stores. The New England magistrates replied that they would contribute to the expedition only if the province could be annexed to their government. Otherwise, they would rather the possession of New York remain with The Netherlands "than to come under such a person as Colonel Lovelace who might prove a worse neighbor." Wyborne, who already disapproved of the New Englanders, their autonomous trading practices, and their disdain for the Duke of York, was himself less than popular in Boston, a city filled with numerous English seamen fleeing impressment back home. Indeed, the captain was so unpopular during his stay that he was attacked by a mob, wounded, and barely escaped with his life. It was thus not surprising that his offer to lead an expedition of New Englanders against New Netherland fell on deaf ears.[8]

The war had remained at a distance from Massachusetts, and the colony leaders, though voicing a need for action, were content to let sleeping dogs lie. Now, with the *Expectation* incident, the situation changed radically. The seizure of the four New England ketches, they felt, demanded redress. The Boston government sent Nathaniel Davenport and Arthur Mason, to carry Governor Leverett's and his council's protest against the action and to demand the release of the vessels.[9]

Boston's ire was aroused, and with it the urge to abandon the restraint exercised earlier. If the vessels were not released, the government threatened, "We doe declare our Selves bound & Resolved by ye help and assistance of god to Endeavour a full Reparation by force of Armes."[10]

The gauntlet, it appeared to Colve, had been tossed. The unwavering Dutch government responded with a straightforward recounting of the sequence of events concerning the Connecticut usurpation of the towns, of the East Riding country—"your allies, with your approbation, as they give out"—the seizure of *Expectation*, and the subsequent reprisals against the four ketches. Massachusetts, Colve noted coldly, was the aggressor, not New Netherland.[11] He made it abundantly clear that his administration was not about to yield. Military escalation seemed unavoidable.

The English governments to the north were threat enough to the Dutch, but their employment of spies and provocateurs was a dangerous nuisance that seemed to continue without respite. Governor Colve was particularly upset that the New Englanders had added insult to injury by sending Nathaniel Davenport as one of their official emmissaries. Davenport, Colve insisted, was a spy of the first order. But there were others, some of whom had caused considerable problems.[12]

In November, Francis Beado, a 27-year-old native of London, one of several reported troublemakers in New Haerlem, was arrested after having claimed to possess a commission "to attack, rob, burn and destroy" by fire and sword the village of Fordham. He had, his accusers charged, been very near to success when apprehended, and had confessed to his crime without torture. On November 28 he was sentenced to be placed at the stake and branded on the back with a red-hot iron. Thereafter he was banished from the colony for 25 years and warned that he would be put to death if he returned. The Beado incident was disquieting enough to convince several inhabitants of the town that a conspiracy existed, and they left with their families and property soon afterwards.[13]

The Beado affair was endemic to the problems of securing a vast border that was sparsely populated by Dutch and English settlers who communicated freely with New England and other enemies. Several days after the Beado trial, the Colve government, seeking to address the problem, published a decree notifying the citizens of New Netherland that all correspondence with New England or other enemies was strictly forbidden. All messengers, captains, and travelers entering the colony were to first deliver their letters to Secretary Bayard for examination, on pain of a fine of 100 guilders in beaverskins for failure to do so.[14]

Colve did not take the direct threat of attack by Massachusetts lightly. Following the New Englander's ultimatum, his rule of New Orange grew more strict with every passing day. The governor was increasingly concerned about the vulnerability of the loyal Dutch towns on Long Island and the Dutch inhabitants of those towns with mixed population. Soon after receiving Massachusetts's ultimatum, he visited the village of Midwout, on the island, in company with several officers and local dignitaries, to confer with the magistrates and chief persons of the towns of Amersfoort, Brooklyn, New Utrecht, and Bushwick. The tidings he presented were grave. The New Englanders, he had been repeatedly informed, were making preparations and were, he was told, "already on their way to attack this Province in a hostile manner." Though he attached little credit to the reports, he may have suggested, to soothe the growing concern, that he felt it imperative "to encourage them [the Dutch towns] in their plight." He recommended that they thresh their grain with all possible expedition and send as much to New Orange as they could. Upon his summons, they and their people were to immediately take refuge in the city. In the meantime, they were to maintain a careful watch on the English towns to the east and keep him informed of "occuring events." The militia companies of the towns, with the exception of six men left behind in each village to maintain order, were to muster, fully armed, in front of Fort Willem Hendrick on Friday, December 19. One-third of each company would be furloughed every third day in rotation. Thus, the city would maintain a substantial guard while imposing minimal demand upon the citizen soldiers.[15]

Many citizens of the outlying towns were, in fact, well aware of the escalating situation and had already sought permission to move to New Orange. Colve saw to it that buildings in the city were found to house the refugees, and he ordered that the Long Island Ferry be readied to transport the expected influx of citizens to the city with all possible expedition. And finally, though the governor could not possibly visit all of the towns of New Netherland, he did dispatch messengers to those most likely to be affected by any military adventures of the enemy. These he ordered to remain vigilant and to be ready to remove to New Orange at a moment's notice.[16]

Colve was pleased with the work that the companies of New Orange militia and the troop of horse had undertaken in fortifying the city. Not satisfied with the militia's strength in numbers, however, he ordered an additional company of foot raised and placed under the command of Cornelis Steenwyck, who had formerly commanded the company of horse. With the exception of the guard, it was decreed, no one in New Orange, whatever his status, was to be permitted on the fort walls, bastions, or batteries between sunset and sunrise at the risk of corporal punishment; anyone entering the city other than through the guarded city gate would do so on pain of death.[17]

Even during the military emergency, Colve wrestled with daily administrative problems, often with the aid of the Council of War and his civilian councillors. There were many issues to be adjudicated, such as the petulant rivalry between the upper Hudson towns of Willemstadt and Schenectady, both vying for the Indian trade. The New Orange magistrates bickered incessantly over the reorganization of civil powers and the courts in the city. And, of course, there were the ever-present state affairs, such as negotiations with the Crossweeke Indians over the accidental shooting of a drunken brave beneath the fort by a Dutch guard. Public complaints against officials appointed by the government were also daily grist for Colve's administrative mill. To his and his council and advisors' credit, such matters were firmly but judiciously attended to in the face of potential enemy attack.[18]

The refortification of New Orange, though vastly improving the city's defenses, was proving inordinately painful for those obliged to bear the burden of expense. In late January, the burgomasters and schepens of the city complained of the excessive expenses of the construction work. Many owed considerable sums of money and were daily beset by creditors for payment. They petitioned Colve to devise some expedient to discharge the expenses already incurred or expected to arise. The governor responded by imposing a tax on the wealthiest and most affluent inhabitants. The estates of individuals worth more than 1,000 guilders "Wampum value" would be appraised by six impartial persons, two of whom would be selected by the magistrates from their own number. When completed, the list contained 133 names. As such a tax would be time consuming to collect, Colve decreed on March 7 that an advanced loan would be collected from individuals worth more than 4,000 guilders, paid in beaver skins or wheat "at Wampum price," and to be repaid from the proceeds of dues from a temporarily imposed "extraordinary" customs on export products. The revised list totalled 65 persons, with property assets amounting to 520,900 guilders.[18]

With the increase in militia manpower in New Orange, and the growing population of refugees, the maintenance of military discipline was bound to be affected. Colve, realizing the need for a civilian-military liaison, appointed one Jacobus van de Waeter to the newly created post of Town Major of New Orange and Auditor of its Court Martial. Nevertheless, discipline, in light of the degenerating situation on the periphery of the colony, continued to be a problem, and strong punishment the favored remedy. When *Zeehond*'s boatswain's mate scolded and threatened his captain, Colve ordered Captain Evert Evertsen, senior naval officer in the colony, to administer the punishment. The boatswain's mate, Jan Pieterse, was ordered to "be thrown, on board your ship [*Suriname*], three times from the yard-arm, and then be flogged as long as you and Captn Ewoutsen will think he can bear it."[20]

Colve was again forced to address the problem of alcohol, which was having a detrimental effect on his men. By mid-January the problem had grown to such an extent that he was once more obliged to issue a proclamation forbidding all persons to sell, barter, or give credit, without permission, for strong liquor to the soldiers and sailors. They were also forbidden to receive, pawn, or purchase clothing, arms, ammunition, or other materials from those in the military, presumably to prevent black market operations from gaining head.[21]

With the potential of an attack from Massachusetts in the offing and amid pervasive uncertainty about whether the Fatherland was still ignorant of the Dutch plight in New Netherland, Colve authorized another effort to inform the States General, Zeeland, and Amsterdam of the situation. Captain Vonck, having been released from New England, was appointed to the command of the ketch *Hope* on January 1, 1674, and given orders to sail for home as soon as wind and weather permitted. He was directed to steer for the Azores, then the English Channel, making the "best port that opportunity presents" in Holland, Zeeland, Flanders, or even along the northwest coast of Spain or Galicia. Vonck was entrusted with a thick set of packages filled with letters and communiques for the Admiralty of Amsterdam, the Staten of Zeeland, and others, which, upon reaching Europe, he was to forward with a note of his arrival. If unable to make a Dutch port, the captain was sternly ordered to retain the three smallest packets for two or three weeks before sending them off. He would then be at liberty to make a run up the English Channel for home if winds were favorable. If taken by the enemy, he was directed to "take good heed to throw the letters overboard into the sea, well fastened to weights."[22]

Now Colve could afford to return his attentions to the dissident towns of the East Riding of Yorkshire.

Throughout the winter Massachusetts blustered mightily about action against New Netherland, but could not decide upon a course. It was, in fact, Connecticut, spurred by the prospect of finally securing the East Riding country of Long Island as its own, that caused Colve the greatest discomfort. In recognition of his October confrontation at Southold, Fitz-John Winthrop had been promoted to the rank of major by the Governor and Council at Hartford. They then directed him to raise a force to secure the East Riding towns. Accompanied by several Massachusetts observers, Major Winthrop secured ready assistance at New London and Stonington for his mission across the Sound. Finally, in late February 1674, he sailed for Long Island, which was now ready to accept Connecticut's dominion with open arms.[23]

With a fair wind behind him, the major soon arrived at Shelter Island to secure intelligence regarding the Dutch foe, but aside from a convivial meeting with Captain Sylvester, he learned little of value, so he pressed on to Southold. He had no sooner landed there than a post rider from Setauket arrived with an urgent dispatch intended for the local militia commander. The major was immediately informed that *Zeehond*, a ketch, and two sloops, then anchored near White Stone, were waiting the first fair wind to sail for Southold. Added to this news, "a person from New York of credible intelligence" reported that the Dutch ships "were bound hither with great resolution to reduce or destroy the towns on the East end of Long Island," and to take on provisions from Shelter Island. Governor Colve, it appeared to the English, was at last going to attempt to make good his threat to punish the towns of the East Riding with fire and sword for their failure to submit to his government.[24]

Winthrop quickly dispatched an express to Captain Howell, commander of the Southampton militia, and to the chief officer at Easthampton to inform them of the impending danger, and to request a meeting at Southold to consider "the best way for the preservation of these towns." Within hours, the three officers and the several observers from Boston were immersed in conference, discussing the best way to defend the provisions, which, it was learned, the Dutch hoped to take on at Shelter Island. After due consideration, the Bostonians suggested that the officers totally ignore the provisions and concentrate their attention on the defense of Southold.[25]

Major Winthrop agreed and ordered Howell to raise 40 soldiers from Southampton and place them under the command of a lieutenant (presumably to leave the captain free to defend his own town should the Dutch turn their attentions in that direction). This force was to be ready to march at an hour's warning. The lieutenant at Easthampton was to raise an additional 20 men to be commanded by his eldest sergeant. With these mobile forces, the major hoped to be in a condition to give the Dutch a warm welcome wherever they might land.[26]

At 7:00 A.M., Sunday, February 23, Fitz-John Winthrop was informed that the snaauw, a ketch, and two sloops were within gun shot of Plum Gut, with a fair wind and tide to bring them in. The sudden appearance of the Dutch warship and her little consorts, despite a watch that had been established to prevent a surprise, managed to startle everyone, especially the local inhabitants. With Winthrop's example, however, they soon recovered their composure and "thought it was then time to look about us, and provide for our defence." The major immediately summoned the 60 militiamen from Southampton and Easthampton to Southold. The diminutive Dutch squadron did not press toward the town, but came to anchor off Shelter Island to demand provisions from Captain Sylvester, the proprietor of the island. Sylvester,

> with the advice of the officers the day before, thought it might be most for his safety, and the peace of his family, being then at the mercy of an enemy (they having landed 50 armed men) to comply with their demands, and by their order was forced to deliver the provisions the same hour, which they immediately shipped.[27]

Captain Eewoutsen's flotilla remained anchored off Shelter Island throughout the night. The next morning, with Sylvester aboard, the fleet, "having an easy gale and the advantage of the tide," had soon come to off Southold. Eewoutsen anchored his flotilla in "an handsome order," and brought all of his great guns to bear, while preparing his men for a landing in force. Fearful of the bloodletting that appeared imminent, Sylvester beseeched Eewoutsen for permission to personally deliver the Dutch surrender terms to Winthrop. The captain agreed. Winthrop was soon informed that the enemy had come to demand "subjection" to the States General and the Prince of Orange. Upon surrender, it was promised, Southold would enjoy the same privileges that had been conferred upon the other towns of New Netherland. Refusal would only bring swift and total destruction.[28]

Upon receipt of the terms, Winthrop consulted with his officers and the troops, who were unanimous in their resolve to oppose the enemy. The major quickly drafted a reply to be delivered by Sylvester.

> That I am here appointed by the authority of his Majesty's colony of Connecticut, to secure these people in obedience to his Majesty, and by God's assistance, I hope to give a good account thereof, and you may assure yourself, that I will receive you in the same condition, as a person that disturbs his Majesty's subjects.[29]

Having received Winthrop's reply, Eewoutsen resolutely began filling his sloops with men preparatory to landing. Watching the Dutch motions, the major prepared to "entertain" the foe with a "forlorn-hope," or advance guard, of 50 men. As the sloops prepared to press for shore, *Zeehond* opened the engagement with a single shot, to no effect. The English quickly replied in kind, the ball splashing harmlessly in the water near the snaauw's bow. Then commenced a flurry of small arms fire from both sides, accentuated now and then by a few cannon rounds. The Dutch fire, "which fell thick" upon the English, however, did no damage, and the English fire accomplished little more than to splinter the sides of the warship. But for troops in open boats, Eewoutsen must have considered, the defender's fire was all too hot. Thinking better of conducting a costly assault on a town that would only continue to refuse subjugation, he called off the attack. Soon afterwards, he ordered anchors raised and all sail made for New Orange.[30]

The skirmish at Southold, though preserving, perhaps strengthening, Connecticut's hold on the East Riding towns, had been for Major Winthrop an apparently harrowing experience. Soon afterwards he requested that he be replaced by "some fitter person to manage the great affairs, which I find too heavy for me." His dispatch, telling of the successful repulse of the Dutch, reached Hartford on March 1, giving his father the governor and the Council much more about which to rejoice. But the major's request for a replacement was solemnly denied. He was instead ordered to remain on Long Island "till at least these present motions of the Dutch be over." Reinforcements, he was told, were on the way. In fact, Connecticut had recently requested that the Massachusetts Bay colony send a man-of-war to clear the coast of the enemy's ships, without which action the East Riding towns might readily be assaulted at any time. Only after the arrival of the warship, which guaranteed the security of the Long Islanders, would the major have the liberty to return to the mainland.[31]

Fitz-John Winthrop undoubtedly chafed under his father's orders, but Governor Winthrop saw a larger picture than his son. Both the governor and the Council of Connecticut were of the correct opinion that the Dutch, strapped for manpower, had committed what little strength they could spare to facilitate their designs on the East Riding towns. The repulse at Southold, they were confident, would undoubtedly prevent them from venturing forth on such an adventure again in the near future. Yet young Major Winthrop must have blanched when his father added that he must continue management of the Long Island militia to quell any further proceedings of the Dutch, at least "until they [the Dutch] receive more forraine Assistance." Though the governor indicated that he hoped fresh English recruits would soon be arriving, the thought of the arrival of enemy reinforcements was undoubtedly depressing.[32]

Despite Major Winthrop's concern, for once, the governor of Connecticut's appeal to the Massachusetts Bay Colony did not fall on deaf ears, for that colony now also claimed injury at the hands of the Dutch. Unlike some in his government, Governor John Leverett had, from the outset, been a strong advocate of action to secure the East Riding towns. Yet the colony he governed was still mixed in its sympathies. Even after word of the skirmish at Southold arrived in Boston, Leverett was obliged to apologize to Winthrop for his colony's indecisiveness. On March 3, he wrote,

I cannot answere your expectation, and desire I cannot be wholy sylent least I should render myselfe negligent of that respect I owe you and your Counsell: truth is the generall voague of the averseness of the people to ingage in any acts of hostility against the dutch, occations retarding of comeing to any conclusion tending thereto. . . . I may be accounted by some too forward to take armes and by some too backward, I doe write in truth I doe not delight in warr, and must likewise say I am against delays in dangers, and fore slowing oppertunitys, and gieveing advantage to the enimy that insults, upon pretences that will not lye square at all times upon any ground. . . . Sir I really pitty the townes of [the] East End of Long Island, and will not be wanting to apply myselfe to endeavour their reliefe and am not without hopes that the next weeks upon the Courts comeing together we may doe some thing.[33]

Leverett and his supporters were, in fact, able to do something. On March 14, he informed Winthrop that help was on the way. The General Court had ordered two vessels to be outfitted as men-of-war. They were to secure the passage through Long Island Sound and "repress the present insolency of the Dutch." The court had further resolved that the ships would transport 200 soldiers for the defense of navigation and "to Joyne with our Confederates as matters may present."[34] Two weeks later, Massachusetts was ready to field the two vessels, both fully outfitted and furnished with ammunition and provisions. The first of these vessels was the 60-ton ketch *Swallow*, of Salem, with 12 guns and 60 men, and commanded by Captain Richard Sprague. The eight-gun, 40-man ketch *Salisbury*, similar in burthen to *Swallow*, was commanded by Captain Samuel Mosely. Massachusetts eventually surpassed its own objectives, for within a short time, a force of 560 foot soldiers and two troop of horse had also been raised. The Plymouth settlement followed with an additional 100 men for the cause of country and king.[35]

The active preparations of Massachusetts and Connecticut for aggressive warfare only added to the siege mentality of the Dutch. Colve no longer suffered any illusions as to which side the English of Long Island would take, even among those villages that had declared their allegiance. Again he issued a proclamation, but this time it was intended for the Dutch. The fortifications of New Orange were "on the eve of perfection" and in such a state as to be capable of resisting all attacks.[36] The walls now bristled with 180 great guns, and by English accounts, the garrison numbered nearly 800 regulars and militiamen. New Orange would not be easily subdued.[37] Again Colve informed the Dutch "out people" from the surrounding towns that they were to retire to the city on notice of the enemy's approach, but this time they were directed to come "provided with proper hand and side arms." Those who failed to come in at the first alarm would be considered traitors and enemies, and would be punished by death and the confiscation of their property. Departure from the city during such an emergency and the holding of correspondence with the enemy were to be punished in a like manner.[38] Any arms that had been loaned or furnished during past administrations to the inhabitants of such towns as Flushing were to be delivered up on 24 hours' notice. And to make certain that there was no negligence in following orders, the Dutch deputies from each of the adjacent towns were summoned and sternly instructed to follow all of the governor's orders.[39]

During the meeting with the deputies, several from the towns of Bergen, New Utrecht, and Bushwick asked that boats be provided to carry inhabitants from the out areas of the colony to safety. Colve approved, and empowered Cornelis Steenwyck and Cornelis van Ruijven to handle the request. He was well aware that without boats Manhattan could not be escaped from, reached by friends, or attacked by foes. Boats could offer an obstruction, as in the case of *Suriname*, which was permanently anchored in a defensive posture as a floating battery near the lower rondeel, or could be a detriment to defensive fire if in the way. The harbor near the public weighing house was cluttered with small craft, which were obstructions to the waterfront defenses. Thus, Colve ordered that all such vessels be removed by the skippers, bargemen, and boatmen of the city to an area behind a defensive float that had been erected. The boats were to be placed under the protection of the guns of *Suriname* and the rondeel. All vessels that were not promptly removed were to be burned.[40]

Colve labored tirelessly. But even as rumors circulated, the long-feared attack on New Orange failed to materialize. Though many said Charles II was determined to retake the province by force, there were also whispers of a different kind in the air; whispers of peace.

20

NEWS FROM THE COAST
OF SPAIN

Along the Gulf of Cadiz, between Cape St. Vincent at its western-most extremity and the Strait of Gibraltar on the east, the southwest coast of Spain was generally low and indented by few geographic features. Though the meandering Guadiana and Guadalquivir rivers, the latter leading to the fabled city of Seville, sent their accumulated waters into the gulf's bosom, to mariners of the seventeenth century the Bay of Cadiz and the ancient metropolis of the same name provided the chief interest. Strategically ensconced on a small peninsular promotory at the mouth of the bay sixty miles west-northwest of Gibraltar, the city was frequently the center of major events and military actions. After the discovery of the New World, Cadiz had grown dramatically in importance as Spain's premier port for colonial traffic, a place where majestic galleons departed with goods for the Americas and returned with their holds filled with gold, silver, pearls, and precious stones. As a consequence, the galleons and the port they arrived at became the unfortunate targets of enemy attacks. In 1587, the dashing English seadog, Sir Francis Drake, destroyed the city, and in 1596, Queen Elizabeth's ill-fated consort, the Earl of Essex, also sacked it.

The military and political turmoils of the seventeenth century were no less harrowing for Cadiz, for Spain's fortunes as a major European naval power had begun to wane. At the outbreak of the Third Anglo-Dutch War, the Spanish government, having already fought long and bloody wars of empire with both antagonists, was economically beholden to the Dutch and attempted to remain neutral. Cadiz, already the primary international entrepôt on Spain's Atlantic coast, became, for all intents and purposes, an open port. There, Dutch warships of

Raid on America

Amsterdam assembled to escort richly laden Spanish galleons through perilous waters—in full view of Royal Navy warships and French traders. There, Dutch privateers operated with growing impunity as French merchants, hated but tolerated by the Spanish, watched and reported to their king. There, Tunisian or Mediterranean-bound British convoys put in for repairs and supplies, and English spies monitored Dutch capers, their accounts turning up in the pages of the *London Gazette* only days later. And there, Cornelis Evertsen and Jacob Benckes sought to bring their own rag-tag armada to refit, reprovision, await their government's orders, and perhaps undertake one or two last flings against the enemy before returning home.

On December 4, 1673, though only three tantalizing miles from Cadiz Harbor, the Dutch fleet found entry all but impossible. A cold, offshore wind had come up during the night, and on the following day the entire flotilla was obliged to tack laboriously back and forth, seeming to lose more ground than it gained. The heavily laden prizes, having retarded the fleet's passage across the Atlantic, continued to cause problems. They could make little, if any, headway and *Swaenenburgh* was, at one point, forced to take in tow one of the worst sailers among them. About midday on the 5th, their travails were temporarily forgotten as a Spanish armada, 13 or 14 ships strong, passed in magnificent procession, bound for the West Indies and the Americas with the Viceroy of Peru.[1] The following days were no less frustrating as the Netherlanders continued to battle the winds within sight of their objective, their advance measured in yards rather than miles.

On December 6, *Swaenenburgh* was boarded by the Dutch Consul in Cadiz, Gaspar van Collen, who had come out with urgent dispatches from Middleburgh. After an undoubtedly warm welcome aboard, he delivered into Evertsen's hands three letters from the Raden of Zeeland, the long-awaited orders from home. Unfortunately, they were not what Kees the Devil had expected; upon reading them, he learned that news of the conquest of New Netherland had caused considerable tumult at the highest levels of government in Middleburg and Amsterdam, and, indeed, in the very halls of the States General.[2]

The government of Zeeland, it seemed, was more irritated than pleased by the brash young commander they had sent out a year before to take St. Helena, capture rich English East Indiamen, and raid in the Americas. The Raden had been in the dark concerning his actions until the end of September 1673, a period of nearly three months. Only from the frigate *America*, which had gone to Curaçao with slaves, had there been any tidings of his arrival in the Americas. Then there were two letters dispatched by Benckes to the Admiralty of Amsterdam in June, by which they had learned second hand of the juncture of the two squadrons, the raid on Virginia, and the fate of the tobacco flotilla. From the commander of Suriname, they had received word of the terrible conditions in his own colony, which was nearing starvation, something "fully known" but unreported by Evertsen. Yet, the government complained, they had not received a single letter from him since his arrival in the Canaries almost eight months before. The deputized Raden of Zeeland were growing more perturbed daily, particularly as rumors had surfaced in Middleburg "giving us some appearance of truth" that the Terre Neuf expedition, which they had hoped had been launched, had been captured and ruined.[3]

On September 30, the Raden, still unaware of the magnitude of the odyssey that the tiny squadrons of Evertsen and Benckes had actually undertaken, or of Evertsen's efforts to keep the government informed, dispatched secret orders, along with a chastisement, to their young commander. He was directed (if he had not already arrived there) to sail to Cadiz or another harbor in neutral Spain rather than attempt a circumvention of the British Isles to return home as previously ordered. There Evertsen was to sell the fish they assumed he had taken in Newfoundland for the highest price possible, or, failing to do so in that country, to send some through the Strait of Gibraltar to Mediterranean markets. In the event he had already arrived at Cadiz, he was instructed "to make all ships as quickly as possible clean and shipshape," and to revictual for two or three months, but not to sail before receiving further instructions. The Raden also asked Benckes to do the same, but to await specific orders from his own masters, the Admiralty of Amsterdam, "who apparently agree with us to keep both squadrons together" to inflict further damage on the enemy with common force.[4]

The Raden were not lacking in optimism, however, and, in fact, expected more from their commander than may have been fair. They hoped that the conquests and prizes taken would prove to be so numerous that the commander could pay his men their wages and provide whatever new equipment was necessary for the squadron from the plunder. He was, of course, instructed to take special care that, whatever portion he might use for pay and repairs, there should be a large surplus left for the country. Ever concerned over the objective of the raid—profits to be derived from the booty of war—the government instructed Evertsen that it

> will greatly contribute to that end if everything is truthfully justified and accounted for, that the fish taken and conquered [goods] be sold for the highest price and the names be faithfully received and remitted here, or if the abovementioned fish be sent further Straitwards, upon judgement

of greatest, and in such a case that it be insured, and the other conquests
of greater value be preserved there [at Cadiz] until further order, unless
it be something subject to decay or something that for some other evident
reason cannot await further order.[5]

The Raden, apparently only mildly concerned over the starvation
reported at Suriname, suggested that some of the prize cargo, assumed
taken by the Terre Neuf expedition, including dried fish, olive oil, flour,
salt, Spanish wine, meat, and bacon, might be shipped off in a small
ship with ten or twelve men from Evertsen's squadron to the aid of that
beleaguered colony as quickly as possible, but only if the exercise were
to be commercially profitable for Zeeland. In fact, Evertsen was instructed to do so only if the meat and bacon could be purchased in
Suriname "for a reasonable price and that the booty taken from the
enemy is considerable and can easily spare the cost." The Raden assumed the Terre Neuf expedition to have been under Zeelander management, and thus dispatched a letter to Benckes requesting that if
Evertsen did not join him in Cadiz, he was to send the aforementioned
supplies with one of the Newfoundland contingent to Suriname.[6]

When news of the capture of New Netherland, received at Whitehall
on October 3, reached The Netherlands a full three weeks later, it was
the Admiralty of Amsterdam and not Zeeland that had learned of it
first. The effect was electrifying, and the Dutch were as stunned by the
dramatic turnabout as their counterparts across the North Sea had
been. Unlike the British Admiralty, which benefited from regular intelligence data, Amsterdam, owing to the capture of one of the express
vessels and the wreckage and capture of the second sent from New
Netherland, was still ignorant of all but the barest details.[7]

Upon learning of the colony's capture, Amsterdam Admiralty Secretary de Wildt immediately dispatched a letter to Lord Grand Pensionary Fagel of the States General confessing that the Admiralty board
was "completely blind as to what ought to be undertaken for the conservation of the Colony, as well as the concepts [intentions] of the Officers who had performed the said capture." Fagel was, however, moved
by the urgency of the situation and presented the letter the next day to
a meeting of the deputies of the States General. After due deliberation,
a series of secret resolutions was agreed upon. Lord de Huijbert, Grand
Pensionary of Zeeland, was to be immediately informed of the news.
He was asked to disclose to his own government "in the best, most
efficient, most fitting and most secret manner," the dramatic news and
to send a committee of deputies to attend a full briefing at The Hague
on the evening of October 19. Fagel hoped that, thus informed, the
deputies from Zeeland and Amsterdam might jointly develop an effec-

tive plan of action "to the holding and conservation" of New Netherland, the employment of ships already there, recommendation of a policy relative to the Evertsen and Benckes squadrons, "and resolve as shall be found to be of best service to the Country."[8]

There were serious problems between Zeeland and Holland to be considered, primarily pertaining to who would bear the expense incurred by the garrisoning of the colony, and who would be the beneficiaries of any profits that might be derived from the conquest. A jointly shared operation, given the rivalries and jealousies traditionally exhibited by both states, was unlikely. Holland and Zeeland, the two most powerful members of the States General, had often acted more as independent but allied states than members of a single national federation. Yet the harmony exhibited by Evertsen and Benckes during their joint expedition was exemplary of what could be accomplished, and had, to the undoubted astonishment of all, resulted in far more than anyone in The Netherlands might have expected. On the other hand, their harmony had also resulted in the acquisition of a territorial responsibility that neither the nation nor Zeeland and Holland had been prepared to shoulder. The two expeditionary forces had been sent out to replenish the distressed war chests of both provinces with revenues derived from plunder and to injure the enemy. Instead they had subjugated a vast chunk of territory squarely in the middle of England's American empire. The first inclination of the States General, undoubtedly born of pride in the recovery of lost territories, was to consider the best means to hold it. Inevitably, however, closer examination of the situation was bound to lead to alternative avenues of action, not the least of which was to employ the territory as a bargaining chip in the inevitable peace talks.

Having met in secret, the representatives of Zeeland and the Admiralty of Amsterdam returned to their provinces to deliberate further over the knotty issue. For Zeeland, whose soldiers and ships had been left to garrison New Netherland, the issue was one of economics as well as national integrity and pride. On October 30, the Grand Pensionary of Zeeland, having for two weeks meticulously dissected the problems and promise of the situation, convened a meeting of the state council to consider the issue. He pointed out that the conquest of New Netherland had produced a serious dilemma for Zeeland—primarily how the province could hope to maintain this vast region, along with its other responsibilities and dependencies, such as Suriname. No one seemed at first to question whether such an action should be undertaken, but rather how it might be implemented. It was, at the outset of discussion, considered a purely military problem, and thus it was not unexpected that a military solution be suggested. One proposal was that a small squadron of at least one 18- or 24-gun warship, several fireships, and other small vessels might be assembled and fielded to provide naval support for the colonies, and, as opportunity permitted, inflict damage upon the enemy. And there was, of course, still the option of employing the Evertsen squadron, thought to be somewhere at sea, which had been ordered to refit at Cadiz for a voyage of up to three months. But the first solutions were not necessarily the most acceptable. De Huijbert went to great pains to brief the Council as fully as possible so that they might determine a viable, cost-effective resolution of the issue. All of the communications from Evertsen and Benckes, from the commander of Suriname, as well as "further information concerning the debated sea affairs," were read in closed session and evaluated in depth over the course of the next several days. Gradually, but perceptibly, economic considerations began to outweigh patriotic fervor.[9]

On November 4, it was finally agreed that if Evertsen arrived at Cadiz or any other Spanish harbor, he should, as earlier directed, remain there for three or four months to refit, "and then be employed again in concert with the Amsterdam squadron to do most damage to the enemy." But more importantly, as the Admiralty of Amsterdam had also concluded that it was necessary to hold New Netherland—if Zeeland agreed—and since the operation that had captured it in the first place had been a joint expedition (albeit one not sanctioned as a campaign of conquest by either government), it was resolved that support be sent as quickly as possible. Therein, however, lay the rub. Zeeland, burdened by what it believed to be more than its fair share of economic and military committments to the war effort, and deprived of the hoped for treasures from the East Indiamen Evertsen had been sent out to capture, was willing to step back from the project and its promises. The province would do so, however, only with the provision that it receive just compensation for its initial investment, namely the cost of fielding the Evertsen squadron. The Admiralty of Amsterdam, the Zeelanders proposed among themselves,

> will take the half, in addition to their contingent, also to provide that some portion of the contingent, to the account of the one party, on the condition that this Province is compensated out of the aforementioned conquest of New Netherland.[10]

An extract of the resolution was sent to Lord de Mauregnault, one of Zeeland's deputies to the States General and also a foreign minister for the United Provinces. De Mauregnault was directed to inform the general government of his province's intentions and to secure approval for the action. At the same time, de Huijbert would attempt to handle the touchy business of dealing with Secretary de Wilde.

Though all of the deliberations had been conducted behind closed doors, the news of the many rich prizes said to have been taken in America could not remain a secret and soon spread rapidly in the merchant community. By late November, the Zeeland Assembly was informed that some merchants were preparing (well before the fleet ever reached Cadiz) to put in a claim for the goods believed to have been captured by Evertsen and Benckes in the Virginias and New Netherland. Indeed, they had already notified the admiralties of both Zeeland and Amsterdam of their intentions. The Zeeland government, though quietly prepared to relinquish authority over the reconquered colony of New Netherland, was not willing to lose the fruits of its labors, taken at great risk and expense for the benefit of the state, to powerful private interests—at least not without restitution. The Raden thus resolved to freeze approval of any such actions until further "necessary information be provided." The Assembly, concurring, dispatched a recommendation to the Admiralty of Amsterdam that they should consider the same course of action. It was becoming increasingly clear, however, that the raid on America had given birth to more problems of a military, commercial, and domestic nature than anyone cared to deal with.[11]

Not until December 5, and after a packet of dispatches from Commander Benckes had arrived, did the States General reach a preliminary consensus as to what should be done concerning New Netherland. With Zeeland apparently willing to relinquish its primary role, it was ordered that the Admiralty of Amsterdam, on behalf of the States General, be provisionally charged with the administration of the colony, as well as any militia forces sent there, and citizens residing there. The Admiralty was also directed to send a fit person as governor and commander in chief "to obey the orders of the said College of the Admiralty of Amsterdam." The officer was to be deputized and commissioned by Secretary of the Fleet of the Netherlands, Joris Andringa. All officers of companies to be sent there, however, were to be answerable to the orders of the Admiralty of Amsterdam.[12] Unfortunately, the Hollanders charged with this burden were not in complete accord with the States General's directives, and Zeeland, who had shared in the conquest, and whose troops and ships garrisoned it, was not even consulted on, much less informed of, the decision.

On the surface, it appeared that some of those charged with the administration of the new colony could hardly await word from those who had carried out its subjugation before rushing to address the issues of its management and defense. Yet given the information vacuum in which they operated, and the inordinate time lapse between sending and receiving of data across vast expanses of sea and land, such predictive measures were imperative. Indeed, second-guessing had been honed to a fine diplomatic and military art, geared to such lapses, often supplemented and occasionally directed by only the barest details of distant events. Ironically, one of the primary outlets for information concerning affairs in North America was the United Provinces' mortal foe, England, whose newspapers, merchants, and even diplomats provided a steady stream of information that soon filtered into the Dutch outports across the North Sea. Secrets were difficult if not impossible to maintain, particularly those pertaining to large-scale military motions. Although Secretary Fagel had already been informed of the conquest of New Netherland by De Wilde of Amsterdam, it was not until after January 3, when Lord de Huijbert dispatched additional intelligence from Middleburg, that he discovered the extent to which Evertsen and Benckes had gone to hold the colony. De Huijbert's communique informed the Secretary

> that there are tidings that a ship with a dispatch boat from the squadron of Captain Cornelis Evertsen and the greater part of his enlisted Marines have been left in New Netherland for the occupation and defense of the fort and the city of [New] Amsterdam.[13]

By then, however, secret negotiations for peace were well underway.

Entirely unaware of the concerns he had aroused in the Fatherland, with the exceptions of those noted in the fall letters from the Raden, Cornelis Evertsen was, for the moment, more intent on bringing his bedraggled fleet into Cadiz Harbor than with issues of state. On the evening of December 6, though *Schaeckerloo* and two of the prizes had managed to work their way into the bay, northerly winds continued to frustrate the remainder of the flotilla. The following evening the fleet of capers, which had returned from their cruise empty-handed, as well as Benckes's *Noordhollandt* and a few others, finally made the bay, but Evertsen, De Witte, Richewijn and the rest were obliged to drop anchor outside. Finally, at daybreak on the 8th, an easterly breeze picked up, the Zeelanders and their prizes again weighed anchor and stood in, only to be forced to a frustrating standstill by a powerful flood tide. So close to his objective, after taking nearly four days to gain only three miles, Evertsen resolved to press as many of his ships in as possible in any manner necessary. "As the fluit and fireship were well to our lee," he recorded in *Swaenenburgh*'s log, "[I] Sent Capt. de Wit with Commander Richwijn to tow them in. After midday weighed anchor and tacked into the Bay."[14]

As the Zeelanders finally entered the estuary, Evertsen observed *Noordhollandt* sailing toward him with the entire fleet of capers. Pausing long enough to board *Swaenenburgh*, Commander Benckes excitedly informed him that a fleet of nine ships, presumed to be English, were coming through the Strait of Gibraltar, and that he and the capers were en route to intercept them. The inclination of the Zeeland commander to join the sortie was undoubtedly strong, but his own ship's rudder was in a serious state of disrepair, the vessels under his command "had neither water nor soup," and all were in great need of service. Evertsen had little choice but to proceed and, excusing himself from Benckes's sally, continued into the bay, coming to anchor at 7:00 P.M. By December 10, De Witte, Richewijn, and the gaggle of prizes had also entered and were soon busily engaged in watering, revictualling, and making repairs.[15]

Evertsen's arrival at Cadiz did not go unnoticed by English agents in that metropolis, and word of his appearance was soon in the hands of the British Admiralty Secretary Samuel Pepys. But Evertsen paid little attention to such matters, certainly well aware that the enemy could not help but be apprised of his presence. His first concern was to attend to his ships, for it was not until December 13 that he even took time to pen a letter to the Raden of Zeeland. The communique was long and detailed, informing the government of his recent travails from the Azores to his arrival in Cadiz Roads on December 10, and the dreadful physical condition of his little flotilla. He expressed surprise that none of his earlier letters had reached Zeeland, as he had taken every opportunity to write. Evertsen thus dispatched copies of his last two letters, written while in New Netherland, to update the government on his proceedings while there and in Virginia. He apologized for not sending any information aboard *America,* noting that he "had intended to be back in the Fatherland before the small ship . . . and therefore had not sent a letter with her." Having received from Consul van Collen the government's orders to provide an account of the prizes and goods taken during the expedition, as well as directions to supply Suriname from the prize cargoes, Evertsen sought to comply as much as possible. He explained that it had been his intention, before arriving at Cadiz, to send a small vessel to New Netherland and another to Suriname, but the scattering of part of his prize fleet off Cape St. Vincent by the Levantine winds had set back such plans. Nevertheless, in token acknowledgment of the Raden's directives, he volunteered to send two pipes of wine and two of oil with the Berbice-bound privateer *Eendracht,* Captain Jan Laurens commanding, who offered to bring them to Suriname. It was not much, but considering the Raden's orders concerning the limitations of what might be spared, it was undoubtedly all the commander dared send.[16]

Evertsen provided the Raden with a meticulously itemized list of every prize taken during the expedition, both before and after the juncture with Benckes, as well as their current dispositions, and of the various conquests made on land and sea. Of the vessels taken from the enemy, he documented a total of 34, of which only half a dozen had survived the travails of the past months and now lay with the fleet at Cadiz. The remainder had either been lost in storm, wrecked, abandoned as worthless, sold or traded for the benefit of Zeeland, or separated from the squadron by weather or enemy action. Of the prizes that had survived, four contained over 3,060 hogsheads of tobacco, and the remainder were heavily laden with sugar, freight goods, tobacco, and fish. Though the profits expected from the sale of these cargoes and ships would undoubtedly not equal those from a richly laden East Indiaman, they were certain to be substantial. There were also returns expected from the sale of slaves at the markets of Curaçao, as well as the proceeds from confiscated properties taken in English America and St. Eustatius. The Terre Neuf squadron had burned or wrecked 150 sloops, decimated England's coastal drying stations in Newfoundland, and all but destroyed her fishery operations in that part of the world. Evertsen also reminded the Raden of the capture of New Netherland, including three colonies, three islands, three cities, two forts, and 32 villages, wherein 12,000 to 14,000 souls resided.[17]

Kees the Devil Evertsen and Jacob Benckes, in their raid on America, with but nine ships, had been successful far beyond their own expectations. Neither of the two, however, believed their mission completed. There were 14 strong Vlissingen privateers cruising about Cadiz, several of which carried between 20 and 36 guns, which had been specifically sent "to cruise for a richly loaded English fleet, under convoy of a few ships of war." And the enemy convoy was expected to pass the strait at any time. Not long after Eversen's arrival at Cadiz, Benckes and the capers returned from their brief cruise, empty-handed but undaunted. Both Dutch commanders now hoped to take advantage of the timely opportunity, and formally contracted with eleven capers to sail as a combined fleet to search for the expected convoy. It was thus agreed, Evertsen informed the Raden, that each of the capers would receive a sixteenth share of all prizes jointly taken, and the remainder would be shared half and half by the Zeelanders and Hollanders. He offered as his reason for agreeing to this seemingly lopsided division in favor of the privateers, that they were 400 men stronger than his and Bencke's forces combined and therefore deserved it.[18]

Cornelis Evertsen was eager to set off in search of the rich enemy convoy, and had already made cursory repairs and "cleaned up as much as possible as quickly as possible in order to put to sea to cruise for this fleet." He dutifully assured the Raden that he fully intended to return to Cadiz after the sortie to complete the provisioning of the fleet and to fulfill all instructions sent to him by the Zeeland government. But, he cautioned, there would be problems in such undertakings. Ships stores were purchased at a dear price in the city, and filling the numerous vacancies in the fleet's greatly diminished manpower complement would be nearly impossible. It had also, he noted, become necessary to maintain a constant vigil over the prizes and their cargoes to prevent plundering. *Sint Joris* was in need of a sloop tender, and *Swaenenburgh* was in serious want of certain repairs and cable. Indeed, the ship, he wrote, "is very leaky, and the rudder must be held to the sternpost with chains, whereunto the hard winds, which we have had since our departure from New Netherland, have done us much evil."[19]

Despite the difficulties, Commander Evertsen's report seemed optimistic; with its long list of prizes, plunder, conquests achieved, and enemy property destroyed, it could not help but stir a certain quiet admiration. The commander was well aware, however, that the day of reckoning for his decision to abort the mission against St. Helena and to concentrate his efforts in the Americas would soon be at hand. Having made such a decision, he was also aware that the expedition's success would be measured by his superiors, not in terms of victories achieved or defeats sustained, or even in lands taken, but by weighing the expenses incurred against the market value of the goods captured. Possibly hoping to increase his final tally by a successful raid on the Strait convoy, Evertsen excused himself from producing a comprehensive accounting of the prize vessels by noting that "their cargoes cannot be precisely reported, as the majority of ships were taken from under the forts and in the rivers of the enemy, from which the masters escaped to land with all papers."[20]

He dutifully promised to send "a detail of the price of all our prize goods" by his next letter, and also declared his intention to send Colve's communiques overland at the first convenience. Ironically, half a continent away, the Raden of Zeeland were also writing, even as Evertsen sat in his great cabin composing his report. The Raden's missive, however, was of considerable import, for though they were not yet aware of his arrival at Cadiz, or of the condition of his fleet, they had resolved to order Cornelis Evertsen home.[21]

The Vlissingen privateers and the squadrons of Amsterdam and Zeeland were a formidable force whose presence in Cadiz was certain to arouse concern among English and French mariners obliged to pass in the vicinity of the Bay of Cadiz. The Dutch were equally anxious to put to sea to justify enemy anxieties, lest the slightest delay permit the enemy convoy from slipping by undetected. Thus, at daylight on December 16, *Swaenenburgh* (presumably with *Noordhollandt*) and the eleven capers set sail, but "held on and off the wind in front of the Bay" awaiting Captains de Witte, Van Zijl, and Richewijn who were rushing to complete repairs on the fireship. Two days later all but the fireship, which was still being repaired, had come out. Evertsen was undoubtedly perturbed, for a fireship was a necessity in any large squadron encounters in seventeenth century warfare, and he quickly dispatched De Witte in *Schaeckerloo* back to fetch her. Soon afterwards, as the flotilla drifted listlessly about the mouth of the bay, patiently awaiting the tardy ship, a sail was sighted and five capers immediately set off in hot pursuit.[22]

Slowly, the remainder of the fleet drifted westward under light sails, sighting Cape Maria on Friday, December 19, and coming abeam of Villa Nova the next day. On the morning of December 21, *Swaenenburgh* sighted three sails on the horizon, but coming up on them discovered them to be Van Zijl, De Witte, and the long-awaited fireship. Finally, the fleet was complete, but, by now was spread for miles over the ocean. Soon another sail was sighted, but could not be overtaken. Then followed a string of sightings and pursuits. The predatory acumen of the Dutch warships and privateers was of no avail, as each potential victim proved to be one of their own ships. Time and again fruitless pursuits were taken up only to end in disgust as the prey proved to be a Dutch warship or privateer. Then, on the evening of December 22, *Swaenenburgh* and several capers chased and overtook a Frenchman laden with a cargo of figs, bound from Faro, Portugal, to Nantes, France. The victim was taken by a privateer under the command of Captain Mels Cornelissen after a brief exchange in which the merchantman's master, one Olloene, was shot and killed.[23]

At daybreak on December 26, the fleet was cruising south of Cape St. Vincent, having experienced several successive days of missed opportunities and sour fortunes. The French prize had somehow become separated from the fleet and disappeared entirely. Though several sails had been sighted and pursued, she was not to be found again. Almost without warning, yet another sail was sighted on the horizon, pressing out of the west and upwind of the fleet. Quickly, all of the Dutch ships "let our English flags fly, whereby he came within musket shot where he saw what ship we were, intending to continue on." Two capers, under the commands of captains Warwijck and Van Goethem, which were closest to the oncoming vessel, closed as quickly as possible. The prey, however, which proved to be a Turk called *Oraenjen Boom* (*Or-*

ange Tree), carried twelve guns and a crew of 100 and was not about to be subdued without a fight. For half an hour the two capers pounded her into submission in an unequal battle. Finally, upon boarding, it was discovered that her crew included a dozen Christian slaves, and several "renegades," or Moslem converts from Christianity. In fact, the captain of *Oraenjen Boom* was himself a renegade Scotsman. Within a short time, the crew of the prize was distributed around the fleet, undoubtedly to prevent the possibility of a prisoner uprising on any single ship.[24]

Despite the capture of the Turk, the Dutch raiders were growing daily more frustrated at the prospect of success. On December 29, their numbers diminished as captains Cornelis Marijnisse and Jan Lourissen broke away from the flotilla and pointed their bows toward Berbice and, they hoped, better hunting. With them, Evertsen, as he had promised the Raden, sent several pipes of oil and wine for Commander Versterre in Suriname.[25]

By January 2, 1674, 19 days out and but a single prize to show for all their efforts, the capers were resigned to failure and turned toward Cadiz, "as they no longer wished to cruise."[26] And with them went the Dutch warships, more the worse for wear.

There was much for the Dutch to attend to upon their return to the Spanish port. On January 6, the Moslem prisoners were sold as slaves, and *Oraenjen Boom* was sold to the highest bidder. By mid-month, fifteen capers and men-of-war, including *Schaeckerloo*, had been beached behind the fort protecting the entry into the bay to begin much needed cleaning and repairs on their hulls. Work progressed swiftly and within a few days the privateers, which had been at sea for three months, and the warship, which had been out for more than a year, were back in service. *Swaenenburgh* was not attended to until *Schaeckerloo* was afloat. Evertsen had undoubtedly staggered repairs on his flotilla to provide the least possible vulnerability at any given time. Efforts to locate the source of *Swaenenburgh's* severe leaking, however, failed miserably, and it was resolved to remove her cannons to the shore and fully careen her "as it was so unsuited to operate on the high seas."[27]

On January 24, Benckes again put to sea with his squadron intent on conducting an independent cruise without the capers in company, despite Evertsen's advice to the contrary. *Schaeckerloo* and *Sint Joris* did not accompany the Hollanders, but sailed soon afterwards with eleven of the Vlissingen privateers.[28]

In the meantime, Evertsen's crew began working day and night to repair the leak in *Swaenenburgh's* hull. On February 7, Captain Abraham Ferdinand van Zijl came in with a French ketch that had been

The Dutch squadron before Cadiz, February 13, 1674. This romanticized depiction of the engagement between *Schaeckerloo* and *Tiger* suggests the contest was waged amidst Spanish galleys and the Dutch squadron, quite close to shore. The fighting ships are at center, as local citizens and soldiers watch from the shores. *Courtesy Royal Netherlands Embassy.*

bound from Tangier to Lisbon with a cargo of almonds, goatskins, and copperware. The crew of *Swaenenburgh,* engaged in the cold, wet work of ship repair, undoubtedly groaned in envy, for as long as they were in port, there was no chance to earn prize money.[29] Evertsen, however, provided the Zeelanders with every opportunity possible. Not long after *Schaeckerloo*'s return to port (empty-handed), he ordered her out again to rejoin the caper fleet.[30] Though this patrol proved as fruitless as those that had preceeded it, the consequences of De Witte's return would prove disasterous.

Schaeckerloo cruised for several days in the Bay of Cadiz, and though she had set off short of water, she had been unable to rejoin Evertsen in Cadiz Harbor owing to heavy weather. At about midday on February 12, the big pinnace was finally able to beat into the bay. An hour and a half later, the 453-ton English frigate *Tiger*, Captain Thomas Harman commanding, fresh from patrol off Tangier, followed suit.[31]

Harman, who had served as a lieutenant aboard the frigate *Adventure* in 1671, had been appointed by the king the following year to the command of *Tiger.*[32] The captain was filled with bravado as he entered the harbor, for *Swaenenburgh,* was lying on her side, Benckes's squadron was somewhere at sea, and the caper fleet was nowhere in sight. Soon after his arrival, he declared for all to hear that "he had driven the *Schaeckerloo* in before him," and that De Witte had left his station "fearing to meet the English Frigat." The charge caused an instant scandal, "whereby," Evertsen recorded, "terribly villainous words were exchanged by the English and the Spanish as well as our own country." Although De Witte declared he had seen no ships, the accusations, Evertsen felt, clearly demeaned his honor.[33] The fire-eating commander, perhaps recalling De Witte's "convenient" absence at São Tiago a year earlier, advised him "that there was no better redress for his Honor then to challenge the Englishman." Ignoring the fact that his own ship was heavily outgunned and outmanned, De Witte agreed. Harman instantly accepted the tossed gauntlet of combat. *Schaeckerloo*, it was decided, would put to sea the following morning to prove that her captain "was neither fearful nor weak before the English."[34]

The contending forces were far from evenly matched. After a year-long expedition, *Schaeckerloo* was well below her normal complement of 156 men as a result of attrition in battles fought and from her share of the men left behind as a garrison at New Orange. The *London Gazette*, soon after the engagement, placed her strength at the time she entered Cadiz Bay at 140 men, which was, if not accurate, at least in

The Naval Engagement between H.M.S. *Tiger* and *Schaeckerloo* February 13, 1674. A sequential illustration of the battle, beginning at right, as viewed from Spanish fortifications at Rota. *Courtesy National Maritime Museum, Greenwich.*

all probability, close to the correct complement. Though English sources claimed that the pinnace was armed with 36 guns, her actual count was undoubtedly closer to 28 or 30, all of various light calibers, the same number with which she had started out on the expedition a year earlier. According to Evertsen, the fourth-rate frigate, *Tiger*, on the other hand, mounted 44 cannon and 22 swivel guns, an estimate that coincides with Pepys' armament rating for the ship's wartime at-home service.[35] Evertsen later claimed that before the engagement Harman had declared that he had only 160 crewmen, but The *London Gazette* claimed *Tiger*'s full strength to be 184 men.[36]

Cornelis Evertsen, having prodded his captain to accept combat for the preservation of his honor and, by implication, that of Zeeland, sought to at least improve the odds for De Witte's outgunned and out-manned ship. On the eve of battle, he transferred 170 of his own complement of marines, seamen, and landsmen to double-crew *Schaeckerloo*. The move practically stripped *Swaenenburgh* of her own manpower, but clearly suggested that De Witte's battle tactic had al-ready been determined. Outgunned, the smaller Dutch ship stood little chance of emerging victorious in broadside-to-broadside combat. By double-manning the pinnace's complement, she might succeed in clos-ing quickly and taking *Tiger* by boarding.[37]

The Dutch preparations did not go unnoticed, and *Tiger* "put herself also in the best disposition she could for the encounter." Observing that *Schaeckerloo* was double-manning, Harman may have attempted a similar tactic, for as Evertsen noted in *Swaenenburgh*'s log after the engagement, the English captain bragged of having 300 to 315 men aboard.[39]

On the morning of February 13, *Schaeckerloo* weighed anchor and sailed out of the harbor, followed soon afterwards by *Tiger*. Coming up off Rota, on the northern side of the Bay of Cadiz, the Dutch warship patiently awaited her antagonist. The battle would be fought in full view of the inhabitants, about a league from the bay. As *Tiger* finally came up, approaching to within a half-pistol shot of the Dutchman, the sea suddenly shuddered with the roar of broadsides. There were no formalities, only blood, fire, smoke, and the screams of the injured and dying.[39]

Schaeckerloo gave "good fight" on that fateful morning, but Har-man's fire was "so well directed, that it disabled the adversaries Top-mast Yard, killed and wounded eighty Men, without any considerable damage to himself." The superior number of British guns, fired at close range, and the density of men crowded upon the pinnace's decks pro-vided the setting for a veritable slaughter. Twice De Witte closed to board his nemesis, and each time was repulsed in bloody fighting and a terrible cost in human life. And still the cannons roared. *Tiger* was not without her own casualties, however. Below, a lower deck gun, in the heat of fight, suddenly split open while firing, killing four of the gun crew and wounding others. But it was the pinnace that clearly suffered the most, her casualties rapidly mounting.[40]

It was now Harman's turn to attempt a boarding of the shattered Dutchman. Adeptly, he maneuvered *Tiger* across the disabled enemy bow. Boarding parties were ordered out, and hand-to-hand fighting ensued. The brave Harman did not refrain from the fray and was struck by a musket shot. The ball entered his skull under the left eye and exited between his ear and jawbone, but did not kill him. De Witte was also wounded as the contest rapidly turned against him. Yet for half an hour the savage fight continued, though for the Dutchman bent on redeeming his sullied honor, there was no longer a chance for victory. With over 80 percent of his crew casualties, most of his officers dead or wounded and fewer than 50 healthy men left, Passchier de Witte surrendered his ship.[41]

The slaughter had lasted for a little more than two hours, and the bloody victory clearly belonged to Captain Thomas Harman. De Witte's honor had indeed been preserved, but at a terrible price. *Schaeckerloo* "was so shot through that it was unsuitable to ever be used again." And by English accounts, the Dutch had suffered 140 men killed and 86 wounded, while *Tiger* had lost nine dead and 15 wounded.[42]

About midday, *Tiger* sailed triumphantly into Cadiz Harbor in company with her battered prize, the English flag flying over that of the Dutch "to the great admiration of all that saw it."[43] Word of the English victory raced about Cadiz, and was soon carried to England where Thomas Harman was lionized in song and print. Within a short time a popular ditty describing the engagement, called "News from the Coast of Spain" and sung to the tune of "Digby's Farewell," was circulating in town and tavern. For a war-weary nation that had suffered a seemingly endless string of naval defeats, the victory provided a needed boost. In a war that had provided England with precious few naval heroes, Thomas Harman became an instant celebrity.

> Then cheer up brave seamen and Englishmen bold
> You here, by this story, which I have told,
> No sea-men nor souldiers can with us compare;
> Although they have odds yet to fight them we dare.
> Throughout the whole world a terrour shall prove

If we can continue in union and love:
And thus you may see by these lines I have writ,
How stout Captain Harman did conquer De Wit.[44]

Sadly, though honor had been retained, the battle proved irrevelant, for many miles away, in the halls of Westminster, a treaty of peace between England and the United Provinces had already been ratified.

21

TO HOLD THEM OR LEAVE THEM

By the beginning of 1674, the war on the high seas against England and France had gone well for the United Provinces. Though inferior in size, guns, and manpower, her naval forces had been brilliantly led by the likes of De Ruyter and Tromp, and had fought the combined might of her powerful rivals to a standstill in four major bloody engagements. Her capers, taking over 2,800 prizes,[1] had harassed the allied merchant marine to the point of collapse. And raiders such as Evertsen and Benckes had brought the allies' far-flung colonial dominions to the brink of chaos. The conflict ashore, on the mainland of Europe, however, had become a nightmare of retreat and defeat. The forces of Louis XIV had marched inexorably forward across four of the seven Dutch provinces, a powerful war machine whose nearly unchecked successes had startled and frightened all of Europe, including many leaders of allied England. Many members of Parliament and the king's personal advisors had begun to sense, for the first time, more danger from the waxing power of France than from the commercial rivalry of The Netherlands. Increasingly outspoken, Parliament was becoming vociferous on the danger of resurgent Catholicism in England, unrestricted power of the monarchy, and the acute royal need for money. Some feared the relationship between Charles II and the Catholic King Louis to be the foundation stone for the restoration of popery in England. Others suspected another secret cabal between the two monarchs such as the Treaty of Dover, which had led England into the war with The Netherlands in the first place. Slowly at first, but with increasing momentum, Parliament was withdrawing its support of the crown in the conflict with the Dutch. It was not alone.

As the armies of France had pressed relentlessly forward, entering the ancient city of Utrecht (a scant 22 miles from Amsterdam) in June 1673, the nonaligned powers of Europe, fearful of Louis XIV's flowering imperialism, began to consolidate against him. The Emperor of Germany and the Elector of Brandenburg allied themselves with the Dutch. Secret negotiations between the United Provinces and their ancient enemy, Spain, which had flickered on and off throughout the conflict, were rekindled. Threatened by the power of France, Spain finally agreed to join the war against Louis, but only on the condition that The Netherlands make peace with England and agree to the restoration of all recent conquests.[2]

For Evertsen and Benckes, whose raid on America had inadvertently brought about the Fatherland's largest single territorial acquisition of the war, such terms would be hard to accept. Zeeland and Holland would scurry to divest themselves of the burden of colonial management well before such a peace might be finalized, and emerge with fewer expenditures than would otherwise be the case. But for the thousands of Dutch citizens of New Netherland who had provided their allegiance, money, and sweat to the States General and the Prince of Orange upon request, such terms could only be construed as betrayal.

On January 3, 1674, Secretary de Huijbert presented to the Raden of Zeeland a secret missive sent by States General Secretary Fagel five days earlier. It concerned the question of whether to maintain Evertsen's small squadron on the coast of Spain, in the Strait of Gibraltar, or in more distant regions. From all indications the Spanish government was anxious to lease the fleet, and the Staten, with French forces poised for another blow against The Netherlands, was understandably eager to support any measures likely to secure a Spanish alliance. Only days before, Fagel had received a secret communique from the Minister of Spain, don Bernardo de Salinas, requesting that the Dutch remain at Cadiz, for as his nation inched closer to outright participation in the war, the port took on an enormous strategic importance.[3] It was, however, woefully ill-equipped to manage its own defense.

Through the intelligence-gathering efforts of Consul Gaspar van Collen, the Raden of Zeeland was well aware of Spain's vulnerability in these regions and of its hurried efforts to improve the naval defense of Cadiz. On December 14, the consul informed them that the Spanish king had ordered the construction of a fleet of twenty ships at the port with construction scheduled to begin after the Christmas holy days. The carpenters and artificers had even been paid in advance and had guaranteed a wildly optimistic completion date of the end of March. "The King," he also advised, "has resolved to construct a castle at the mouth of the Bay on the porcose, the better to close off the Bay."[4] The presence of the Dutch warships, it was implied though not stated, would provide a welcome deterrence to enemy attack during this period.

De Huijbert presented Fagel's missive to "those whom it concerned" in the Raden of Zeeland. It was undoubtedly clear that should the United Provinces enter into an alliance with Spain and if the terms concerning the divestiture of recent conquests were honored, the loss of New Netherland would likely follow. De Huijbert and the Raden, however, perceived the situation as both a problem and an opportunity— but in either case one that had to be acted upon quickly. The Zeeland ships at Cadiz might be used as leverage or bargaining chips in an agreement to secure relief from what seemed otherwise certain to be a costly, if temporary, burden. A profit might even be realized. Zeeland, it was secretly decided, would refuse to maintain her ships at Cadiz unless she was relieved of her role in the administration and expenses incurred by the conquest of New Netherland and its subsequent support, and was to be recompensed for her efforts already undertaken. Without Dutch ships of force at Cadiz, especially during the delicate period of securing Spain as an ally, the States General might well lose one of its own bargaining points with the Spanish, something Zeeland was certain the Staten wished to avoid.

As an opening gambit, De Huijbert offered a reply to the Grand Pensionary that there would be considerable difficulty in leaving the small squadron at Cadiz, particularly for a distressed province such as Zeeland, "which in these financial troubles gambles more than many others." The province could ill afford to leave its prizes in the Spanish harbor, or sustain a loss that might result from transporting them and the captured booty home through enemy-infested waters. Evertsen's warships, he implied, were necessary for such work. And the prizes were important to Zeeland's treasury.[5] De Huijbert was, of course, jousting in the dark, for he was as yet uninformed about the Admiralty of Amsterdam's official views concerning the New Netherland issue, of the decision by the States General that Amsterdam would govern New Netherland, or of the Staten's intentions for the future deployment of the Benckes squadron.

The Raden of Zeeland wisely moved to prepare Evertsen for any eventuality. Having learned that the commander had already exceeded their orders of the previous October, they resolved to dispatch a new set of instructions adapted to the rapidly evolving situation. On January 3, sealed orders were sent to Van Collen via an Ostend convoy bound for Cadiz. The consul was instructed to deliver them "in the fastest and the most secret manner" to Evertsen. The orders specifically directed the commander to remain at Cadiz until further word, but to hold himself in readiness to sail. Upon the first notice from the Raden, he was to be permitted to go to sea with his ships and prizes, "prepared in such a way to be able to return to the Fatherland." He was specifically instructed to take good care of the captured prizes and booty so that "these in no way will be diminished or spoiled."[6]

By mid-January The Hague was rife with whispered tales of impending peace negotiations and the alliance with Spain as the Prince of Orange and the States General hammered out a proposal for an end to the war with England. Though the proposals were bound to influence the fate of New Netherland, the government continued to superficially address the problems of the colony's administration as if the United Provinces intended to maintain control forever. The show of concern was undoubtedly designed to counter the influences of rampant speculation, but primarily stemmed from the prevalent opinion that there was little or no prospect for peace. By January 14, after several rebuffs, the government of The Netherlands was able to dispatch a secret set of peace terms to the king of England, asking for a revival of the 1667 Treaty of Breda. The singularly most important issue of the proposal was The Netherlands' willingness to give up its "ancient domain" in America, the New Netherland colony. The States General and the Prince of Orange then turned their attention back to the problem of managing the colony they were offering to England as if nothing had happened.[7]

On January 15, the letter from Cornelis Evertsen, written soon after his arrival at Cadiz on December 13, reached Middleburg, apparently at the same time as did word of the proposed terms of the peace. The two missives struck the Zeeland government with the impact of twin cannon shots. The following day, the continued deliberations of the Raden on the future of New Netherland and the fleet at Cadiz were brought to a perfunctory, if temporary, halt as that august body digested the news. Here, at long last, was word from Zeeland's squadron commander in the field—no rumors, no second-hand, six-month-old intelligence, but direct confirmation of and extensive data on the campaign in America, prizes and booty taken, and losses inflicted upon the enemy. Here were details of the capture and current disposition of New Netherland. But more importantly, here was the first solid indication that the conquest might have to be sacrificed to secure a separate peace with England. What had been mere speculation a few days before had become hard reality.[8]

Though Evertsen could certainly not be faulted for the timing of his letter's arrival, its effect, in conjunction with the news from The Hague, was disturbing. It was also undoubtedly central to the course of action the Raden immediately chose to take, a course communicated to the States General in a set of resolutions dispatched on January 16.[9] The commander's raid on America, though inflicting enormous damage and raising great havoc among the enemies' colonies, had failed to produce the large monetary profit for Zeeland for which the Raden had hoped. Indeed, quite to the contrary, it had, by the conquest and garrisoning of New Netherland, created a major unexpected military and economic responsibility certain to prove logistically difficult to maintain and expensive for the province to absorb.

As peace talks with England sputtered to life, with the now substantial possibility that the colony might be traded off to obtain Spain's entry into the war against France, the Raden wasted little time in deciding its own course. Despite the commitments made by its commander, Cornelis Evertsen, and the fervent pleas for aid from the citizens of New Netherland, Zeeland would divest itself of responsibility to the colony in the fastest and most inexpensive way. The obvious first step, of course, would be to investigate the possibility of turning the colony over, at cost, to Zeeland's partner in conquest, the Admiralty of Amsterdam—if Amsterdam, with a French army at its threshold, would have it!

After closed deliberation, the Raden resolved to immediately send a delegation of two of the Deputized Raden, Lords van der Beke and Muenicx, with a set of secret resolutions to The Hague to meet with the Prince of Orange and the States General. There they were to diplomatically "sound out the intentions of the Board of the Admiralty of Amsterdam as to their inclinations with regard to the joint conquests of New Netherland, whether to hold them or leave them." The delegation was also to seek assurances that control of Zeeland's share of goods and property in the colony "may not be torn free from our control," whatever decision was reached. The Raden hoped to convince the prince and the Staten to bring the issue to speedy resolution by forcing Amsterdam to accept responsibility for the colony, while at the same time ensuring that Zeeland's share of the conquest would not be usurped. Once a decision had been reached, it was felt, the Raden would be free to order Evertsen home from Cadiz, without recriminations, unless some marked advantage for him to remain appeared.[10]

If, indeed, Amsterdam expressed a willingness to accept the burden, the delegates from Middleburg were instructed to formally let them know that Zeeland would not be unwilling to transfer her share of the conquests, including debts and profits, the salary and wages of the garrison, and use and ownership of *Suriname* and *Zeehond,* "for some advantage," of course. In point of fact, Zeeland was by now so eager to be rid of the burden handed her by Evertsen that the delegates were instructed, if the Admiralty of Amsterdam displayed no interest, to negotiate with the City of Amsterdam or even some wealthy merchants from that place to take over Zeeland's share of the responsibility. The Raden was, it seemed, practically willing to deal with anyone provided recompense be offered, "be it only something material such as Cannon and Shell." The delegates were directed to promote the virtues of the newly acquired colony and make its potential value seem attractive. They were instructed to point out the prospect of profitable commerce between New Netherland and Suriname.[11] If, however, the decision was made by the Prince of Orange and the States General to abandon the colony,

> it may then be resolved immediately to send a vessel to New Netherland with orders to those there in Command, to break off there and load all the cannon, ammunition of war and what further may be there into the ships and then return to the Fatherland, and even should there be no willingness to do so, that it should be required as a case of necessity.[12]

The Raden were well aware that there were not one, but two, Dutch squadrons at Cadiz. Both squadrons, they felt, should be returned to the Fatherland as quickly as possible. At the very least, they suggested that, in accordance with De Huijbert's strategy, Evertsen's tiny force must be ordered home by the first post. In the event the Prince of Orange and the States General, "for good and pregnant reason," judged it necessary to keep the squadrons in Spain to harass the enemy, the delegates were to try to dissuade them. The expense of the ships, they were to point out, had already far exceeded Zeeland's estimations. Those left in New Netherland would not return home for some time, and it would therefore be objectionable and costly to hold Evertsen at Cadiz any longer. There prizes there would "suffer neglect and always drop considerably in value" if allowed to remain—a loss the penurious Zeelanders felt they could ill afford.[13]

But what if the Prince and the Staten insisted that the Zeeland ships remain in Spain? In such an event, the delegates were directed to counter by bending every effort to divest their province of all fiscal responsibilities relative to New Netherland by aggressively seeking a transfer of its own share of authority over the colony to the administrative purview of Amsterdam. Simultaneously, Zeeland would demand a distribution of all booty taken or yet to be realized as a profit. If the national government agreed to pursue such a course, the delegates were to urge Amsterdam to assume the cost of equipping, feeding, and paying the wages of Evertsen's fleet from the day of departure to its return to the Fatherland, but only if there was clear advantage in it all for Zeeland.

Refitting and repairing Evertsen's ships at Cadiz were certain to be expensive. The Admiralty of Amsterdam would be permitted to take them into service provided it assumed their expenses from the day of their arrival at that port onward. There was a proviso, however, that Amsterdam must "also take over the captured prizes at a reasonable valuation, by which this Province [Zeeland] can close its accounts to advantage." In return, the Admiralty of Amsterdam would also be asked to deliver to the Admiralty of Zeeland a well-equipped and fully manned ship of 50 guns and a frigate of 26 to 28 guns to replace *Swaenenburgh* and *Schaeckerloo*. To force the prince's and the Staten's approval, the Raden determined "that the presence of Captain Cornelis Evertsen in Cadiz shall not be given consent unless this shall occur in some way or another to the advantage and relief of this province."[14]

If for reasons of state New Netherland was to be held until the end of the war with France, despite the Raden's efforts to pull out, the Zeeland delegates were to press for more concessions. They were to demand that all expenses incurred for wages, board, equipment, and rental of ships from the conquest onward were to be at the cost of the state. The charges for the garrison left behind in the colony would thus fall upon the States General and not upon Zeeland.[15]

Satisfied for the moment with its aggressive initiative to divert and liquidate its unsought conquest, the Raden then turned their attentions back to Kees the Devil. In a letter dispatched on January 18, the officials rebuked their young commander for his failure to provide a complete roster of all individuals dead, left behind, or taken into service during the voyage. He was authorized to pay his crews one month's salary from the revenues from "food money or from salt and dried fish sold." The Raden were, as yet, unaware of the fragile negotiations underway in The Hague concerning the issue of the government's prizes, but were cautious enough to warn Evertsen against disposing of the main prizes, "which are specifically to remain untouched and unsold."[16]

On January 19, Lord de Mauregnault, a Zeelander and one of the Staten's deputies for foreign affairs, reported the submission by the

Admiralty of Amsterdam of an agenda of points to be considered by the States General concerning New Netherland. Amsterdam, stalling for time before assuming the burden of administration of a colony it did not wish to administer, requested clarification of a number of issues concerning property. Interestingly, it also suggested seeking neutrality for the colony so that it might maintain commerce with the surrounding colonies, even though they were English and a state of war existed in Europe.[17] The Admiralty of Amsterdam, like the Raden of Zeeland, with which it had yet to consult on the issue, had become inordinately nervous about the ultimate status of New Netherland. Yet, unlike Zeeland, and concerned about being left holding the bag, Amsterdam reserved her council against the most favorable moment.

When the Raden discovered that Holland had, in fact, been directed by the States General to dispatch aid to New Netherland, the haughty Zeelanders took the news as nothing less than a direct insult. They were outraged that they had not been informed of the move and of not having "our advice and approval heard," for which they had provided every opportunity. They were equally distressed that the States General had placed an Amsterdammer in command of the colony without consulting Zeeland, whose own commanders were already in charge there. But most of all, they feared that the new commander would pay little attention to Zeeland's holdings, goods, and property still in the colony. The doubtful status of New Netherland, they informed the Staten on January 23, had been completely clarified by Evertsen's letters. They complained bitterly to De Mauregnault, "seeing that the State[s General] of the Country repeatedly proposes restitution of the Conquest back to the English, it isn't so strange that we are in doubt as to holding of the same."[18]

Nevertheless, the Raden resolved to press on with the question of whether to abandon New Netherland and haul everything away or to hold on and try to obtain concessions. "We suggest," they wrote,

> that, although restitution of this considerable Conquest was so liberally proposed, there are nonetheless still means and proposals conceivable to hold on to it, even with the willingness of the English, for some equivalent of money, which we could judge would match quite well with Amsterdam's capacity.[19]

The Raden decided to abstain from involvement, though its ships were being maintained in New Netherland at Zeeland's expense. They were deeply concerned, however, that their expenditures would continue to climb, and that control over their property and booty in the colony would not be recognized by the Admiralty of Amsterdam, which would be in overall command there. They thus instructed De

Mauregnault to discuss the matter with the Lord Deputies of Amsterdam "to hold everything together and undivided until the whole affair between us and them be adjusted." Having learned that two companies of soldiers were to be sent to garrison the colony, soon to be an Amsterdam stronghold, the Raden also suggested, almost facetiously, that two more might be sent to the relief of Zeeland's colony of Suriname while they were at it.[20]

The following day, January 24, Lords van der Beke and Muenicx requested a meeting with the Prince of Orange to seek his support in the matter, but were put off until the following afternoon. Prince Willem, taken up with "multifarious occupations," undoubtedly regarding the peace initiative, appeared sympathetic to Zeeland's concerns and promised "to be helpful to us in case of need." Reinforced by the prince's support, the Zeelanders met with the deputation from the Admiralty of Amsterdam that evening. The delegation from the Raden was not long in getting to the point. They were eager for the repatriation of Evertsen's ships and prizes in Cadiz harbor. The Hollanders were absolutely opposed and told the men from Middleburg exactly why. For the first time, the Zeelanders learned that two weeks earlier the Admiralty of Amsterdam had written to all places in the vicinity of the Strait of Gibraltar—indeed, wherever their merchantmen might be—that all such vessels should proceed to the port of Livorne to be picked up by Benckes' squadron and escorted to Cadiz. The flotilla was then to remain at Cadiz until it was transferred into Spanish service for eventual deployment about Jamaica or elsewhere. In fact, the Zeelanders were shocked to learn that a contract for Benckes' ships had already been drafted and handed to the Spanish Minister to The Hague, don Bernardo de Salines.[21]

When the Zeelanders pressed the Hollanders on the issue of New Netherland and learned that two ships with two companies of soldiers and supplies, two private ships, and a fluit were not only designated to sail for the colony, but were preparing to depart, they were undoubtedly stunned. The Hollanders shrugged off the news with the comment that it was a move that "one would be content to start with, until one sees how the peace will fall out, of which, however, people believe there is none or little prospect." The Zeelanders persisted. How much was New Netherland worth to Holland, they asked? The Hollanders demurred, saying that they were not empowered to make such decisions, but as the peacetime produce of the colony had been worth only 40,000 guilders, "they wouldn't want to take it for free."[22] The meeting, which seemed to be going nowhere for the Zeelanders, was at an end.

Later, the delegates from Zeeland and Holland, conferred with States General deputies Lords de Mauregnault and van Beuningen on the matter of Evertsen's tiny squadron. The Hollanders insisted that it should remain with Benckes, but the Zeelanders, anxious for the prizes at Cadiz to be brought home, were opposed. Again the conference ended in deadlock, with both sides resolved to appeal to the Prince of Orange.[23] Neither side in the dispute, however, was aware that larger affairs of state, namely the latest peace initiative, was about to overtake and finally inundate their disagreements.

Spain continued to actively pressure the United Provinces to seek peace with England as the price for her entry in the war against France. She had, more often than not, suffered at the hands of the English navy in previous conflicts and had no desire to wage a war on two national fronts at once. The States General, however, which had entrusted the Marquis de Fresno, the Spanish ambassador to England, with power of attorney in all matters concerning the peace initiative, were hesitant and mistrusting of the Stuart king. Many feared that he had, or was about to conclude, yet another secret treaty with France, a treaty that would guarantee another war. Despite such misgivings, progress was made. On December 12, 1673, two days after Evertsen's arrival at Cadiz, it was learned at Whitehall that the "Spanish ambassador has at last brought some propositions which his Mistress will undertake shall [it] be consented to by the States [General] from whom as yet we hear nothing, but a trumpeter is daily expected with a reply." For nearly a month, nothing more was heard. Then, on the evening of January 7, 1674, a packet boat arrived at Harwich bearing a Dutch trumpeter who delivered two letters into the hands of the town mayor. The letters were for the Spanish ambassador.[24]

Though the trumpeter was detained, the letters were immediately dispatched to Secretary Arlington in London, who personally delivered them to the ambassador. One communique was from the States General and was addressed to King Charles II. Ironically, it contained points to be discussed in the development of a treaty of peace, points that had some time earlier been distributed in print (though branded a forgery by some) to certain pro-Dutch and anti-war members in the House of Commons.[25]

The issue of pro- and anti-Dutch sentiments was reaching new heights in Parliament, which had, since November, moved ever farther from support of the war. Plans to recapture New York, which in October proved an issue of burning importance, had been all but forgotten as Parliament's ardor cooled. Clamors for peace were heard far and wide across the land, from the West Country mariners whose fisheries had been destroyed by Dutch raiders to the streets of London where merchants were forced to close their shops for lack of goods to sell. On

Raid on America

January 15, Secretary Arlington, condemned by some as pro-Dutch, was impeached by Sir Gilbert Gerard in an act seconded by Sir Charles Wheeler. Arlington was specifically accused of corresponding with the King's enemies and of disclosing his secrets to foreign ministers and consequently of high treason. Yet the move for peace and its support in Parliament had taken hold. One official wrote that

> People here are possessed with an opinion that the Dutch are content to make the peace upon any reasonable terms so much have the Dutch arrived by their artifices upon the generality of the people and some no inconsiderable number.[26]

On January 24, the Spanish ambassador presented the king with the letter from the States General, drafted January 14, agreeing to a six-point peace proposal. As Charles reviewed the proposal, point by point, he was well aware that his options to continue a war that few in his government wished to support were dwindling. The Royal Navy had suffered defeat after defeat, and its seamen lacked the willingness to again do battle. Parliament, stirred by the secret intrigues of the king's nephew and England's national enemy, Willem, Prince of Orange, and by a growing disgust for the conflict that seemed increasingly pointless, had been prorogued by the king in late 1673. Still the cabals continued. The crown's coffers were empty, yet could not be refilled without Parliament. Despite the great opposition to the war, which mounted with every new day, Charles knew he would have to summon the government back into session, if for nothing else than to answer the royal need for funds. Parliament, however, titillated by the intrigues for a separate peace with the United Provinces, fearful of the growing power of France, and bone weary of the royal debt, had already ceased to support the war. To recall Parliament was to end the war.

Carefully, the king examined the document before him. The latest Dutch proposal was to the point and quite amenable to England's pre-war demands. England would receive two million guilders in war reparations from the States General, to be paid over three years. England would receive recognition of its beloved "dominium mares" on British seas from Lands End to Staten Land in Norway, with the British flag on ships and fleets alike receiving proper recognition by vessels of the United Provinces. The latter point was conditional in that such recognition would not imply or lead to the hindering of a free fishery. The trade and shipping treaty of 1668 would be reconfirmed. Both nations would agree not to support each other's enemies.[27] But key to the proposal was the following article:

> That whatsoever countries, islands, towns, ports, castles, or forts have or shall be taken on both sides, since the time the late unhappy war broke

out, either in Europe or elsewhere, shall be restored to the former lord or proprietor, in the same condition they shall be in when the peace itself shall be proclaimed.[28]

With conditions so positive for England and opposition to the continuance of the war growing stronger in Parliament and the countryside, Charles had little choice but to accept. Failure to do so could only lead to catastrophe. He would not, like his ill-fated father before him, challenge Parliament, and he could no longer prosecute the conflict without it.

The king girded himself for the opening session of Parliament on January 24 when he was to address both houses. Well aware of the seething distrust many members held for his intentions toward France, he was obliged to offer his personal assurances, albeit nervously (for it was a lie), that there was no secret treaty with Louis XIV and that there never had been one. The presentation of the letter from the States General containing the peace proposal, however, was the meat of his speech, and Parliament had, after the years of war, finally developed a healthy appetite for such rare food. After several days of active debate, both houses voted to accept the proposals offered by the Dutch. It now seemed that there would be peace at last with the United Provinces.[29]

The approval by Parliament met with instant popular support among the citizenry of England. "These resolutions," wrote Francis Lord Aungier, "have given very great and general satisfaction to his Majesty's subjects here."[30] Across the North Sea, the news met with equal acceptance. King Charles's trumpeter arrived in The Hague on February 1, bearing letters to the Prince of Orange informing him that the king had "absolutely" deferred to Parliament on the matter of peace. The Dutch, who had believed chances for an agreement were minimal at best, were stunned. Some, such as Willem Adriaen van Nassau, bastard cousin and confidant to the Prince of Orange, as well as his substitute as First Nobel of Zeeland, noted, however, that "it was in no way doubted whether that work could be brought to a desired conclusion in a few short days, be it not even already done, of which issue people have been prepared to learn for days now."[31]

The Dutch response to Charles's letter was immediate. On February 5, a trumpeter from Holland arrived in London with a reply confirming the willingness to accept a peace on the terms provided. On the same day, both houses of Parliament presented an address to the king at the Banqueting House offering "their humble advice that he would be pleased to proceed in a treaty with the States General upon their proposals in order to a speedy peace." The reluctant king thanked the two houses for their advice, vowing that he would indeed "endeavour a peace."[32] A commission was immediately appointed to handle the details.

"People in general," wrote one Whitehall official the next day, "are in great expectation of peace, and nothing but peace will be able to satisfy them." The commissioners did not prolong their work, and on February 9, the final document was completed and signed at Westminster. On the following day the Lord Keeper was authorized to place the Great Seal to the ratification of the treaty, and Sir Gabriel Sylvius, envoy to the Prince of Orange, was dispatched to The Hague with the ratification. On February 11 Parliament was officially notified of the conclusion of the peace. Two days later, both houses expressed their heartfelt thanks to the king, for, as the Lord Lieutenant of the Tower of London noted, "the peace is mightily adored here."[33]

On February 27, James, Earl of Suffolk, deputy to Henry, Earl of Norwich, Earl Marshal of England, was warranted to issue orders to the king's heralds and "pursuivants at arms" to appear the following morning, at 10:00 A.M., at the gate of Whitehall, where the sergeant-at-arms and trumpeters would be "ordered to attend and to publish the peace with the States General there and in all places in London where it has been unusually proclaimed.[34] For England, the war was at last over.

At The Hague the States of Holland and Friesland were the first to read the Treaty of Peace and to officially offer a resolution that it be ratified. Accordingly, on March 4, they gave their consent to the ratification by their deputies in the Assembly of the States General. Little notice was taken that day of the messages just arrived from the commander and burgomasters of the colony of New Netherland, an ocean away, begging for reinforcements, settlers, and assistance. Few paid attention to their pathetic but sincere declarations of allegiance. Peace with England was at hand. What mattered the future of a few thousand settlers in a far away frontier that could barely pay its way? The letters were set aside and forgotten.

On March 5, the Prince of Orange entered the Ridderzaal, or Knights Hall, at The Hague, striding across the checkered floor, and beneath flag-festooned ceiling. The delegates from the seven provinces of The Netherlands, seated on both sides at the far end of the hall were in festive spirits, for in the Prince's presence, the peace was to be ratified. "The Ratification," it was remarked in the *London Gazette* soon afterwards, have been exchanged with Sir Gabriel Silvius; and this day, the Peace was Proclaimed here in the usual manner; which, as it occasioned a great and universal joy, so the publick expressions of it were extraordinary. The States have resolved to make a noble present to the Marquess del Fresno, Ambassador of Spain in England, as likewise to the Spanish Minister here, Don Bernardo de Salinas, on the occasion of the Peace.[35]

Peace with England had been achieved at last. But for the brash young commanders who had ravaged the Americas, conquering its strongest bastion in the name of Zeeland, Holland, the States General, and the Prince of Orange, there would be no peace, only recriminations, battles, and more bloodshed, for there was still a war with France to be fought. And for the loyal Dutch of New Netherland, there was a future fraught with uncertainty, disillusionment, and new hatreds.

22

VLISSINGEN

The Treaty of Westminster specified a series of dates on which hostilities between England and the United Provinces were to end at various points around the world. Owing to the delays to be expected in the transmittal of news over the vast expanse of the globe on which the two great powers had fought, there was not a single moment for universal peace, but staggered dates upon which hostilities were to cease. From the Soundings of England north to Norway, fighting would be terminated after March 8, 1674; from the Soundings south to Tangier, after April 7; from Tangier to the Equinoctial Line, after May 5; and everywhere else in the world, peace between the two powers would be observed after October 24, more than seven months later. Any acts of war committed by commissioned warships or letters of marque in any region after the published dates would result in "pain of the actors making reparations for damage done and being punished as violators of the public peace."[1] Thus, for Cornelis Evertsen and Jacob Benckes, the war against England would not officially be over until after April 7. Ironically, the bloody engagement between *Schaeckerloo* and *Tiger* had been fought several days after the actual ratification of the treaty in England, yet technically had been enjoined while the two nations were still belligerents in that region.

In the most bitter exercise in irony and honor, *Schaeckerloo* had struck her flag and had been on the verge of sinking with scores of casualties and dead aboard when Captain Harman, himself desperately wounded, took her under tow to Cadiz as a prize. The Englishman was undoubtedly unprepared for the reception awaiting him there. Pressure to release the wounded Captain de Witte and his men was immediately brought to bear by the Spanish governor, possibly at the behest of Gaspar van Collen or even Evertsen. Harman was equally unprepared for Commander Benckes' squadron, which had chosen this particular moment to return to Cadiz from an unsuccessful cruise in search of the elusive English Strait convoy. At nightfall on February 13, Benckes, Boes, and Richewijn had entered the harbor quite unexpectedly, much to the dismay of *Tiger's* commander. As soon as the Hollanders had discovered what had transpired, an angry Benckes dispatched a warning to the English that he would sink *Tiger* where she lay, neutrality or no neutrality, unless the Dutch prisoners were released. The gallant but shattered De Witte and his comrades were soon in friendly company once again.[2]

With only *Swaenenburgh* and *Sint Joris* in harbor, and Benckes' flotilla only just returned from sea, the Dutch as Cadiz, particularly the Zeelanders, were in no position to take further aggressive actions. Evertsen's crew, part of which had been transferred to *Schaeckerloo* before the battle, had now been reduced to a skeleton, many of its members having been killed or wounded aboard the pinnace. Manpower problems aside, the flagship was in urgent need of repair. Evertsen had little choice but to careen the big frigate to attend to the long-needed cleaning and repairwork. A full three days were needed to haul *Swaenenburgh* over on her side to expose enough of her stern to permit removal of her damaged rudder. When it was finally brought onboard, it was "found that her pins were completely loose so that some could be pulled off by hand." The ship was then heeled over on her opposite side in order that her chronic leak might be located. Even after she was hauled over as far as human endeavor dared, her keel remained seven to eight feet under water. Divers were sent down in an effort to locate the leaks, but to no avail. A second attempt was made to heel her over even farther, but the net result was only more trouble— a cracked foremast top and shattered crosstree. Frustrated, Evertsen decided to give up the search for the elusive leak and ordered the crew to scrape the ship's bottom and smear it with a mixture of soot and lime to retard marine growth and prevent damage by shipworms and other borers. *Swaenenburgh* was then righted and her foremast stripped to repair damage to the top and the broken crosstrees. On February 24, the cannons, which had been removed to permit careening, were brought back aboard and the ship made ready for sea. As if on cue, on the same day Evertsen received the Raden's explicit instructions to return home with his ships and prizes.[3]

Commander Benckes, too, was soon the recipient of sailing orders from his own masters, the Admiralty of Amsterdam. With his fleet in a suitable state of repair, he prepared to sail the following day. On the eve of departure, however, the governor of Cadiz requested a final meeting, to which Benckes agreed. At the meeting, Benckes was informed that the king of Spain, "who could not do without the presence of these ships," had sent last-minute orders that the Hollanders not be permitted to sail for five or six days, and until further orders were sent. The commander, who had received quite specific instructions from the Admiralty of Amsterdam to proceed to Livorne, "could hardly agree." But the governor persisted until the Dutchman finally consented to remain until March 1.[4]

Though both Dutch commanders were now ready to sail, on February 26, the weather turned sour as heavy, unremitting storms began to batter the Spanish coast. On February 28, the gale dashed a hapless Danish fluit and its Norwegian cargo to pieces upon the reefs outside the harbor entrance. Not until March 2, was the weather suitable for departure. Having already overstayed his promised extension, Benckes paid a final visit to the governor of Cadiz, who had received no additional word from the king. On March 3, with no further reason to remain in port, Jacob Benckes parted company with his young companion in arms and conquest, Cornelis Evertsen, for the last time.[5]

Two days after the departure of the Amsterdam squadron, Evertsen witnessed what must have been a most disturbing scene, the expected event that had undoubtedly caused the king of Spain to request Benckes to remain at Cadiz. At about midday, March 5, the entrance to Cadiz Bay was blanketed by a cloud of sails—English sails. It was an enormous convoy of 82 ships, shepherded by approximately 14 warships, the least of which, the excited Dutch Consul van Collen said, carried 54 guns, and 2 fireships. The convoy was commanded by Captain Sir Richard Rooth, aboard H.M.S. *Swiftsure*. Assembled with considerable difficulty over the preceeding months, his flotilla was, for the most part, bound for the Strait of Gibraltar and the relief of the British bastion at Tangier, which guarded the approach to the Mediterranean.[6] Owing to advance intelligence, Rooth was well aware of Evertsen's presence at Cadiz, but may have overestimated the number of hostile vessels in the harbor. On December 22, Admiralty Secretary Samuel Pepys had sent the then-departing captain an urgent message warning of the recent arrival of a nine-ship Dutch squadron at Cadiz "to which also is added their expectation of a Spanish squadron to join with them."[7] Possibly hoping to avoid a confrontation, Rooth failed to move against the tiny Dutch force remaining in the harbor.

Sir Richard, whose primary mission was to provision the British at Tangier, had been ordered not to lose a minute in setting out from Portsmouth, "as the garrison of Tangier may be in some distress for want of victuals."[8] Though H.M.S. *Tiger* sailed out to join him, and undoubtedly informed him of the weakened state of the Dutch forces, much to Evertsen's relief, Rooth honored the Spanish neutrality and pressed on toward his primary objective. Fourteen merchantmen, however, entered the Bay of Cadiz to trade, all unescorted. On March 9, the British fleet set sail, four warships and the greatest part of the merchant fleet pressing on toward the strait, and the remainder for Tangier. Rooth did not ignore the danger to his rear or to the merchantmen left behind. He took particular precautions to assign several men-of-war and a fireship to patrol the entrance to Cadiz harbor on the chance that Evertsen might soon sail.[9]

While the Zeelanders may have been willing to run the blockade, nature once again intervened. The day after the main British fleet sailed off, a storm blew out of the southeast, delaying the Dutch departure for several days more. On the 14th, as the weather finally began to improve, *Swaenenburgh* was moved from her anchorage behind the Puntael to another before the city, possibly to top off her provisions and water. The British patrols maintained a keen watch on all such movements, and from time to time one of his majesty's warships would slip into the harbor to monitor the enemy at close range and seize whatever opportunities that might be presented. By late March, seven warships and a fireship had come to anchor in the crowded, neutral harbor. With so many belligerants anchored so close together, incidents were bound to occur.[10]

On the night of March 23, another storm erupted over Cadiz and continued unabated for nearly a week. During the foul weather, on the night of March 25, the prize ship *Batchelor* mysteriously disappeared. It was at first supposed by the Dutch that she had snapped her cables during the storm and was driven out to sea. Desperate to recover the rich prize, Evertsen immediately hired a bark, furnished her with a spare cable and anchor, and sent her off in search of the missing ship. The supposition that the prize had been driven out to sea was given credence the following day when another vessel, which did not belong to the Dutch flotilla, was also forced out of the bay by the foul weather. Then came the shocking news that *Batchelor* had not drifted out at all, but had been quietly cut out by an English small-boat expedition. Evertsen was understandably infuriated, for he had apparently learned, immediately before the raid, that peace between England and the United Provinces had been proclaimed. Although they were not officially to cease hostilities until after April 7 in the Cadiz region, it appeared that the British had violated the intention of the peace and, what was even more important, the neutrality of Spain.[11]

Evertsen immediately filed a complaint with the governor of Cadiz and requested that "he be so kind as to free his roads, it being no safer here than in open sea," and further demanded that order be restored. The English must leave. The governor agreed to all of Evertsen's requests, provided he could prove that the English had done what he had accused them of doing. The governor's response was as good as a challenge to the Dutchman. Kees the Devil immediately dispatched an express along the Iberian coast as far as Lisbon, Portugal, with a letter from the governor to enforce his demand that if *Batchelor* should happen to come in, she be held for him. She would be easily recognized, Evertsen noted, for she had neither anchor nor cable.[12]

Though the weather continued foul for several days more, it did not prevent the British from sending more warships into the harbor to monitor the activities of the Zeelanders, or to seek shelter from the storms. Evertsen paid small heed, for he had problems enough with the loss of his prize. He would be hard pressed indeed to explain the loss to his superiors back home. Nevertheless, he persisted in his efforts to prove to the governor that the English had stolen the prize, in violation of Spanish neutrality. Only when the governor officially accepted his claim would he be absolved from blame for the loss back in Zeeland.

Evertsen launched into a full investigation with zeal, and began to collect depositions from seamen aboard ships that had been moored near the site of the alleged deed. One witness declared that on the night the prize disappeared, a bark with fifteen or sixteen Englishmen onboard that had been at the anchorage remained there until dark, "and then made off, rowing to the shore." The witness paid scant attention to *Batchelor*, which lay at anchor (apparently unattended) to the landward of himself, and had been unable to see whether the bark had sailed near her or not. However, the crew of another ship, lying closer, declared that the crew of the same bark had been observed leaving its own vessel, rowing over to *Batchelor*, and "that about midnight had sailed off from close alongside her, her foresail hoisted."[13]

Convinced now that the English had cut out his prize, Evertsen pressed on with his investigation. On April 4, in the presence of the harbor master and a clerk summoned for the purpose by the governor of Cadiz, he located and raised *Batchelor*'s anchors. His objective was to discover whether the ship's cables had snapped under the force of the storm or if they had been intentionally cut. Both cables, it was soon observed, had been cut, "one on the bitts and the other about two feet into the hawsehole, which was sufficiently clear to show that the English had done it."[14]

Satisfied that he had proven his point, with reputable witnesses to verify the findings, the Zeeland commander called upon the governor to see what he intended to do about it. Once skeptical, the governor was now deeply embarrassed. What did Evertsen want him to do about it, he asked? Would he, replied the Zeelander, "be so kind as to liberate his roads and persuade the English that the ship be brought back from where they had taken it?" The governor agreed, and after collecting pertinent data, forwarded the request to the appropriate authority.[15]

On April 8, hostilities against England officially ended in the waters of Spain, and Cornelis Evertsen, satisfied that he had done his best to recover *Batchelor*, began to make final preparations for the perilous voyage home. Instructions were distributed to merchant ships wishing to sail under *Swaenenburgh*'s protection, and on the 13th Kees the Devil raised a blue flag, announcing his intentions to sail with the next morning's tide. On the eve of his departure, however, yet another storm blew up over Cadiz Bay, "with hard wind and thunder" out of the southwest.[16]

For the next five days, the fleet was forced to remain in harbor. Then, at dawn on the 19th, there was a brief break as an easterly sprung up. *Swaenenburgh* rushed to make immediate sail, only to be driven back to a precarious anchorage just outside the harbor. Despite the frustration, the day was not without its satisfactions, for upon his returning to anchor, Evertsen received papers confirming

> that the Governor would speak to the Consul of the English nation [regarding the *Batchelor* affair], and if he could not prove the case to the contrary would take him under arrest.[17]

Finally, on April 25, the winds and seas turned favorable. Evertsen's convoy, 25 ships strong, including *Swaenenburgh*, *Sint Joris*, five prizes, 18 Dutch, Swedish, Hamburg, and (ironically) English merchantmen, sailed out of Cadiz Harbor. Simultaneously, the eight Royal Navy ships, with whom the Dutch had co-existed in forced neutrality for many long weeks, sailed for the Strait of Gibraltar with their own convoy. Many Dutch seamen undoubtedly looked back with some sadness at the bones of the once proud *Schaeckerloo*, left behind in the harbor as a worthless hulk. Many more looked back with a mixture of regret and pride, in final goodbye to their mates that had died in her gallant but pointless fight.[18]

Evertsen's voyage west, across the Gulf of Cadiz, was mercifully un-
eventful. Although Faro, Lagos, and Cape St. Vincent were passed
without incident, the ocean that lay ahead could not be expected to be
traversed without certain risks. The war with England was over, but
the conflict with France was as deadly as ever. The French fleet had
emerged from two years of warfare practically unscathed, and might
well be cruising in the waters off her coast—waters through which the
Dutch convoy must sail. On May 2, a ripple of concern passed through
the convoy when 16 or 17 sails were sighted to the west of Cape St.
Vincent. Fortunately, they were discovered to be either English or Portuguese. Five days later, approximately 54 miles off Cape Roca and the
city of Lisbon, the flotilla turned north. By the 13th, Cape Finesterre,
the westernmost point of northern Spain, was less than eight miles
distant. Here Evertsen took up pursuit of a strange sail but failed to
come up with his prey. The following day, he spoke with the commander of a Flemish caper, Captain Guilliaem Willems, who was four days
out of La Coruña, Spain. During the course of the next few weeks,
such encounters with friends and potential enemies alike would increase as proximity to the English Channel narrowed.[19]

On May 18, the weather was thick with freezing sleet and all visibil-
ity obscured. Fortunately, a brief glimpse of the coast through the curtain of icy rain was enough to tell the seasoned Dutch navigators that
they were but a short distance from the Coruña Channel. Evertsen now
sought to shepherd the flotilla, which had been at sea a full month,
into the waterway to take on water for his prizes. After several days of
incessant beating about against adverse winds, the flotilla finally entered the channel. Then, after a visit of several days more, Evertsen
again met with delay as equally contrary winds and an accident with
one of the prize fluits frustrated efforts to depart.[20]

By the evening of June 1, however, the fleet was finally on the open
sea again, heading north and skimming the western perimeter of the
Bay of Biscay, bound for home. A chance encounter with an English
ship on June 2 provided the Dutch with welcome news. The Englishman had left the Downs only a few days earlier and had encountered a
massive Dutch warfleet of over 100 sail in the English Channel. Several
days later, his report was confirmed by a Dutch captain out of Texel
bound for Guinea who had also sighted the fleet.[21]

Slowly, but perceptibly, Evertsen's flotilla closed with the northwest
coast of Bretagne, the triangular peninsula that thrust its way westward from the heart of France to divide the Bay of Biscay from the
English Channel. There, located at the tip of the peninsula, on the
northwest shore of a bay called the Rade de Brest, as every Dutch

seaman worth his salt knew, lay the main French naval base on the Atlantic coast, the heavily fortified City of Brest. Evertsen was well aware that even now warships might be fanning out from Brest, patrolling in search of Channel-bound ships and convoys such as his own. Safe passage into the Channel, he knew, required more than favorable winds and a mariner's skills. Much depended upon pure luck.

On June 7 the convoy had, by the navigator's calculations, crept to within 30 miles of the Ile d'Ouessant, the westernmost island landfall of the Bretagne peninsula. The following day the winds were from the west, driving the fleet ever closer to the supposed shoreline, when it was suddenly overtaken by a "flying fog." The flotilla crept cautiously onward. On the morning of the 9th, soundings were taken and bottom struck in 96 fathoms, leading to the conclusion that the convoy was much further west than had been estimated. Evertsen called for a navigational fix on Friday, June 12. The convoy's position was then fixed at 49° 20', well within or parallel to the throat of the English Channel.[22]

Soon after the midday position fix, *Swaenenburgh* encountered an English vessel that had sailed from Brest the previous day. Again the news was good. Though twelve French warships were in port, they were

> so far up river that one couldn't approach them, the French being quite alarmed and scared, had closed off the river with a chain and were very busy fortifying the place and laying batteries, making use of the ship's cannons, and there also being 6,000 soldiers there, the cause being the [Dutch] fleet was appearing daily before Heyssent [Ile d'Ouessant].[23]

Evertsen undoubtedly could not have been more delighted, for with the French bottled up at Brest, there was every reason to believe that the chances of his own convoy being intercepted were minimal. That evening, the lookout spotted the Lizard, the southernmost landfall on the coast of England, a welcome signpost to the English Channel and the final leg of the voyage.[24]

The flotilla entered the Channel confidently, passing many English ships sailing westward, unafraid and in peace. On June 15, the convoy was off Beachy Head, and on the following evening was barely three miles off Dover. But passage through the Strait of Dover was not for the textbook sailor. On the 17th, while at anchor in 14 fathoms off Dover, *Swaenenburgh*'s cable snapped. Evertsen dropped another anchor, while at the same time dispatching a boat to retrieve the lost anchor by its buoy rope. Unfortunately, the buoy line also snapped and the anchor was irretrievably lost. When the flotilla finally got underway again, the breeze began to blow out of the east, bringing progress to a halt; then, during the night, a "running wind," swinging from all points of the compass, began to blow, further frustrating the advance. By the morning of the 19th, the fleet found itself well below Dover and losing ground. Navigating the Strait was proving anything but easy. When the ships were obliged to come to anchor against the usually stiff northeast winds, the anchors often failed to take hold, forcing them to tack laboriously back and forth simply to hold position. On the morning of June 21, *Swaenenburgh* found herself only two miles from Calais; by evening she had managed to struggle up only as far as Dover, on the opposite side of the Channel.[25]

Finally, on June 22, the winds picked up from the west and Evertsen's convoy broke free into the North Sea. With winged sails they pressed northeast, along the fringes of the Ruytigen Banks, with the cities of Dunkirk, Ostend, and Blankenburgh mere shadows on a distant horizon. Soon they came to the Wielinghe Channel and the approach to Vlissingen. But as it was calm and Evertsen's pilot was unsure of the passage, the flotilla came to anchor within sight of the Fatherland.[26]

On Tuesday, June 23, the log of *Swaenenburgh*, in the pages of which were recorded the remarkable 570-day odyssey of exploits, battles, and conquests, was closed with a final entry. "Wind due north with rough winds; sailed further out and entered the Spleet; anchored about midday before Vlissingen."[27] Cornelis Evertsen had returned home.

23

TEARE OUT THE GOVERNOURS' THROATS

For Governor General Anthony Colve, the spring of 1674 brought scant relief from the threat of attack. Still patiently awaiting instructions from The Netherlands, he was well aware that the fate of New Orange would be decided in Europe. He knew that his worst foe was demoralization—from enemy intimidation and propaganda, and from unrest among the citizens. Stung by the military stance of New England and the cruel winter destruction of Hoeren Kill, Colve's resolve only stiffened, for such motions could not be ignored. Retaliation for the English actions was effected by confiscating goods belonging to the inhabitants of New England, Virginia, and Maryland. These had been intentionally exempted from the earlier September 10, 1673, Proclamation and Act of Confiscation in hopes that the region would be spared the hostilities prevalent elsewhere in the world.[1]

Few placed any credence in the recurrent rumors of peace that filtered in from New England and Virginia, including Colve, who doggedly continued to perfect New Orange's fortifications, as much to occupy the citizenry as to improve the works. Unfortunately, the colony administration was by this time completely destitute. The governor, in a desperate measure to meet the continuing defense expenditures, was obliged to borrow the monies from Nicholas Bayard, offering "as a special mortgage and pledge" for his "security and satisfaction" the very "bronze cannon" in the fort, upon which defense depended.[2]

Colve had continued to expand friendly relations with the Mohawks to the north, a people with whom a renewed alliance might provide a buffer between the isolated Dutch settlements on the upper Hudson and the French in Canada. On May 12, he concluded, in negotiations with the two Mohawk villages closest to Fort Nassau, Kaghenewage and Kanagro, a renewal of peace and agreement for mutual defense against the French.[3]

Undoubtedly hoping to keep the New Englanders, who were moving to dispatch their own naval force, off balance, Colve fielded Eewoutsen's *Zeehond* as frequently as possible, sending her on patrols in Long Island Sound and along the coast of New England. In May the snaauw was sent into the sound specifically to raid enemy shipping. Sailing eastward along the north coast of Long Island, Captain Eewoutsen descended on the unsuspecting English like a fury. On May 8, a vessel commanded by one Captain Fleet of Long Island, bound from Narragansett for Huntington, was the first to spy the odd-looking Dutch warship to the west of Block Island. The snaauw was making directly for him. Terrified, Fleet pointed his bow toward Point Judith, on the north shore of the sound, and sought to outrun the Dutchman, which was coming up fast. As Fleet passed the point, *Zeehond*, which had closed to within three miles, refused to be shaken. Desperately, the merchantman pressed on toward Concencut Point, when suddenly, her nemesis "brought her tacks aboard and stood of to sea with her Antient out." The Dutchman, however, had come close enough that Fleet was later able to provide a rough description. He judged

> that shee was a man of warre, and that frigat called the Snow shee chasing him with studding sails had no head no missen mast her foresailes out of proportion with her after sayles.[4]

The following day, lingering off Point Judith, Eewoutsen sighted another potential victim, the sloop *Swan*, Samuel Woodbury of Swansea, skipper and part owner with the widow of one John Dixy (or Dicksy). The sloop, which had been bound from Milford for Swansea laden with 7,800 bushels of wheat, 60 or 70 bushels of peas, and 60 bushels of maize, made immediately for Narragansett Bay with *Zeehond* hot on her heels. The Dutchman opened fire, but *Swan* failed to stop. For the next three hours Eewoutsen continued the pursuit, firing the whole time, and finally overtaking his prey barely six miles from Swansea. *Swan* surrendered within sight of home and many witnesses. The alarm was promptly spread along the coast. Governor William Coddington of Rhode Island immediately dispatched warnings to Governor Leverett in Boston, as well as to Plymouth and Martha's Vineyard.[5]

Eewoutsen continued to cruise off Block Island and two days later took the sloop *Egmond and Mathew*, Richard Pattishall, captain and part owner with John Daffom and Thomas Russel, all of Boston. The sloop, which had sailed from Virginia on May 6, laden with 59 hogsheads of tobacco, was taken near the east end of Long Island. On the same day, *Zeehond* captured the New England ketch *Prosperous*, William Lewes skipper, belonging to Richard Cuts of Piscattaway. This vessel, which departed from Maryland on May 2 bound for New England, was also taken near the east end of Long Island with a cargo of 67 tubs of tobacco, 70 to 80 bushels of corn, 600 pounds of iron, 10 hides, and assorted private goods. On May 16, all three vessels, together with sails, rigging, anchors, and cargoes, were ordered confiscated.[6]

While the Colve administration pressed on with defensive preparations and aggressive naval patrols, New England was beset and confused by contradictory rumors. On March 16, Matthias Nicholls, writing from Stamford, Connecticut, to Governor Winthrop, reported that "Wee have here our share of the various Rumours and Reports as well from Boston and those parts Eastward, as Virginia and Maryland westward." The most prevalent accounts were that the king had designated some ships for the reduction of New York. But verifiable news from Europe was slow to come in.[7] On March 30, Governor Leverett informed Winthrop of the most recent account to reach his colony directly from London, which was a letter dated October 28, 1673—five months previously.[8] By mid-April, hopes for the arrival of a naval reinforcement from England to retake New York had begun to falter, and New England's aggressive stance was noticeably calmed by mutterings that peace was in the offing. "Mee thinks it strange," Nicholls wrote Winthrop on the 11th, that

> there hath beene no further confirmacon of the Newes from Maryland or Virginia, the Alarum whereof was at first so hot, in some short time wee may have I hope better satisfaction. Wee have of late had Intelligence by the way of Roade Island of great hopes of peace, how true wee must expect with Patience.[9]

Then, on May 7, a vessel belonging to Charlestown, arriving at Boston after a month's passage from Scotland, delivered the first positive news and a copy of the peace treaty between England and the United Provinces. Furthermore, it was said that a frigate and four ships would shortly bring a new governor to New York. The following day, Governor John Leverett sent an express with full details of the treaty to Governor Winthrop, who received it a week later.[10] Reception of the same news on Manhattan Island shortly afterward was far more imprecise, and was destined to be anything but well-received by the inhabitants.

On May 12, John Sharpe wrote from Milford, Connecticut, to Governor Winthrop describing a particularly tortuous sequence of events in New Orange when the peace became known. Sharpe, who had been banished from New Netherland, claimed he had petitioned Colve for permission to visit New Orange to see his wife and children. The plea was carried by one Isaac Melyn[11] (a Dutch property owner in New Orange who lived in Connecticut) and delivered to Colve with word of the peace. But Melyn failed to inform the governor general that one of the conditions was the surrender of the province of New Netherland. Sharpe later claimed that Colve then agreed to admit him, although the council records of New Netherland suggest that the Englishman had entered the province without approval. On arriving in the city and calling upon the governor (or being called by him), Sharpe dutifully turned over a number of letters that he had promised to deliver to various inhabitants. Again, the Dutch records suggest otherwise. When Colve opened and inspected the letters, he began to question the visitor closely and then induced him to turn over two copies of original communiques taken at Boston, which detailed the terms for the surrender of New Netherland. Colve was undoubtedly shocked by the dramatic turn of events, for the abandonment of his colony was certain to have repercussions among the citizens who had been promised aid, not abandonment. Thus, the governor ordered Sharpe to speak only of the peace and not of the terms of surrender.[12]

Though Sharpe claims to have obeyed Colve's order, Melyn, who retired to his home in the city, was not so easily intimidated. He, too, had been apprised of the terms of the peace while in Connecticut and was angered at what he considered to be betrayal by the States General. When a crowd of burghers, hungry for news from the north, gathered outside his house, Melyn "ragingly" informed them that they had been slaving not for The Netherlands, but for Charles II. The States General, he said, had surrendered New Netherland to the king of England. The enraged inhabitants began crying out passionately, "wee'l fyre the Town, Pluck downe the ffortifications teare out the Governours throats, who had compelled them to slave soe contrary to their priveledges."[13]

Colve, learning of the near-mutinous situation but sensing that an end to the war was in sight, acted with calm resolve to restore order. He quickly sent for Melyn, who stoically denied nothing and was immediately committed to the dungeon of Fort Willem Hendrick on charges of uttering seditious and mutinous language. Melyn was advised to prepare for his execution, for in two days he would die "by the french man who hanged in Chaines on the Gallowes."[14] After being so confined for a day and a night, this "unfaithfull Judasly and treacherous travailour" sought to soften his sentence and affirm his innocence by accusing Sharpe of spreading damaging news about the country—news that

Colve's reign was to be short-lived and his government at an end. When brought before the governor, Sharpe was also accused of bringing letters from Captain Nicholls of Connecticut to a certain French merchant named Mirviele without review by the proper authorities. During two days of interrogations, Sharpe was not permitted to speak in his own defense. After the interrogations, he was committed "to the inner and nethermost Dungeon Cousin german to the Stygeon Lake," where he was kept for three days on charges of mutiny and disturbance. The prisoner was then released but ordered banished from the colony for a period of ten years upon pain of death.[15]

Sharpe's sentence was handed down with great solemnity on May 2, after which the townhouse bell was rung three times. A large portion of the city population turned out to watch as the prisoner was placed in a canoe and set out for Connecticut. He had not achieved the purported purpose of his visit—to see his wife and children—and was sent off without even having secured his boots or a shirt. The showy banishment, Sharpe later declared, had been set up to convince the people that "the States of Holland would never part with such municiple strong hold or fort."[16]

For his own part, Isaac Melyn was not sentenced to die after all, but was committed to hard labor working on the city defenses "from morning to night every day untill the works were fully compleated." It was a hard sentence, for it was said that it would be quite some time before the work was completed, since the governor was "dayly projecting more and new inventions to fortefy and employ the people, on purpose to keep them out of idlenesse."[17]

Upon his arrival at Milford, Sharpe immediately informed Governor Winthrop, in a somewhat melodramatic letter composed on May 12, of the situation in New Orange. The commonalty, he claimed,

> belch forth their curses and execration against the Prince of Orange and States of Holland, the Dutch Admiralls who took it, and their taskmaster the Governour saying, they will not on demand, and by authority of the States or Prince, surrender, but keepe it by fighting soe long as they can stand with one Legg and fight with one hand, which resolution will create I feare, further trouble to both nations.[18]

Despite their initial rage, the citizenry did not permit the more hotheaded inhabitants to explode into open mutiny. By mid-June, news of unquestionable veracity concerning the peace arrived in New Orange from New England. Coolly and methodically, the Governor General of New Netherland prepared for the inevitable transition. On June 18, he released all arrested goods and effects in the colony belonging to the inhabitants of New England, Virginia, and Maryland on the stipulation that the governments of those colonies do likewise with the property of New Netherlanders. Six days later, the three vessels Eewoutsen had seized in May were released and restored to their skippers. Having received official word from Holland, on July 1, Colve publicly proclaimed the Treaty of Westminster.[19]

The news caused "no little emotion" among the Dutch of New Netherland, who were now obliged to accept another new set of rulers. Yet they were now stoically resolved to make the best of it; anger had turned to acquiescence. As one Dutchman, Jeremias van Rensselaer, philosophically wrote: "Well, if it has to bee, we commend the matter to God, who knows what is best for us."[20]

On July 1, the same day that Governor Anthony Colve proclaimed the Treaty of Westminster in New Orange, James, Duke of York, an ocean away, officially commissioned Major Edmund Andros (or Andrews) "to bee my Lieut and Governour" of New York. This was apparently only a formality, for four months earlier, in March, the crown had deputed the major to receive the province on his behalf. The 35 year old Andros was a distinguished officer who had proven himself on the battlefield during the last two wars with The Netherlands. In 1672, he had commanded his majesty's forces in Barbados and gained a reputation for his skill and understanding of American affairs. His regiment was the first to be armed "with the bayonet or great knife" upon its introduction to the British army. In the same year he was confirmed as Landgrave of the Province of Carolina, and 1674 he became Seigneur of the Fiefs and Bailiff of Guernsey, a post granted by the king. When his regiment was disbanded at the peace, he was considered fit to receive his commission as governor general of New York.[21]

By the terms of the peace, Great Britain officially demanded restitution of New Netherland on March 31, and that it be turned over to Andros, with all its "appurtenances, artillery, ammunition and war equipment, of whatever type there might be and in the same condition they were at the time of the publication of the peace." Upon receipt of the communication in The Hague, the States General sent copies of the terms to the Raden of Zeeland and the Board of Admiralty of Amsterdam requesting that they see that the evacuation of troops be carried out together with all arms, goods, and equipment brought in prior to publication of the peace. They were to order Governor Colve to restore New Netherland into the hands of Sir Edmund Andros "without doing or caused to be done any exploitation, plundering or removal of residents . . . guns, gunpowder or any tool of war" that were there prior to the conquest. Furthermore, the Assembly directed that the king of

England be requested and expected to permit the residents of New Netherland to live in peace

> and to that end shall once forgive and remove from all thought all offenses, injuries, damage and loss which during the present war or in times past were done there or may have been suffered, and permit the residents of the said New Netherland to enjoy their lands, farms, and all their goods to which they have right in that country, all with the same right, privilege and freedom which the said residents enjoyed before the date of the said war.

The request was to be handed over to the king of England by Lord Van de Lier, Ambassador Extraordinary to England.[22]

Six days later, on April 6, the States General formally resolved to order the evacuation of the forts and restore New Netherland to the king of England. Having received the resolution, the Raden of Zeeland informed the Admiralty of Amsterdam that there was no longer any other course than to obey the directives. They thereupon immediately prepared orders for Captain Evert Evertsen, commander of *Suriname*, and all of the forces under his command, with the troops, the snaauw *Zeehond*, "and such other vessels as there may be present" to return to the Fatherland "in the shortest possible time." A missive was also prepared for Colve indicating the States General's resolution to evacuate New Netherland. He was instructed to see to an orderly transition, taking care "that with the vacating of the conquest no well founded reason for complaint shall be given to the English people."[23]

Not until June 25, 1674, was a warship readied at Amsterdam to convey the official orders of evacuation to New Orange. Two days later the States General resolved that the master of the ship, Captain Hendrick van Tholl (or Toll), who was just arriving at Scheveningen to convey the Dutch ambassadors extraordinary to England, should carry the Staten's resolution of April 6 to Colve. Governor Colve, in turn, was directed to turn the colony over to Edmund Andros. In the event that Andros had not yet arrived and no orders had been received in the colony from England, the Dutch, after inventorying their goods, were to vacate the place nevertheless. The ambassadors extraordinary, Lords van Reede, Cornelis van Beuningen, and van Haren, were to formally inform the king of the Dutch's intentions.[24]

Captain van Tholl came to anchor before the austere walls of Fort Willem Hendrick on October 9, with instructions for Colve to surrender and vacate New Netherland. Five people of his choice were to administer to the colony government until the arrival of Major Andros. Colve immediately began the removal of arms and goods, but before he was fully prepared to depart, the major arrived. Coming to within a mile and a half of the city on October 22 in the frigate *Diamond*, and accompanied by another called *Castle*, he anchored under Staten Island and promptly dispatched his credentials to the Dutch governor. Colve replied with a request that he be permitted eight days to complete the evacuation and to conclude his administrative and personal affairs. In the meantime, the city government dispatched a welcoming delegation to the soon-to-be-governor of New York, consisting of Councillor Steenwyck and Burgomasters van Brugh and Beeckman. The delegation carried with it a request that various privileges and securities might be permitted the citizenry. Anxious for an orderly transition, Andros reassured the three Dutchmen that all inhabitants would retain all of the rights and privileges which they enjoyed before the war.[25]

With English and Dutch troops temporarily billeted together in one small town occasional disorders were bound to erupt, but Colve's strict remedies—including the arrest of drunken English soldiers—maintained order. On October 27, the Dutch commander requested Andros' approval of eleven articles for the inhabitants of the colony. These included guarantees of religious liberty, freedom from impressment, upholding the validating of judgments passed in the colony courts during the Dutch administration, the maintenance of actual owners in possession of confiscated properties, and a number of minor rights and privileges. Noting that he had been directed to act with justice and kindness, Andros promised to consider the requests as soon as he assumed office.

Colve was careful to attend to the needs of the Dutch Reformed Church as well as he could by giving the consistory of the church, who were terrified at the prospect of being dispossessed, the deed for the church within Fort Willem Hendrick. Then, assembling the municipal and militia officers of New Orange, the last Dutch governor general of New Netherland formally absolved them from their oaths of allegiance and bade them a sad but dignified farewell. The magistrates with whom he had struggled shoulder to shoulder to build a new government, to promote law and order, and to improve industry amid many enemies and obstacles presented him with a gift of 250 guilders for his services during his year-long tenure. The final entry of the short Court Records of New Orange, the last to be written by an official of sworn allegiance to The Netherlands in the tiny city, reads:

On the 10th November [October 31 English calendar], the Province of New Netherland is surrendered by Governor Colve to Governor Major Edmund Andros in behalf of His Majesty of Great Britain.[26]

With that, the Dutch flag was lowered in the fort as Colve and his veterans relinquished the works and the city to its new rulers, retiring to their frigate in the harbor. On November 2, Governor Andros, as promised, dispatched his somewhat belated reply to Colve's requested eleven Articles. He agreed to most of them. As a final gesture, he wished the Captain Godspeed and his heartfelt thanks for the gift of a coach and three horses being left behind by the Dutchman.

Upon his return to Middleburg, Cornelis Evertsen was not, as the conquerors of New Netherland might have expected, well-received by the Staten of Zeeland. He was summoned on July 15, 1674, before the Assembly to present an account of his expedition and to answer many charges brought against him concerning the failures (but not the successes) of his odyssey.[27]

The first charge concerned his late arrival at São Tiago in the Cape Verdes, a result of making port at and lingering in and around the Canary Islands for nine days. Evertsen's inquisitors were perplexed that the hoecker, which separated from the squadron on December 24, had managed, though poorly equipped with sails, to reach São Tiago 25 days earlier than Evertsen's main force. Thus, it was stated, he had lost time, with the delay resulting in the aborting of the primary mission with which the squadron had been charged.[28]

The French colony of Cayenne was not attacked, though Evertsen's orders had clearly stated that the colony was to be the first military action to be taken against that enemy. And the lengthy delay in Suriname could not, they reminded him, be overlooked. Then there was the overlong stay in New Netherland to be considered. Because of the delay there, and the arrival of the stormy season, the fleet had been unable to sail around the north end of England to return to the Fatherland as ordered. Instead it sailed to Cadiz, which it had been ordered not to do. Because of such delays, the Staten complained, "the Land has been saddled with the heavy expense of having to pay seven months additional keep and wages than would otherwise have been the case without any service at all having been enjoyed for them."[29]

And finally, there was the issue of "the unnecessary, audacious and unequal battle" that Evertsen had ordered Captain Passchier de Witte to enter into against H.M.S. *Tiger*.[30]

There was much debate over the questions. The Grand Pensionary, who diplomatically remained unavailable, stated through the person of Lord van Odijck, who stood in his place as First Noble, that he could not advise the Staten on such matters, but that the issue be continued.

In the meantime, until the questions were resolved, he advised, Captain Evertsen should not be given new employment.[31]

Evertsen was not without his supporters. The Lords Deputies of Middleburg noted that "exploits at sea were very uncertain and subject to many accidents," and were overcome only through experience. The loss of time, they said, was not Evertsen's fault. The attack on Cayenne had been hindered by the shoally bottom and the sea approaches, which had been sounded and found inadvisable to attempt. Had they been unsuccessfully tried, it was likely that the squadron would have been incapable of conducting future actions against the enemy. The long stay in New Netherland, they pointed out, was done to insure the stability of his important conquest. For this singular reason, the optimum season for sailing home via the route north of England passed, making it necessary to sail for Cadiz. The battle with *Tiger* "was done in order to preserve the Honor and reputation of the Land." The Middleburgers felt that Evertsen's actions were entirely justifiable and that the Lords of the Admiralty should be free to employ the captain again.[32]

Still unsatisfied with Evertsen's case, the Lords Deputies of Zierikzee demanded that the captain's "instruction and other papers and proofs" be turned over to the state's attorney and answered before the Court, and that Evertsen be denied a return to command until then. The Lords of Goes and Tholen supported the views of the deputies of Zierikzee.[33]

It is not surprising that the Lords Deputies of Vlissingen, home of the most daring of the United Provinces' capers, were completely supportive of Evertsen. He had, they stated in his defense, "fulfilled his orders in all ways." Indeed, he was a member of one of the country's foremost seafaring families, "a family which had certainly shown merit," and he had comported himself well in every instance. They cast their lot with the Middleburgers.[34]

The final voices heard were those of the Lords of Veere. They were not content with the report given, but were against the passage of any resolution denying the captain a command. They "judged that Captain Cornelis Evertsen had not erred in lack of courage." Yet the Staten could not bring itself to a decision. The Lords of the Admiralty, which had yet to provide the captain with a new assignment, declared that they would "not do so without the approval of the Lords States of Zeeland."[35]

Kees the Devil Evertsen, for once, humbled himself. On July 24, the Staten read a petition from the captain "in which he explained his great sorrow" that the Staten was not content with the conduct of his expedition. Swallowing his pride, he requested that they "graciously overlook the same." After due deliberation upon the matter, five of the members indicated their willingness to support the captain's request. The Lords of Zierikzee grudgingly accepted, but only conditionally upon the advice of the Lords of Tholen. Not until September 11, however, was the affair again presented for deliberation. This time the Lords of Zierikzee gave their assent to "overlook with favor the unhappy outcome of the primary goal and other affairs of his expedition" and to permit him to resume service. Finally, on the following day, "because of the good services of the ancestors of the said Captain, which could also be hoped and expected of him," Cornelis Evertsen de Jongste was forgiven and officially permitted to return to the service of his Fatherland.[36]

24

EPILOGUE

Though the raid on America was quickly forgotten in the swirl of events that swept the United Provinces through four more years of war with France, its consequences were not ephemeral. The battle against England had marked Holland's zenith as a world maritime power. The Dutch warriors who had followed the flag to sea had miraculously held the overwhelming forces of both England and France at bay in home waters and had subdued, through force of arms and pure bravado, a vast colonial frontier empire in America. With a population of barely two million souls, The Netherlands had blunted, if not defeated, the assaults of both France, with a population of fourteen million, and England, with a population of seven million. The cost of this glory, however, was her preeminent position in the naval and commercial hierarchy of European nations.

The superb defensive campaigns of Michiel de Ruyter, one of history's greatest naval commanders, which had repeatedly fended off attack and seaborne invasion, could not compensate the terrible drain on the republic's limited resources. Not until the signing of the Treaty of Nijmegen in August 1678, would the flow of blood and national resources be even momentarily staunched. Few by then recalled the brief moment on October 31, 1674, when the red, white, and blue flag of the United Provinces of the Netherlands was lowered over Fort Willem Hendrick to make way for the English jack. Fewer still were aware that it marked for all time the termination of major Dutch involvement in New World empire-building. For most, the changing of the guard merely signalled the emergence of a new order.

Had Great Britain not prevailed in the reordering of New Netherland, then most certainly France would have, with its dynamic imperialism and the able leadership of Frontenac in Canada. Though blessed with an abundance of capable military leaders, the republic, beset by rivalry between states and by indecisive and occasionally avaricious political leadership (with a few glowing exceptions), could no longer sustain such an empire. The golden age of the Dutch Republic had waxed magnificently, and had then begun its fade from the world scene.

Yet the daring raid on America had significantly influenced the course of subsequent events at almost every point at which the Zeeland and Amsterdam squadrons had touched. This was also true for many whose lives had been affected by the Dutch expedition.

The unhappy governor of Suriname, who had pleaded for a replacement to take over his command of that fever-ridden, starving colony, was all but ignored by Zeeland and would be obliged to serve out the war there. The depopulated island of St. Eustatius, by the terms of the Treaty of Westminster, would eventually be returned to Dutch authority and would remain, with a brief exception, a Dutch colony through the present.[1]

In Virginia, Sir William Berkeley's corrupt and heavy-handed autocracy, which had dragged the colony through its developing years, was to be short-lived. Combined with the bitter fruits of England's disastrous Navigation Acts and numerous natural catastrophes, it might be said that his dictatorial regime began its descent with the Dutch raid on the Chesapeake in 1673. Defection to the Dutch during the war and open revolt by the citizenry had been feared throughout the trying days of 1672–73. The vulnerability of the colony to naval attack was clearly illustrated by the Evertsen-Benckes raid in July 1673, and improvement of the defenses had been considered paramount—but it was costly. In 1674, following the announcement of the necessity to levy excessively heavy taxes to pay for colony defenses and improvement of the forts—which had proved practically useless during the Evertsen raid—appeared the first hint of outright mutiny in the colony. There was insurrection at Lawn Creek, nurtured by the call for increased taxes to be exacted from the impoverished population. Though the Lawn Creek Rebellion was quickly suppressed, it was a worrisome harbinger of things to come. In 1675 and 1676, after the governor failed to repel a series of disastrous Indian raids, his inaction and the rot within his regime germinated open rebellion, which all but brought down his government. Finally, in the spring of 1677, Berkeley was relieved of office and returned to England a bitter, dying man.[2]

On the Delaware, the little settlement that had, with the exception of a single thatched barn, been wiped out by Maryland raiders did not disappear. Huddled together in the miserable little hut, several families faced the terrible winter. Somehow they survived, and with the spring came relief from New Castle. Those who remained, the families of Hermanus Wiltbanck, John Kiphaven, Alexander Moultson, Harman Cornellinson, Anthony Inclose, and Elizabeth Roads, the widow of John Roads, Sr., formed the nucleus of a new town. In May 1676 the residents living at Hoeren Kill pressed the new government at New Castle for patents for their lands, for there were disputes over where they lived and under whose government they were to be administered. Rumors that Marylanders were again surveying their lands and intending to retake the place reached Governor Andros. Contention between New York and Maryland again blossomed, even as the town began to grow and flourish. Still, fear of invasion by Lord Baltimore's forces permeated the settlement well after it was legalized as part of the new colony of Pennsylvania in 1685. Indeed, the boundary dispute between Pennsylvania and Maryland would continue for nearly another century, until the 1760s, when a survey line between those two colonies was drawn by Charles Mason and Jeremiah Dixon. By then, Hoeren Kill had become Whore Kill, and the tragic affair in the winter of 1673 was but a dim footnote to history.[3]

Upon the inauguration of the Andros government in New York, the magistrates who had been in office on the Delaware at the time of the Dutch attack were reinstated. The new government at New Castle, led by Captain Edmund Cantwell and William Tom, readily secured oaths of allegiance to the Duke of York from the Dutch, Swedish, Finnish, and English settlers of the Delaware country. Tired of conflict, and perhaps aware of the inevitable course of empire, they docilely accepted the new order.[4]

In New York those associated with the defeat administered by the Dutch suffered ignominy and censure. Captain John Manning was disgraced for his surrender of Fort James by having his sword broken over his head.[5] On January 11, 1675, Colonel Francis Lovelace was arrested in London and committed briefly to the tower "for not having defended the colony and fort of New York according to his commission and duty."[6] Ironically, the colonel's grandson, the Fourth Lord Lovelace, would also serve as governor of the colony his grandfather had surrendered, but would die in office in 1709. For the most part, the Dutch citizens and magistrates who had sworn allegiance to the United Provinces and the Prince of Orange retained their homes and estates. Only a few, such as Cornelis van Ruijven, who had served the Colve administration with zeal and loyalty, returned to The Netherlands, unable to compromise their allegiance as easily as did their countrymen. The remarkable Captain Anthony Colve, the cement with which the disparate elements of New Netherland were held together against a whirlwind of difficulties, returned to the Fatherland and obscurity, a loyal and brave soldier who deserved much more respect than history would allot him. The colony he had administered was returned by King Charles to the dominion of the Duke of York, James Stuart, by Royal patent on June 29, 1674, and immediately plunged into disputes with neighboring New Jersey over the old territorial issues.

The New Jersey proprietorship itself underwent a dynamic change in the years following the war. In March 1674 two Quakers, Edward Billing (or Byllyne) and John Fenwick, purchased Lord John Berkeley's share of the proprietorship. Two years later Sir George Carteret agreed to partition the province into two territories, East and West Jersey. Governor Philip Carteret returned to resume command in 1674, and would administer a colony destined to stagnation and strife for a total of 16 years. And to Captain James Carteret, the onetime president of the colony, fate was less than kind. Though his decline is not well-documented, it was said that, addicted to strong liquor, he took to spending nights in whatever barn he could find shelter, disavowed by family, fame, and fortune.[7]

Both of the principal Dutch protagonists in the drama that swept up the coasts of the Americas in 1673 were destined for greater glories. Upon his return home from Cadiz, Benckes, unlike Evertsen, was well received and promoted to the rank of vice admiral of Amsterdam. He was too valuable a leader to keep pent up in port over spurious charges by armchair strategists and politicians.

Benckes was given command of seven Amsterdam men-of-war, a fireship, and five lesser ships and sent out to recover the colony of Cayenne from the French. His flotilla set sail from Holland on March 16, 1676, and arrived before Cayenne on May 4 after a brief stop at Puerto Rico for provisions. After landing 900 men, he directed a furious assault against the French fort, which was armed with 37 cannon, and carried it after a desperate fight. Soon afterwards, he sailed for the island of St. Martin, which he also captured, and then to the once-again Dutch-held island of Tobago, where he assumed command as governor.[8]

Following closely in Benckes' wake was a French fleet under the command of the Comte d'Estree. The French arrived before Tobago on February 23, 1677, landed their troops, and on March 3 engaged the Dutch in a furious fight on both land and sea. Benckes directed the Dutch naval squadron, and after a day-long combat emerged victorious, having watched d'Estree's flagship and part of the French fleet go down. Two weeks later, d'Estree sailed away with the remnants of his squadron, arriving at Brest on June 21.[9]

Soon after his return, d'Estree was commanded by an irate Louis XIV to return to Tobago with 16 ships and defeat the obstinate Dutchman once and for all. Returning to the island on December 7, the French admiral landed his troops and set his sights on a strong Dutch fort, key to the island's defense and defended by Governor Benckes. Five days later, the battle began. "The French," wrote the famed buccaneer John Esquemeling a few years later,

> made a beginning to their attack by casting fire-balls into the castle with main violence. The very third ball that was cast in happened to fall in the path-way that led to the store-house, where the powder and ammunition was kept, belonging to the castle. In this path was much powder scattered up and down, through the negligence of those that carried it to and fro for the necessary supplies of the defendents. By this means the powder took fire in the path, and there ran in a moment as far as the storehouse above mentioned, so that suddenly both the storehouse was blown up, and with it Vice-Admiral Benckes himself, the Governor of the island, and all his officers.[10]

The French, taking advantage of the catastrophe, stormed the fort with 500 men and took it, along with 300 prisoners. The Comte d'Estree ordered the fort and every house on the island demolished, and then sailed for France. Thus perished on December 12, 1677, the brilliant seaman who had overseen the brief resumption of The Netherlands' American empire.[11]

Zeeland could not long permit its own brilliant commander to molt. In 1675, the charges brought against Cornelis Evertsen concerning the raid on America were all but forgotten as the war with France dragged on. Kees the Devil was appointed rear admiral by the Admiralty of Zeeland. Four years later he succeeded his illustrious father, who was killed in the Four Day Battle in 1666, as vice admiral of the province. In 1684, he was elevated to lieutenant admiral, and four years later he became supreme admiral of the state of Zeeland.

In the fall of 1688, when Prince Willem of Orange was preparing for his famous descent upon England that was destined to secure for him the throne of that nation in the Glorious Revolution, Cornelis Evertsen commanded The Netherlands fleet of 50 ships-of-war, 25 frigates, 25 fireships, and 400 transports that was to carry Willem's 4,092 cavalry and 11,090 infantry to British shores. Evertsen commanded the invasion fleet until October 17, when command was given, for diplomatic reasons, to a brave but less-than-capable Englishman, Admiral Arthur Herbert, later the Earl of Torrington, who hoisted his flag in the 62-gun *Liefde*. Willem was borne on a Protestant breeze, and on February 21, 1689, was crowned King William III of England in Westminster Abbey.[12]

With the Dutch William on the throne of England with his English Queen Mary, and ex-King James carried to Ireland by a French fleet on March 12, 1689, conflict was inevitable. The incompetent Lord Torrington, who now commanded the combined Anglo-Dutch fleet, was ably seconded by Evertsen and opposed by the French Admiral Tourville. In late June, Tourville and Torrington met off Beachy Head on the coast of England. Twenty-two of the allied fleet, which were in the van, were commanded by Admiral Cornelis Evertsen, then 46 years of age.[13]

The allied council of war conferred on June 26, and, wisely deciding that the Anglo-Dutch fleet was far too weak to do battle with Tourville, dispatched its decision to London. Three days later, however, the field commanders were overridden and directed by Whitehall to engage the French. The battle began approximately ten miles south of Beachy Head; the allies had the benefit of the wind. Torrington's line, with Evertsen in the van, Torrington in the center, and Sir Ralph Delavall in the rear, bore down on the French line. Evertsen closed upon the enemy van at about 9:00 A.M., and Delavall with the enemy rear half an hour later, but Torrington held back, having decided at the last moment to change his attack and cut off the French rear. An inevitable muddle ensued, with the English center and the Dutch van drawing farther and farther apart. The French were quick to seize the opportunity offered, and through the gap created by Torrington's last-minute maneuver poured the French White squadron from Tourville's center, while the French van commanded by Chateaurenault "doubled" him at about 1:00 P.M. Evertsen's squadron, with French warships on either side of the line, fought broadside-to-broadside for two hours, until the wind suddenly fell and the fleets drifted apart. Though saved by nature, Evertsen would likely not have surrendered even had the battle continued. Despite the terrible casualties suffered by the Dutch, only one small ship, which had drifted among the enemy, was overwhelmed and taken. The allied fleet stopped, anchored, and began to lick its wounds, but the French had had enough and did not come up again.[14]

Kees the Devil, his brave men, and their shattered but unbeaten fleet were loudly applauded by England for their unyielding stand at Beachy Head. Evertsen was later given a letter from Queen Mary apologizing for the feebleness of the English fleet during the battle. Torrington was committed to the Tower of London. Fortunately for Willem, the French did not capitalize on their victory or attempt a landing in England to restore James.[15]

Evertsen continued to command the Dutch squadron for a short time. Though he participated in an expedition against Cork, Ireland, politics and rivalry between Zeeland and Holland again exacted their toll. Evertsen was replaced in late 1690 as commander of The Netherlands fleet by Admiral van Almonde of Amsterdam as a result of intensive infighting and state patrimony concerning naval affairs. He would never again command a major fighting fleet.

On November 16, 1706, exactly 64 years to the day from his birth, Kees the Devil died in his beloved Middleburg. His body was interred there in St. Peter's Church. In 1918, his tomb was removed to the Nieuwe Kerk [New Church]. In May 1940, the church was heavily damaged in fighting, but the tomb was well-protected and survives today in the auditorium of the restored church, a modest memorial to the man whose raid on America nearly altered the course of history.[16]

NOTES

The following are abbreviations and short titles for the notes presented hereafter. In each citation, the series number, if any, follows the initial or short title. The volume number follows the series. In the *Acts of the Privy Council* and certain volumes of the *Calendar of State Papers, Colonial Series*, item numbers are employed rather than page numbers. In several instances, multiple item numbers are further divided by paragraph or segment letters. Books are cited by author, or in collected documents by editor, and are followed by volume number and page number. For further particulars, complete citations may be found in the Bibliography.

Acts P.C., Col.—Acts of the Privy Council, Colonial Series.
Cal. S.P., Col.—Calendar of State Papers, Colonial Series, America and West Indies.
Cal. S.P., Dom.—Calendar of State Papers, Domestic Series.
Cal. S.P., Ven.—Calendar of State Papers, Venetian Series.
Christoph—*Book of General Entries of the Colony of New York.*
Conn. Col. Rec.—The Public Records of the Colony of Connecticut, 1636–1776.
EJC—Executive Journals of the Council of Colonial Virginia, 1680–1754.
Fernow—*Records of New Netherland, From 1653 to 1674 Anno Domini.*
JHB—Journal of the House of Burgess of Virginia 1619–1776.
Lords Journal—Journals of the House of Lords.
MCNY—Minutes of the Executive Council of the Province of New York.
MCV—Minutes of the Council and General Court of Colonial Virginia 1622–1632, 1670–1676.
Md. Archives—Archives of Maryland.
O'Callaghan—*Documents Relative to the Colonial History of the State of New York; Procured in Holland, England, and France.*
Pa. Archives—Pennsylvania Archives.
Tanner—*Catalogue of the Naval Manuscripts in the Pepsyian Library at Magdalene College, Cambridge.*
Va. Magazine—Virginia Magazine of History and Biography.

Notes to Pages 3–12

1. PROLOGUE: MAD FOR A DUTCH WAR

1. Boxer, 11. Cf. G. J. Renier, 16–31; M. H. M. Vlekke, 162–166; and S. J. Fockema Andrae, for a comprehensive synthesis of the system of government in the Dutch republican era.
2. Boxer, 12.
3. Ibid.
4. Ibid., *passim*.
5. J. H. Plumb, xxii.
6. De Vries, "The Population and Economy," 661–682.
7. Ibid., 675, 676.
8. Cf. *The Journal of Maarten Harpertszoon Tromp, Anno 1639*, trans. and ed. by C. R. Boxer, (Cambridge, 1930), for account of the engagement; and Francis Vere, 49–54, and Carla Rahn Phillips, 214–219 for an overview of strategy.
9. Rogers, 4, 5, 11.
10. Boxer, 69.
11. The seven-man delegation from the United Provinces was composed of Van Ommeren, Van Strevelshoek, Van Purmerland, Jacob Veth, Van Reynswoude, Schuyrmans, and Wolffren. Stegan.
12. Clowse, II, 150–184; Andrews, 13.
13. Rogers, 26–27.
14. Andrews, 203; Thurloe, V, 80, 81.
15. Barbour, *passim;* Andrews, chp. I, XIII.
16. Williams, 114, 115.
17. [1620, Apr.7. 18.Jac.I.: Commissio specialis concernens le herbae Nicotianae. 17.Ry.190. W]; [1620, Jun 29. 18.Jac.I. : A Proclamation for restraint of the disordered trading of tobacco. 17.Rym.233. W]; [1624, Sep 29. 22.Jac.I: A proclamation concerning tobacco. 17.Rym.621.W]; [1625, Mar 2. 22.Jac.I.: A proclamation for the utter prohibiting the importation and use of all tobacco which is not of the proper growth of the colony of Virginia and the Somer islands, or one of them. 17.Rym.668 W]; [1625, Apr 9. I.Car.I.: Proclamatio de herbe Nicotiana. 18.Rym.19 W]; [1626, Feb 17. 2.Car.I.: A Proclamation concerning tobacco. Ry.848 W]; [1627. Mar 30. 3.Car.I.: De proclamatione de signatione de tobacco. 18.Ry.886 W]; [1627, Aug 9. 3.Car.I.: De proclamatione pro ordinatione de tobacco. 18.Ry.920 W ; 1630, Jan 6. 5.Car.I.: A proclamation concerning tobacco. 19.Ry.235 W], in Thomas Jefferson, 305ff.
18. Ibid., [1633, Aug 13. 9.Car.I.: A proclamation to prevent abuses growing by the unordered retailing of tobacco. Mention 3. Rushw. 191 W]; [1633, Oct 13. 9.Car.I.: A proclamation for preventing of the abuses growing by the unordered retailing of tobacco. 19.Ry.474 W]; [1634, Mar 13. Car.I.: A proclamation restraining the abusive venting (vending) of tobacco. 19.Ry.522 W]; [1634, May 19. 10.Car.I.: A proclamation concerning the landing of tobacco, and also forbidding the planting thereof in the king's dominion. 19.Ry.533 W]; [1634, June 19. 10.Car.I.: A commission concerning tobacco. M.S. W]; [1637, Mar 14. Car. I. A proclamation concerning tobacco. Title in 3. Rush. 617 W; 1636-7, Mar 16. 12.Car.I.: De commissione speciali Georgio domino Goring et aliis concessa concernente venditionem de tobacco adsque licentia regina. 20.Ry. 116 W]; [1639, Mar

25. Car.I.: A proclamation concerning tobacco. Title 4. Rush.1060. W];
(1639, Aug 19. 15.Car.I.: A proclamation declaring his majesty's pleasure
to continue his commission and letters patents for licensing retailers of
tobacco. 20.Ry.348. W]; [1639, Car.I.: A proclamation concerning retailers of tobacco. 4.Ry.996 W].

19. Ibid., [1644, June 20. Car.2. An Act for changing of tobacco brought from
New England with custom and excise. 99.8].

20. Ibid., [1650, Oct 3. 2.Car.2.: An act prohibiting trade with the Barbadoes, Virginia, Bermudas and Antego. Scoble's Acts. 1027. W].

21. Ibid., [1651, Oct 9. 3.Car.2.: An act for increase of shipping and encouragement of the navigation of the nation. Scoble's Acts. 1449. W].

22. U.S. Bureau of the Census, 748.

23. Van Winter, 40.

24. O'Callaghan, III, 48; Thurloe, V, 80, 81.

25. Proceedings and debates of the British Parliament respecting North America, I, 281, cited in Van Winter. 38.

26. *Va. Magazine*, III, 15–20.

27. Van Winter, 42.

28. Van Brakel, 104.

29. [1675, Oct 1. 27.Car.2. W.], Jefferson.

30. O'Callaghan, III, 55–56.

31. *Pa. Archives*, 2nd ser., V, 529.

32. Ibid., 553.

33. Charles II, 164.

34. Pepys, V, April 30, 1664.

35. Vere, 115.

36. Clowse, II, 258–265; Fraser, 243–244.

37. Clowse II, 269–278, Vere, 124–132; Fraser, 242–243. English casualties
were estimated at 6,000 men, most of whom were burned to death aboard
their ships. Eight English ships were sunk and nine captured. Dutch losses
were placed at 2,000 men.

38. Fraser, 160; Vere, 140.

39. Fraser, 243–247, 250.

40. Pepys, VIII, June 22, 1667; Clowse, II, 289–296; Rogers, 109; Vere, 143–150.

41. Pepys, VIII, 260–262, 268–269, 310; Vere, 145; Marcus, 162; Fraser, 251.

2. OUR BUSINESS IS TO BREAK WITH THEM

1. Van Winter, 45ff.

2. Marcus, 163; Fraser, 262.

3. The text of the original undated document is preserved at Ugbrooke Park
in the care of Lord Clifford of Chudleigh, descendent of one of the signa-
tors, Lord Thomas Clifford of Chudleigh. Fraser, 275, 479n.

4. Fraser, 276. Details of the Cabal and the Secret Treaty of Dover remained
largely unknown until 1830 when the text was first published. As late as
the 1930s the deleted aspects of transactions leading to the treaty which
were contained in the Clifford Papers, remained unknown.

5. De Jonge, II, 246; *Cal. S.P., Ven., 1671-72*, 244; Fraser, 274–278.

6. De Jonge, II, 246–247.

7. Fraser, 308; Vere, 161–162.
8. *Cal. S.P., Dom., 1672*, 220.
9. Vere, 153.
10. Ibid.; Haswell, 185.
11. Vere, 153.
12. Ibid., *passim.*
13. Ibid., 152; Haswell, 185.
14. Evelyn, III, 406.
15. Ibid., 407.
16. Pepys, II, 82.
17. Clowse, II, 442–443. Clowse notes that De Haes' first lieutenant, Tobijas Post, bravely kept the ship's pennant flying and concealed the death of his commander. The loss of the projected booty, initially estimated at a million pounds, was downplayed by the British so much that figures as low as £60,000 were offered as an objective estimate as to the worth of the entire Smyrna Fleet. Clowse, II, 441–444; De Jonge, II, 250ff; Vere, 152–153.
18. Blok, III, 166–176.
19. Ibid.
20. Barbour, 52, 75; *Cal. S.P., Ven., 1671–72*, 170.
21. James Nipho to Joseph Williamson, June 8/18, 1672, in Barbour, 58.
22. R. Bulstrode to [S. Cottington], June 14/24, 1672, in Barbour, 58.
23. Barbour, fn. 58: H. Brugmans, "Handel en Nijverheid," *Amsterdam in de Zeventiende Eeuw*, II, 40; J. Grossman, 15ff, 111–112; Z. W. Sneller, 11. Barbour points out that owing to its high metallic coverage, "for the f. 7,201,433 owing its depositors, the bank could produce coin and bullion to the value of f.6,654,277, and unimpeachable securities for the missing half million florins." Barbour, 44fn: Van Dillen, "The Bank of Amsterdam," in *History of the Principal Public Banks* (The Hague: 1934), 91–92.
24. De Jonge, II, 246–247, 259, 264–265. Cf. 259n for Resolution of the States General March 28, April 2, and April 13. On January 25/February 4, 1672, the States General agreed to fund a fleet of 48 warships, the size of the 1671 peacetime fleet, though all were aware of the impending hostilities. Ultimately, the decision came down as follows: 36 warships of 60 to 80 guns, each with crews of 360 sailors and 80 soldiers; 12 other ships of war manned by 200 sailors and 50 soldiers; 24 fireships with crews of 22 each; 24 snaauws with crews of 25 each; and 24 hired galliots to carry messages and supplies. The budget, good for seven months rather than the requested eight, would amount to 4,776,248 guilders. Only when England declared war, on March 28, did the States General approve an additional 12 warships of 60 to 80 guns; 12 more of the second class; 24 frigates of 20 to 30 guns, manned by 80 sailors and 20 soldiers each; for an additional expenditure of 2,200,000 guilders.
25. Bruijn, 79–93.
26. De Jonge, II, 265.
27. Ibid., 272n for War Council decision May 7/17, 1672.
28. For a complete account of the Battle of Southwold, or Sole Bay, see Clowse 302–309, and De Jonge, II, 291ff.

3. SIMPLE SURRENDER

1. Barbour, 141.
2. Bruijn, 83ff.

3. Ibid., 92.
4. Ibid., 85.
5. *The London Gazette*, February 6–February 10, 1672/73.
6. Tanner, I, 274–275; *Cal. S.P., Dom., 1666–67*, 34.
7. *Cal. S.P., Dom., 1666–67*, 42.
8. Clowse, II, 435.
9. *Cal. S.P., Dom., 1666–67*, 84, 380.
10. De Waard, 107; Clowse, II, 436; *Cal. S.P., Dom., 1666–67*, 496, 523, 549.
11. De Waard, 104–107.
12. Ibid., 104; Brandt, 652; Clowse, II, 435.
13. De Waard, 104, 107.
14. Brandt, *passim*.
   When *Zeehond* sailed from the great privateering port of Vlissingen in the late fall of 1672, she carried a crew of 22 men under Captain Thijssen's command. According to the record of the ammunition masters she carried the following: 6 iron cannon [ijzer geschut], firing 3 lb shot [gotelingen]; 6 muskets; 14 carbines; 20 pistols; 25 cutless; 600 lbs of gunpowder; 350 lbs of match or fuse; 20 long pikes; 300 rounds of 3 lb shot; 100 rounds of 1 lb shot; 200 lbs of musket lead ball; 50 lbs of pistol lead ball; 133 lbs of scrap iron; 36 hand grenades; and 12 boarding axes. De Waard, 106–107.
15. De Waard, 104–107.
16. Ibid.
17. Evertsen Papers, Item 1, First Instructions.
18. Ibid., Articles 1 and 2.
19. Ibid., Articles 3 and 4.
20. Ibid., Articles 5 and 6.
21. Ibid., Article 7.
22. Ibid., Articles 9, 10, 11, and 12.
23. Ibid., Article 8.
24. Ibid., Articles 14 and 15.
25. Ibid., Article 16.
26. Ibid., Article 17.
27. Ibid., Article 18.
28. Ibid., Article 19.

4. PUT EVERYTHING TO RIGHTS

1. De Waard, 1.
2. *The London Gazette*, Thursday, February 6 to Monday, February 10, 1672/73.
3. De Waard, 1.
4. Ibid., 1–2.
5. Ibid., 2.
6. Ibid.
7. Ibid.
8. Ibid., 3.
9. Ibid.
10. De Waard, 3; Bruijn, 92.
11. De Waard, 4.
12. Ibid.; Du Bois, 2–3.
13. De Waard, 4.
14. Ibid., 4–5.

15. Ibid., 5.
16. Ibid.
17. Ibid., 6.
18. Ibid.
19. Van Hoorn was brother to an important and influential boekhouder, Jacob van Hoorn, but was apparently less than scrupulous in keeping his own records. In 1674 he was recalled by the States General for improperly maintaining accounts of his administration in Cadiz. On January 29, 1673, three years after the capture of *Isaac and Benjamin* and *St. Maria*, the Admiralty of Zeeland and Van Hoorn finally settled their accounts. See Admiralty of Zeeland Minutes, January 30, 1675, and De Waard, 6n.
20. De Waard, 6–7.
21. De Waard, 7.
22. Du Bois, 2–3.
23. Lindeström, 41–47.
24. De Waard, 7.
25. Ibid., 8.
26. Ibid.
27. Ibid.
28. Ibid., 8–9.
29. Ibid., 9.
30. Ibid.
31. Ibid., Everaert, 608–609.
32. De Waard, 9–10.
33. Ibid., 10.

5. TO THE LAST MAN

1. De Waard, 11.
2. Ibid.
3. Dampier, 60.
4. Ibid.
5. De Waard, 11–12.
6. Ibid., 12
7. Ibid.
8. Ibid., 12–13.
9. Munden's squadron assembled at the Hope in January, where it took on gunners stores. Its destination remained a secret, and its departure from the Downs, sometime prior to January 19, 1673, was carried off without any intelligence reaching the enemy, or even circulating about the waterfront. Munden picked up a small prize en route to, or at, the Cape Verde Islands, which accounts for the discrepancy in the number of vessels with the squadron in the Downs, and that which was encountered by Evertsen at São Tiago. *Cal. S.P., Dom., 1672–73*, 387, 453.
10. De Waard, 12.
11. Ibid., 12–13.
12. Ibid.
13. Ibid., 13.
14. Ibid.
15. Ibid.

16. Ibid.
17. Ibid.
18. Ibid.
19. Ibid., 14.
20. Ibid.
21. Ibid. De Witte rejoined the main squadron on the 14th, presumably with *De Eendracht* in company. The hoecker, unfortunately, does not appear in the Dutch records after her disappearance during the early storms encountered by the squadron until after Evertsen's departure from Suriname in the spring of 1673. Evertsen was later castigated by the Raden of Zeeland for delaying his voyage at the Canaries while the tubby little victual ship had already arrived at the Cape Verdes, alone and unprotected.
22. Ibid., 14–15.
23. Ibid., 15.
24. Ibid.
25. Ibid., 16. Had Evertsen been aware of the recent sequence of events at St. Helena, he would have felt less than justified in the actions he eventually took to abandon the mission to that place. The English-held island had been reinforced on November 16, 1672 when a 36-gun man-of-war of 400 tons, 120 seamen, and 75 soldiers landed, bringing with them 30 great guns and 150 muskets with which to fortify. On December 20, four ships of the Dutch East India Company, of 40, 36, and 32 guns, and a pinnace of 16 guns, arrived on the scene and attacked the man-of-war and attempted a landing, but were twice repulsed. Though the English took heart with the arrival of a 22-gun French ship from India, the aid was offset by the arrival of yet another Dutch East Indiaman of 26 guns. The Dutch persisted, and on January 1, landed 400 men. The English were driven into their fort, and then onto their warship. Humiliated and short of supplies, they sailed for Brazil to reprovision, leaving behind a hired Portuguese vessel to watch the newly ensconced VOC garrison. For the English, the occupation of St. Helena by the Dutch posed an even greater potential loss, for a rich flotilla or eight to twelve English East India ships from India, with cargoes valued at between £400,000 and £500,000, was expected to pass at any time.
Though four of the heavily laden ships eventually passed the island safely, on April 22, the fate of the remainder was uncertain. Munden's mission was clear. The delay at São Tiago was quickly forgotten. On May 4, 1673, the English squadron arrived at St. Helena, and two days later captured the Dutch VOC garrison. With the VOC unaware that their recently captured station was now in enemy hands, Munden sought to insure that his enemy remained uninformed as long as possible. The Dutch signals and ciphers were extracted from his captures, and on May 11, when a VOC ship was sighted approaching, she was lured in and captured with ease. Onboard was the new Dutch Governor of St. Helena. Fifteen days later, a fleet of six VOC ships were sighted, and on the following day, three were taken.
With the treasure-laden Dutchmen in hand, Munden patiently awaited the arrival of the English East Indiamen. When five of the English Indiamen arrived, Munden determined to return to England as their escort.

He returned as a national hero. *Cal. S.P., Dom., 1672–73*, 296, 312, 495, 496, 505, 506–507; De Jonge, II, 472.

26. De Waard, 16–17.
27. Ibid., 15.
28. See Evertsen Papers, Item 2, Second Secret Instructions for complete text of instructions.

6. THE WILD COAST

1. See Hemming for a synthesis of European attitudes and concepts of Guiana, and South America, and, of course, Raleigh's classic work.
2. Carpenter, 32–34; Nystrom, 17–18.
3. Fermin, 11–12.
4. *Cal. S.P., Col., 1669–74*, no. 920.
5. Ibid.
6. There is no mention of how Captain Evertsen's corpse was preserved from January 31 to March 25 (when it was interred at Fort Zeelandia), a period of 53 days, much of which was in the heated climes of the Equatorial regions. It is probable that the corpse was kept immersed in brine or beer. There are several records of similar occurrences in later years, when corpses were preserved at sea for long stretches of time while immersed in brine or rum.
7. De Waard, 18.
8. See Robert Harcourt for a description of difficulties in navigating the uncharted and dangerous Guiana coast.
9. De Waard, 18.
10. Cf. Henry Bolingbroke for an exquisite description of the approaches to Guiana and the coast in the nineteenth century. It becomes readily apparent upon comparison of Harcourt and others that the region remained in a virtual wilderness state for nearly three hundred years after the coming of the European settlers.
11. De Waard, 18.
12. Ibid.
13. Ibid., 19.
14. Ibid.
15. Ibid.
16. Collis, 89.
17. Ibid.; Fermin, 122.
18. Collis, 89.
19. De Waard, 19.
20. Ibid., 19–20.
21. Ibid., 20.
22. Ibid.
23. Ibid. The shallowest portion of the river channel was noted as 19 feet in depth, and the deepest was 21 feet.
24. Ibid.
25. Ibid.
26. Ibid., 21.
27. Falconer, 78.
28. De Waard, 21.

29. Captain Wroth was the brother of Sir John Wroth of Kent, England, and had been commissioned by Governor Stapleton, of the Leeward Islands, to seek "purchase in the Dutch plantations of Guiana." Having fought in Suriname during the last Dutch war, he was quite familiar with the waters and the inhabitants. *Cal. S.P., Col., 1669–74*, nos. 1132, 1132 I, 1132 II.
30. Wroth estimated that, in addition to the small population of Dutch and English settlers, there were an additional 7,000 to 12,000 slaves in Suriname. He was quick to point out that both Dutch and English inhabitants "were very sickly and died fast." His captive, John Madder, estimated that in addition to 300 Dutch in the colony, there were 200 Englishmen, and that the slave population numbered between 5,000 and 6,000 souls. *Cal. S.P., Col., 1669–74*, nos. 1132 I, 1132 II.
31. Ibid.
32. De Waard, 21.
33. Ibid.
34. Ibid., 22.
35. Ibid.
36. Ibid., 23.

7. IN THE FACE OF THE WHIRLWINDS

1. De Waard, 23.
2. Willoughby, "Proposals Concerning the West Indies," Egerton MSS, 2395, f. 470.
3. *Acts P.C., Col.*, I, no. 937.
4. *Cal. S.P., Col., 1669–74*, nos. 38, 39.
5. Harlow, 208.
6. Williams, 112.
7. Ibid., 114, 119.
8. *Cal. S.P., Col., 1669–74*, nos. 59, 59 I–59 III.
9. On May 28 an inventory of "great artillery, powder, arms and ammunition, in the magazines and forts in Barbadoes" noted the following resources: 152 culverins, demi-culverins, sackers, minions, falconets, drakes or small field pieces; 10,430 shot for service, 10 hand grenades, 260 pikes, 480 muskets, 1,002 swords, 804 bandoliers, 21,000 lbs. small shot, 6,500 cut flints, 368 barrels of powder, and 1,800 lbs. of match. *Cal. S.P., Col., 1669–74*, no. 1101 I.
10. Ibid., nos. 995 VIII, 997, 1000, 1000 I–1000 III, 1029, 1098, 1131; Ottley, 17; Harlow, 209–210.
11. *Cal. S.P., Col., 1669–74*, no. 1070; Harlow, 211–212.
12. Tanner, I, 276–277.
13. Wyborne had served as commander of the fireship *Joseph* (1666), *Portsmouth* ketch (1668), *Portsmouth* pink (1669), *Garland* (1672), and would later command *Speedwell* (1675), *Pearl* (1675), *James* galley (1677), *Bristol* (1679), *Rupert* (1679), and *Happy Return* (1681). Tanner, II, 428.
14. De Waard, 24.
15. Ibid., 22, 24.
16. Ibid., 24.
17. Ibid., 24–25.
18. Ibid., 25.

19. For a synthesis of the colonial establishment at Martinique see De Jonge, II, 493ff, and Sidney Daney.
20. *Cal. S.P., Col., 1669–74*, no. 1029; De Waard, 25.
21. De Waard, 25.
22. Brandt, 739ff.
23. Record Book of Netherlands Ships.
24. Brandt, *passim*.
25. De Waard, 25.
26. *Cal. S.P., Col., 1669–74*, no. 1097; Tanner, I, 276– 277; De Waard, 25.
27. In 1672 Sir Charles Wheeler noted that on Martinique "the most winderly island, the French King's Lieut.-General lives, and about 600 men bearing arms; it is happy in a most secure harbor, the Culesac [Cul-de-Sac] in which they are raising a very strong fortification, the King of France having sent an engineer on purpose, and the talk is of 60,000 livres [expenses]. *Cal. S.P., Col., 1669–74*, no. 987.
28. De Waard, 25.
29. Ibid., 26; *Cal. S.P., Col., 1669–74*, no. 492.
30. *Cal. S.P., Col., 1669–74*, nos. 1097, 1098.
31. De Waard, 26.

8. AS FAR AS THE EYE CAN SEE

1. *Cal. S.P., Col., 1669–74*, no. 987.
2. Williams, 114. For a comprehensive overview of the history and geopolitical position of Guadeloupe during the seventeenth century see M. A. Lacour.
3. *Cal. S.P., Col., 1669–74*, no. 896 I.
4. Ibid., no. 987.
5. Ibid.
6. De Waard, 26, 122.
7. Ibid., 26.
8. Ibid., 26, 122.
9. *Cal. S.P., Col., 1669–74*, nos. 1082, 1097. Bertram Ogeron had been sent as governor of the island of Tortuga by the French West India Company in 1664. He took possession of the island for France in an effort to divert trade from the Spanish, much as the Dutch had from their base at Curaçao. A full account of the travails of Governor Bertram Ogeron and his men, the shipwreck of *Grand Infant*, also known as *Ogeron*, or *l'Ecueil* which had been built at Tortuga, and was lost on the west side of St. Johns island, is recounted in Esquemeling, 259–266, and Burney, 73–74.
10. *Cal. S.P., Col., 1669–74*, no. 987.
11. Ibid., nos. 977, 987.
12. Ibid., nos. 986 I–986 VII.
13. Ibid., no. 1038.
14. De Waard, 26.
15. Ibid.; *Cal. S.P., Col., 1669–74*, no. 1109.
16. De Waard, 26–27.
17. Ibid., 27.
18. *Cal. S.P., Col., 1669–74*, no. 1109.
19. De Waard, 27.
20. Ibid.

21. *Cal. S.P., Col., 1669–74*, no. 977.
22. Innis, 2–3.
23. Ibid., 11.
24. *Cal. S.P., Col., 1669–74*, no. 987.
25. Ibid., no. 446.
26. Ibid., no. 987. The guns, when itemized by type, included three culverins, 22 sackers, three minions, and one falcon, a total of 29, not 30. Ibid., no. 896 VI.
27. Ibid., no. 987.
28. Innis, 12.
29. *Cal. S.P., Col., 1669–74*, no. 891.
30. Ibid., no. 977.
31. *Cal. S.P., Col., 1669–74*, no. 1109. The Dutch may have employed several of the smaller prizes in the cutting-out exercise, although there is no mention of such actions in De Waard.
32. De Waard, 27; *Cal. S.P., Col., 1669–74*, no. 1109.
33. Innis, 10.
34. Ibid., 11.
35. *Cal. S.P., Col., 1669–74*, no. 987.
36. Ibid.
37. Ibid.
38. Ibid., nos. 805, 986 I–986 VII.
39. De Waard, 27.
40. Ibid., 27, 122; *Cal. S.P., Col., 1669–74*, no. 1109.

9. TREACHEROUSLY DESERTED

1. De Waard, 27–28.
2. Attema, 13.
3. Attema, 16. See Hartog for excellent overview of St. Eustatius' history.
4. Goslinga, 261–262; Van Grol, I, 48; Attema, 17; Hamelberg, II, 17.
5. O'Callaghan, III, 186.
6. Attema, 20.
7. Ibid.
8. *Cal. S.P., Col., 1669–74*, no. 896 VII.
9. De Waard, 27–28.
10. Ibid., 28.
11. Ibid.
12. Ibid.
13. Ibid.
14. Ibid., 28–29.
15. Ibid., 29.
16. Ibid.
17. Ibid.
18. Ibid.
19. Ibid., 27–29.
20. *Cal. S.P., Col., 1669–74*, no. 1109.
21. De Waard, 30.
22. Ibid.
23. Ibid.
24. Ibid., 30–31.

25. Ibid., 30.
26. Ibid.
27. Ibid.
28. Ibid.
29. Ibid. There are two notes of interest regarding the sailing of *America* for Curaçao. Evertsen indicates in the journal of *Swaenenburgh* that the prize sailed with 1,801 pieces of eight assigned to the States General. A certificate of transferral, undated, included in the Everten Papers, Item 8a, states "There has yet been in said prize, in money, sent along as freight, more than 2300 pieces of Eight, at one per Cent. Further a barrel of claret and a small barrel of Indigo." The note further states that Lieutenant Goossen Janssen had been charged with the business of attending to the prize goods but had ordered one Joris Vincentius to handle the transactions. By a second accounting, primarily of ammunition that had been transferred to *America* from *Swaenenburgh, Suriname,* and *Schaeckerloo,* made when the prize reached Amsterdam in October 1673, Vincentius delivered a quantity of 1,801 pieces of eight to vendue master J. Elbert. This account, which is Item 8b in the Evertsen Papers, suggests a possible collusion to embezzle prize goods and treasure prior to its delivery to the States General. A difference of 499 pieces of eight was never noticed.
30. De Waard, 30.
31. *Cal. S.P., Col., 1669–74,* no. 1138 IV.

10.   FORTS IN THE MOST CONVENIENT PLACES

1. Dabney, 53.
2. *MCV,* 486; *Cal. S.P., Col., 1669–74,* no. 1145.
3. *MCV,* 484–485.
4. Ibid., 485; Shea, 87–88.
5. *MCV,* 486.
6. Ibid., 487.
7. Berkeley and Council to Arlington, July 13, 1666, CO 1/20 f. 199 and Ludwell to Arlington, February 2, 1666/67, CO 1/21 f. 38; *JHB,* November 8, 1666, 42.
8. *EJC,* I, 534–535. Not only was Point Comfort inconvenient, it also afforded little in the way of a foundation to build upon, or materials to build with. The expense, complained colony officials, was more than the colony could bear. In 1673, Berkeley pointed out, when pressed to construct a fort on the point, that the cost would be at least £15,000 sterling. Virginia's entire annual revenue did not exceed £22,000, of which he received £1,200, and the Council was paid £200. The remainder went to public works.
9. *Acts P.C., Col.,* I, no. 423.
10. Ludwell to Arlington, June 24, 1667, CO 1/21 (3217) indicates *Elizabeth* was mounting 46 guns when she arrived. Pepys rated her as mounting 32 guns in peacetime and 40 during home duty in war. Hayward rated her at 45 to 48 guns. Ludwell reported that the vessel had been in the country only five days before she was lost, which would place her arrival time at May 1, 1667.

11. *MCV*, 490–491; Warnsinck, *passim;* Wertenbacker, 129; Shea, 90–91; Shomette, 43–46.
12. Shomette, 43–46.
13. Ludwell to Lord Berkeley, November 7, 1667, CO 1/21.
14. Ibid.
15. *MCV*, 490; Ludwell to Lord Berkeley, November 7, 1667, CO 1/21; *Cal. S.P., Col., 1669–74*, no. 71.
16. Ludwell to Lord Berkeley, November 7, 1667, CO 1/21.
17. Ibid.
18. Ibid.; Ludwell to Arlington, June 24, 1667, CO 1/21.
19. *Cal. S.P., Col., 1669–74*, no. 63.
20. *Acts P.C., Col.*, I, no. 761.
21. *Cal. S.P., Col., 1669–74*, no. 71.
22. *EJC*, I, 535.
23. Shea, 92.
24. "An Answer to the Inquiries of the . . . Lords Commissioners for Forreigne Plantations," June 20, 1671, CO 1/24.
25. *Cal. S.P., Col., 1669–74*, no. 771.
26. Ibid., nos. 780, 781.
27. *MCV*, 334.
28. Wertenbaker, 142.
29. *Va. Magazine*, III, 142.
30. *Cal. S.P., Col., 1669–74*, no. 1057.
31. *EJC*, I, 533–534.
32. Ibid.
33. *MCV*, 334.
34. Ibid.
35. Ibid.
36. Ibid.
37. Ibid., 342.
38. Ibid.
39. *Cal. S.P., Dom., 1673*, 438.
40. Cotterell was commissioned as captain of *Signett* (1661), *Paradox* (1662), *Forrester* (1664), *Delph* (1666), and *Angier* (1670). He also served as lieutenant aboard *Warwick* (1669), and as first lieutenant aboard *Revenge* (1669), the only two commissioned Royal Navy vessels he was destined to serve aboard. Tanner, I, 339.
41. Gardiner served as an officer aboard *Henry* (1666), *Tyger* (1666), and *Bristol* (1668). Tanner, I, 353.
42. *Cal. S.P., Dom., 1671–72*, 98.
43. *Cal. S.P., Dom., 1672*, 14.
44. Ibid., 35.
45. *Cal. S.P., Dom., 1672–73*, 321.
46. *Cal. S.P., Dom., 1672*, 35.
47. Ibid., *1672*, 124.
48. *Cal. S.P., Dom., 1672*, 520.
49. *Cal. S.P., Dom., 1671–72*, 422.
50. *Cal. S.P., Dom., 1672*, 290, 333.
51. Ibid., 520–521, 600, 645, 647, 661, 670; *1672–73*, 180, 187.

52. *Cal. S.P., Dom., 1672–73*, 321–322, 434, 439, 573, 614.
53. *Cal. S.P., Dom., 1673*, 7, 438.
54. *Augustine* underwent alterations to her breadroom to assure that there would be enough space for bread storage for a transatlantic voyage. Shortages of vinegar, a necessity on all "foreign voyages to sweeten the ship for the preservation of the seamen," and a collision with the ship *Happy Return* were among the problems that delayed her scheduled departure. *Cal. S.P., Dom., 1673*, 57, 84, 129, 188.
55. Ibid., 438; *EJC*, I, 533.
56. *EJC*, I, 533.

11. COURAGE AND CONDUCT

1. *EJC*, I, 532.
2. De Waard, 34.
3. Ibid.
4. *EJC*, I, 532.
5. Ibid.; De Waard, 34. Governor Berkeley states in his report of the raid that the Maryland fleet was comprised of eight ships. Evertsen records in *Swaenenburgh*'s journal that there were eleven ships.
6. De Waard, 34.
7. Ibid.; *EJC*, I, 532.
8. The Zeeland raiders were entirely unfamiliar with the Chesapeake. Indeed, in 1673 there were no hydrographic charts available to assist mariners entering or departing the bay and its rivers. Navigation amidst the shifting shoals of the Tidewater was largely dependent upon local pilots. As late as 1660, ship masters trading in Virginia complained of the lack of buoys or beacons to mark the shoals, as well as the absence of knowledgeable pilots to steer their ships up the James River. The following year, the office of Chief Pilot of James River was created. Among his duties was the establishment and maintenance of "good and sufficient beacons in all necessary places from Willoughbies Shole . . . to James Cittie." Hening, II, 35.
9. De Waard, 34.
10. *EJC*, I, 532.
11. De Waard, 34.
12. *EJC*, I, 532; De Waard, 34.
13. Ibid.
14. *EJC*, I, 532–533; De Waard, 34.
15. De Waard, 34.
16. Berkeley reports Gardiner and Cotterell fought for three hours, and then Gardiner fought on alone for another hour, disengaging at 8:15 P.M. *EJC*, I, 532–533. Evertsen, however, notes that he opened fire one half hour before sunset, which suggests his position may not have been in the van of the fleet, but further back, with the bulk of fighting being carried on by other ships of the squadron. De Waard, 34.
17. De Waard, 34–35.
18. Ibid.; *EJC*, I, 533.
19. De Waard, 35.
20. *EJC*, I, 533.

21. De Waard, 35; *EJC*, I, 533.
22. De Waard, 35.
23. Ibid. The vessel in question may have belonged to Colonel John Custis.
24. Ibid.
25. Evertsen writes: "another 20 [ships], sailed up the James." Berkeley, in his official report, writes: "Two and twenty" ships went up the James, and the remainder into the Nansemond. If the earlier total of 40 ships, offered by Berkeley, is accurate, this would leave a disparity of six to eight vessels unaccounted for, possibly the Maryland fleet. De Waard, 35. See also *EJC*, I, 533.
26. De Waard, 35.
27. Ibid.
28. Ibid., 36.
29. Ibid.
30. Ibid.
31. Ibid.
32. Ibid.
33. Ibid., 36–37. Van Zijl's ship was freed on the 15th, and Benckes on the 16th.
34. Ibid., 37.
35. Ibid.
36. Ibid.
37. Ibid.
38. Ibid.
39. Ibid., 37–38. Carteret and his wife, Frances Delavall, were married on April 15, 1673. See Whitehead for details on Carteret's rise and fall.

12. ALL THEYR CRY WAS FOR NEW YORKE

1. Whithead, 62–63.
2. Ibid., 64–65.
3. Ibid., 66–68; O'Callaghan, III, 214.
4. Whitehead, 69.
5. Ibid., 69–71.
6. Mrs. Schuyler Van Rensselaer, 199, states that Carteret was ordered to leave by the New Jersey government.
7. That Carteret was a somewhat unwelcome individual in the Delavall household is suggested by an entry in Danker's Journal, 45, reprinted in Whitehead, 72n, which accuses him of "all the time drinking" and being a "very profligate person" whose wife was eventually taken back into the family fold by her father.
8. De Waard, 38.
9. Ibid.
10. De Waard, 38.
11. Ibid.
12. Ibid., 39.
13. Ibid.
14. Ibid. The anchorage, though snug, was obtained with some difficulty as one of the fluits was grounded, but later freed.
15. Ibid., 40.

16. O'Callaghan, III, 213; *Cal. S.P., Col., 1669–74*, no. 1138 IV. Davis is reported to have been told by Evertsen that if his information regarding New York was true, "I will give him his sloop and cargo again."
17. O'Callaghan, III, 200.
18. *Cal. S.P., Col., 1669–74*, no. 1138 IV.
19. O'Callaghan, III, 204, 205, 213.
20. Moulton, 39–40.
21. Ibid., 40.
22. Ibid., 25.
23. Ibid., 27–28.
24. The site of the public wharf is now well beneath modern Whitehall Street.
25. Moulton, 29–30. The public house was located on what is now Whitehall and Broad Streets.
26. Ibid., 31–33.
27. Ibid., 35.
28. De Waard, 40.
29. Ibid.
30. Ibid., 41.

13.   STUCK IN THE MUZZLE OF THE CANNON

1. Hazelton, I, 115–116.
2. Ibid.
3. Ibid., 117.
4. Van Rensselaer, 97.
5. Ibid.
6. Ibid., 97–98.
7. Ibid., 97–98. Van Rensselaer notes that the earliest indication that knowledge of the outbreak of hostilities had reached the governor's ear came when he wrote Governor Winthrop of Connecticut that all New York vessels in Dutch parts, including one of his own, the ship *Good Fortune*, had been placed under arrest, although not yet confiscated.
8. See *MCNY*, II, for various movements of troops to outposts in Delaware and New York for the defense of the city.
9. Van Rensselaer, 100.
10. Ibid., 101. A limited narrative of the capture of New York, from a decidedly English viewpoint, was penned by John Sharpe, one of the defenders of Fort James. Sharpe carried a narrative letter, published in *Cal. S.P., Col., 1669–74*, to Governor Winthrop's son, Fitz-John Winthrop, who copied it and passed it on to his father, possibly providing the earliest detailed account of the attack to reach Connecticut.
11. O'Callaghan, III, 62.
12. Ibid., 203.
13. *Cal. S.P., Col., 1669–74*, no. 1122.
14. Van Rensselaer, 102; *Cal. S.P., Col., 1669–74*, no. 1122.
15. Van Rensselaer, 102, 104.
16. Ibid., 102.
17. De Waard, 43; . Ibid. *Cal. S.P., Col., 1669–74*, no 1122. Governor Lovelace was thoroughly castigated by Delavall's son-in-law, William Dervell, for his "neglect," and Manning for "ye treachery." O'Callaghan, III, 206.

18. De Waard, 41.
19. Ibid.
20. Van Rensselaer, 104.
21. De Waard, 42. Robert Hodges claimed that the Dutch reply "was that they came to take the place, which they said was theyr owne and theyre owne they would have." O'Callaghan, III, 199.
22. Van Rensselaer, 103.
23. De Waard, 42; O'Callaghan, III, 199.
24. De Waard, 42; O'Callaghan, III, 201, 206; Van Rensselaer, 103.
25. Van Rensselaer, 103.
26. De Waard, 42.
27. Ibid. Van der Zee, 485, suggests that the entire fleet was spun around by the formidable currents although Evertsen is explicit in noting that his ship lay at anchor behind the crescent formed by the rest of the fleet.
28. De Waard, 42–43.
29. Ibid.; Van Rensselaer, 103.
30. Ibid., 43.
31. Ibid., 42–43; Van Rensselaer, 103.
32. O'Callaghan, III, 199.
33. Evertsen specifically states in De Waard, 43, that the Dutch landing force consisted of 600 men. English accounts, O'Callaghan, III, 199, 201, 206, state between 500 and 800. One observer, Nathan Gould, who viewed the proceedings from onboard *Swaenenburgh*, wrote that "he was very confident there could not be above twelve hundred fighting men in the whole fleete not above sixteene hundred in all."
34. O'Callaghan, III, 199, Robert Hodges claimed that the fort held out for four hours, "which was as long as they had any Cartriges."
35. Ibid., 206.
36. Ibid., 199.
37. Van Rensselaer, 105.
38. De Waard, 43; *Cal. S.P., Col., 1669–74*, no. 1122.
39. *Cal. S.P., Col., 1669–74*, no. 1122; De Waard, 43; Van Rensselaer, 104.
40. *Cal. S.P., Col., 1669–74*, no. 1122.
41. De Waard, 43.
42. De Waard, 43; O'Callaghan, III 199–200. Hodges states that the soldiers from the fort were formed into a ring and commanded to lay down their arms. Sharpe claims that Colve broke his promise but no other English account even mentions such a promise. Dutch records indicate the place was surrendered without any terms at all, or "without making any other capitulation." Cf. *Cal. S.P., Col., 1669–74*, no. 1122 for John Manning's, and Dudley and Thomas Lovelace's version of the surrender and Colve's conversation, and De Waard, 43, for the brief Dutch account.
43. O'Callaghan, III, 199–200; Van Rensselaer, 105; De Waard, 43.
44. De Waard, 43. Hodges mentions the two vessels taken before New York, but there is no other note of such being taken, in either Dutch prize records, or in English accounts. It is possible that the two vessels may be one and the same as *Expectation* and *Batchelor*. O'Callaghan, III, 200.
45. Ibid.
46. De Waard, 44; O'Callaghan, III, 201–202.
47. De Waard, 44.

48. Ibid., 37.
49. O'Callaghan, III, 198.
50. The Winthrop Papers, X, 87.
51. De Waard, 44; O'Callaghan, III, 201, 205.
52. *Cal. S.P., Col., 1674–74,* no. 1144.
53. O'Callaghan, III, 205.
54. De Waard, 44.
55. Ibid.; *Cal. S.P., Col., 1674–75,* no. 495.

14. **CONSTABLE STAVES AND ENGLISH FLAGS**

1. O'Callaghan, II, 609.
2. Ibid., 610, 612–613; Moulton, 10; Van Rensselaer, 106–107.
3. O'Callaghan, II, 571–572, 573.
4. O'Callaghan, II, 574–575.
5. O'Callaghan, II, 573, 601; III, 202; *Oyster Bay Town Rec.,* I, 679–680.
6. O'Callaghan, II, 571–572.
7. Ibid., 571, 572, 576.
8. Ibid., 576, 579–582.
9. Ibid., 604–605.
10. Ibid., 578.
11. Van Rensselaer, 108.
12. Ibid.
13. O'Callaghan, II, 578.
14. Ibid., 602–603, 608.
15. Ibid., 608.
16. Ibid., III, 206.
17. O'Callaghan, II, 588–589, 590.
18. Van Rensselaer, 109.
19. De Waard, 47; O'Callaghan, II, 592, 595.
20. O'Callaghan, II, 593–595, 597.
21. Ibid., 595.
22. Ibid., 600, 607. Lapriere was an alias used by Robert Vanquellin, a native of Caen, France, who emigrated to New Jersey. He was eventually appointed Surveyor General for the colony and in 1668 became one of the governor's Council.
23. Ibid., 600, 603, 605–606.
24. Ibid., 600–607.
25. Ibid., 597.
26. Van der Zee, 486.
27. Winthrop Letters, 5th Series, VIII, 150; Van der Zee, 487.
28. Van der Zee, 487.
29. O'Callaghan, II, 585.
30. Ibid., 595–586, 602. The vessel in question belonged to one Jonathan Silck, or Slick.
31. De Waard, 45.
32. O'Callaghan, II, 585.
33. Ibid.
34. De Waard, 47.
35. Ibid.
36. Ibid., 109.

37. Ibid.
38. Ibid., 110.
39. O'Callaghan, II, 598.
40. Ibid., 598–599.
41. Ibid., 599–600.
42. De Waard, 110.
43. Ibid., 109.
44. O'Callaghan, II, 600.
45. De Waard, 166–168.
46. Ibid.
47. O'Callaghan, II, 606, 608.
48. De Waard, 110–112.
49. Ibid., 111–112, 124. *Expectation* sailed on September 4, 1673.
50. Ibid., 48; O'Callaghan, 609–611.

15. IT IS THEIRS WHO ARE STRONGEST AT SEA

1. See James A. Williamson, *The Cabot Voyages and Bristol Discovery under Henry VII, with the Cartography of the Voyages by R. A. Skelton* (London: 1962) for the most comprehensive sources in translation and interpretations of Cabot's voyages.
2. For a full account of the Spanish and Basque fisheries, see H. A. Innis.
3. Morison, 574. On August 8, 1563, Sir Humphrey Gilbert wrote: "On the fifth of August, I entred here in the right of the Crowne of England; and have engraven the Armes of Englande, divers Spaniardes, Portugals, and other strangers, witnessing the same." Morison gives the date of this occurrence as August 8. Cf. full account in Sir Humphrey Gilbert.
4. Two excellent overviews of the English fisheries in Newfoundland and the problems of their administration during the seventeenth century are to be found in Ralph Greenlee Lounsbury and in Charles Burnet Judah, Jr. The principal work on the history of Newfoundland, and one that contains numerous valuable depositions, petitions, and narratives pertaining to the Newfoundland fisheries in the seventeenth century is D[avid] W[ordley] Prowse.
5. Judah, 125.
6. Child, 205–215.
7. Prowse, 190. A quintal was the measurement for a lot of fish, weighing 112 pounds in Cabot's day. The unit measured in terms of modern metrics is 100 kilograms.
8. Ibid., 173.
9. See Judah, 109–115, for the evolution of English policy regarding settlement at Newfoundland prior to 1668.
10. Deposition of John Raynor and John Mathews, in Prowse, 178–179; Judah, 111.
11. "John Downing's Petition," in Prowse, 207.
12. John Downing, "Narrative," Prowse, 206.
13. For a comprehensive account of the contest between the West Countrymen and the London and Bristol mercantile interest for control of the Newfoundland fisheries, see Judah, 107–127.
14. Prowse, 182. English intelligence reports claimed that after the Second Anglo-Dutch War, in 1668, Placentia was defended by 20 guns and 90 to

100 soldiers. In 1676, John Downing reported that "in y^r 1670 [the] French had Placential fortified with ordinance a Garrison of Sodiers and Chaine also St. Peters fortified with great gunns garris'n of Sodrs at both places many inhabitants great stores of Cattle and sheepe." By 1676, Placentia was defended by two forts mounting 13 guns, but populated by only 15 familes, four of which were English. Within four years the forts were in ruins and only three cannon were mounted. Prowse, 181, 185; *Cal. S.P., Col., 1661–68*, no. 65.

15. Prowse, 181.
16. Judah, 114, 121, 122; *Cal. S.P., Col., 1661–69*, no. 1732.
17. *Cal. S.P., Col., 1669–74*, no. 362; Order in Council February 12, 1675, CO 1/67, no. 15.
18. *Cal. S.P., Col., 1669–74*, no. 809.
19. Ibid., 751.
20. Ibid., no. 809.
21. *Cal. S.P., Dom., 1672–73*, 15, 123.
22. Ibid., 127–128.
23. Ibid., 136, 211.
24. Ibid., 602.
25. Judah, 130.
26. *Cal. S.P., Col., 1674–75*, no. 495. The fort, "being out of repair," provided absolutely no defense, and the Dutch carried off four of its guns. Estates plundered included the following: Lady Kirke's, Lady Hopkins's, George Kirke's, Sir David Kirke's, William Jones', Ez. Dibble's, John Kent's, Philip Davis's, William Robins's, Charles Holland's, John Heard's, Robert Love's, William Pollards', and others.
27. Ibid.
28. The inhabitants, observed one of the English prisoners aboard Boes' squadron, were forced to provide six hogs and a bullock for each of the Dutch vessels "as a composition for what the Dutch had left behind." *Cal. S.P., Col., 1674–75*, no. 495.
29. Prowse, 174–175.
30. Ibid., 175.
31. Ibid., 197; Judah, 113. During the course of his raid, De Ruyter entered St. Johns Harbor, Bay of Butts, and Petty Harbor, capturing English shipping and destroying English property and plantations.
32. There is some question as to the degree of destruction carried out by the Dutch squadron. Captain Dudley Lovelace, a prisoner aboard the squadron, accounts for 70 vessels destroyed at Newfoundland. Evertsen, in a report to the Raden of Zeeland written December 13/23, 1673 states "that they had ruined and burned at least 150 sloops." *Cal. S.P., Col., 1674–75*, no. 495; De Waard, 119.
33. The size of the Newfoundland fishing fleet of 1673 was well below that of the previous season owing to the terrible losses sustained in 1672, and, undoubtedly, to the demands for seamen to fill the ranks of the Royal Navy. The extent of the Dutch raid on the fishing fleet might be gauged by a report in New England that the invaders had "taken all the English vessels in the country, five or six belonging to Massachusetts." *Cal. S.P., Col., 1669–74*, no. 1144.

16. BLOWN INTO A THOUSAND PIECES

1. De Waard, 49.
2. Ibid.
3. Ibid., 49–51.
4. Ibid., 51.
5. Ibid.
6. Ibid., 52.
7. Flores has been termed "the most isolated and stormiest, and except as aids to navigation, the least significant of the Azores." Barely 55 square miles in extent, it was probably discovered in 1452 by Diego Teive, a Madeiran navigator and sugar merchant. Eventually settled, by the end of the seventeenth century the island boasted a population of 3,239 people, 938 households, 2 *vilas*, 4 villages, 6 parish churches, and a Franciscan convent. Duncan, 12, 144, 146.
8. De Waard, 52, 53.
9. Ibid., 53.
10. Ibid., 119.
11. Judah, 130.
12. The town of Horta was sacked and burned by Sir Walter Raleigh in 1597 and damaged by a terrible storm in 1669, but by the 1670s had become a major entrepôt lying between the Americas and Europe. It served as a major stopover and victualling center for the Newfoundland codfishing ships, ships bound for the West Indies, New England and New York vessels bound to England and Madeira, and South Atlantic ships from Angola, Brazil, and the East. Fayal's main export was wheat, and Pico's was primarily wine. Duncan, 137, 138.
13. Duncan, 139.
14. Ibid., 119.
15. De Waard, 53.
16. Ibid.
17. It is uncertain which vessel named *Pearl* was lost, that of Bristol or that of London, the former believed to have also been referred to as *Peace*. *Pearl* (*Peace*) of Bristol, however, is the more likely candidate since the total loss between *Pearl* and *Elias* amounted to 1,300 hogsheads. *Elias* carried 700 hogsheads, while *Pearl* of Bristol carried between 600 and 700 hogshead. *Pearl* of London carried between 700 and 1,000 hogsheads, suggesting that she was the likely survivor of the two *Pearls*.
18. De Waard, 54.
19. Ibid., 54–55.
20. Ibid., 55.
21. Ibid.
22. Ibid.; Duncan, 118–119.
23. Duncan, 115, 119, 120.
24. De Waard, 55.
25. Ibid., 55–56, 119.
26. Ibid., 119.
27. Ibid., 56.
28. Ibid., 57, 58.

29. Ibid., 58.
30. Ibid.

17. VERY ILL AND DANGEROUS CONSEQUENCES

1. *Cal. S.P., Dom.*, *1673*, 372, 387, 396, 398, 410, 411, 414, 415, 421, 434.
2. Ibid., 369.
3. *Cal. S.P., Col.*, *1669–74*, no. 1165.
4. *Cal. S.P., Dom.*, *1673*, 323.
5. Ibid., 438, 448.
6. Tanner, II, no. 49.
7. Ibid., nos. 59, 92; *Cal. S.P., Dom.*, *1673*, 439, 448. On July 18, it was reported from Plymouth that the frigates *Adventure* and *Morning Star* "are gone out cruising," and that *Speedwell* had sailed the same day for the same purpose.
8. Tanner, II, nos. 89, 92.
9. The two convoys, which apparently rendezvoused at sea, arrived at Kinsale on July 28 under the protection of *St. David* included four heavily armed East Indiamen, and 35 West Indiamen from Barbados. They had apparently been entirely missed by the *Adventure* squadron sent out to escort them. *Cal. S.P., Dom.*, *1673*, 484.
10. Ibid., 479.
11. Tanner, II, no. 127. Eight of the Barbados convoy broke off from the main fleet at Kinsale and arrived safely at Bristol on August 10. *Cal. S.P., Dom.*, *1673*, p. 503.
12. Tanner, II, no. 156, Cf. Clowse II, 312–316 for an account of the Battle of Schoneveld and its military implications.
13. *Cal. S.P., Col.*, *1669–74*, no. 1132 I.
14. Ibid., no. 1131.
15. Ibid., no. 1132 I. Captain Wroth's deposition was read by a committee of the Council for Trade and Plantations on October 21, 1673.
16. Tanner, II, no. 277.
17. Ibid., no. 298.
18. Ibid., nos. 321, 324.
19. *Cal. S.P., Dom.*, *1673*, 555.
20. Tanner, II, no. 331.
21. Ibid., nos. 343, 346.
22. Tanner I, 421. On September 25, 1673, Pepys instructed Captain Gardiner that upon his arrival in the Downs, a Royal inquiry "into the behavior of his ship and Augustine" would be conducted, taking "such notice of Captain Cotterell's failure as his behavior shall deserve" Tanner, II, 371. Cotterell was found guilty of cowardice and cashiered from the navy. Gardiner was cleared and continued in service. Captain James Watt, formerly first lieutenant of H.M.S. *St. Michael*, who had been in town awaiting his majesty's pleasure for a command, was appointed to *Augustine*. On September 27, Pepys directed the Navy Board to arrange with the owners of *Augustine* for stores and refitting, and provisions enough to bring her into the Thames. The vessel was in a serious condition, with many sick and wounded aboard, for whom Pepys went to some pains to provide assistance. An evaluation of her munitions revealed she had expended most of her powder and shot. Tanner, II, nos. 360, 386, 387, 396, 422, 471.

23. *EJC*, I, 532–535.
24. O'Callaghan, III, 204. Lieutenant Price is noted in Tanner, I, 395, as having served under appointment by the king aboard *Augustine* in 1673. He never served in another naval command, possibly owing to the onus of cowardice attached to *Augustine*, even though he was the nephew of Sir Herbert Price, and was highly recommended by Ludwell, who noted "he behaved himself wth extraordinary courage."
25. *Cal. S.P., Dom., 1673*, 566.
26. Cf. *Cal. S.P., Col., 1669–74*, nos. 1138, 1138 I–IV, and O'Callaghan, III, 198, 199, 200–202 for news accounts and depositions evaluated by the British government.
27. O'Callaghan, III, 207.
28. Ibid.
29. *Cal. S.P., Col., 1669–74*, no. 1145. Dyer was appointed Collector of New York on July 2, 1674. O'Callaghan, III, 221– 222.
30. Ibid., 208.
31. Ibid.
32. *Cal. S.P., Col., 1669–74*, no. 1145.
33. O'Callaghan, III, 209.
34. Ibid., 209–210.
35. Ibid., 210.
36. Ibid.
37. *Cal. S.P., Col., 1669–74*, no. 1160.
37. Ibid., no. 1164.
38. Ibid., no. 1165.
40. Ibid.
41. Ibid. One Bostonian, Richard Wharton, writing about the Dutch attack on September 24 suggested: "If speedy care be taken before the enemy send further supplies, two or three frigates with two or three hundred men for land service with such force as may be raised there will be sufficient, but in such case the frigates must be there in February or March at furthest, and the soldiers must have warm clothing and bedding aboard, or the frost will unfit them for service." He further advised that a general officer be elected in America, where his majesty has many worthy subjects fit for command. *Cal. S.P., Col., 1669–74*, no. 1144.

18.   WE ARE NOW COME TO DEFEND YOU

1. O'Callaghan, II, 614.
2. Ibid., 604, 605, 614–615, 617, 619.
3. Ibid., 619, 629.
4. Ibid., 622.
5. Ibid., 618.
6. Ibid., 618, 662; Van Rensselaer, 115.
7. O'Callaghan, II, 622–623.
8. Ibid., 622–624, 650.
9. Ibid., 623–624.
10. Ibid.
11. Ibid., 629.
12. Ibid., 629–630, 681, 685.
13. Ibid., 633.

14. Ibid., 634; Van Rensselaer, 111; Fernow, IV, 407.
15. O'Callaghan, II, 628.
16. Ibid., 616, 628–629.
17. Ibid., 620.
18. Ibid., 620–622.
19. Ibid., 638.
20. The Winthrop Papers, X, 86–88.
22. O'Callaghan, II, 639–640.
23. Ibid., 640.
24. Ibid., 641.
25. Ibid., 641–642.
26. Ibid., 642.
27. Ibid., 643.
28. Ibid., 647, 648.
29. Ibid., 649.
30. Ibid., 651–652.
31. Ibid., 652, 660.
32. Ibid., 660.
33. Steenwyck's journal of *Zeehond*'s diplomatic voyage to eastern Long Island is reprinted in its entirety in O'Callaghan, II, 654–658.
34. Ibid., 655.
35. Ibid., 656.
36. Ibid., 583–584, 656.
37. Ibid., 656.
38. Ibid.
39. Ibid.
40. Ibid., 657.
41. Ibid.
42. Ibid.
43. Ibid.
44. Ibid., 657–658.
45. *Md. Archives*, V, 55, 57, 63, 108–109.
46. Ibid., 80–81, 111.
47. *MCNY*, I, 124, 125, 677; II, 669, 670, 671–672. Hermanius Wiltbanck was appointed schout, Otto Wolgast, William Claesen, and Isaack Savay were appointed commissioners for Hoeren Kill.
48. Cf. Wiltbanck deposition concerning the incident in De Valinger, 478, and Weslager (1967), 198–202, for accounts of events leading to the capture and destruction of Hoeren Kill.
49. *MCNY*, II, 678–679.
50. De Valinger, 478.
51. *MCNY*, II, 679–680; Christoph, 502–503.
52. Ibid., 737–739; Christoph, 570.
53. Jenkins had secured a tract of land at Hoeren Kill called Pershore, upon which he established a plantation. Cf. Philemon Lloyd Deposition in Weslager (1961), and context of action in De Valinger, 479.
54. See depositions of Hermanius Wiltbanck, Alexander Moulston, Harmon Cornelison, Anthony Inclose, and Elizabeth Roads, May 16, 1683, in De Valinger, 475–476.
55. Howell had served as a member of the Maryland Burgesses in 1665, 1666, and 1671. *Md. Archives*, II, 10, 239, 416; XV, 27–29.

56. De Valinger, 476, 479.
57. Ibid., 476; *Md. Archives*, V, 116.
58. De Valinger, 476, 481.
59. Weslager (1961), 297.
60. De Valinger, 482.
61. Ibid., 476, 481.
62. Ibid., 476.
63. Ibid., 481.
64. Ibid., 476.
65. Ibid., 476–477.
66. Ibid., 482–483.
67. Ibid., 481.
68. Ibid., 477, 479. In a deposition provided by Philemon Lloyd, in Queen Anne County, Maryland on April 6, 1728, nearly 55 years after the destruction of Hoeren Kill, it was stated that Howell's forces continued on the Delaware "for almost Three months; but the poor Circumstances of the people Incapable of furnishing them with Provisions; Together with the Great Severity of a Cold Season then came on; Obliged the Said Soldiers to think of Leaving the place," whereupon they burned it. The troops returned to Somerset County, Maryland "about the End of December." Philemon Lloyd Deposition, in Weslager (1961), 295–297.
69. *Md. Archives*, II, 416.
70. O'Callaghan, II, 511.

19. THE NAVEL OF HIS MAJESTY'S TERRITORY

1. De Waard, 48.
2. O'Callaghan, II, 662–663.
3. Ibid.
4. The Winthrop Papers, X, 103.
5. O'Callaghan, II, 663–664.
6. Van Rensselaer, 113.
7. *Cal. S.P., Col., 1669–74*, no. 1144.
8. Van Rensselaer, 113–114.
9. O'Callaghan, II, 666.
10. Ibid.
11. Ibid., 667–668.
12. Ibid., 668.
13. Ibid., 665–666.
14. Ibid., 666.
15. Ibid., 669–670, 673.
16. Ibid., 669–673.
17. Ibid., 670–671, 674.
18. Ibid., 680–681, 684.
19. Ibid., 685, 686, 697, 699, 700; Van Rensselaer, 116.
20. O'Callaghan, II, 674–675, 677–678, 682.
21. Ibid., 687.
22. Ibid., 677. Vonck's ship arrived safely in The Netherlands at the beginning of March. The messages Vonck bore arrived in The Hague on the day before the ratification of the peace treaty between England and The Netherlands, too late to have any influence on those important proceedings.

23. The Winthrop Papers, X, 91.
24. Ibid., 92.
25. Ibid.
26. Ibid.
27. Ibid., 92, 93.
28. Ibid., 93.
29. Ibid., 93–94.
30. Ibid., 94.
31. Ibid., 95.
32. Ibid.
33. Ibid., 96–97.
34. *Conn. Col. Rec.*, II, 20.
35. The Winthrop Papers, X, 97, 100, 101.
36. O'Callaghan, II, 696.
37. Van der Zee, 490.
38. O'Callaghan, II, 696–697.
39. Ibid., 701–702.
40. Ibid., 702.

20. NEWS FROM THE COAST OF SPAIN

1. De Waard, 58.
2. Ibid.
3. Ibid., 112, 113.
4. Ibid., 113.
5. Ibid., 113.
6. Ibid., 113–114.
7. Ibid., 174.
8. Ibid., 174–175.
9. Ibid., 115–117.
10. Ibid., 117–118.
11. Ibid., 118.
12. Ibid., 175–176.
13. Ibid., 117.
14. Ibid., 58–59.
15. Ibid., 59.
16. Ibid., 118–120.
17. Ibid., 121–125.
18. De Waard, 120. The following capers were specifically contracted "to join the Squadron of Captains Binckes and Evertsen": *'d Offerhande Abrahams (Abraham's Sacrifice)*, Adrian Centsz Vos; 36 guns, 160 crew; *Salamander*, Constant, 32 guns, 150 crew; *Ram*, Pieter Marcusz, 36 guns, 160 crew; *Elena (Helen)*, Thomas Nett (Nith), 24 guns, 100 crew; *Nassow (Nassau)*, Cornelis Marinusz (Marijnisse), 28 guns, 120 men; *Eendracht (Unity)*, Jan Lawrensen (Lourissen), 28 guns, 150 men; *Wulpenburgh*, Thobias Thobias, 28 guns, 120 men; Mels Cornelissen, 14 guns, 80 crew; *Jager (Hunter)*, Jannes Warwyck, 26 guns; *de Brack (Beagle)*, Jan Spaignaert, 10 guns; *Eenhoorn (Unicorn)*, Clement, 14 guns. Abraham Lourissen and two others failed to join. Evertsen Papers, Item 10c; De Waard, 58.
19. Ibid.

20. Ibid., 119.
21. Ibid., 188.
22. Ibid., 59–60.
23. Ibid., 60.
24. Ibid., 60–61.
25. Ibid., 61.
26. Ibid., 62.
27. Ibid., 62–63.
28. Ibid., 188.
29. Ibid., 189.
30. Although not specifically stated, it is probable that Evertsen had dispatched *Schaeckerloo* on picket duty beyond the entrance to the roads to maintain a vigil over enemy arrivals and departures. De Waard, 62–63.
31. Ibid., 63.
32. Tanner, I, 360.
33. De Waard, 63.
34. *The London Gazette*, March 19 to March 23, 1673/74; De Waard, 63. *Swaenenburgh's* journal notes the date of Harman's challenge on January 31/February 9, but as the following dates between February 10 and 22 are missing, and the sequence of events noted in all other works and references regarding the challenge and engagement that followed suggest that no more than a day's time elapsed, the journal entry date of February 12/22 is undoubtedly inaccurate, and was probably filled in after the fact.
35. Tanner, I, 274; De Waard, 63; *The London Gazette*, March 19 to March 23, 1673/74.
36. De Waard, 63; *The London Gazette*, op. cit. The *Gazette's* account of the battle between *Tiger* and *Schaeckerloo*, the first to appear in print, has become the source for most accepted English accounts of the affair. Such notable historians as Clowse have incorporated, almost verbatim, the *Gazette's* description.
37. De Waard, 63. The *Gazette* notes that only two lieutenants, 70 soldiers, and 60 seamen were transferred to *Schaeckerloo*, which is 38 short of the 170 reported by Evertsen.
38. Ibid.
39. Ibid.
40. Ibid.
41. Ibid.
42. Ibid.
43. *The London Gazette*, op. cit.
44. *Naval Songs and Ballads*, 85.

21. TO HOLD THEM OR LEAVE THEM

1. Motley, 846.
2. Van Rensselaer, 119.
3. De Waard, 176–177.
4. Ibid., 126.
5. Ibid., 177–178.
6. Ibid., 178–179.
7. Ibid., 190; Van Rensselaer, 120–121; Gosses and Japikse, 590.

8. De Waard, 179.
9. Ibid.
10. Ibid., 180, 181, 186.
11. Ibid., 187.
12. Ibid., 180.
13. Ibid.
14. Ibid., 180–181.
15. Ibid., 181–182.
16. Ibid., 182.
17. Ibid., 183–185.
18. Ibid., 185.
19. Ibid., 186.
20. Ibid., 187.
21. Ibid., 190.
22. Ibid.
23. Ibid.
24. *Cal. S.P., Dom., 1673–75*, 57, 96.
25. Ibid., xi–xii, 69.
26. Ibid., 107.
27. *Lords Journal*, XII, 616–618; Weslager (1967), 216.
28. Weslager (1967), 219.
29. *Cal. S.P., Dom., 1673–75*, 116. Cf. *Lords Journal*, XII, 616ff. for text of full speech.
30. *Cal. S.P., Dom., 1673–75*, 125.
31. De Waard, 191–192.
32. *Cal. S.P., Dom., 1673–75*, 139–140.
33. Ibid., xii, 140, 144, 145, 147, 148, 154.
34. Ibid., 182.
35. *The London Gazette*, February 26 to March 2, 1673/74.

22. VLISSINGEN

1. *Cal. S.P., Col., 1673–75*, 182.
2. Vere, 177–78; De Waard, 63.
3. De Waard, 63–64.
4. Ibid., 192.
5. Ibid., 64–65, 193.
6. De Waard, 65, 193; Tanner, II, nos. 243, 430, 958, 1969. Evertsen estimated the English convoy at 70 ships, 10 warships, and two fireships. Pepys lists the Royal Navy warships that accompanied the merchant fleet as follows: Rooth's flagship *Swiftsure*, 3rd rate; *Dreadnaught*, 3rd rate, Trevanian; *Plymouth*, 3rd rate, Young; *Constant Warwick*, 4th rate, Harris; *Bonaventure*, 4th rate, Wood; *Swallow*, 4th rate, Russell; *Falcon*, 4th rate, Andrews; *Reserve*, 4th rate, Wellshaw; *Advice*, 4th rate, Dawson; *Sweepstakes*, 4th rate; *Richmond*, 5th rate; *Speedwell*, 5th rate, Skelton; *Well*, dogger; *Ann and Christopher*, fireship; *Olive Branch*, fireship.
7. Tanner, II, no. 958.
8. Ibid., no. 1192.
9. De Waard, 65, 193.
10. A total of seven men-of-war and a single fireship were present in Cadiz Harbor at the end of the month, although Evertsen noted the entrance of

only two by date, on March 15/25 and March 23/April 2, 1674. De Waard, 65.

11. Van Collen did not write a protest for the Raden of Zeeland until April 23/May 3, 1674, two days before the final departure of Evertsen's remaining squadron for The Netherlands. De Waard, 66.

12. Ibid., 65–66.

13. Ibid., 66.

14. Ibid.

15. Ibid. The seizure of *Batchelor* had been effected on the night of March 24, by her master, William Idle, who had been carried from New York to Cadiz as a prisoner aboard the Dutch squadron. Carefully biding his time and "wayting his opportunity," Idle, with eight men and a boat, escaped, boarded *Batchelor*, "secured the Dutchmen [aboard], and brought safe off through 140 sayle of Shipps in the Road with what Loading shee had then in her, without Anchor, or Cable, to Plymouth." This daring act counted little in the eyes of the British Admiralty. Since the vessel had been recaptured from an enemy, but in neutral waters, the admiralty reacted cautiously to avoid potential disputes with Spain over the issue. The crown was entitled to a share of the cargo, or its value, as prize goods since they had been in possession of the enemy when taken. On April 22, 1674 Idle petitioned the admiralty, in whose charge the vessel had been placed, for the return of his ship and lading. Although he was eventually awarded "the King's bounty for his exploit in regaining the ship and his losses by its detention," final adjudication of the case was not made until May 1675. *Acts P.C., Col.*, II, nos. 986, 989, 999, 1008, 1015, and 1022.

16. De Waard, 67.

17. Ibid.

18. Ibid.

19. Evertsen's encounters at sea, all peaceful, included the following: a Flemish caper on May 17/27; an unidentified polacer on May 18/28; Captains Cooreman and Willem Anteunissen, bound from La Coruña for Vlissingen on May 21/31; an Englishman bound from the Downs for Port a Port on June 1/11; Captain Jan van Haerle, ten days out of the Texel, on June 5/15; an Englishman, bound from Brest, on June 12/22; and Captain Cornelis Clement, four weeks out of Cadiz with a Flemish prize, on June 20/30. De Waard, 70–73.

20. Ibid., 70–71.

21. Ibid., 71.

22. Ibid., 72.

23. Ibid.

24. Ibid.; Cf. Evertsen Papers, Item 7, for Evertsen's notes concerning the defenses of Brest.

25. De Waard, 73–74.

26. Ibid.

27. Ibid., 74.

23. TEARE OUT THE GOVERNORS' THROATS

1. O'Callaghan, II, 710.

2. Ibid.

3. Ibid., 712–713.

4. The Winthrop Papers, X, 106–107.
5. The Winthrop Papers, X, 106–107 indicates *Swan* was taken on May 9, while the Dutch records in O'Callaghan, II, 715, suggest she was taken on May 11.
6. O'Callaghan, II, 715–716. *Egmond and Mathew* was later released for a voyage to New England after her captain had petitioned for her release. He was obliged, however, to post security and offload her cargo before sailing. There is no indication of her disposition afterwards. Ibid., 725.
7. The Winthrop Papers, X, 99.
8. Ibid., 101.
9. Ibid., 103.
10. Ibid., 104–106.
11. Isaac Melyn was the son of Cornelis Melyn, who, years before, had transferred his allegiance to Connecticut, but retained a home in New York. Van Rensselaer, 122.
12. The Winthrop Papers, X, 108.
13. Ibid., 108–109.
14. O'Callaghan, II, 709. There is little to suggest the presence of incarcerated French soldiers in the city gaol. Dutch records in O'Callaghan, II, 720, mention several French soldiers, apparently deserters from the northward, who had caused mischief while drunk in the city.
15. The Winthrop Papers, X, 108–109.
16. Ibid., 109–110.
17. Ibid., 110.
18. Ibid.
19. Van Rensselaer, 124; O'Callaghan, II, 726, 727; Van der Zee, 493.
20. Van Rensselaer, *Correspondence*, 464.
21. O'Callaghan, II, 740–741; III, 215.
22. De Waard, 194–196.
23. Ibid., 197.
24. De Waard, 197–199.
25. Van Rensselaer gives the date as October 16, but employs the "new" style calendar, providing an incorrect sequence. Van Rensselaer, 124, 125; De Waard, 200–201; O'Callaghan, II, 548.
26. Van Rensselaer, 125.
27. De Waard, 202.
28. Ibid.
29. Ibid.
30. Ibid.
31. Ibid., 203.
32. Ibid.
33. Ibid.
34. Ibid.
35. Ibid., 203–204
36. Ibid.

24. EPILOGUE

1. *Cal. S.P., Col., 1669–74*, no. 1380.
2. Wertenbaker, *passim*.

3. Weslager (1967), 218–221, 223, 224, 227, 230.
4. Ibid., 217.
5. The ceremony was carried out with a symbolic wooden sword.
6. *Cal. S.P., Dom., 1673–75*, 193, 527.
7. Pomfret, 38–48.
8. Esquemeling, 267–268.
9. Ibid., 268–271.
10. Ibid., 271–272.
11. Ibid., 272.
12. Vere, 197.
13. Ibid., 198; Clowse, II, 335–344.
14. Vere, 199–200. Evertsen's flag was on the 68-gun *Veluwe*.
15. Vere, 200.
16. Ibid., 211.

BIBLIOGRAPHY

Account of His Majesty's Island of Barbadoes and the Government Thereof, An." *Journal of the Barbados Museum and Historical Society*, III, No. 1 (November 1935), pp. 45–57.

Acts of the Privy Council, Colonial Series. Edited by William L. Grant and James Munro. 6 vols. Hereford, England, 1908–1912.

Andrews, Charles McLean. *Colonial Self-Government, 1652– 1689*. New York and London, 1904.

Answer to the Inquiries of the Lords Commissioners for Forreign Plantations, June 20, 1671. Public Record Office, Colonial Office 1/24. London, England.

Archives of Maryland. Baltimore, 1883–present.

Attema, Ypie. *St. Eustatius: A Short History of the Island and its Monuments*. Translation by Peter Daniels. Holland, 1976.

Balmer, Randall. "Anglo-Dutch Wars and the Demise of the Dutch Reformed Power 1664–1682." *De Halve Maen*, LXIII, No. 1 (December 1983), pp. 5–8.

Barbour, Violet. *Capitalism in Amsterdam in the Seventeenth Century*. Baltimore, 1950.

Blok, P. J. *Geschiedenis van het Nederlandsche volk*. 8 vols. Groningen, 1892–1908.

Bolingbroke, Henry. *A Voyage to the Demerary, Containing a Statistical Account of the Settlements There, and of Those of Essequebo, the Berbice, and Other Contiguous Rivers of Guyana*. London, 1807.

Book of General Entries of the Colony of New York. Edited by Peter R. Christoph and Florence A. Christoph. New York Historical Manuscripts: English. Baltimore, 1982.

Boxer, C. R. *The Dutch Seaborne Empire 1600–1800*. London, 1965.

Brakel, S. van. "Eene Memorie over den Handel der West-Indisch Compagnie omstreeks 1670." *Bijdragen en Mededeelingen van het historisch genootschap* (Gevestigd te Utrecht), XXXV. Amsterdam, 1914. pp. 87–104.

Brandt, Gerard. *Het leven en bedryf van den Heere Michiel de Ruiter, hertog, ridder, &c. It. admiraal generaal van Hollandt en Westvrieslandt.* Amsterdam, 1687.

Bruijn, J. R. "Dutch Privateering During the Second and Third Anglo-Dutch Wars." *Acta Historicae Neerlandicae.* N.p., 1976, pp. 79–93.

Burney, James. *History of the Buccaneers of America.* London, 1816.

Calendar of State Papers. Colonial Series, 1661–1675. 4 vols. Edited by Noël Sainsbury. London, 1889–1891.

Calendar of State Papers, Domestic Series, 1672–1675. 4 vols. Edited by F. H. Blackburne Daniell. London, 1901–1904.

Calendar of State Papers, Venetian Series, 1661–1675. 6 vols. Edited by Allen B. Hindes. London, 1932–1940.

Carpenter, John Allan. *French Guiana.* Chicago, 1970.

Catalogue of The Naval Manuscripts in the Pepsyian Library at Magdalene College, Cambridge. Edited by J[oseph] R[obson] Tanner. 2 vols. Cambridge, 1903.

Charles II. *The Letters, Speeches, and Declarations of King Charles II.* Edited by Sir Arthur Bryant. [1935]; Reprint, London, 1968.

Child, Sir Josiah. *A New Discourse on Trade.* London, 1694.

Clowes, William Laird. *The Royal Navy: A History from the Earliest Times to the Present.* 7 vols. Boston and London, 1898–1903.

Colledge, J. J. *Ships of the Royal Navy: An Historical Index.* 2 vols. New York, 1969.

Collis, Louise. *Soldier in Paradise: The Life of Captain John Stedman 1744–1797.* New York, 1965.

Dabney, Virginius. *Virginia: The New Dominion.* Garden City, New York, 1971.

Dampier, William. *A New Voyage Round the World.* [1697]; Reprint, New York, 1968.

Daney, Sidney. *Histoire de la Martinique: Dupuis la Colonisation Jusqu 'en 1815.* 3 vols. Fort Royal, 1846.

Documents Relative to the Colonial History of the State of New York; Procured in Holland, England and France. Edited by E. B. O'Callaghan. 15 vols. Albany, 1853–1887.

D[u] B[ois]. *Les Voyages fait par le Sieur D B Aux Isles Dauphine ou Madagascar, & Bourbon, ou Mascarebbe, és Années 1669.70.71 & 72. Dans lequelle il est curieusement traité du cap Vert de la ville de Surate des isles de Sainte Helene, ou de l'Ascension.* Paris, 1674.

Duncan, T. Bentley. *Atlantic Islands: Madeira, the Azores and the Cape Verdes in Seventeenth Century Commerce and Navigation.* Chicago and London, 1972.

Du Tertre, R. P. J. B. *Histoire Generale des Antilles.* 4 vols. Forte-de-France, Martinique, Paris, et Pointe-à-Pitre, Guadeloupe, 1973.

Engleschen Alarm: of Oorlogs-teyken. Te Bespeuren in haren ontrovwen en Goddeloose Handel; tegen de Regenten en onderdanen van de seven vrye vereenigde provincien. Edited by Hendrick vander Stegen. Amsterdam, 1652.

Esquemeling, John. *The Buccaneers of America: A True Account of the Most Remarkable Assaults Committed of Late Years Upon the Coasts of the West Indies by the Buccaneers of Jamaica and Tortuga (both English and French).*[1684]. Reprint, New York, 1967.

Evelyn, John. *The Diary of John Evelyn.* Edited by E. S. de Beer. 6 vols. Oxford, 1955.

Everaert, John. *De Handel der Vlaamse Firma's te Cadiz 1600–1700,* Rijksuniversiteit te Gent, Faculteit van de Letteren en Wijsbegeerte, publicatie 154. Brugge, 1973.

Evertsen Papers, 1672–1673, The Hans Bontemantel Collection. New York Public Library.

Executive Journals of the Council of Colonial Virginia, 1680– 1754. Edited by Henry R. McIlwaine and Wilmer L. Hall. 5 vols. Richmond, 1925–1945.

Falconer, William. *An Universal Dictionary of the Marine: or, A Copious Explanation of the Technical Terms and Phrases Employed in the Construction, Equipment, Furniture, Machinery, Movements, and Military Operations of a Ship.* [1780] Reprint, Devon, England, 1970.

Fermin, Philippe. *An Historical and Political View of the Present and Ancient State of the Colony of Surinam in South America.* London, 1781.

Fockema Andreae, S. J. *De Nederlandse staat onder de Republiek.* Amsterdam, 1962.

Fraser, Antonia. *Royal Charles: Charles II and the Restoration.* New York, 1980.

Gilbert, Sir Humphrey. *The Voyages and Colonising Enterprises of Sir Humphrey Gilbert.* Introduction and notes by David B. Quinn. 2 vols. London, 1939–1940.

Goslinga, C. Charles. *The Dutch in the Caribbean and on the Wild Coast, 1580–1680.* Assen, 1971.

Gosses, I. H. and N. Japikse. *Handboek tot de Staatkundige Geschiedenis van Nederland.* 3rd rev. ed. The Hague, 1947.

Grossman, J. *Die Amsterdamer Boerse voor 200 Jahren.* Den Haag, 1876.

Hamelberg, J. H. J. *De Nederlanders op de Westindische Eilanden.* 2 vols., II: De Boven-windsche Eilanden St. Eustatius, Saba, St. Martin. Amsterdam, 1901.

Harcourt, Robert. *A Relation of a Voyage to Guiana, 1613.* Edited by Sir C. Alexander Harris. London, 1928.

Harlow, Vincent T. *A History of Barbados 1625–1685.* 1926. Reprint, New York, 1969.

Hartog, J[ohannes]. *Geschiedenis van Sint Eustatius.* Aruba, 1976.

Haswell, Jack. *James II: Soldier and Sailor.* New York, 1972.

Hayward, Edward. *The Sizes and Lengths of Rigging.* [1654]; Reprint, London, 1967. Introduction by R. C. Anderson.

Hazard, Samuel. *Annal's of Pennsylvania, from the Discovery of the Delaware 1609–1682.* Philadelphia, 1850.

Hazard's Register of Pennsylvania, Devoted to the Preservation of Facts and

Documents, and Every Kind of Useful Information Respecting the State of Pennsylvania. Edited by Samuel Hazard. 16 vols. Philadelphia, 1828–1834.

Hazelton, Henry Isham. *The Boroughs of Brooklyn and Queens, Counties of Nassau and Suffolk, Long Island, New York, 1609– 1926.* Vol. I. New York and Chicago, 1925.

Hemming, John. *Red Gold: The Conquest of the Brazilian Indians, 1500– 1760.* Cambridge, Massachusetts, 1978.

Hening, William Waller, ed. *The Statutes-at-Large, Being a Collection of All the Laws of Virginia.* 13 vols. Richmond, 1819–1823.

Hussey, Frank. *Suffolk Invasion: The Dutch Attack on Languard Fort, 1667.* Lavenham, Suffolk, 1983.

Innis, H. A. "Rise and Fall of the Spanish Fishery in Newfoundland." *Transactions* of the Royal Society of Canada. 3rd series, XXV (1931), pp. 50–71.

Inniss, Sir Probyn. *Whither Bound St. Kitts-Nevis?* Antiqua, West Indies, 1983.

Jefferson, Thomas. *Jefferson's Writings,* I. New York, 1986.

Jonge, J. C. de. *Geschiedenis van het Nederlandsche Zeewezen.* 4 vols. Haarlem, 1859.

Journal of the House of Burgesses of Virginia 1619–1776. Edited by John P. Kennedy and Henry R. McIlwaine. 13 vols. Richmond, 1905–1915.

Journals of the House of Lords. 133 vols. London, 1860–1903.

Judah, Charles Burnet, Jr. "The North American Fisheries and British Policy to 1713." *Illinois Studies in the Social Sciences,* XVIII, Nos. 3–4. University of Illinois Bulletin, XXXI, No. 1 (September 5, 1933).

Lacour, M. A[uguste]. *Histoire de la Guadeloupe.* 4 vols. Basse-Terre, 1855– 1860.

Lindeström, Peter. *Geographia Americae.* Trans. Amandus Johnson. 1925; Reprint, New York, 1979.

London Gazette, 1665–1674.

Lounsbury, Ralph Greenlee. *The British Fishery at Newfoundland 1634–1763.* New Haven and London, 1934.

Ludwell, Thomas, to Lord Arlington, June 24, 1667. Public Record Office, Colonial Office 1/21. London, England.

Ludwell, Thomas, to Lord Berkeley, November 7, 1667. Public Record Office, Colonial Office 1/21. London, England.

Marcus, G. J. *A Naval History of England: The Formative Centuries.* Boston and Toronto, 1961.

Minutes of the Council and General Court of Colonial Virginia 1622–1632, 1670–1676, With Notes and Excerpts from the Original and General Court Court Records, Ante 1683, Now Lost. Edited by Henry R. McIlwaine. Richmond, 1924.

Minutes of the Executive Council of the Province of New York. Edited by Victor Paltsits. 2 vols. Albany, 1910.

Morison, Samuel Eliot. *The European Discovery of America: The Northern Voyages* A.D. *500–1600.* New York, 1971.

Motley, John Lothrop. *The Rise of the Dutch Republic.* London and New York, 1898.

Moulton, Joseph W. *View of the City of New-Orange, (Now New York) as it was in the Year 1673.* New York, 1825.

Naval Songs and Ballads. Selected and edited by C. H. Firth. Cambridge and London, 1908.

Nystrom, J[ohn] Warren. *Surinam.* New York, [1948].

Order in Council, February 12, 1675. Public Record Office, Colonial Office 1/67. London, England.

Ottley, C. R. *The Story of Tobago: Robinson Crusoe's Island in the Caribbean.* Trinidad and Tobago, 1973.

Oyster Bay Town Records, I (1653–1690). Edited by John Cox, Jr. New York, N.d.

Pennsylvania Archives. Edited by Samuel Hazard, et al. Philadelphia, 1852–1856. Harrisburg, 1874.

Pepys, Samuel. *The Diary of Samuel Pepys.* 11 vols. Edited by Robert Latham and William Matthews. Berkeley and Los Angeles, 1971–1983.

Phillips, Carla Rahn. *Six Galleons for the King of Spain: Imperial Defense in the Early Seventeenth Century.* Baltimore and London, 1986.

Plumb, J. H. "Introduction." In *The Dutch Seaborne Empire 1600–1800,* by C. R. Boxer. London, 1965.

Pomfret, John E. *Colonial New Jersey: A History.* New York, 1973.

Proposals Concerning the West Indies. Egerton Manuscripts, no. 2395. British Museum. London, England.

Prowse, D[aniel] W[ordley]. *A History of Newfoundland from the English, Colonial, and Foreign Records.* London, 1896.

Public Record Office, London. Colonial Office Files 1/20, 1/21, 1/24, 1/67.

Public Records of the Colony of Connecticut, 1636–1776, The. Edited by J. H. Trumbull, et al. 15 vols. Hartford, 1850–1890.

Raleigh, Sir Walter. *The Discoverie of the Large, Rich, and Beautiful Empire of Guiana, with a Relation of the Great and Golden City of Manoa.* [1596]; Reprint, London, 1848. Edited by Sir Robert H. Schomburgh.

Record Book of Netherlands Ships. Rijksmuseum, Nederlands Scheepvaart Museum. Amsterdam.

Records of New Netherlands: From 1653 to 1674 Anno Domini, The. Edited by Berthold Fernow [1898]. 7 vols. Reprint, Baltimore, 1976.

Renier, G. J. *The Dutch Nation: An historical study.* London, 1944.

Rensselaer, Jeremias van. *Correspondence of Jeremias van Rensselaer.* Translated and edited by A. J. F. van Laer. Albany, 1932.

Rensselaer, Mrs. Schuyler van. *History of the City of New York in the Seventeenth Century.* New York, 1901.

Rogers, P. G. *The Dutch on the Medway.* London, 1970.

"Seventeenth Century Commentary on Labor and Military Problems in Barbados, A." *Journal of the Barbados Museum and Historical Society,* XXXIV, No. 3 (March 1973), pp. 117–121.

Shea, William L. *The Virginia Militia in the Seventeenth Century.* Baton Rouge and London, 1983.

Shomette, Donald G. *Pirates on the Chesapeake: Being a True History of Pirates, Picaroons, and Raiders on Chesapeake Bay, 1610–1807.* Centreville, Maryland. 1985.

Sneller, Z. W. *Economische Crisissen in Vroeger Tyd.* Kampen, 1932.

Thurloe, John. *A Collection of the State Papers of John Thurloe. Containing Authentic Memorials of the English Affairs from the Year 1638, to the Restoration of King Charles II.* London, 1742.

Tromp, Maarten Harpertszoon. *The Journal of Maarten Harpertszoon Tromp Anno 1639.* Translated and edited by C. R. Boxer. Cambridge, 1930.

U.S. Bureau of the Census. *Historical Abstracts of the United States, Colonial Times to 1957.* 2nd Printing. Washington, 1961.

Valinger, Leon de. "The Burning of the Whorekill, 1673." *Pennsylvania Magazine* (October 1950), pp. 473–487.

Van Grol, G. J. *De Grondpolitiek in het West-Indische Domein der Generaliteit.* 3 vols. Algemeen Historische Inleiding. 's-Gravenhage, 1934.

Vere, Francis. *Salt in their Blood: The Lives of the Famous Dutch Admirals.* London, 1955.

Virginia Magazine of History and Biography, III, No. 1 (July 1895).

Vlekke, B. H. M. *Evolution of the Dutch Nation.* New York, 1945.

Vries, Jan de. "The Population and Economy of Preindustrial Netherlands." *Journal of Interdisciplinary History*, XV, 4, pp. 661–682.

——— "The Decline and Rise of the Dutch Economy, 1675–1900." *Technique, Spirit, and Form in the Making of Modern Economies. Essays in Honor of William N. Parker.* Research in Economic History, Supplement 3, pp. 148–189. 1984.

Waard, C. de, ed. *De Zeeuwsche Expeditie Naar de West onder Cornelis Evertsen den Jonge 1672–1674.*'s Gravenhage, 1928.

Warnsinck, J[ohan] C[arel] M[arinus]. *Abraham Crynssen der Verovering van Suriname en zijn Aanslag op Virginië in 1667.* Amsterdam, 1936.

Wertenbaker, Thomas J. *Virginia Under the Stuarts, 1607–1688.* Princeton, 1914.

Weslager, C[linton] A[lfred]. *Dutch Explorers, Traders, and Settlers in the Delaware Valley 1609–1664.* Philadelphia, 1961.

——— *The English on the Delaware 1610–1682.* New Brunswick, New Jersey, 1967.

Whitehead, William A[dee]. *East Jersey Under the Proprietary Government: A Narrative of Events Connected with the Settlement and Progress of the Province, Until the Surrender of the Government to the Crown in 1703.* Newark, New Jersey, 1875.

Williams, Eric. *From Columbus to Castro: The History of the Caribbean.* New York, 1970.

Williamson, James A. *The Cabot Voyages and Bristol Discovery under Henry VII*, with the Cartography of the Voyages by R. A. Skelton. London, 1962.

Winthrop Papers, The. *Collections of the Massachusetts Historical Society.* 9 vols. Boston, 1846–1892.

Winter, Jhr. P. J. van. "De Akte van Navigatie en de Vrede van Breda." *Bijdragen voor de Geschiedenis der Nederlanden*, IV, 1–2. The Hague, 1949. pp. 27–65.

Zee, Henri and Barbara van der. *The Story of Dutch New York.* New York, 1978.

Index